DF
OF
SQUIRE JACOBI

*Neil McIntire
Best Wishes*

By D. J. HILL

DREAMS OF SQUIRE JACOBI

Copyright © 2015 by D. J. HILL

This book is a total work of fiction, and, any names, characters, locales, or incidents are products of the author's imagination, or, are used fictitiously, and, any resemblance to actual events, persons, living or dead, or locations is entirely coincidental.

All rights reserved. No part of this book may be reproduced, scanned, transmitted by any means, or stored in any retrieval system, electronically, or distributed without prior permission, except as provided by USA Copyright law and the author's rights.

ISBN-13 978-0-9980746-0-3

Library of Congress Control Number 2016915817

Printed in the USA by Morris Publishing*
3212 E. Highway 30, Kearney, NE 68848.
1-800-650-7888 www.morrispublishing.com

Cover Design © Morris Publishing

CONTENTS

Orval The Marvel - 2

Hereford McAbeley - 17

Young Abe's Axe - 73

The Ringerless Ding-a-ling - 83

The Birds - 114

Uncovering the Covered up Cover-up - 127

The Last Fast Talking Angel - 145

The Patient with Patience - 163

Docker Ying Yang - 178

The Brain Game - 187

The Spy That Came Down with A Cold - 208

Aliens Unawares - 222

The Horse Sale - 244

Ooma and Woma - 255

The Last Leprechaun Standing - 271

Thomas and Elias Tall Tale - 288

Interesting Interest - 364

The First and Last Interview of the Patient - 377

Jake Kelly's Tale - 393

How to Tell a Story Well - 436

ORVAL THE MARVEL   (because nothing else rhymes)

Orval woke up in the middle of the night squirming, clawing and scratching. He was in a panic.   "Lorena, Lorena, wake up, wake up." He yelled out. "Somethin', is a-crawlin" all over me. Fetch the candle, light the lamp, hurry, before they all get gone."

Lorena rolled out of bed, got the burning night candle from the hall, came back into the bedroom, and, lit up the coal oil lamp. She turned up the wick to get a good flame, got her glasses from off of the night stand, and came over to where Orval was sitting on the other side of the bed.

"Here, here, hold the lamp here, on my back." He said, as he pulled up his night shirt. "Do you see'em a-crawlin', hurry, look, before they done up and get gone again."

Lorena moved the lamp back and forth, up and down, pulled up the top of his long under shirt ever further and adjusted the lamp's wick for even a better flame, then, she said. "Orval, this is the third night in a row that you done been got up with invisible bugs a-crawlin' all over you. So far, I ain't seen the first bug a-crawlin' or even a-layin' tryin' to hide. Maybe you just done been dreamin'."

Orval responded. "Lorena, I'm tellin' you, I think we us got a bad infestation of bed bugs, especially on my side of the bed. Maybe they like the flavor of me better'n you. Maybe they all run off and hide the minute you light up the lamp or when I get up. Maybe they all crawl up in my hair and hide. You ain't looked up there once. Why don't you look up there now?" He said, while pulling his night shirt down and bending over for her to look.

Lorena took the lamp in one hand, and, brushed Orval's hair backwards with the other hand, checking his hair. "I don't see anythin' up here either Orval." She said.

"Maybe they got wings, maybe, that's it. They all got wings, and, when you light up the lamp, or I move, or I pull up my night shirt, they all fly off some where's and hide somewhere else in the dark." Orval said.

"I never seen any bugs a-flyin' no where's, Orval. So, you might as well crawl back in bed and try to get some sleep. If you want to stay up and chase the bugs, go to it full barrel, but for me, I am goin' back to bed." With that, Lorena took the candle back out to the pedestal in the hallway, brought the coal oil lamp back into the bedroom, set it down on the night stand, turned down the wick, blew out the flame, crawled back in bed and covered herself up, turning her face away from Orval.

Orval sat on the side of the bed for a while, then, got up, went into the hallway, got the pee potty from under the hall table, took the lid off, relieved himself, put the lid back on and set the potty down on the hall floor. He noticed that the candle in the hall was more than halfway melted down. Lorena hasn't made up any new candles of late. He thought to himself. Maybe he might have to start buyin' store bought candles for night lights.

"Make sure you push that potty back under the table there, Orval, I don't need you a-kickin' it over when you get up next. I got no hankerin' to be a-moppin' up pee in the middle of the night." She yelled from the bedroom.

Orval came back into the bedroom, but instead of crawling in bed, he went to the back window, pulled the curtains apart and peered out. "The chickens are a-cacklin', they are awake in the roost, somethin' must be out there, a-tryin' to get in the chicken house." He said.

"Well, if there were somethin' out there, like a fox, or a coyote, or maybe a big rat, they would really be creatin' a rukus. They're probably just restless because it's a moonlit night." Lorena said. "So, let'm go, and, come on back to bed, you need your rest."

Orval stayed at the window, still peering out. "I don't know, maybe I got some mites on me from off'n them chickens. Maybe that's what is a-causin' my itch. Maybe that's what it is. I don't know. I've wallowed every one of those chickens morning and night in a pan of wood ash. I've even spent good money on that stuff they call diatomaceous earth and I've put both in their dust box every week, I spray them down every two weeks with garlic, and, I've even sprayed down their coop with store bought pesticide every other week and that stuff ain't cheap. I don't know how they could be havin' any mites on'em at all. I ain't ever seen any kind of mite eggs on their feathers." He said, as if talking to himself but obviously talking out loud.

Lorena did not respond, was apparently asleep, or, at least pretending.

Then, Orval traipsed around the house for a while, got a drink of water from the water bucket in the kitchen, then, finally came back into the bedroom, and crawled back into bed with Lorena. He squirmed around for a while; flip flopped from one side to the other a few times, and then finally fell off to asleep again.

Morning came early, and, Orval got up just as the sun was coming up. He went to the kitchen, started a fire in the wood stove, put a couple of eggs on to boil and put the coffee pot on. He assumed that Lorena was sleeping in again, as she had been doing lately, so, he thought that he would just let her get her rest. He went out to get the newspaper, came back in the house, stoked up the fire in the kitchen stove and waited for the coffee and eggs to boil.

After breakfast, Orval started out his day by feeding and watering the chickens and his team of mules, and then went to doing minor repairs and maintenance around the outside of the house. His work today, was to include the addition a new toilet seat on the outhouse. Lorena had complained that the old seat was just too cold. He had even gone so far previously as to get her some of that store bought toilet paper on rolls, but, for himself, he continued to use the pages from the old Sears & Roebuck's catalog. He noted that he was now already up to page 173. Too, he had also noticed that she had not used much of the last roll that he had put on, but assumed that maybe she was still using the catalog paper like he did, and, dismissed any further thought of the matter.

Orval then went to shelling his sweet corn in the barn. He planned to take the shelled corn into town to the mill to make cornmeal. Then, his plan was, to trade most of it off to the general store or barter some of it off for other things that he and Lorena needed around the house. He had been shelling corn now for three or four days, as, he couldn't remember just exactly how many, but, he did know, that he now had four gunny sacks, each about two-thirds full of newly shelled sweet corn. Sweet corn, or dried roastin' ear corn, makes the best cornmeal ever he thought to himself. He tied the new gunny sack up and carried it to the wagon and loaded it on with the other three bags along with his empty coal oil can.

He went to the other end of the barn and harnessed up his mules while they were still in their stalls. Then, he led them out and around the barn to where the wagon was, and, hooked them up to the wagon. He got his rain slick, threw it on the wagon, mounted up on the wagon, yelled "giddyup there ya'll", and headed out for town less than a half mile away. No sense whatsoever a-walkin' when you could ride, he thought to himself.

Orval got to the mill, showed the miller what corn he had and what he wanted, argued a little with him about what percentage that the mill held back for the milling of his corn, then, finally agreed on the common ten percent by weight, and told the miller that he wanted his gunny sacks back as part of the deal. The miller ground Orval's corn, and, put the cornmeal into ten twenty pound paper bags. Orval argued that he must have had at least sixty pounds of shelled corn per the four gunny sacks that he had brought in, and, that ten percent of about two hundred and forty pounds minus ten percent should at least more than that. The miller argued back, that the weight was not there, that there was too much moisture in the corn, besides, he told Orval that he had not counted the two bags of cracked corn that he had asked for to feed his chickens, and, it was what it was, and, to either take that trade off, as it was, or, just pay him in cash, outright for the total milling of the cornmeal. And, he added, both he and the mill preferred cash on the barrel head with no percentage held back at all, then, Orval could take it all back for all he cared, as, it was a small job anyway, and, he was only doing it out of the goodness of his heart. Orval accepted it as it was, loaded the ten twenty pound sacks on his wagon, along with the two bags of cracked corn, left the mill, and headed his wagon on down to the general store.

Orval tied his mules up in front of the store, because there was a lot of noise and traffic in town, with those newfangled automobiles rollin' up and down the street, and, he didn't want his mules takin' off on their own, as, there was no tellin' where they would ever wind up.

Why, they could even run off in the river and drown, he thought to himself. He went into the store, shopped around some, looking at this and that, until the owner John Autrey was free from ringing out customers, so he could finally get a word in edgewise with him.

"John, I've got a deal for you that you can't afford to pass up." Orval started off with.

"I know all about your deals, Orval, you've been in here before, and, we've both been to the State Fair and seen a goat ropin'. What do you have now?" John said.

"John, I have, out there in my wagon, ten bags of right at two hunnert or so pounds of some of the best freshly milled corn meal to be found around town, if I must say so myself." Orval said.

"My next guess is, Orval, that you want to trade a little, maybe even barter some, for some of the stuff you need, is that right?" John said.

"John, you hit the nail right on the head." Orval added.

"Ok, Orval, I don't know yet, if I can take all two hundred pounds of your cornmeal. I haven't got all of that figured out in my head yet. But, if I make a deal with you on the lot, minus what you want to keep yourself for your own home cookin', will you promise me that you won't go peddlin' the rest of your cornmeal out on the streets? I mean, after all Orval, I have a business to run here, and, I don't need any secondary back handed competition." John said.

Orval responded. "OK, I think I need to hold back two bags of the ten, which would give you eight bags of twenty pounds each, or, you getting right at a hunnert and sixty pounds. How would that be?"

John, came back with another plan. "OK, Orval, I might be able to work with you on it, but, you know, I have to break those twenty pound bags down into five pound bags, just to sell them in the store. So, now hear this, for an agreement. I sell cornmeal for a dollar for a five pound bag. Five into one hundred and sixty is thirty-two bags. I need to make at least twenty percent just to break even. So, I will pay you twenty-five dollars for the lot. If, that is, if, you want to use my scales, with me providing the five pound bags, with you a-weighing out the five pounds each back there in the back room, you unloading your wagon yourself, and, you doing that work as part of the deal. Would you agree to that? Money is really getting' hard to come by in these times, you know. Twenty-five dollars is twenty-five dollars, you know." He said.

Orval turned around, appeared to be counting on his fingers, then, turned back around to talk with John, and said. "OK, John, I know, that you are going to come out better on the deal than I am, by about a half a bag of cornmeal, but I'll agree to that, but, if, I don't need twenty-five dollars' worth of goods here today, out of that what is left, that you'll pay me out cash for the difference?" He asked.

John nodded his head, said OK, and, they shook hands on the deal. John showed Orval where the five pound bags and scoops were, where the scales were, how to operate the scales, got him some string to tie the bags with, and showed him how he wanted the bags tied. Orval then went out to the wagon and started bring in the eighteen bags of cornmeal to break down for John bag by bag.

Orval finished the agreed upon chores of weighing out the cornmeal and bagging it up, neatly tying each bag, then, went around the store gathering up what he needed. Dried beans, oats, flour, sugar, a slab of salt pork, a couple of cheap candles, and, a couple of 12 gage shotgun shells of double ought buck shot type. He asked John where the coal oil was, and John yelled back that it was now out back of the store and that it was now called kerosene. Orval went looking out back with can in hand, found the drum and filled up his can. He then stacked his stuff up and went up to the counter for John to ring him out. Orval's total owed amounted to eleven dollars and fifty cents. John then gave Orval thirteen dollars and fifty cents in change. Orval asked if John would slice up the slab of salt pork, and, John told him that he could do it himself, and, showed him where the hand crank slicer was. After Orval sliced up his salt pork and wrapped it up in a piece of paper, then, he put it all into a gunny sack.
"You got your stuff all together?" John asked.

Orval looked down at his gunny sack, then, replied to John. "Well, yes and no, John, I mean, yes that I have everything I come to town to get today, but, as for the rest of me, I'm not so sure. You know, I remember, years and years ago, when I had the finest team of mules in the County, and, even won a prize or two down at the County Fair. Nowadays, I'm hard put to even know of anyone else in the County that even has a team of mules. John, I'm a-livin' in yesteryear, I'm a has been, I have lived long enough to have become a livin' memory. I don't see horses and buggies and wagons on the streets anymore, everywhere you look, all you see is those automobiles, and, they scare my mules, hells bells, they even scare me! Years ago, no one had any money, but they got by, didn't they? Today, everyone has money and they can't even make it payday to payday. I am the only one that I know, that don't have electric in my house, I still live by candle and oil lamp. I am the only one I know, that don't have runnin' water, I still pull my water out of the well with a bucket. I am the only one I know, that don't have a toilet inside the house, I still have an outhouse that is mighty cold on a winter's morn. Now, today, I eat and sleep very little and it don't take much to get me by. I want you to know, that I appreciate everythin' you have done for me over the years, and, I don't know if I can every repay you. You are one of the few folks in town that even understands me, I mean, think about it, if I had me one of those newfangled automobiles, do you suppose that the dealer would let me trade ten or fifteen pounds of cornmeal to grease it and change the oil on the thing?"

John looked at Orval and said. "Orval, we been friends for a long time. Let's keep it that way on into our future. Someday, maybe, we might just be the oldest two codgers still alive and kickin' around this town."

Orval said thanks to John, again, for everything, and headed out the door for home.

When Orval arrived at home, he unhitched and unharnessed the mules and put them away after feeding them and giving them water. He also feed the chickens some of the cracked corn and put the rest away in a barrel and put the lid on top. You have to keep other little critters out, he thought to himself. Then, he took his goods into the house and put them away in the kitchen. Lorena was not about the house. Orval thought that she must be visiting her lady friends. Later, when she did not come home before dark, he figured that she must have gone on to evening church with the ladies. He fixed himself a bite of supper and being tired as he was, not getting any more sleep than he had, he crawled in early, figuring that Lorena would be along home soon.

During the night, the chicken's a-cackling woke Orval again. He got up, opened the bedroom curtains and peered out into the darkness. A partial moon shined off and on from behind clouds which lighted the field and trees in back of the house. He thought that he caught a glimpse of something moving amongst the trees. He stood and watched, then, he again saw what he thought to be something moving again, but now, from tree to tree. He called out. "Lorena, Lorena, wake up, get my shotgun, I've got the shells here. There is someone out in the woods moving around from tree to tree, they might be chicken thieves, or, a-tryin' to get in the barn to steal my mules. Quick, get my shotgun."

Lorena rolled out of bed and got Orval's shotgun from where it was hanging in the hallway near the lighted night candle. She brought the gun to him and said. "Now, Orval, don't you be shootin' someone for no reason. Maybe it's someone lost from a huntin' party. Or, maybe it's some runaway child. Maybe they is a-lookin' for their lost dog. There ain't no tellin' what they might be, or, what help they might need."

Orval loaded the double barrel shot gun with the two double ought buckshot shells that he had bought from John. He kept watching. "Lorena, I know, that they ain't no tellin' what in the world that they might be up to, but, I'm gonna make sure that they ain't tryin' to steal the chickens, or maybe even get in the barn to steal my mules. Those mules is our very livelihood. Those chickens are too, we have enough eggs to eat and some to sell or trade, and, have chicken for Sunday dinner once in a while, and, I just ain't a-gonna let no one take away something for free that we have worked so hard to get." He said.

Lorena was now right behind and pushing up against Orval, trying to see out the window herself. "Where are you a-lookin', I don't see much of anything out there." She said.

"Here, look over my right shoulder and I'll point out the trees that someone is a-movin' back and forth from, from one tree to the other, then, back again. If that ain't dang suspicious, I don't know what is." He said.

"I still ain't seein' anythin', anywhere, anyhow." She said, while again pushing all the way up to the window with her forehead pushed up on the glass.

"You watch, Lorena, I'm getting' my pants on, and, I'm goin' out there to see what they are up to." Orval said.

Lorena came right back at him. "No you ain't, you ain't goin' out there, if there was someone up to no good, they would sure see you before you seen them. They have been out there in the dark, and their eyes are already used to the dark, while you have been here in the house with the candle lit up a-showin' yourself off." She said.

Orval was getting his pants on anyway, despite what Lorena was saying. "Lorena, I've got a double barrel shotgun fully loaded. If someone ain't got sense enough to back down from that, then, they deserve to be shot." He said.

Lorena was now to the point of pleading with him. "Orval, come to your senses, I can't let you go out there, you don't know what you might be up against. What if they are drunk out of their minds, what if they are murderers on the run in the night, what if they are just tryin' to tempt you or trick you to just come out of the house?" She said.

Orval went back to the window. "I'm still a-watchin', and, if I see them come up close to the barn or the chicken house, I'm-a going out there come hell or high water." He said.

From that point on, for the next hour or so, neither Orval nor Lorena, either one, saw anyone else move out in the woods. The chickens had settled down, and the clouds had gone away, and, the moonlight had become brighter where you could see much better. "Maybe they gave it up for the night because of the bright moonlight." Orval said.

Lorena had already gone back to bed, but, she woke up enough to say.

"I'm sure that that's most likely the case, and, I am sure that maybe you ought to give it up too and come on to bed."

Orval sat his shotgun up next to the window, but he didn't unload it. He finally took his pants back off and climbed back into bed. "I'm a-leavin' my shotgun loaded, just in case we get woke up again." He said.

"That's good." Lorena said while patting her pillow and turning over to go back to sleep.

The next few nights were all the same. First it was the itches, then, it was the chickens a-cacklin, then, it was someone walking about in the woods close by, sometimes getting closer, sometimes not so, sometimes with Orval getting the shotgun, loading it, then, unloading it in the morning. Orval had all that he could take. He decided that he would go to the Sheriff first thing in the morning. Maybe the Sheriff could assign a deputy to look into what was going on. Do an investigation, or, whatever they called it. With that decision being made, Orval finally fell off to sleep.

When morning came, Orval could hardly wait to get to town to see the Sheriff. He didn't even build a fire in the kitchen stove or fix himself breakfast. He did need to get some of his money to buy more shotgun shells, he thought. He hurriedly fed and watered the mules and the chickens. He was obviously impatient while the mules had their breakfast of corn. He didn't even want to wait until they finished eating to harness up the mules to take the wagon into town. He decided that that it would be faster, if he would just saddle up one of the mules, whichever one finished eating first, and, he would ride him into town, since it was faster than him walking the half-mile into town. He went up to the back door and yelled to Lorena that he was headed for town and that he would be back before lunch. He let one of the mules out of the stall for pasture, then saddled the other mule, led it out of the stall, opened the gate, led the mule out, then, closed the gate and tied it tight shut. Orval then mounted up and headed toward town.

Coming into town, he rode up to the Sheriff's office, dismounted and tied his mule up to the closest post out front. He went in to meet the

Sheriff's clerk in the front office. "Good morning, Miss Sarah, I come to see Sheriff Sam. Is he come in yet?" He asked.

"Why yes he is, Orval. Let me see if he is free. He has been back in the jail feeding a couple of our overnight client's breakfast. Let me check." She said. With that, Sarah went back down the hall. Orval sat down in the lobby area to wait and see. He thought. It was always right to be polite. You get a lot more things your way if you are polite.

In a short time, Sheriff Sam came down the hall with Miss Sarah following. "Orval." He said. "Good to see you. Come on in the office. I saw your wagon and mules in town last week. I haven't heard much from your part of the County lately, what's new with you?"

Orval got up and walked back to the office with the Sheriff. "Well, I don't know much new, except all them automobiles a-runnin' up and down the street sure makes my mules skittish." He said.

"Yeah, I know, but that's what the world is coming to. Why, would you believe that the County has already bought the Department two of those automobiles, just in case one of them breaks down? I never thought I would see such in my life time. So, what do you have going on that I need to know about?" Sheriff Sam said.

Orval sat down across from Sam's desk and started his previously thought out explanation of his perceived problem. "Well, Sam, it is like this. For some time now, every night, it all starts with the itches, or, if not the itches, it's my chicken's a-cacklin', which wakes me up. Then, I gets myself up, and looks out of the bedroom winder, just to maybe see what is disturbing my chickens. Then, out in the woods, just behind my barn and chicken house, I can make out someone, sometimes someone a-walkin', sometimes, someone a-hidin' behind a tree. One night, it's this tree, then, another night, it's another tree, sometimes they move, and sometimes they don't. I have tried to think it all out, and, I have come to the conclusion, that someone is a-casing my house, or, my barn, or, my chicken house."

The Sheriff looked at Orval, thought a little, and then said. "Well, Orval, I can relieve some of your anxiety, maybe a little. First, I have been Sheriff now for more than ten years, and, in that whole time, we have not had one horse or mule stole in the entire County. In this day and time, the horse thieves have now moved on up with the industrial age, and now, they have gone to stealing those newfangled automobiles which have all but taken over almost all transportation. So, I don't think you have a horse thief, or, in your case, a mule thief hiding out there in your woods. Second, I only have two chicken thief suspects and they both live on the other side of the County. One is on probation, and, he is behaving right nicely and working steady. The other has no transportation, other than his walking everywhere, and, he is completely on the other side of the County from where you live. So, I don't think you got yourself a chicken thief."

Orval looked up at the Sheriff and asked. "Then, just what do you suppose that I got a-goin' on out at my place then?"

The Sheriff hesitated a little, and then said. "Well, maybe, just maybe, you got someone out there in your part of the country that likes to watch folks, or, look in their windows, something like that."

"You mean like a peepin' Tom?" Orval asked.

The Sheriff continued. "Orval, just about the time that I think that I have seen or heard of everything, something comes along to just bust me up that I can hardly believe. Do you know, that there are more women than there are men, who are out and about looking in other folk's windows? Why, I caught one woman, a church woman no less, who had fallen in love with another man who had married some other woman. She used to go look just hoping to see that he was unhappy. She even sent the other woman flowers, with no name on the card, just to see if it could cause a rukus between the man and woman. Hoping maybe, that, if they separated, somehow, that maybe she would have another chance at him. Another time, I caught a man, that did the same thing, but, he was looking in windows to see his son growing up. You see, this man and woman had an affair but she was married, and, she had the boy, and it was not her husbands, but she never told her husband, and, the other guy just wanted to see his son. Why, he even volunteered to be a coach on the little league baseball team, but would only coach on the team that the boy was playing on, and, he did other things like that just to have some closeness with the boy as he was growing up. I remember another woman, who was also a church goer, who didn't like the deacon, and who thought that her husband would make a better deacon, and, who thought that the deacon's wife was drinking too much wine, and, she went to watching her at night just to prove she was right so she could bring a complaint against her and her husband, just so her husband could get a chance at the deaconship, or, another woman who was so much in love with a man, and, vice-a-versa, the same for a man much in love with a woman, but neither one, could not bring themselves to make some direct contact for whatever reason, being embarrassed to do so or whatever, so, they just watched one another from afar. I could go on and on about this type of thing, but, maybe that is something similar going on out at your place." He said.

"So, you think I got a peeper, that can't get close enough to peep, because of my chickens a-cacklin' and that is what keeps them scared away? Is that what you are sayin' Sam?" Orval asked.

"Well, I'm just saying that that is one of the most likely possibilities. Just think about it. If it were raccoon hunters, they would move on out of the woods and you would hear their dogs barking on the trail. Fishermen usually go out early in the morning, not at night just before bed. By the same token, hunters and fishermen never go alone, they always have a buddy, because they know that if something happened to them out in the woods or out on the lake, that they could die in bad weather out there in some field, or drown in the river of the lake, just being by themselves." Sam said.

Orval looked up again and said. "Well, I never thought of such. I mean, I never ever had any other woman take a dandy toward me, and I knew to leave well enough alone to never do anything like that myself, why my wife would have killed me and the woman both had I ever done something like that, and, she would have probably have known it, if I had ever even thought about doing something like that."

Sam looked at Orval and asked. "Orval, how long has it been now since your wife died? What was her name? Lenora?"

"Lorena, Lorena that was her name. It will be three years next month since she died. She had memory problems, you know, not that I don't have some now and then myself." Orval responded.

"How long were you and Lorena married when she died?" Sam asked.

"Fifty-seven years. We were married fifty-seven very too short years. It seems, that it all went by faster'n one of them fallin' stars a-flashin'' by in the sky." Orval said

Sam looked at Orval, hesitated, and then said. "Well, you know, Orval, I have both seen and heard, that folks who were married a long time, some, not even as long as you and Lorena were married, that those folks come to be joined together, like the preacher says when they marry someone, that they become one, and, that no one should or could ever tear them asunder, and, you can see it if you look for it. Do you know what I mean?"

Orval looked up at Sam. "Sam, I know, that I'm a-livin; in the past. I am a has been, and have been, for some time now. I don't have either electric or water hooked up to my house, I live by candle light and a coal oil lamp, I don't have an indoor toilet, I still have an outhouse. I draw water in a bucket from the well, and, I drink out of the bucket. I never go anywhere other than where my mules can take me, or, where I can walk. Sometimes, Sam, I get overloaded on my thinkin' anymore. I just might have to think about that on the way home." He said, as he got up to leave.

The Sheriff got up to walk Orval out of the office and told him. "Now, Orval, if you just happen to see an automobile, parked along the road near your house, a little before dark now and then, over the next few days, don't think anything about it. I will have one of my deputies stake your place out, and, maybe bring that person in for questioning, the one who has been skulking around in the edge of the woods behind your house. I will keep you posted if anything turns up. You understand? So, I don't want you worrying none further, do you hear me?" Sam added.

"Thanks Sam, I appreciate that, just be sure to let him know, that I have a double barreled 12 gage shotgun in the house to protect myself." Orval said.

"I'll tell him, Orval, I'll be sure to mention that." Sam said, as they walked out to the street. Then, he waved goodbye as Orval mounted up on his mule for his ride back home.

On the way home, plodding along on his mule, Orval talked to himself some, argued with himself a little, why, he even tried to converse with the mule a little, then, he finally come to some agreement with himself, that he had more to think about in this day and time, than he had ever previously thought about.

HEREFORD MCABELEY

Early on, in this dream, it is required, so as, that the dreamer may understand what is to come later, a short introductory or pre-emptory dream if you will, just to try to explain things up proper, so, please bear with that requirement for the time being, and by the time you too get well on into the dream along with me, it may assist and help you to more fully understand the overall purposes and intents to try to make some understanding of the story out of the dream, if at all, if you will.

Now, while dreaming about it all in the pre-emptory, before I first met, or remember for that matter, or had anything to do with, that I had come to know of, a certain character named Hereford McAbeley, I remembered from the pre-emptory dream, of having thought to myself, that I had never met anyone, over my entire lifetime, at that particular moment in time or in any of my dreams either, by the name of Hereford. I had heard of a cow, that a local farmer had, that he had confirmed was of a certain Hereford brand, but he had never used that name on her too much, but instead, had given her the name of "Bessie", and he used that name, Bessie the cow, when he called her in at milking time, and, he said that she always came in both to it and by it and would have made her Hereford genealogy proud. By the same token, when I thought about it further, I had never known anyone with the name of McAbeley, either Hereford or his father for that matter, and, I do not ever recollect of ever hearing of Hereford's middle name, ever, but some ingrained instinct, well inside of me, kind of just told me, that if he did have a middle name, that it would be something most likely, and most probably, just as odd. I do not know why I thought this to be significant, at that time, but I did.

Sometimes, Hereford would pronounce his name "Mac-abe-ly" while, at other times he would pronounce it "Mac-able-ly". Generally, in most cases, later on, when working with him, I just always called him Hereford. Now, to further this thought, I have known many folks that sometimes, declared that they only had initials for their names, like G.W., and, that is all that they were called, I always thought that G.W. would stand for George Washington, but was never really fully sure. I knew several folks named J. R., but never came to know what that ever stood for either, except maybe Junior, or James Robert, or, something equivalent. But, Hereford was not a Junior to his father, although they did act alike in some ways. By the same token, so as, that I should think to mention it, was, that I, at one time or another, and, on several other various multiple occasions, considered Hereford to be somewhat more than as odd as his name, but other than that, I found him to be generally acceptable in nature, a fairly outgoing kind of personality, and, he seemed to have established for himself a most definite place in the community, as, he was forever doing things for folks, to no end, just not for the ones who bought insurance from him, I might add, but almost anyone and everyone, in our little community of Central Falls, where most of the folks around town, were somehow touched by him in one very positive way or another. Hereford was a "do-gooder" in my book, and I kept a tight book, for the most part, that is, on occasion.

Now, our fine community of Central Falls, Rhode Island, was neither large nor small, it was kind of what you would, or, might call, somehow caught in between the other two. It was large enough, that it was not possible for you to get to know everyone in the community by name, yet, small enough that you knew most of the folks that you had to directly deal with, and, for the most part, generally, could call those folks by their first name. Hereford probably knew more folks than most, because he was an insurance man. Actually, Hereford was the one of the few insurance men in and around Central Falls. In some sense, that made business good for Herford McAbleley and the Community Insurance that his father before him had founded, and now, the business being Hereford's, it also made it a little easier for him. Now, Hereford sold all kinds and all types of insurance, insurance for your car, insurance for your house, insurance for your life, cancer insurance, polio insurance, and, other types of health insurance, with some of his insurances being kind of out on the fringes, for instance, or, for example, whichever, like his pet insurance program, or, his disaster insurance, which I just have to address later, for it to be believed.

Hereford, was what you call, an independent multiple line insurance man, selling anything and everything needed by the community at large, which, the way he operated his line of business, was anything and everything, whichever, and, both he and his father before him, had most of the folks in all of Central Falls, insured for one thing or another, at one time or another, over the years that have gone by. Hereford's dad sold insurance, but to tell the truth, Hereford, himself, was never much of a salesman as compared to his father. If you needed insurance, you just went to Hereford, and he wrote you up for whatever you needed, or wanted, at the time, for that matter. Hereford was not the kind of man that would ever go door to door trying to sell anyone anything, although, he was usually out and about, here and there, all over Central Falls and sometimes on up into Pawtucket, and all over, maybe even up around Woonsocket, or, over at Providence, all over, just about like a stink. Hereford may not have known everyone in Central Falls by name, but you could say that most folks in town knew him and his, and what his business was.

Now, there were some of the folks in Central Falls, that had insurance elsewhere, like on up in Woonsocket, with the French, other than with Hereford, but most of them were the type of folks who did not want other folks knowing much about their personal business, or, knowing any more than they wanted them to know, anyway, so, they took most of their insurance business out of town. Most of those folks also took their banking business and other personal business out of town too, shopping and all, mostly, so other local folks, would never know either how much money they had, or, just how little money that they actually had, some, because of family secrecy, or, for whatever purpose, or, other reason that I never quite figured out, and, others because of the potential possible embarrassment to their families otherwise. Hereford, I might mention, was my insurance man, and, I had no problem with that, as I had little to hide from most of the folks in Central Falls, and, they all knew, or, had either seen first-hand or heard about most of my capers, and knew first hand of most of my deficiencies, I might add, that I either had attempted or fully accomplished at one time or another, or some, which had come to fruition for that matter, in my younger years, mostly. Not to say, that I was nearly perfect in any way, shape, form or fashion, but folks around town did not point very many of their skinny bony fingers at me, signal me with a certain selected elected finger, or, whisper things to one another, too much, behind my back, that I took note of, at least in my more recent years, and, as for all the rest of the whole bunch congregated in town, the millers, the jewelers, and even some of the fishermen included, I, for the better part, could have cared less overall.

Now, I did not grow up with Hereford, and, I honestly have to say, that I do not know where he came from, other, than that, he just came home one day from some boarding school, from somewhere else, and, just up and took over his father's insurance business, called, the "Community Insurance". I had previously worked for Hereford's father, doing odd jobs, off and on for some years, before Hereford came back from school, that is. When Hereford came back, his father then retired from the insurance business and he and his wife, whom I took to be Hereford's mother, but was never told directly or right out, were said to have retired and moved down to Florida, to a more favorable climate for their bones in their old age, or, somewhere else that I can't remember, right off, and, Hereford took over the business in the same house where his father ran the insurance business for as long as anyone around Central Falls, or, Pawtucket, for that matter, can remember. Now, personally, if you had asked me for my opinion, which, you did not, but, I am going to give it to you anyway, as I said before, Hereford's father was a much better insurance salesman, than Hereford ever dared to be. Hereford was too straight-forward, too direct, too matter-of-fact, too down-to-earth, and, if I might add, too much like Hereford, which, most folks agreed to or had to put up with, sooner or later.

Now, Hereford did not have to do much to get his job as an insurance man, as, he did not even have to make application or interview, as, it was just kind of handed over, given up, and turned over to him in one fell swoop by his father. Hereford did not even have to put up a new sign, as, his father's sign "Community Insurance", was out in front of the house, and, served the most suitable purpose. Hereford did not even have to go to the trouble to repair or repaint it, as, it stood out fine enough on its own. Now, I am sure that Hereford had to pass some State test in order to qualify to be able to sell insurance, but that was just something else, another little detail, amongst other multiple little details, that I really had no particular business whatsoever to know, however, but it is mentioned, because that, just happens to be another little bit of information, that I never quite got all put together in my brain, or got to know directly, about Hereford. My work with Hereford's dad, was what most folks call "part time" and "on call", a kind of a "Jack of all trades", handyman status, on an "as needed" basis. But, I might mention, that the work, overall, helped me to pay my bills, and, I did not have to put myself out too much, overall, like as if I had to work at one of the mills around town, working from daylight to dark. Now, as far as I knew, because no one told me any different, I was to continue with the same arrangements with Hereford at the helm, although I never got that in writing, only in general verbal discussion.

In trying to get to know Hereford a little better, I first tried to make small talk by asking him where he went to school, and he said flatly, "back east". When I asked him where back east, because Rhode Island is not exactly very much west of anything, he said "on the coast". When I asked him the name of the school, he said that "it did not particularly matter, as the school was so small that very few folks in this area had probably never heard of it, and, that it would most likely just embarrass him more just to talk about it". So, I let it go, I let it drop, and, I just figured it was probably somewhere up around Boston, somewhere in that area, where folks are forever saying things like, "Ahh, Boston, land of the baked beans and cod, where the Lodges only speak to the Cabot's, and the Cabot's speak only to God". Well, maybe, they might have talked at one time or another, to

21

the rest of those folks up there that were either related to the Fitzgerald's or the Kennedy's, or, some other shirt-tail-kin that had tight lips, but never with a definite answer to anything to speak of in public. I think that is why those folks mostly make for good salesmen and politicians, if there is such of a thing for either. That was the way with Hereford, you never really ever got a definite clear cut answer out of him either, even when he explained things, and, he was the same way when he dealt with his clients in his insurance business. "How is business?" folks would ask Hereford, "So-So", or "Samo-Samo", "What are you doing Hereford?", "Oh, this and that", "Where you doing this and that Hereford?", "Oh, here and there." When you doing this and that here and there Hereford?' "Oh, now and then." He would say. Or, "Community Insurance is-sure-a-cookin' on the front burner", or, "We're rollin' right along and walkin' on back home." was about all you would ever hear him say. Not to say, that that was bad, in anyway, that was just Hereford being Hereford, and, that is the way that he was, and, you could tell, that he was not likely to change anytime into the near future, as he was kind of "set in his ways" so to speak, even though he was still young.

Now, when you needed Hereford, for some insurance matter, you would have to go hunt him up or hunt him down, to find him somewhere, as, he was never in his office, and, when you did not need him at all, you would forever be bumping into him or see him out and about, around town, talking up business, finding out what was new, filling in where he was needed, looking out and about to fill some of the odd ball needs of the folks in Central Falls and on up around Pawtucket. Hereford did more good, mostly volunteer kind of stuff, than anyone else that I have ever met in my lifetime, even up to this day, and the energy that he had, going from daylight to dark, and even after sometimes, if he needed to do something for someone that needed something done immediately that couldn't wait, that kind of thing, never ending, it would get done, but not ever to the point of attracting any attention back to Hereford, but, I am not exactly sure how he came to accomplish all that. A lot of town folks said, and, just not under their breath, that Hereford was a most "precious man", out to do good in every way that he could, but never seeking recognition in any way, shape, form or fashion, and, the same could be said of his wife Anielia, who folks also called a "precious lady", who was also always out and about with a helping hand, doing good for someone or another, at no cost to anyone, ever. Hereford and Anielia were the absolute perfect pair, and most folks in Central Falls felt fortunate and were glad to have them living within the community.

Folks in town, knew Hereford as being married to this most delightful lady that most folks called Anielia, by name, but some in town, called her Nelly, and, I might add, that, it was kind of the word around town, and, the rumored supposition was, that most folks thought, that she had to have been his high-school sweetheart, no other explanation being ever given, but no children born between the two of them had ever come along, that anyone had ever seen or heard of, with Anielia being the most private kind of lady that she was, but, I might mention, very out-going, for the most part, generally, and, on regular occasion. Like clockwork, day in and day out, she would set out on her daily missions with a joyful fervor that you could see a block away, even on the weekend, instead of them going to church, because, I never, ever remember either of them attending any of the churches around Central Falls, although, they did work in the soup kitchens and things like that. When Aniela set out in the morning, she was always flitting around town like a sweet little Angel, helping folks, baking birthday cakes for the little children in the community, baking pies and cookies for the old folks to eat after them going to funerals, picking wild flowers and taking bouquets to sick folks at home or in the hospital, taking poor folks sacks of groceries and leaving the sack on their porch sometimes, so that they never knew who delivered it or where it came from, buying winter coats down at the Salvation Army store, and giving them out to children on the street, that type or sort of thing, working at the food pantry, and the "soup kitchen" where she would sneak some folks extra beans or mashed potatoes with a big grin, too, she packed up lunches and dinners and delivered them to the "shut-ins" and other needy folk around town, all of which was what I called "a good work". Anielia also volunteered at the grade schools helping out in the kitchens to fix the kids lunch, then, afterward, helping them with their studies until lunch was over, then, on into the study hall with them. She was not a busy body, in any way, as she did not attract attention in doing anything that she ever did, and, sometimes, it seemed that she just caused things to happen, something like magic, and, no one quite knew just how it all came about, but mostly she was a most helpful and caring person and bore evidence of such, and, was the kind of person whom you really appreciated, just getting to know, and, I might add, she did it all with very little acknowledgement by anyone, and, when someone did acknowledge her work, she appeared somewhat embarrassed, which, when I think, about it, that that is how she wanted to do it all, and forever and always, giving everyone or someone else any of the credit.

On the first occasion, where I got to meet Anielia up close, was when I helped Hereford carry in a hide-a-bed couch at his house, he told me that he had gotten a good deal on it at a yard sale, it was one of those kind of couches that had a mattress in it that you could fold out and make it into a bed, and him and Anielia were adding it to their living room furniture. I do remember that it was heavy, and, that Anielia had all but cleared out the living room to get the couch in, then held the door open for us, but, just like a woman, she could not decide exactly where she wanted it to sit, so, she had us move it around two or three times, or more, until it kind of finally settled down, all by itself, over against one wall. "You having company on the way in from out of state, Hereford?", I asked, but his reply was only "Not really", and, it was the kind of a "not really" that had a certain tone or ring to it, that told you, that you would not gain any more information out of him about that, so, you might as well not say anything else about it at all. Anielia made no other comment except to say "thank you, thank you, thank you", and, offered me tea, which I fully accepted, and as, that is how I learned that she was a tea drinker herself.

It was during the time of having tea with Anielia and Hereford, that Anielia explained a simple philosophy to me, as she put it. "Tea is much like mankind in itself, as, the tea plant does not grow everywhere, as it only puts its roots down where it gets equal sunshine and darkness, the right soil, the right climate, and the right amount moisture at the right time of the year, like mankind, everyone in this world, finds someplace to put their roots down, but then, some folks, like the gypsies or the nomads never do, as they just wander on forever here and yon. The rest of us are all looking for some good place to put our roots down, then, when we do, we give of our self, like the tea plant. Now, they do not cut the plant down when they harvest the tea, as that would destroy it, but they trim the leaves at various times during the harvesting season. Rose bushes are like tea plants, and, you have to learn how to cut the rose at the right place on the stem, at the exact right place in order for more roses to come onto the plant, and for it to flourish, if you do not cut them right, the rose plant rebels and ceases to bloom. Like tea, you have to be gentle and trim it, not like a hedge, but by one leaf or at least a few leaves at a time." She went on. "Also, mankind is much like that, in that you cannot cut someone down physically or psychologically, as it could totally destroy them, or, at least set them back several years. We give of ourselves, not too much, but just enough to enrich the lives of others. We all have to let one another give of themselves, like the tea plant or the rose bush, gives of itself for our enjoyment year after year, but then, sometimes we expect too much. too soon, of some folks. Too, in tea, it is not the leaf, or the bud, or the stem that flavors the tea, it is how the tea leaves are processed after being picked. All of mankind is in the mode of being processed, one way or another, for better or for worse." I had to stop and think about that for a moment, but, she went on. "Too, the flavor of the tea is enhanced, by the way or methods that the tea leaves are processed, and, additionally; by the way we make the tea, dependent upon our habits and cultures. Mankind is like that, in that, our best or worst can be brought out by our fellow man dependent upon how we interact with one another." I listened, and thought to myself, why is it, that ideas and things like this, this kind of insight, this simple kind of wisdom, is not being taught in our schools and colleges in this day and time. But my brain could not bear to dwell on such thought for too long until it went on and started out on its own to start thinking about something else.

That was the first time, now that I think about it, that I ever was inside of Hereford's house, and, had the gracious opportunity to meet with that young petite and caring lady of the McAbeley household who was Hereford's better half, and, now, there, on that day, I got to know her personally, and finally, I might add. I was more proud for having gotten to meet her. When I worked for Hereford's dad, I never remembered ever being invited into the house, and, I usually took my work orders out on the front porch, not that they were stand-offish, but he and his wife were just a little different breed from Hereford and his wife Anielia, even though they were apparently related.

Now, in some other respects, Hereford was just like his father, in that, they both always said that they could insure almost anything, boats, cars, motorcycles, barns, houses, but then, Hereford pushed the envelope completely out of the box, so to speak, and began to insure pets and farm animals, and whatever other type of insurance that anyone needed along the way, he would even insure them against hell or high water, and, I think that either one of them, Hereford, or his father, could have insured folks even for or against whatever, or with respect to those, whichever. Hereford, however, took it on up another rung up the insurance ladder, on up to another level, so to speak, on the ladder of his success, and also insured things that his father probably had never even dreamed of insuring, or, most likely, if the truth were ever known, had never even crossed his father's mind to do such.

Hereford told me, that one time, he had even insured a farmer's water well, and, had insured it, against it ever drying up, or, "going dry" as they say. Well, the well owner, a farmer, reported that by late summer the same year, the danged well had sure enough gone dry, and, he indicated that he wanted to make a claim and collect against his insurance with Hereford and the Community Insurance, in order to get some of his money back that he had already paid in, of course. That, of all things, is what was to be my first big job working with Hereford since he had taken over the business from his father, and, it jump started my continuing working relationship with Hereford, as, Hereford hired me, based, I guessed, on what his dad had told him about me, I always thought, but not right off of the street, or on the spot kind, if you will, because, at that particular moment in time, I was in the middle of a good pool game, down at Kadise's pool hall, and, Hereford hired me, there, amongst the smell of smoke and whiskey, to help him do what he had to do as an insurance man, and, from that time on, I have continued working with him off and on over the years, doing one thing or another, since that day, and, this is how I got to get to know Hereford, more personally. At that time, Hereford, had already investigated the farmers dry well situation, as, he told me, in the initial briefing for the job, sitting in his truck, that he had already put a bucket down into the well, bounced it around, brought it out, and found that there was still dampness down in the bottom of the well, and, had already told the farmer that the well was only silted in and just needed a good cleaning out, as there was, most likely, still plenty of water down there, and we were going to get to work on it.

We went out to Hereford's house and gathered up everything we were going to need to do the job on the dried up well. Hereford got a lantern, some rope, a flash light, a short handled shovel, an old board with holes in each end, a pair of fishing waders that had a buckle up bib in the front, and, he brought along "Rufus". I never knew what kind of dog Rufus was, but Hereford always said that "Rufus" was a "Jack Daniel's Terrier", or, something like that. Now, I might mention here, early on, that I already knew of Rufus, even before I come to know Hereford, even before Hereford took over the insurance business from his father. Rufus was actually Hereford's dad's dog, which Hereford had inherited, along with the insurance business, I knew that. Now, I always wondered, but never got an answer, as to how old Rufus really was, as, he had to be older than dirt, but, Rufus just didn't ever look as old as he should have been, and, he didn't act old, but he was old, he had to be, even in dog years, that is, if you calculate up the total years of his life, that is, when I remember and think back about it. Prior to Hereford coming back home, Rufus was always with old man McAbeley or his wife, everywhere they went, always with his head stuck out of their car window, enjoying the breeze, and, even when I worked with him, Hereford's dad always brought the dog along, so, I got to know Rufus and Rufus got to know me, and, over a number of years, Rufus accepted me for what I was, I might add, with no further questions asked, but he would still give you a good sniff, just to make sure it was you. Too, Rufus had manners, as, I never seen him hump anyone's leg that I remember, and if you were a friend of Hereford, you were also a friend of Rufus, or, the other way around, whichever, as that is just the way he was. Now, today, in up to date time, Rufus, was always now either with Hereford, or, with his wife Anielia when they were out and about town. Too, as best as I remember, Rufus was also the kind of dog that was just always there, and looking out to be petted or provided with some delicacy that only dogs seem to care for, and, for the most part, you could say, Rufus was fairly well behaved, for a dog, that is. Rufus, on regular occasion, acted smart, smarter than a dog should really be, and, you could even see it in his eyes when he looked at you, as if he wanted to talk to you, and, sometimes, I even think that he tried. Rufus seemed to know things afore hand, like, which way you were going to move, when you were going to get up or stand up, when he needed to move out of the way, when someone was coming, where the cats were, that type of thing. Rufus just knew where he was supposed to be at any given moment in time, and, he just showed up there, "Johnny on the spot", or "Rufus-on-the-spot", I should say.

By the time that Rufus got me checked out by sniffing me up and down, making sure I was who he thought I was, Hereford and I had already arrived at the farm. We met with the farmer and went out to his well, where Hereford lit up the lantern, even though it was broad day light outside, it was dark down in the well, and, he tied a rope on the lantern and lowered it down into the well, "to test the air", he said. He said, that if the lantern went out, that meant that there was not enough breathing air oxygen in the well to be able to work in. But if the lantern stayed lit up brightly he said that "that was a good sign". Hereford then got his rope, looped up several loops, put the loops around "Rufus's" legs, neck and body, and picked him up and lowered "Rufus" down into the well. He said if "Rufus" stayed awake and did not go to sleep, the air was sure to be good down at the bottom of the well, and also, safe enough for me to work in. This was Hereford's "second test". It worked out well, in that "Rufus" was down in the bottom of the well, barking his fool head off, and, Hereford said that "that was a good sign". Hereford then pulled "Rufus" out of the well, muddy paws and all and let him go. Rufus then licked his paws clean, and, lay down by a nearby tree and proceeded to watch us work, which, I might add, he was especially good at.

Hereford asked the farmer where he wanted the silt to be put, and the farmer said put it in his garden, and he even went and got Hereford a wheelbarrow, to carry the silt from the well to the garden. Hereford looked at the wheelbarrow, told the farmer that he did not know anything much about machinery, the farmer looked at Hereford kind of funny, then said that maybe it would be better if he did it himself. Hereford nodded in agreement. Then, Hereford made up what he called a "Bosun's chair", with a couple loops of rope and the old board with the holes in each end of it, dropped the shovel down into the well, and, told me to put on the fishing waders and to buckle up the bib. I did as told, and, I climbed onto the well railing and worked myself into the "Bosun's chair", Hereford then ran the rope through the well pulley, looped the other end of the rope around a limb on a nearby tree, told me to climb over the railing, then, with me sitting on the "Bosun's chair", Hereford eased me down into the well with the lantern hanging on. It was here that I noted that Hereford was one strong kind of guy, much stronger than he looked. He told me that if the lantern acted like it was trying to go out, or to go dim, that that meant that there was little oxygen and that I was to yell up for him to send down the "Bosun's chair" and he would pull me up out of the well. After I got down into the bottom of the well, I hung up the lantern on what looked like a root, then, I sent up the "Bosun's chair", and, Hereford sent down the water bucket, he yelled down to me for me to shovel the silt into the bucket and then he would pull it out and send an empty back down. By the time I had sent up 15-20 buckets, and had been hit in the head with the bucket at least 10 or 12 times, I was already more than up to knee deep in muddy water. Hereford said, that when the water got up to waist deep, for me to yell up and he would send down the "Bosun's chair" and he would pull me out. By now, I did not need the shovel anymore, as I just dipped the silt out of the well with the bucket, which made the job to go faster. Another after another, and a few more wheelbarrow loads, and, the job was all but done. Hereford sent down the "Bosun's chair", pulled me out, and told the farmer to wait a day or so for the stirred up silt to settle before he started using the water. I must say, that the farmer was very pleased with our work, and, he dropped the claim against his insurance policy with Hereford right there on the spot, and, he even talked with Hereford about taking out some other types of insurance, he said talking about things going dry, that he needed some insurance on his Jersey cow against her going dry of milk, and Hereford told him to just let him know when and he would write it up. I had to respect Hereford all the more, with him taking the pains to go out of his way to address the complaints of his policyholders, and, making things right, out of things that had gone wrong, one way or another, just like, and just the same as his father did years ago.

On the way back into town, Hereford talked about the job that we had done, and, how good that it had turned out. Hereford said, "You know, down in a well, there is very little circulation of air, and, as it happens, carbon dioxide as a gas is heavier than the air itself, and, is exuded from the carbonaceous materials in the soils, this can cause the Carbon Dioxide (CO_2) gas to collect in the well right above the water because it is a little heavier than the air. This is bad, in the respect that it displaces the air and oxygen, and, it may be hard to breathe accordingly, or, not able to breathe at all, as this is what killed off quite a number of well diggers years and years ago, before anyone recognized the potential hazard. The CO2 gas is good, in the respect, that it seals off the well water from all of the germs, microbes, pollens and yeast that float around in the air, as they cannot live in such an atmosphere either. So, you see, everything has its good side and its bad side, dependent upon how you look at it, or how you are affected by it. This was another thing I found out about Hereford, was, that he kept the work that we did more interesting than not, overall, without question, and, most of the time, I learned something new, that I had never dreamed of learning, and, my brain accepted it.

Hereford one time said, when we were out on a job, and, he said it kind of proudly, that he had once insured a tree, for a widow woman, against it ever being struck by lightning, and, of all things, before the year was out, wouldn't you know it, the woman reported to Hereford that the tree had done up and been struck by a lightning from some passing storm, and had burn marks all over it, from top to bottom, or bottom to top, whichever, and, wanted to file a claim on it against her insurance and the Community Insurance, that she had just recently bought. Well, Hereford said, that he investigated the woman's claim, and said that his finding were, that the lighting actually had not come down from the sky to strike the tree, but had come up from the ground, and, that it was the tree that actually did the striking of the clouds in the sky instead, as, in that fashion, by definition, the tree had not really been struck, and, anyway, that is not what the woman had insurance for, and, besides that, the tree was not totally dead as it still had green leaves on it, and, he added, that if the tree ever did die, it would probably be just from old age, as, in addition, in Hereford's estimation, the tree was already well over past it's prime, and he told her so on the spot. Hereford even showed the widow woman the humped up ground from whence he said the lightning had come. She said that she thought that those humps had been caused by pesky moles, but Hereford said that she was no more than what he graded as a "lay person", and, only a goodly trained insurance man could ever really tell the difference between the two. He said that Rufus probably even thought that the humps were caused by moles, and tried to dig them up, but he said that he corrected Rufus on the spot, as he couldn't even tell the difference.

So, upon Hereford's recommendation, the woman initially dropped her claim against her insurance policy on the tree, but, decided on her own, to continue to pay the premiums of the policy, just from what he said and what I understood. Now, later on, when the tree did not leave out, on the following spring, and the woman again complained to Hereford, and he followed up with another investigation, which was where I came in, because he picked me up, and, we went out to her house just to look things over. Hereford told the woman that it had been a very hard winter and that if the truth was ever to be known to man, that the tree had probably frozen to death in the process and that he was sorry for it. Well, the woman wanted the tree cut down, as she said that she did not want any dead limbs falling out of it and hitting her on the head, whence she was mowing the grass. Hereford agreed with the woman, and mentioned that she did not have any insurance against that sort of thing, then, he had me get the chain saw, an axe and a wedge, and, put me to work, he put me on his schedule again, kind of off of the street, if you will, as I was not at Kadise's pool hall at that time, he told me to cut the tree down, then, to cut it up piece meal, which, I did, from the top down, climbing all over that tree like a monkey before I was through, and, I also split the log parts into firewood size, load it up, and haul it over and delivered it, in Hereford's truck, over to Hereford's house, and stacked it by the cord, out in his front yard, right in front of the Community Insurance sign. Whereupon, Hereford implanted a big hand painted sign which said, "Firewood For Sale – You Pick Up And Haul Off, Please Pay inside at Community Insurance". Hereford sold the fire wood almost immediately thereafter, and, I estimate, as a best guess, for, as a total, of more than a $200, at the going price of what I knew cord wood to be, then, Hereford paid me $50 cash, for the tree cutting, then, we both made another trip, over to the woman's house, immediately thereafter, that is, and Hereford wrote the woman out a Community Insurance refund check for $25 declaring it a bonafied benefit and refund against her insurance policy that she had had on the tree. He reminded the woman that it did not cost her one thin silver Mercury dime to have the tree cut down, and, that she got a better return on her money, which was more than what she had paid in, in insurance premiums on the insurance on the tree, in the first place. The lady took the check in a heartbeat and said that she was tickled and more than delighted that we had stopped by, she then offered us some tea and cookies, which we partook of gingerly, amongst happy discussion about the now missing tree.

While we partook of the tea and cookies, the lady told us that she had taught school years and years ago, but now, she had been retired for years, and, that she had always considered herself to be an environmentalist, and, had used earthy examples of such to teach the pupils in her classes. She said that she had one heard a little sing-song years before, that she used in her teachings, and asked if we would like to hear it. Hereford and I looked at one another, took another sip of tea, and nodded in the affirmative, in unison. The lady went into an adjoining room, and came out with a ukulele, tuned it up as she was saying "my dog has fleas", or something like that, then she began to sing and play.

"There was a bug, A pretty little bug,

The prettiest little bug that you ever did see,

bug on the hair.

hair on the dog,

dog on the porch,

porch on the house,

house on the ground,

And the green grass grew on around, on around

And the green grass grew all around."

It was a pretty little tune, and, the lady said that she made it up from another song about a pretty little bug, on a feather, with the feather on a bird, and the bird on an egg, and an egg in a nest, and the nest on a limb, and the limb on the tree, and, the tree on the roots, and the roots in the ground, and, the green grass grew all around. She said she also had one about a pretty little bug on a hair, with the hair on a cat, with the cat on a board, and the board on a fence, and the fence on a post, and the post in the ground, and the green grass grew on around, on around, and the green grass grew all around. She kind of sing-songed it all and run it all together and, it did not sound all that bad, not as bad as I had expected it to. Now, I had that little jingle ringing all around inside my brain bouncing from one side to another, and, could not for the life of me get it out, or, get it to quit. She then came up with another similar jingle, about a log in a hole in the bottom of the sea, then, there was a knot on the log, then there was a frog on the knot, then, there was a wart on the frog, then, there was a hair on the wart, then, there was a bug on the hair, in a hole in the bottom of the sea, all being sing-songed much like the similar aforementioned. I might say, that she seemed to enjoy singing and performing, and, Hereford and I expressed our enjoyment of it all.

Then, the lady put her hands up on each side of her face, with her palms forward an thumbs pushing into her cheeks, and she said. "Look, Mister Chubby Face, your face is so chubby, you can't even smile." And, then, she would say. "Oh, yes I can.... see." And, she would smile so sweetly. Then, she would put her hands up, one hand above her forehead at her hairline, with palm forward, and, the other other hand, palm forward below her chin. And, she would say. "Look, Mister Long Face, your face is so long, you can't even smile." And, then, she would say. "Oh, yes I can.... see." And, she would again smile so sweetly. And, I could see, just how she could be with children, and, why all of the neighborhood children loved to be around her.

Later, the lady brought up some questions on insurances and talked to Hereford about some of her other various needs. Hereford was a man who knew how to listen, how to do business, how to take care of a customer, how to do what was needed to be done at the time, how to give back whence was given, that sort of thing. Hereford had a knack and a special way to either help folks directly or somehow get them the help that they needed, whether they knew it or not, and, I respected Hereford all the more, and, in addition, was proud to be his employee but mostly glad to just have a job to make a little money to pay my bills.

On a more personal note, Hereford once told me, that on one occasion, that he had even insured a young man, from becoming an alcoholic. I had never heard of such. He said that that particular insurance policy was probably the easiest policy that he had ever sold, as the young man's mother had come to him, looked him up, or hunted him down, whichever, with her hands a-wringing, and immediately demanded such an insurance policy out of him, which was, as it happened, coincidentally, and immediately after the mother had found her only darling beloved son in a stumbling-falling-down drunken stupor, but, of first thought, had considered that her only beloved had possibly come down with that dreaded disease called Polio, and, that she had not had the opportunity to buy him a lick of Polio insurance beforehand, and, it just about scared her to a dropping off the face of the earth death. So, when she found out that the boy way only drunk, from too much wine, that of all things, his uncle had made, and had hid away, with the boy, innocently enough, getting into his uncle's wine cellar on pure unadulterated happenstance alone, through some inviting unbarred and unlocked door, and, that he had somehow guzzled up too much of it down in too little time, so, at that particular moment in time, she got on the band wagon real quick, and hunted up Hereford for some additional insurance to cover the matter. Hereford said that the mother was somewhat actually relieved, that her dearly beloved was only drunk and did not have the dreaded polio, when it all eventually dawned upon her, or when she came to her senses about it all, and after she had gotten a smell of his breath, of course, and it all came to a head, but she then saw a greater need for another type of insurance, against what she saw as being an even greater danger to the very eternal life of her beloved. So, that is how Hereford wrote up the policy against the boy from ever becoming an alcoholic. However, he said, that it was not too long hence, that the boy acted up again, fell off the wagon, so to speak, somewhat, and, pulled the same caper, and did the same thing all over again, and, wouldn't you know it, before the boy had even sobered up, here comes the mother traipsing in to the Community Insurance office, calling for Hereford, and wanting to file a claim against her insurance policy, on behalf of her drunken son. Hereford said that he told her that just getting drunk a couple of times did not qualify, or for that matter, as the act did not make the boy out to be an alcoholic, by a long shot, and, that bonafied alcoholism was something that took years and years of practice, and, besides that, that she had purchased the "long term policy", he explained that alcoholism requires the taking on of daily overdoses of excessively strong spirits, of which wine did not qualify, and, for years and years on end, which requires the ruining of you liver, and, maybe even your pancreas, in order to accomplish. Hereford told the mother that maybe she did not need insurance against the boy becoming an alcoholic as much as she needed insurance to prevent the boy from drinking at all. However, he added, he did not sell that line because that there was very little money to be made in that type of insurance policy anyway, as, most wives would be wanting to either cash it in, or file some claim on it, on behalf of most of their husbands living in Central Falls and some on up into Pawtucket, maybe even all the way up to Woonsocket. Hereford did say that he had went out of his way, and counseled the boy later, telling him that he ought to make some attempt to generate a much closer relationship and a better bond with his uncle, and encouraged the boy to try to extend himself a little and have his uncle teach him how to make wine, which would bring about a little camaraderie with the uncle and ultimately prevent hard feelings within or throughout the family. Hereford said, that the uncle came to him later, thanking him for not making his sister mad at him and settling things with his nephew, and, inquired if Hereford could insure some of his wine against it turning to vinegar. I think Hereford said that he could and he did help the uncle out in that matter.

Hereford had all kinds of stories like this, the dog that he insured against getting the distemper, but then Hereford required the owner to build the dog a dog house, in order to qualify for such a purchase, or, the parakeet that he insured against it never learning how to talk, but then, he made special trips over to see it and try to help it along a little to get it to talk, then, there was the cow that he insured not to ever go dry of milk, but required the farmer to provide her with extra corn, and good alfalfa hay, or, the chickens that he insured against them quitting laying eggs, that he required the chickens to be provided some "scratch" and added vitamins to their water, on and on and on and on, most of the time, unless you were there, first hand, like I was, on occasion, you never got to know what farmer's well it was, or what, or whose tree it was, or who the drunken boy was, who owned the chickens, or whose dog or whose parakeet, or whatever, as, that was information that Hereford kept close to his heart, it was, as Hereford said, "proprietary for an insurance man", so to speak, or, not to speak of it to any great detail. I might mention here, that Hereford's father did not go this far out, as far as I ever knew, on selling these types of insurance policies, and, if the truth were known, Hereford's father probably never had such a thought cross his mind about such kinds of insurance.

Now, it was not just the odd ball interesting things that Hereford handled, as, it was not too interesting when old man Tuck hit a deer out on the edge of town, and all but totaled his pickup truck out on what they called Running Dummy road by the old mill. Hereford was right on that case, all over it, about like stink, getting old man Tuck's truck towed to a local body shop, right here in town, then, he traipsed all over three counties to find here a fender, there a hood, now a bumper, a windshield, then a headlight with brackets, him getting all of the bits, parts and pieces, hauling them back to Central Falls in his own truck, then, helping to bring old man Tuck's truck back to almost rebuilt condition, and, I might say, at a fraction of the cost that any other similar accident would have cost, or, any other out of town body shop's cost would have been. Why, Hereford even let Old man Tuck use The Community Insurance pickup for a few days, until Tuck's truck was repaired and back on the road. Old man Tuck was so happy and pleased with what Hereford did for him, that word around town was, that old man Tuck had done up and talked Hereford into insuring the nose of his blue tick hound dog, against the dog from ever loosing it's sense of smell. But then, I only heard what I heard, and, maybe he did, and then, on the other hand, maybe he didn't. Nevertheless, Hereford was a special and at oftentimes an unbelievably capable personage in the form of an insurance man, and it was almost uncanny as how he knew exactly what needed to be done, and, he did it, whatever it was, wherever and whenever, and, on time, and, I might add, within the Community Insurance budget.

I might throw in here, that old man Puckett, years and years ago, had an old maid school teacher sister that lived with him for years out on the farm, until she died, that is, and, Hereford said that he had her insured to pay for her funeral, as, she did not want to leave any debt when she died, and Community Insurance not only paid for her funeral but even bought flowers, and paid for her grave with a proper head stone, name date and all. But then, I have to tell you this, since it came to my brain's fogged memory, just thinking about her. When I was in school, she was one of my teachers in grade school, and, we all rode the school bus, we had this sing song poem about "Old Maid Puckett", which the boys would sing on the way to school, which went something like this... as best as I can remember.

"Now, Old Maid Puckett, Done lost her bucket

She reported it stolen, But the Sheriff found out

That Paw-tucket", and, she said... "Oh Yuck"

This busted up almost all the girls on the bus to and from Pawtucket, and they always threatened to report us for being stupid one day, and, ignorant the next, but they never did, as all the boys thought it was funny, and, I always suspected that the girls thought that it was funny too, and we could tell, as some of them even rolled their eyes or acted like they were going to puke after poking their fingers down their throats, so, we knew that they liked it.

I remember one time where Hereford and I had to go out and about the town and help locate a lady's cat that he had insured, and, to also, as a side job, to help get rid of a dead cat that we had found out in the street, over by the lady's house, but not quite in front of. Now, some folks called the lady, "the cat lady", but with an endearing flavor, not a negative one, as she had a good heart and took in quite a number of strays. The lady was popular for finding the most mangy ratty old dirty cats, and, cleaning them up, taming them down, feeding them and fattening them up, then, giving them away to good homes, collar and all. Anyway, we went out on that job for her, and, after we did what we had to do, and, returned the lady's cat, or, I should say cats, because we had caught two and did not know which one was hers, the lady had thanked us and had provided us with a cup of tea.

While we were there, having tea, I remember the lady talked to Hereford and I about cats, and, related some things that I had never considered about cats. I remember, she said, "All members of the cat family are ambush predators, and, house cats are no different than their larger cousins, the tigers, lions, cougars and panthers. All cats are curious and naturally inquisitive. Cats will clear your house of multiple pests such as mice, rats, cockroaches, bugs, and even ants. All of those things which may infringe upon their territory, as, all cats are territorial and will defend that territory. Cats love to roam and hunt, and, oftentimes play with their catches. When cats are hungry, they set themselves up in the ambush position in the areas where they have had success in finding food on previous occasions. Sometimes, at feeding times, the cats will set and await their "prey", and, watch you with baited breath, until they get you to feeling downright guilty, and then get up and feed them. Cats coexist with man only to the extent where it suits their own purpose, and, do not make for good pets as do dogs, as, dogs look forward to cohabiting with man, and, that in itself is their reward, cats on the other hand, usually being independent in their ways, just automatically always expect some reward, for little or no reason, as they have it figured out that they are doing you and everyone else a gracious favor by them just hanging around your house in the first place, so, if you give them something to drink, they will want something to eat, and, if you give them something to eat, they will want somewhere to dump, and if you provide a place for them to dump, the will want someplace quiet to sleep, and, if you give them some place to sleep, they will take over the whole damn house."

I thought about that a little, I guess, but not ever having had a cat for a pet left me with very little understanding of what all that she had said. I didn't doubt what the lady said about cats, and considered that she probably knew more than most about cats, because she looked out after them, but, I thought that between us all, Hereford, the lady, me or Rufus, that most likely, Rufus knew more and forgotten more about cats than the rest of us all combined as he took them a lot more serious than the rest of us.

It was either shortly after, or, a little before, or, around about this time, one or the other, or either, but not neither, that I was duly served up with a subpoena by the High Sheriff's selected deputy, one fine evening, while I just happened to be down at Kadise's pool hall, with the subpoena, greeting me, inviting me, and giving me the opportunity, to come and testify before a Grand Jury, down at the Court House, in a case being set up, in the County, possibly, as I had heard beforehand, to be brought against the Community Insurance in some matter. At first, I had no direct idea as to what it was all about, but, as time went on, more information on the matter, little by little, here and there, began to come out or leak out, whichever, as folks talked, my information, came directly, or, mainly from down at Kadise's pool hall, or, I should also mention the Masonic Hall upstairs (although they are not supposed to say anything one way or the other as those folks are normally supposed to be taught to bite their tongue and be tight lipped), which, brought out more of the nitty-gritty details of the Grand Jury's case into a more brighter light.

Apparently, what started it all, was, that Hereford had insured a ladies black cat, and, he had written up a life insurance policy on the cat, with the lady paying monthly premiums and all, and, had also, apparently, had the lady put into her last will and testament, an annuity of sorts, to be set aside, for the continuing care of the said cat, in the event of the ladies early demise, if, that was prior to that of the said cat, and, that the cat, if it so happened to have outlived the lady, would also, as a live cat, be willed to Hereford. Which, in that respect, would make Hereford, and perhaps Community Insurance in some part, also be, the custodian of such an annuity, which was specifically set aside for care of the lady's said cat. However, the most dreaded thing happened, and, the old lady up and died, before that is, of the demise of her said black cat. Something of that order, as well as I can explain, with what I have to work with, that is. Furthermore, just so as to cloud up the issue a little, the supposed extended family of the lady, as the woman had no real near immediate kinfolk around Central Falls that anyone could recall or remember, had immediately, upon hearing first word of the aforementioned ladies demise, showed up forth with, all the way up from Fall River, Massachusetts area, with a duly appointed attorney, and had filed up papers with the County Clerk, and was said to have even prayed the County Court, just a little short of bribing the Judge himself, to try to get the results of the will changed, backed off, turned upside down or backwards, or, at least jacked around some, so as, that they could get their hands on at least some, if not the better part, of the deceased ladies estate, including her money, and, including the annuity, or course, that was set aside for the said cat, and, all of which was, they felt, theirs by all human rights known to man, since they were of some supposed extended blood relation and kin, as they felt that it should rightly be theirs, more so, than for it all to go to some danged old mangy hairy black cat. In the detailed reading of the will, again, apparently, the lady had not just left the annuity to care for the said cat, she, and, again apparently, had left the said cat her entire estate, including her life's savings, the value of her residence and her very domicile, with everything in it, furniture and all, and also including her 1970 Plymouth Road Runner that only had 23,000 miles on it, to wit, to none other than that particular danged old said mangy hairy black cat. That was what the case was all about, as, like I said before, as well as I can explain it, with what I have to work with, brain and all.

That was where I came in, or come in, whichever or whenever. I had to properly appear, and, was called upon, after waiting some sufficient time out in the lobby of the County Court house, by the subpoena, to testify before the said Grand Jury, presented with the known evidence in the case and the matter at hand, as it was called, and of what was referred to as "the cat lady", and then, after first being sworn in, just like I was in some sort of court, to tell the truth, the whole truth, and, nothing but the truth, whereon, I was called in before that most august group of concerned citizens, and found out that I was partly required to testify on the behalf of the contestants, those folks who claimed to be the supposed extended family of the said deceased lady that had owned the said black cat in question, that is. It also turned out, that I was also to testify on behalf of said Plaintiff Hereford McAbeley and the said Community Insurance, to determine, to the satisfaction of the said Grand Jury, the, "is", the "is or", the "or", the "or is not", or, the "is or is not", of the said matter, whichever and whenever known. It was the "is or is not" question that was further to be brought out by the said august body of the Grand Jury, supported by the multitudinous testimony of all the said participants, for, and, or against, the said extended family of the said deceased lady and the said aforementioned black cat, and, or, for, or against, said Hereford and the said Community Insurance, whichever, however, or, whenever.

The prosecutor, and, I call him that because he acted like one, called for me from the lobby, and, I, in the custody of the Sergeant of or at Arms, whichever, brought me in before the said Jury which were seated at a conference table, and, initially put me on the stand, being duly sworn, and, the Bailiff swearing me in before testimony began. The Chairman of the Grand Jury, introduced himself and the members of the Jury, and, then, immediately began asking me if I knew anything of the certain said cat in question, the said cat's life insurance policy, the said cats annuity, the said deceased lady, or anything else which may be of some pertinent said interest, but not in that said order, as he kind of said bouncing around somewhat in his said questioning. I replied that it was most likely the said latter in the said list without getting too said deep or too said much into said specifics and said details. The said prosecutor asked me if I ever worked for the said Mr. McAbeley, and I replied in the said affirmative that I had, and had for some said time, and, that I had said worked for both said Mr. McAbeley's, both said Hereford and his said father before him. He then asked me "if I had ever been over to the said deceased ladies house, when she was said still alive of course, that is before she said died, and, also, there, while in the said employ of either of the said Mr. McAbeleys?", and, I said that I had, on said occasion, specifically with the said latter Mr. McAbeley, but not with the said former Mr. McAbeley. "What was that said occasion?" The prosecutor asked me. I told him and the said Jury who were all gawking my way, making me feel a little said uncomfortable, that I had gone over with said Hereford, one said evening in the said not too distant or said recent past, with a said shovel, and a said garbage bag, to help said Hereford scoop up a said dead black cat off of the said street, not from said right out in front of said ladies house that is, but just down the said block, a said little, from the said ladies house, and, that the said black dead cat looked like it had been run over by a said car, as that it had been squashed, and, was, at the time of said scoop up, nearly flat as a said pancake, and, said Hereford and I shoveled the said remains of the said dead black cat, into the said garbage bag. The Prosecutor asked me, "Did you see the said car run over and squash the said cat?" I told him that I had not. He then said, "Then you do not know what it was that killed the said cat, or, just exactly how the said cat died, do you? I told him that I did not, although it did look like some of the other dead cats that I had seen in the streets over the years. The prosecutor then said to the Jury , "Disregard the testimony as to what it was that killed the said cat, as no one really knows, or no testimony has been received to date on the said matter, so disregard it totally, and, also disregard the second, fourth and seventh saids, as, those saids had not been said yet", but then, he continued, The prosecutor then asked me, "What did you do with the said garbage bag, the one that had the said dead black cat in it?" I told him and the said Jury, looking most of them straight in the said eyes, as, I had nothing to hide at the time, that I put said garbage bag in the said bed of said Hereford's said pickup truck. The Prosecutor then advised the Jury to also disregard, as that that the second and third said had not been said yet either. "Then what happened" the prosecutor asked me. Well, I told the said prosecutor and the said Jury that said I went with said Hereford out to the said edge of town, near a said bridge along said Pigeon's Creek, by the said old mill, where said I dug a said hole alongside the said road, and, buried the aforementioned said scooped up dead black cat which was in the said garbage bag, said cat, said bag and said all. The said Prosecutor again advised the said Jury to disregard the two latter saids, but could consider the one previous aforementioned said, if they so choose. "Were you in any further employ in this matter of said Mr. McAbeley?" The prosecutor went on and asked. Yes, I went on, and said, that I assisted said Hereford in driving up and down most of the said streets of the said entire town of said Central Falls, helping said Hereford to look for and tying to retrieve the said ladies lost black cat, and, after a few hours into such a said endeavor, we located, or, I should say that said Hereford's dog Rufus located, two identical twin black cats, running alongside together, or side by side, maybe one just a little in front of the other, whichever, just east of the said Kopka's Phillips 66 auto service station parking lot, which said Hereford's said dog Rufus chased down, and cornered, while said Hereford and said I caught both of them said cats in a gunny sack, and, took them both back up to the said ladies house to return them to their rightful said home and said rightful owner, the aforementioned said lady in the aforementioned said house. The said prosecutor advised the Jury to disregard two of the first three and also the last two of the aforementioned saids, as, he said that they were said redundant. The said prosecutor then asked me if I knew if either of the said black cats to have belonged to the said lady, or, if I knew that the said scooped up dead black cat that I had helped bury, which could have possibly really been the said black cat that belonged to the said lady. I told him that I did not know for sure, but I knew that said Hereford did, because for one thing, I thought that said Hereford had mentioned to said me that he had a picture or photo of the said ladies black cat, that he had said insured, and, when we returned the said cats to the said lady, even though she first questioned whether or not that either one of the said caught black cats were hers, because she said, that neither of the caught said black cats quite acted like her said black cat, and, that she thought that her said black cat was a little fatter than either of the caught said black cats. However, said Hereford had a long talk with the said lady, showed her the said picture that he had of the said insured black cat, and, afterward, the said lady appeared to be quite relieved on the return of her said cat, whichever one it was, and, in the end, decided to keep both of the said black cats, until she could get it all figured out, and, said that she appreciated our kind efforts, offered us both some tea and cookies, and, told said Hereford that she wanted to talk to him later on about some other insurance. The prosecutor then advised me that I did not have to say anymore saids before him or the Jury during my testimony. The prosecutor then asked me, "Do you know the name of this said lady, the said lady with the said cats? I said that I thought that her name was Stephanie Franusiak. "No further questions at this time ", said the prosecutor, and reminded me again that I did not have to say said anymore, at all, and with that, I was excused from further testimony and also from the further presence of this fine august body of concerned citizens on the Jury, and, the Sergeant at or of Arms, whichever, escorted me back out to the lobby, advising me not to discuss my testimony with anyone, at any time, forthwith, and said that he thought that I had try to run my saids into the ground and break them off. I told him that I would try to said behave and watch all of my other saids, on his said behalf.

In small talk in the hallway, I learned of another lady that had found out about Hereford insuring cats, and she was saying that she had had a calico cat that she wanted him to insure, but Hereford did not appear to be too interested, she said, because her cat was "mottled", Hereford had told her that no two "mottled" cats are alike, they don't look alike or act alike, and, all of them are independently unpredictable, do not come when they are called, have a mind of their own, do not normally make for a good pets around the house, as, they only want to eat, sleep, be left alone, have their litter box changed more often than that which is really needed, and, if they ever get out, they never come back, and, besides that, they are very hard to catch, and, to top it all off, that calico cats hark up hair balls so large that they usually choke to death in the process, and, are thereby uninsurable on that account because cat suicide is totally uninsurable. That sounded like Hereford, getting all of that said right out, in one long breath, just like a good insurance man, I thought, and, I was all the more proud for having worked for him. The lady continued to complain to others and saying things like that all calico cats are mottled to begin with and that is why they were named calico in the first place. This, in all, was more than what my brain could take, as I never really wanted to know anything more about cats or listen anymore to such chitter chatter for that matter.

While I was there in the lobby, different folks from Central Falls kept coming in, some, being called into the Jury room, some idling about, some wandering around, or whatever, all pairing off with others to discuss the happenings. I recognized the farmer whose well I had helped clean out, I talked to him and he said that he still had good water, and, there was a young boy there, about 15-16 years old, I imagine, in the escort of an older lady, probably his mother, I thought, and, I wondered if he was the boy that Hereford said that he had insured against him becoming an alcoholic. He was a little pale, but he looked stone cold sober to me at the time. I did not inquire into this matter, I might add. Other folks kept coming and going, until such time as I was called again into the Jury room, and escorted by the Sergeant of, or, at Arms, whichever, or, whatever.

Again, I was reminded by the bailiff that I was still "duly sworn", as I entered into the Jury room. I duly noted this time before the Jury, that all the comments and questions, regarding the particular said cat in question, had moved on up, and had been elevated from just a "cat", then to the "black cat", then, to the to "the dead black cat", then, promoted again to "the said black dead cat", then, back again to the "said scooped-up dead black cat", or, referred to on occasion, as "the scooped up said dead black cat", whichever variation, they so choose at the time, all of which, taking place during my questioning, regarding any involvement which I may have had in any of the matters in question before this august body called up as a Grand Jury. I was careful to watch my saids, by the way, just for your information. I was asked if I knew anything about Community Insurance and their policies on selling, writing up or issuing insurance policies. I replied that I had no knowledge of such, was otherwise unfamiliar with the business, had not been to insurance school, nor was I trained in the trade as an apprentice. The Jury seemed pleased with my answers, and, I continued watching my saids. I was asked if I had been given a policy for any insurance that I had bought from, throughout, by, or with the Community Insurance or with Hereford as an administrator. I responded, that Hereford told me that he kept my policies on file, for both my car and house belongings at the Community Insurance office, so that they would not be misplaced, lost, ever burned up in a fire, lost in a flood, blown away by the wind, or whatever. I was asked if I had seen any of my papers which I could identify specifically as my insurance policies, at any time, but especially while inside the McAbeley household, and, I replied that I had not, as I never got past their living room, in the times that I was in the house. I was asked if I had seen anything that even looked anything like an insurance policy while in the household of the deceased lady Stephanie Franusiak,, that had the said (whoops) black cat insured. I replied that I had not, but then, I had never gotten beyond the ladies kitchen, where I been provided tea and cookies. I was asked if I had ever seen or knew anyone who had or had even seen any insurance policy or anything looking like an insurance policy, which had the Community Insurance name on it, on any that had Hereford's name on it, and, I replied that I had not, but, could only speak for myself in that matter, and that that for me was no, zero, none, negatory, or zilch, as, I had always taken the word of Hereford that I had such insurance and such an insurance policy, and had only been provided a certificate to put in my car in the event that I had an accident, or, to prove to the police, that I had insurance with the Community Insurance. At this time, I was duly dismissed and again reminded to not discuss anything about the Jury proceedings to anyone while waiting outside the Jury room. The Sergeant of or at Arms, again, whichever, then escorted me, again, but arm in arm this time, out to the lobby, and, he openly commented by complementing me in front of the other folks in the lobby, that I was doing pretty well by watching my saids. A So, I asked him if that was a said compliment.

Apparently, some alarming things had come about while I was inside the Jury room testifying. The talk in the lobby, was now, that the High Sherriff was looking for both Hereford McAbeley and his wife Anielia, and, had put out an all-points bulletin in at least the 5 surrounding Counties, including Fall River, MA, with orders to bring them both into "custody", to arrest them on sight, charge them with anything, their choice, but if nothing else, charge them with "Fraud", in order to hold them, and immediately deliver them to the Court house and the High Sheriff's presence and the presence of the Grand Jury forthwith as soon as possible.

That was mild, compared to what was to be heard next, which was, that someone, somehow, had gained entrance, whether apparently or not, into the morgue at the funeral home, and, had stolen the body of the lady, apparently or not, that had been the previous owner of the said black cat, that of which was presently in question before the Grand Jury. Now, the High Sheriff, not only had two "Fraud" arrest reports to be generated, but now, he also had the theft, and, or, at least the disappearance, apparently or not, either a missing person or the theft of a dead body from right here in downtown Central Falls. No one in the group in the lobby had ever heard of such a thing having happened in the entire history of the town, or, up in Pawtucket for that matter. What an uproar it all came to be. Someone, asked out loud, and, wanted to know, if anyone knew whether or not, or, had heard, that the lady in question, might have been cremated accidentally, or, at least unintentionally, possibly accounting for her disappearance. One lady said, that the missing dead lady, or, the missing body of the dead lady, whichever way you want to look at it, or call it, was, by name, none other, than that of, Ms. Stephanie Franusiak, also known about and around town as" the cat lady". Other folks vied with other ideas, such as how such a thing could happen, and, kept trying to come to grips with, or, trying to come up with some reasonable reasons or explanation for such odd happenings that were coming about and being reported without anyone having to make anything up just for a little excitement.

About or around that time, the High Sheriff, in the company of the Judge, with two Deputies in tow, emerged from the Jury room, in a hurri-some huff, with the Judge telling the High Sheriff that he was ordered to immediately serve the so issued Search Warrants and begin the searches with all available deputies and to work them overtime if he had to. Word was, as it was passed out amongst us folks in the lobby, was, that it was the McAbeley residence, and the Community Insurance business, which was the ultimate destination of the deputies with at least one of their Search Warrants, with the others to be served at the cat lady's house, and, the Central Falls Bank, initially, and, other banks forthwith, for the immediate freezing of all the accounts and assets of the Community Insurance business. The High Sheriff asked the Judge, who it was he was supposed to serve the Search Warrant on if there was no one at the house. The Judge said that the Search Warrant was to be served "on the houses", posted at the addresses as so listed, with the entries made, the house searched for the items so listed on the Warrant, and, that the contents should be brought to the Jury room forthwith, and kept under guard in the locked containers provided. Also, that the houses in question should be sealed and a deputy posted as a guard until further notice. At this moment in time, I thought that everyone present had completely gone crazy and had completely forgotten about the poor old dead lady Stephanie Franusiak whose body was presently still reported as missing from the morgue, with no one out and about looking for her, either that, or, they had already totally forgotten about her, apparently.

After the Sheriff and his deputies had left the building, and the Judge and jury had went back into the Jury room, all 25-30 folks in the lobby broke out into every type of conversation imaginable. Someone asked whether or not that Stephanie Franusiak's body had been embalmed. The lady that had mentioned the possibility of accidental cremation, mentioned it again. Someone else wondered if she had not of been embalmed, and, had only been in a diabetic coma, maybe she woke up, and had just got up, walked out, and went home. Someone else said that she was a good person, always helping others and taking stray pets into her home, as, at one time she was known as "the cat lady", as, she had taken in, nursed and fed about 30 some odd cats, at one time or another, that kind of thing. Someone else wondered out loud if maybe some of the ladies family, the supposed extended relatives, had come and picked her up, or, better still, maybe they just out rightly took her body, as it would have been in their interest just to confuse the issue of the will. Someone else wondered if maybe it was body snatchers, or whatever. It was a quandary, with folks coming up with all sorts of possible explanations as to what could have happened to her or her body. Someone brought up the idea that it would have been in the interest of Hereford, if the old lady had actually died, because, that would automatically put him in line for her inheritance, via her cat that he had insured, along with the annuity. Someone else chimed in with the idea that Hereford may have or could have been directly responsible for her death, if that were the case, that could now include something even up to crimes including that of murder or at least manslaughter. Then, someone else said that the disappearance of the old lady's body put an end to that idea. Which, in that would be the case, would make both, or either, of the investigations, of the extended family or Hereford, for that matter, both null and void. Then, further discussion turned back to mumble, jumble, jargon, inundated with a little innuendo thrown in or out, whichever, just for good measure.

It was about this time that folks from the local truck stop restaurant came in with tables and folding chairs, and, started to set up the catering of what began to look like a buffet style luncheon. The 25-30 folk's conversation changed to what it was, that we could be having for lunch, and, whether or not that it was actually for us, or, for free for that matter. But, we found out shortly, that it was for us, as we were so blessed, and, after a short prayer by the Chairman of the Grand jury, which had come out for the luncheon, blessing the bounty, we all had our fill, and, for the most part were all fat, happy, and content. We no sooner had lunch, when the High Sheriff come traipsing back in the front door, and, I could not but notice, as I was observant, that he had a number of large envelopes under his arm, as he walked right past me, and, I noticed that one of the envelopes had a return address from the Central Falls State Bank. He immediately went into the Jury room, and then, he came right back out to have lunch, but, he did not have the envelopes with him at this time, and, I assumed, by putting two and two together, which I am really good at, when I have to do it, that it had to do, with what was said by the Judge earlier, about it being or having to do with the Community Insurance accounts with the banks, being locked up, locked down, frozen, or just frosted up a little from the inside out. As the Sheriff was eating his lunch, the personnel of the Grand jury, abruptly got up and traipsed back into the jury room and closed the door, with the Sheriff just nodding his head in their direction.

Now, I had not planned to spend the entire day with these town folks, as, I surely had better things to do, than sit around waiting for something else to happen, and, I was sure, beyond a shadow of doubt that all the other guys down at Kadise's pool hall, were wondering where in the world I was. But, here, in the lobby was I, and here were the other 25-30 were, and none of us were allowed to leave, except to go to the rest room to relieve ourselves, and, if we did, it excited someone's soul, connected to the Sheriff no doubt, to the point, of either coming to look for us, poke their head inside the door, or, at least asking from the outside in, about if we were OK, or if everything was coming out OK.

Shortly after having such a thought run through my brain, about having to go to the rest room, here came one of the Sheriff's deputies, serious as a heart attack, I might add, on, in, and through the lobby and then on through the doors of the Jury room, without knocking I might also add, in hand with a black briefcase, handcuffed to his wrist with the other end of the handcuff hooked on to the handle of the black briefcase. He had not said a word to any of us in the lobby, and, he did not even look at any of us either, as, he appeared to be as intent on his job as anyone could be, under the circumstances at hand. The High Sheriff jumped up, dumped his cake in the trash can and followed the deputy through the door to the Jury room, and, slammed the door. Then, for a moment or so, it was all quiet, and, I thought about going to the restroom again.

"What do you mean, that that is all that there was?" boomed a voice through the door from inside the Jury room, which, dawned upon all of us at the same time, and we looked at one another knowingly, that it was the voice of the Judge talking to the Chairman of the Grand jury, and, immediately thereafter, here came the Sheriff's deputy, like he was shot out of a cannon, having been inside the Jury room not much more than a total of 235 seconds, complete, on the watch, and, here he came back out, minus the briefcase and the handcuffs, I, for one, amongst a couple of others, took careful note of that in special observance. Everyone in the lobby then began to murmur to themselves and turning to those closest to them, as to what could have possibly been in the black briefcase. Some comment, although made ominously, was made, that sooner or later, that they were sure and certain, beyond a shadow of doubt, that most of us would surely, find out one way or another, sooner or later, exactly what was in that mysterious black briefcase container carried by the Sheriff's deputy really was.

It did not take long. Because, about at that moment in time, the Prosecutor, jerked the Jury room door open, looked around the lobby, pointed his boney finger at me and yelled, "Sergeant of Arms, get that man in custody, and, get him in here, now!". I just about jumped out of my drawers, but managed to pull myself together and followed him arm in arm with the Sergeant of Arms, back into the Jury room. The bailiff again reminded me that I was still duly sworn, then, started his questioning. "Do you see what is on the conference table?" The Prosecutor asked me. Yes, I said, looking at a very old thick leather bound book with the word "LEDGER" on the cover. "Have you ever seen this book, or, anything like it before?" He boomed. I said that I had not. "Did you not testify that you were inside of the McAbeley household and the Community Insurance at some time in the recent past?" He asked me. I said that that was true, however, I had only been in the living room and that I had never seen anything that looked like the book that was laying there on the conference table. The Prosecutor seemed perturbed with me, looking at me, then, looking at the "LEDGER", looking inquisitively at the Jury members, then looking at me again, and, it all made me feel uncomfortable down deep inside like I had just swallowed a couple of worms out of an apple, that kind of feeling thing. "Would you have any knowledge as to what is in this "LEDGER"?", he asked. I told him that I had no such knowledge, as I had previously testified that I had never seen the book before, as I did not like books anyway, and had not heard about such a book, had not dreamt about such a book, had not had anyone tell me about such a book, and, had not ever even imagined such a thing like that book even in my darkest days. The Prosecutor stopped me there, dead in my tracks, told the Jury to disregard what I had been trying to say, because most everything that I had said up to that point was all hearsay anyway on what I did not know anything about in the first place. He then dismissed me again, directed the Sergeant of Arms to escort me out and told me to wait in the lobby, and again, told me not to discuss anything with anybody, anywhere, at any time, anyhow, anyway. With that, I was ushered out the door arm in arm again by the Sergeant of or at Arms, whichever, with him reiterating what the prosecutor had said, as if I hadn't heard him say it in the first place. I told him that I was still very carefully watching all of my saids.

While in the lobby, after getting another piece of cake at the buffet, I overheard no little heated discussion about Hereford and his wife Anielia as still being missing. Apparently, the deputies had found their house open, front and back door unlocked and house abandoned, but could not determine if anything was missing at the time, when, they had served the house with the Search Warrant. Nothing in the house appeared to have disturbed, their clothes were still in the closet, the dinner table had been set and lift as was set, tea water was still hot in the pot, some lights were still on, there were wet clothes still in the washer and still dry clothes in the dryer, and, their car and truck were still at the house in the drive way with their keys in the ignitions. Hereford and Anielia were both gone, and, there dog Rufus was missing too, with food even left in his bowl in the kitchen hall. Everyone gone, done sailed out of town on the wind or with the wind kind of thing, whichever. They all have disappeared, totally, just like they all had been raptured, and called up to heaven. Still listening, I found out there was an extended order out with an all-points bulletin put out, now, extended even into the adjoining states of Connecticut and Massachusetts, (both States that I never could spell the name of), for the immediate arrest of both Hereford and his wife for "Fraud", and, since their vehicles were still in the driveway, it was also supposed and speculated on amongst the group, that someone else had picked them up, and took them off, an errant accomplice, if you will, which the Sheriff had already suspected from the very beginning, by the way, and, that the whole bunch of them, whoever or whomever, whichever, including Hereford's father and mother, if anyone knew where they were, were to all be arrested for "Fraud" on sight, however, where ever and whenever, in one fell swoop of the clam shell of the law. This was too exciting for words, and, I just about peed down my leg. I finished my cake, excused myself and went to the rest room. I noticed that one of the Sheriff's deputies had followed me into the rest room, the one that had been watching me like a hawk, and, the same one who had made me feel uncomfortable previously.

The deputy acted like he was washing his hands, and said, "You think you are pretty smart, don't'cha?" I asked him if he was talking to me, even though there was no one else in the rest room at the time. He continued, saying, "You are an insider aren't you, you know everything about what Hereford and his dad did with the Community Insurance, don't'cha?" I said that I did not have any idea what it was that he was talking about, however, I did mention to him that the Prosecutor had so told me not to discuss anything with anyone about the matters at hand. The deputy continued, "But, you have sat out there in the lobby, and, you have listened to everything that everyone has said, and, you haven't chimed in with one word, and, you are the only one that has not done so, so, you are the only one who really knows what is going on ain't'cha?" Then he said, "You worked for both Hereford and his dad, didn't'cha? You know where he is, don't'cha? You know where the old lady, the lady that died, you know where her body is, don't'cha? You know if they can't find her body, they may not have a case, don't'cha? You probably even know how they got her body out of the morgue, don't'cha? You were in Hereford's house, weren't'cha? Not another sole in the entire town of Central Falls was ever in his or his dad's house, but you, you were the only one, weren't'cha? "You were in Hereford's car weren't'cha? You were in Herefords truck, weren't'cha? You drove his truck, didn't'cha? Not another sole in the entire town of Central Falls was ever in his truck or his car, except that damned dog Rufus, but you were, weren't'cha? He went on, but this time he had a quizzical look on his face. "Has it not dawned upon you, or have overdosed yourself on dumb ass pills while you were down on the funny farm, that you, are none other, than one of, and, in fact, the a "person of interest" if not their "numero uno" prime suspect?" Suspect, prime suspect, suspect at what? I asked. "Suspect at Hereford and all of him and his dad's doings, the whole rigmarole of the Community Insurance Fraud that has duped the folks of Central Falls with, that's what", he said. "You were knee deep into their business, and, now you are ass deep in trouble because of it, and, if the truth be known, you are "up to your neck" as guilty as they are and you are going to pay for that excursion." He went on. "You, are a neophyte, just a little cog on a big wheel, but, you are the one who will be sent up the river, penned up and incarcerated for 20 or more years, for something, that someone else did, so, why don't you just open up, and, spill your guts, and, get it over with, and, just tell them the truth, or, at least tell them what they want to hear." He added. I said that I had no idea, not ever a clue, a snitch or a sniveling for that matter, as to what in the world it was, that he was talking about, ranting on or raving on or around about, or, whatever it was that he was trying to verbalize, or, what he was even talking about for that matter, and, with that, I excused myself, then started out of the restroom in a jump with a little lurch and kick thrown in for good measure, making sure that the door closed behind me, before he could get out, trying my best to leave the deputy behind, which I hoped he had been.

As I came back into the lobby, the Jury room door was now open, and several folks were coming out of the room. I took notice that it was the farmer which Hereford had insured his cow against her going dry of milk, the lady who had the parakeet that had eventually learned to talk, the lady who had the calico cat that Hereford did not insure, the chicken egg farmer with the no egg laying problem, and the guy with the dog that never got the distemper, and several others that I could not immediately remember anything of or about, but supposedly mostly associated with the Community Insurance somehow. As the last person came out of the Jury room, the Sergeant of or at Arms, whichever, again came over to me and said "You, come with me"., and, "You need to get back in there!", so, arm in arm, in through the door I went again, but this time, as a result of my conversation with the deputy in the rest room, I thought that I should perhaps watch a little more closely exactly what it was that I was going to say, instead of being so outwardly open with my conversation before this august bunch of folks, as, there was no telling what they were thinking about or what in the world was going through their brains, or what was to happen to me next, for that matter.

The bailiff and prosecutor both reminded me that I was still duly sworn, for whatever reason, and then proceeded with the proceedings. "What kind of vehicles did you ever see at, around, or having seen Hereford and or his wife driving, that you may have drove, or, any vehicles that were parked in the yard, or thereabouts in the neighborhood of the location of the Community Insurance office?" I stated that I had seen Hereford's old pickup truck, and Mrs. McAbeley's old 4-door sedan, that either or both of them had driven at one time or another. The Prosecutor continued, "Have you had occasion to ride, drive or otherwise be on the inside of either of the vehicles in question?, he said. I stated that I had ridden, as a passenger, or, drove as a driver, at one time or another, for one purpose or another, in either, or both, of the vehicles in question. The Prosecutor, then asked, "On any of those occasions, when you were in either, one or the other, or both of the vehicles, did you see anything that looked like a receipt booklet, a receipt, or any paper that looked like a receipt, or, any paper that could have passed for a receipt?" I stated that I had not seen any of the lists of the aforementioned or any of the after as mentioned either, first, last with a second either, or neither, thrown in on the side just for good measure. The Prosecutor continued, "Did you, at or on any occasion, or at any time other, did you ever see Hereford McAbeley, or his father, or his wife, the little Mrs. Anielia, or any other person, acting on behalf of the Community Insurance, or, Hereford or Anielia, did you ever, I say again, did you ever, see anyone, at any time or another, give anything that could pass as a receipt, for services charged, or, services rendered, or claims settled, in any matter, to anyone else, either during your employ or at any other time not aforementioned previous?" I stated that I had not, to the whole said kit and caboodle pre, post afore, before, or after mentioned, including that which I had no knowledge of, or, should not have had knowledge of.

He continued, "Did you ever, on any occasion, see any exchange of money, from anyone, to anyone, directly or indirectly, at any time or another, for, or on behalf of anyone associated with or on behalf of the Community Insurance, during your employ, or before or after at any time not heretofore mentioned again previous?" I stated that I had not to the better part of that part of the kit and caboodle, except when Hereford returned money to the lady with a tree that I had cut down, or, to pay for my insurance with the Community Insurance, or to receive my pay for the work that I did directly for the Community Insurance or with or for Hereford, or Herefords dad when he was in charge. "Were you provided a receipt when you paid your insurance premium? He asked. I said that I had not; as Hereford always said that he kept a good accounting record for and on my behalf. "How did Community Insurance, or Hereford, or Hereford's dad, for that matter, pay you for your work with them?" The Prosecutor asked. I stated that I was always paid by the hours worked, by either Hereford, directly, or, before Hereford came to take over the Community Insurance, I was paid the same way by his father, paid every time with cold hard cash on the barrel head, in bonafied tax deductible American dollars and change calculated according to my hours worked. The Prosecutor asked me at that time, "Do you know the definition, or, do you have a clear understanding as to what the terms "Fraud, Extortion, Grand Theft, Money Laundering, Gang Activity, or, Accessory to such activity, means?" I replied and said no, that I had no specific understanding as to what either meant, under the context, but had heard some talk about the latter on one occasion or another down at Kadise's pool hall at one time or another. However, with that, the Prosecutor just left it there, hanging up in the air, with me wondering what it all meant, as he didn't offer up any definition of either of the aforementioned at the time, and, with that, he signaled the Sergeant of or at Arms, whichever, to escort me back out to the lobby, this time, reminding me to just keep my mouth shut, until further notice, if I knew what was good for me, and, the Sergeant of or at Arms, whichever, told me under his breath, not to take off, or, become absent and unaccounted for, or go AWOL, because there was a deputy with most likely more than one fully loaded gun clip on his person, who was assigned to be keeping me company with an ongoing eye out on me. I told him that I fully appreciated his input and would keep my eye out for the deputy's eye out, and, I asked him how I was doing on my saids, but, he did not respond, except for the roll of one of his eyes that I caught out of one of my own.

Well, the folks in the lobby were up in airs, as, the word now, was, that the lady, Stephanie Franusiak, whose body was missing from the morgue down at the funeral home, had apparently left the clothes that, at the time of her death, that she was wearing, that is, left them laying, on the cold marble slab, where she had been laid out, cold as a cucumber as she was, had left her clothes all folded and laid out nice and neat, with no one knowing where she was, or, how that her clothes came to be laid out in that fashion. The mortician, self-admitted, said that he might have, or, just could have happened to have dropped off to asleep or lost concentration, one or another, or, something else could have happened while he was watching the news on TV, at the time of the disappearance of the body, and, he was said to have said, that he somehow felt some responsibility, being full of evident pain with misery on the conscience of his very soul, and, had already had more than a few fits and bad spells with a couple of hot sweats thrown in, including the loss of sleep, about it all. Someone commented that maybe the lady was really a zombie, out and about, walking around stark butt naked in the woods, and then, someone said that we should be more respectful of the dead, as those folks that have gone on their way to that long home deserve better. Someone else wondered if she had been transfigured on up into heaven in bodily form, like the Holy Jesus. Someone else said that that was borderline sacrilegious, or, in the neighborhood of such, whatever, or whichever.

Someone else again remarked that the lady's extended family absolutely had to be somehow involved, and had to have come in and got the lady's body, and carted it off, naked as a jay bird as she was, as, if it could not be proved that the lady was dead, then, her will could not be executed, and then, they all reiterated all over again, that maybe in some way, that the extended family members could gain some benefit, like getting to live in the old lady's house for free and drive her car for free as it only had 23,000 some odd miles on it and would go over 100 miles per hour on a straight away, while still getting 12 miles per gallon, and, without burning any oil, or, the transmissions slipping, and, being able to pass anything on the road except a gas station. The overall mess just got messier and messier, the more the folks conjectured, the worse it got trying to figure out the matters at hand, and, I was all but ready to give it all up, because my brain was now fully inundated with the mystery of it all.

We were all interrupted at or around about this time, when, in through the front door, comes the High Sheriff in marching order style, with Mr. Frank Kopezinski and Mr. Jan Czerwein, Central Falls finest, Certified Public Accountants, the "KC Firm", they were, CPA's of the first rank and of the first order, I knew them well, as Frank was the one who always did my taxes. Neither of them, nor either of them, said hi, by, kiss my foot or nothing, not to me, or to anyone else in the lobby, they were all on a serious solemn mission, and, they stomped right on through the lobby area and on into the Jury room in the company of the High Sheriff. It seemed that no more than a minute or so had passed, when the door to the Jury room flew open again, banging against the wall, and, here the renowned CPA Firm members came traipsing right back out. However, this time, Frank had a black briefcase hooked onto his right hand with a pair of handcuffs just like the one that the deputy had previously had, when he came in with it earlier. As they went toward the door, I heard Frank say, "Jan, you are going to have to drive as there is no way that I can turn the steering wheel with this dang thing hanging on my arm." And, with that, Frank left the building with Jan in the tow.

Shortly thereafter, the High Sheriff came out of the Jury room, told us all, all 25-30 of us, that we were going to be excused for the day, reminded, remanded, as we were, and, told us all not to discuss any matters with anyone else concerning the matters at hand, and, gave us the order to return to this location tomorrow morning and expect to be expected to testify in further matters at hand. Much complaining was heard about, someone said that they had to go to work, some said that they had sick folks at home, a couple more had a doctor or dentist appointment, some said that they had to get their kids to school and also go pick them up, some said that it was no little inconvenience, but, the High Sheriff shouted them all down and again reminded them of the Order to Appear, and that their Subpoena was still active and in full force, and, if they did not show up the next day, he would send out a deputy to come looking for them, and, the end result would not be a pretty picture. The Sheriff looked at me and said that I was duly released at this time on my own recognizance, which embarrassed me in front of the other folks; however, I kept my mouth shut, saluted the High Sheriff, and, headed out the door and down the street to the Library as I had a mission of my own to pursue.

I must be sick, I thought, as this was the first time that I had any free time and did not go directly to Kadise's pool hall. I went into the Library, went to the reference section, and, proceeded to look up every reference that I could find on fraud, money laundering, extortion, grand theft, gang activity and the like. I found gang information, gangland activity, underworld activity, killings, killing contracts, mobs, mafia activity, shootings, knifings, dope running, everything bad, just one bad thing after the other, with nothing good even crammed in around the edges. How could all of this be, I wondered to myself, how could the Community Insurance, Hereford or Hereford's dad be involved in anything like this? The Community Insurance had been here in Central Falls all of my life that I could remember, and, I worked for both Hereford and his dad, over the years, doing nothing but good, helping folks, picking up and dropping off cars, taking folks to doctor appointments, visiting or picking folks up at the hospital, fixing roofs, painting, repairing, raking, hauling off, hauling in, all nothing but good work for the poor folks in Central Falls and some even up in Pawtucket. I gave my quest up, left the Library, and, headed over to Kadise's pool hall for some form of respite where all the talk is about better whiskey, faster horses, younger women, or more money, if they were not arguing religion or politics, but I just gave it all up early and went on home.

The next morning, I was up early, went out to get the morning newspaper, made coffee, and had breakfast. The headlines of the paper read "Local Insurance Firm scheduled to be indicted for Fraud by Grand Jury". I read it with genuine interest, and, about halfway through, it dawned upon me, it hit me like a ton of bricks, that with everything that was happening, that I was most likely going to be out of a job. How was it that this had not occurred to me before? I read on into the article which had a notice attached to it that said, "Any persons, having procured insurance of any form with the Community Insurance at any time in the past, are remanded to contact the CPA firm of Kopezinski and Czerwien for appointment, immediately upon hearing of this notice. Appointments may be made in person, or, by phone." Well, when I read this, I thought, maybe, this may shed some light on the matters at hand. There was another notice on the front page, that requested information on missing persons, Hereford McAbeley, his wife Anielia, Hereford's father and mother listed only as the senior Mr. McAbeley and wife, as I suppose that no one knew their first names, as I did not, and, that lady Ms. Stephanie Franusiak, 'the cat lady', and, that if anyone had any information, about anyone or anything in the matter, that they were to contact the Sheriff's Department immediately, and, there was an added on reminder about it being a criminal offense to harbor any criminals or suspects and could be charged as an accessory after the fact. I looked a second time, but did not notice any rewards being offered for anything at this time. I finished the articles and called Frank at the accountant firm and made an appointment in the afternoon at 5pm, mostly, because I thought that I would probably be tied up with the Grand Jury the better part of the day, and, secondarily, I thought I might find out a little more about this matter if I could pry or broker anything out of Frank.

I reported at about 9am to the lobby at the Court House, and, about 15-20 folks were already there, with about 10-15 more coming to be expected as best as we could calculate. It was talk, talk, talk, about this, about that, what if this, what if that, who knows what. With everything that was said, someone else would chime in that we were not supposed to talk about this, or talk about that, then, someone would tell them to shut up, only to have someone else chime back in with some other comment. "Did you read the paper", "What did it say?" "What do you think?", on and on and on and on. There was no end, and, we sat, and we sat, and we got up and walked, we went to the rest room, I did not know that I could pee as many times as I did, and, we went and looked outside, we went by the Jury room door, trying to hear what was going on, but nothing, nothing was apparently happening. Some went outside to smoke, got cold and came back in even before finishing their smoke. We wondered aloud if anyone was in the room at all, but then, every once in a while, someone would say, "I heard a klunk", or "They are in there all right", or, "They sure are quiet", "I just heard someone banging on the table", just to make some comment in response to anything that was not happening. Nobody was going in, nobody was coming out, nothing. About lunch time, here comes the truck stop catering crew, setting up again for lunch. I was ready, and, even helped them unload, bring in the meals, and, to set everything up, tables, chairs and all. The catering crew set the tables for us, told us to hit the buffet, then the crew made up 10-12 plates, with drinks and silverware, went and knocked on the Jury room door, the door opened, they went in, and, then, the catering crew came back out empty handed. "They are in there all right" someone said, and, everyone looked somewhat relieved upon gaining such profound knowledge. We then set out to have lunch with two passes and two or three deserts apiece; extra coffee, and then, things finally began to look up, again.

The afternoon was not much better than the morning, no one went in, no one came out, no noises from the room, no one going stir crazy, no one having a heart attack, no one yelling for a doctor, no one asking for water, nothing, Again we fidgeted, time drug by, or, dragged by, whichever. No Sheriff, no deputies, no CPA'a, no one coming, no one going, we waited, and, we waited, but nothing. About 4pm, out into the hall came the High Sheriff, and again remanded all of us, and, (at this time, there was probably 35-40 of us in the lobby), remanded us again, that we were still under the Order to Appear and the power of the Subpoena and that we were not to discuss anything that we had seen or heard, or discussed, or, imagined, with anyone, and, that we were ordered to appear tomorrow morning, again, at 9am, and, with that he dismissed us. I headed out to Kadise's pool hall, hoping to get in a short hot game before my appointment with the accountants. But, no luck at Kadise's, no games, no table open, so, I thought to get on over to the accountants and maybe get in early and get my appointment over with.

As I came through the front door, Frank Kopezinski sometimes also known as Frank Kopka, and his distant cousin of some shirttail kin, namely, Jan Czerwien were bent over a table set up in the waiting room, looking at the "LEDGER" book. Frank looked up, nodded and acknowledged me as I came in, and told me to have a seat, and, that they would be with me shortly. I observed, that Frank and Jan both were pointing here and there on the pages, then turning a page, and, again pointing here and there. "I have never seen anything like it.", Frank said. "Me neither", said Jan. Then, there was me, wondering what it could be that neither one of them had never seen before. Frank said, "I think I saw his name on page 137." Jan began turning the pages, arriving on time, as he called me to come and sit at the table, which I did. Frank looked at me, then at the "LEDGER" book, and said, "We are not fully sure on just how to proceed with this inquiry, as you are one of the first to be interviewed, but let us begin, and we may need to wing it, and, if need be, we may have you set up another appointment, and come back again, just to iron out some of the details." I indicated that that would be fine, as, I was not presently working, and, was available, if needed. Both Frank and Jan asked questions, some, as to what insurance that I had had with the Community Insurance, some, as to what I paid for said insurance, if I ever had a claim on any of my insurance, some of what I was paid, and, how I was paid for my work with Community Insurance, with Hereford, or, with Hereford's dad. I gave them the best answers to their questions that I could readily think of, and, while doing so, I could not help but look at the page "LEDGER" book that had my name on it, as it was on the table right in front of me, but upside down to me. At the top of the page, it had my name, as I could read that easy enough, and, it read, "MONIES OWED", and, page 137. The page was full of entries, on one side, it looked like a record of every payment that I had ever made for my insurances with the Community Insurance, with dates and amounts. Then, on the other side of the page appeared to be the date and amounts which I was paid for the work that I did for Community Insurance. Frank looked at me, and said, "What does the date August 17, 2008, mean to you?" I thought, then I mentioned not much, except that that was just a few days ago, and, asked if that was not the last day that anyone saw Hereford and his wife Anielia, and the day right after that the "cat lady" Stephanie Franusiak had died, or, was that the day that her body disappeared from the morgue?. Jan poked Frank, looking at the book, and said, "If you look at the "LEDGER", that particular date, August 17, 2008, is entered on the bottom of every page in the book, as a last entry. Now, Frank, don't you think something is odd with that, as it looks like someone has all but closed out the book completely by showing closure on both debits and credits?" I asked Jan if he was talking to me, and, he said not in particular, as he was more talking to himself. Frank turned the pages, page by page, and, noted on every page, some with him just flipping through the pages like shuffling cards, verifying that that particular date was indeed entered on each and every page. Jan said, "Go to the very last page in the book, Frank, what do you see entered there?" Frank turned to the back of the "LEDGER", opened the book, and they both looked at the entry with a silence that you could have heard a pin drop in, they were so quiet, the danged pin would have clanged like a twenty-four foot metal ladder falling on a concrete sidewalk in downtown Central Falls. I saw, from across the table a short sentence, but, as it was upside down, and, I could not see it well enough to make the entries out, or, could not quite read it upside down, whichever it was, as it appeared to be either some kind of fancy printing or cursive writing. Frank said, "What in the name of this God forsaken world, do you suppose that that means?", with Jan responding that he had no earthly idea either, as to whatever the entry said, both of them pondering, me stretching my neck and straining to see once more, and even holding my breath, but to no avail, I couldn't make heads or tails out of any of it right side up, much less it being upside down, so, I just gave it up. I answered Frank and Jan's questions about the insurance that I had with the Community Insurance, and, the amounts that I had paid in, and any claims that I had, which was simple enough, but it all was still somewhat of a mystery to me, overall.

The dreamer dreams, that six long months have passed, with very little having changed…

So, now, six long months must have passed on by, come and gone, since my last appointment with the two aforementioned CPA's, and, I have had very little work and a whole lot of bills throughout the winter, and, I sorely missed what work I had previous, along with the money, that I had coming in with the Community Insurance and Hereford's assignments. To top it all off, I was initially disqualified for unemployment compensation, since the Community Insurance had paid very little into that program on my behalf, but on a final State appeal, I finally got $47. per week, which, by the way, did not even help to pay my rent, which, I had also gotten behind on, because I had used the money for food, mostly, and, some, I would have to admit, for playing pool, which made me feel guilty. Too, as the time has went by, I also, missed Hereford, I missed his talk, I missed the smile of his sweet wife Anielia, just as much, if not more, than those folks down at the soup kitchen, where I have been taking most of my meals, I might add, and, the food pantry, where I got groceries almost weekly, and the old folks, and, the shut in's, that Miss Aneila always took meals to. There was a genuine emptiness out and about, since all of this "Fraud" business had come about. Much rumor and innuendo had surfaced, ran the gamut, dive bombed, erupted, crashed, and whatever else you could imagine, over the Community Insurance "Fraud" fiasco. It had been a fiasco, but, during this time, and to this day, six months later, no one to date, has traced, seen or heard of Hereford, his wife, their dog Rufus, or, the old lady Stephanie Franusiak whose body had disappeared, or, Hereford's father or mother. Word on the street, and, down at Kadise's pool hall, was, that there was to be a publication coming forthwith, in the County newspaper, from the Certified Public Accountant firm of Kopezinski and Czerwien, regarding the Community Insurance matter. Every day, folks scoured the Central Falls daily newspaper and the weekly County Courier & Press Journal just yearning to see what it was that could be forth coming.

When the announcement finally did come, no one was ready for it, but then, everyone was eagerly looking for it, and, expected it to be more than what it was. The newspaper publication was in pure unadulterated legal form, saying that disposition of "Fraud" had been made by the Court with Judge " so and so" presiding, and, there was five and a half pages of listings, in small print, of every person that had ever been insured by Community Insurance from its date of inception, way back when Hereford's father had started the business, to and through Hereford's time, date to date, back to back, including the net amount of premiums that folks had paid into their insurance policies, what had been paid out, and, what amount was being returned to them as a form of reimbursement to abate their part of the "Fraud". More than 90 percent of the amounts so listed, I observed, were the same, identical in value, with some, or, a few, being a little greater, but not one entry was noted as being any lesser. Total amount of "Fraud", the paper said, over an extended period of 27 years, six months and 5 days, was in the total amount of $2,627,531.35. I furiously hunted for my name down in the list, finally finding it, and seeing that it was recorded, that I had paid in premiums over the years for various insurances for a total of $ 1,726.15, and, was to receive exactly that same amount in return to compensate for my portion of the "Fraud". The article further stated that everyone so listed was to make appointment with the CPA firm to pick up their monies for final settlement of said "Fraud" upon the folks of Central Falls, and, some parts of Pawtucket, with a few on up in the Woonsocket area.

Very shortly thereafter, Central Falls folks, and, even some of the ones up in Pawtucket went totally haywire, and there was no conversation that did not get started with, come around to, revolve around or involve in some way shape, form or fashion, as to what was going on in the community with respect to the "Fraud". As more information was leaked or just came out, it was determined that the Community Insurance business, did not actually have insurance policies, not even one policy could be found, or, not one policy with any formal and legitimate insurance company was ever found in the Community Insurance office files inside Hereford's house, or, in any bank deposit box, safe, or, anywhere else for that matter, in any of the five operative Counties or eleven banks which had held Community Insurance funds. Apparently, Hereford just as his father before him, had "self-insured" the entire community and their properties, through the Community Insurance "Fraud", and, it appeared, that all losses incurred were paid out, of none other, than the interest off of their money which had been invested, the interest, which, had been gained on the accrued on the money that had been deposited in the eleven banks in the five counties, everywhere and with everyone, that the Community Insurance had done business over the years either with Hereford or his dad before him. Even my pay, that I was paid, in cash, had been recorded, and, just like the other losses, all of my pay, apparently, according to the accountants, had also been paid from the interest that had been gained on the money from the premiums paid in. Roofs had been replaced on houses, shingles replaced, hail damage had been repaired, window glass had been replaced from kids baseball breakage, cars and trucks that had been damaged in wrecks had all been fixed back to as good as new, doctor and hospital bills had been paid in full on the insured's from cradle to grave, funerals had been paid for, graves had been paid for, tombstones had been paid for, things replaced that high winds or tornadoes had blown away, everything that had been insured, had their losses covered, by only the interest, that had been paid on all of the folk's insurance policies, and, now, it appeared that both Hereford and his father had managed those funds accordingly and amazingly over the years with both high, low and variable interest rates through the eleven banks in the five counties;. Even the odd ball stuff that Hereford had insured had been recorded in the "Ledger", with all of the premiums and pay outs recorded, almost religiously. Word was, in general, that folks could not believe that such a "Fraud" could have ever been perpetrated upon the innocent folks of Central Falls by such culprits as Hereford and his father before him for so many years. Another rumor circulated, that there had been a nationwide, if not even a worldwide search especially for Hereford's father and mother, first, where they supposedly had gone to retire in Florida, but were never located, then on from there, just like Hereford and his wife were never located either, or, ever seen again on the face of the earth, or, even the lady Stephanie Franusiak's body had never been recovered, for that matter, and, it came to be, within 6 months or so, as if any of them had ever existed on the face of the earth, or, in Central Falls or around the Pawtucket area in the first place, including Rufus, the dog.

Now, as folks began to settle up with the CPA firm, much griping and growling began to take place. Folks, now, who had had their insurance on their house, or car, or whatever, now had to go somewhere else for their insurance. Most went to an insurance agent up in Pawtucket or Woonsocket, and, found out that their insurance was three to five times as costly as the insurance that they had had with the Community Insurance, when Hereford or his dad was still around. This caused no little furor except for that group of folks who always went shopping elsewhere anyway. Surprise, surprise, those folks didn't know how good that they had had it, in the first place, having not been mixed up in the "Fraud" of Central Falls, or, the Rhode Island "Fraud" of the century, as it has come to be known in these parts. It was always the "Fraud", and was never referred to as the "alleged Fraud", and, I wondered why, in my strained brain.

A couple more weeks went by, and, I had to have my Federal and State taxes done, and Frank Kopezinski had always done my taxes, so, I set up an appointment with his CPA firm to do that and also, expecially, to pick up my portion or return of monies from the "Fraud" situation with Community Insurance. A good way to kill two birds with one stone, I thought, and, maybe, I could get caught up on my rent, and, maybe afford something besides peanut butter and jelly, along with some bologna now and then, and, not have to frequent the local soup kitchens, or, the food pantries at the local churches. When I finally did get in to see Frank, he also provided me a proper W-2 form in order for me to be able to file my taxes, completed my payroll taxes for me, and, I was also able to pick up my check from the "Fraud" settlement, and, we talked a little about the entire "Fraud" fiasco. He said that there were other details, some still forth coming, but none known to date to have any particular change in the overall matter. He said that everyone involved with the "Fraud", got every dime of their money returned that they had paid in for any and all insurances with the Community Insurance, a recovery from the "Fraud", if you will. Even the folks who had died over the last 27 years, the CPA firm had their relatives looked up, and their funds were spread out amongst those kin. I asked Frank why the term "alleged" was never used in any of the charges or newspaper reports, and, he said that the Sheriff thought that he had good evidence in the form of the "Ledger" for the Prosecutor to make a case, if they ever decided to go that far. But, at this time, the "Fraud" charges had either been dropped, or modified, or set aside for the time being by the Grand Jury, and, the Sheriff was said to have rescinded every other charge, except the missing person reports on the McAbeley's, but which did not include Rufus's missing, and, it was odd that there was no mention as to what the disposition was on the missing body of "the cat lady", whose body had disappeared from the morgue. I remarked to Frank, that at my first interview on the matter, and, I also remembered that him and Jan had both been somewhat taken aback by some entry on the very last page of the "LEDGER" when I was there, on the first interview. I asked Frank if it was possible if he could share it with me, just out of curiosity, nonetheless, as to what that particular entry on the very last page of the "LEDGER" was.

Frank looked at me, kind of oddly, hesitated a moment, then, got up, walked over to a book shelf in the office, pulled the old leather bound "LEDGER" book from a shelf, turned it upside down, plopped it down on the table, and said, "I'll let you read it for yourself and you can make up your own mind or put your own definition to it." With that, he opened the "LEDGER" up to the last page, turned the "LEDGER" around, pushed it across the desk, and, looking at the bottom of the page, I read the last entry to myself.

"Last and Final Entry"

On this date, August 17, 2008" "For those who interpret such, <u>it was no more than curiosity that killed the cat.   Now, it is announced to the world, for all to know and take heed of, that, on this date, ALL, of the last SIX "ANGELS'S", previously assigned at Central Falls, have now ascended, to avail on behalf of the local populace ever again.</u>"

Signed, "Wreuphous de Fifth".

When awakening from the dream, I will have to say, here and now, for the first time in my life, I was no little shocked and taken aback, dumified, if you will, and, not fully understanding how curiosity could have killed the cat or comprehending what it was, that I was reading about as to their having been some six "Angels" assigned in the little town of Central Falls and Pawtucket, although I still wondered why Pawtucket had never been mentioned otherwise previous, and, I might also add here, that I did not know that "Wreuphous" had ever spelled his name that way, or, that he was the

"Fifth". Now, I figured, in my own brain, that I finally knew why Hereford had called Rufus a "Jack Daniels" terrier. As Rufus was, just like a fifth of Jack Daniels whiskey, as, most folks cannot stop at just a drop, or, things are here one day and gone the next, whichever, and, the very knowledge coming to me of it, left a sweet but yet bitter taste in my mouth, and, a buzz on the frontal most part of my brain, which I can still feel and remember even to this day, as it drives me on to my next much needed drink.

The only thing that the dreamer cannot fully accept, is that somewhere, there is a poor homeless dog, wandering the streets in the East Providence, RI, area, or maybe a little more to the east, that is really a lot smarter than what he looks, or, is more than what folks would normally give him credit for, having been totally abandoned by those danged ass ended or ascended angels, whichever.

Then, the dreamer rolled over, punched up his pillow, and, went back to sleep.

YOUNG ABE'S AXE

Dreaming away, it soon got noisy, and, a little nosy even.

"Hail the house, hail the house, good neighbor Jesse Keith a-calling." The visitor said.
"Who goes there? Who hails the house? A good neighbor you say? What is it you want from another good neighbor? You say you are Jesse, but a little proof on that would shine." Said the householder, from inside the darkened house.
"You know me, I am Jesse, your very close neighbor, a sore-journier, sore from sitting on a most uncomfortable saddle, but yet, and still, calling with a calling, I might add, of something of interest, which you too may also be interested in, a venture even, which could even be turned into an adventure on short notice, so, bring yourself to the door with your gun lowered to the rest position, so that we may more properly converse". The visitor added.
The house holder came through the door and onto the porch so as to greet the so far unidentified so called close neighbor, but yet held his gun at the ready position rather than the lowered at rest position. "If you are truly Jesse Keith, just what might your father's name be?" Queried the house holder.
"I am Jesse, son of Alexander Keith, and father of my daughter Mary Ann Keith, who is your son Henry Bond's fiancé, no more and no less, but for God's sake, Cornelius, for want of some more formal introduction, or have you caught the rampant "CRS" disease which is worse than the flu." The visitor said.
"CRS? What the hell is CRS?" Cornelius yelled back.
"CRS, also known as Can't Remember Shit! Damn, Cornelius, maybe you have more than a bad case of it and don't even know it." Jesse added
Cornelius responded. "Well, I don't think I have it yet, but, I do think, that it is about time that you and I finally met, with an up and coming marriage between our families, I had heard some of you, but have heard more of your father's good work about the community with his doctoring folks with his collection of herbs and all, but would have expected you to have followed in his footsteps a little more than what you have. So, what is it you are calling about today?"
"Well, Cornelius, if we may so converse a little more in private, the

matter at hand, is one which calls for much security, as, it is a much tenuous story to say the least." Jesse said.

Cornelius responded. "Let us retire to the area of the wood shed, away from the house, so that our conversation may be a little more than private."

With that, the two, retired out and about from the house, and re-congregated out behind the wood shed far enough from the house where any conversation between the two would not have been heard even with someone with very good hearing who might have been listening a little more than most folks considered as intently.

"So, what's your story in a nutshell, Jesse?" Cornelius asked.

"Well, Cornelius, it is like this. I have a relative of mine, on my wife Elizabeth's side, of the James family no less, out of that fine family from Jamestown, Kentucky, itself, a distant cousin, if you will, who has, for the immediate previous past, conducted his family business as a horse trader, throughout the tri-state area of Indiana, Kentucky and Illinois, with some venture as far west as the Missouri at times, and, it is he, in whom I have great faith in his spoken word, that says, that he has all but come upon a certain individual just over in Spencer County, right here close by in Indiana, at less than a half day's ride on a good horse, who is said to have immediate close contact with an old farmer, if you will, who has, in his possession, and is holding, the very axe, with which young Abe hacked out fence rails, cross ties for the railroad, logs for cabins, and even cut some trees to float down the Pigeon Creek to the Ohio River, then on to the Mississippi and on even to New Orleans. The axe itself, being the original and only known remnant of that kind memory of young Abe himself from his life here in Indiana. So, what do you think of that? Jesse queried.

Cornelius responded. "What has any of that got to do with me or any of my kin? Or, why am I being apprised by you of such a fact?"

Jesse's come back was. "Well, according to my wife's direct kin relative, this man, says that the farmer has now put the axe up for sale to the highest bidder, and, is now accepting bids for such. So, what do you think of that?"

"Why in hell would I want anything to do with young Abe's old axe?" Cornelius asked.

"Well, hell, Cornelius, the danged axe is already now probably worth a veritable fortune, if the truth was ever known, or, will be on into the very near future." Jesse responded.

Cornelius came back with. "So, again, what has all this got to do with me and my family?"

Jesse responded. "Well, I thought that I would bring you into the deal, to ask if you were interested in pursuing such a venture to make an offer or even possibly purchase the axe, if the chance presented itself, as I do not have the necessary funds myself."

"What kind of money are we talking about, anyway?" Cornelius asked.

"Well, I do not rightly know, at this moment in time, and, would not know until such time as we would meet with the man and the farmer involved, but, just in case, that there was a chance to purchase such an artifact of history, I would venture to think that it would take more money than what I have saved back, so, that is why I considered you to also to go in on the halves to try to purchase such an item if it were available, or, if you were so interested to do so." Jesse responded.

"What do you suppose his asking price would be?" Queried Cornelius.

Jesse responded. "I would expect the top bid to be somewhere in the range of about $200. more or less, from what I have heard second handedly that is."

"$200. Dollars? Hell's bells, Jesse, I can buy a forty acre field, cleared of all stumps for plowing for that kind of money." Cornelius said. "Why would I ever want to waste that kind of money on nothing more than an axe?" He asked.

Jesse had a response. "Think about it, Cornelius, if we had such an item, we could donate it to some museum, or even to the collection that they are now just setting up over in Springfield, Illinois, and, the donation of such a relict would have our names on it, and, we and our families would go down in recorded history, along with Abe himself. So, what do you think of that?"

"Not much, to tell you the truth, most of us, living in these parts, remember Abe when he was young, and a living around here, wanting to wrestle all the time with whomever, just to show off, along with that habit he had of holding an axe out at arm's length longer than anyone else could, just to show how strong he was. All good memories, but that is all that there is, good memories, he left us for Illinois and then went on from there to his destiny, and, the record of his time in Indiana is just another small remnant of history itself." Cornelius added.

Jesse came back with. "Well, might you just think that it may be something that could cause you to mount up on one of those fine horses of yours and to go on the venture with me on a ride over to Spencer County, just to see? Where is your adventure?"

Cornelius responded. "I have the better part of my adventure right here at home, and, I have my money held tight in one of my front pockets. Besides, who ever heard of anyone ever paying $200. Dollars for no more than a $2. Dollar axe?"

"It is what it is, Cornelius, and, it could be what it could be, too, I am free today, and, it looks like you are too, so, put some cash together, mount up, and, let's go for the ride." Jesse came back with.

"OK, let's see what comes of it, but give me a chance to cover myself, and I'll get my horse and be with you just to see where such a venture could go." Cornelius responded.

Jesse dismounted from his horse, adjusted the cinch and the saddle, and waited on Cornelius to set himself set up for the short trip.

Shortly thereafter, Cornelius came, leading his horse by the bridle, readily saddled, and, ready to go.

"You want to water you horse before we go?" Queried Cornelius.

"May as well, as I don't know of any streams we would cross between here and there except maybe Pigeon creek once or twice." Jesse responded.

With that, both Cornelius and Jesse led their horses to the trough, but, could not make either of them drink. So, they gave it up, and mounted up, for the ride.

Inquiry early on upon entering into Spencer County, Indiana, led them to the farmer who was said to have known the owner of the aforementioned axe that was believed to have been owned and used by the young Abe himself. From there, they were so directed to the said owner, or, holder of the said axe, which was reportedly once owned and used by Abe.

Upon arrival at the directed site of the said reported holder of Abe's axe, both Jesse and Cornelius were careful to introduce themselves as being interested parties in the said holdings of the individual said to have held possession of aforementioned axe, so, they stayed mounted on their horses and held them reined up tight and up right at the fence just in front of the cabin. Both of them could hear the noise of dogs barking and growling from within the cabin, so, that was another reason not to venture any further at the moment.

"Here, here, hail to the house, Cornelius Bond and Jesse Keith, both residents of neighboring Warrick County, come calling with an honest venture at heart, to discuss some trade, transaction, barter, or sale, of some item of mutual interest." Cornelius spoke.

"Who goes there?" Came inquiry from inside the cabin.

"It is we, Cornelius Bond and Jesse Keith, of neighboring Warrick

County, as aforesaid, to do some business with you, but only if you will consider such." Added Jesse.

The resident came to the door, with double barreled shotgun in hand, at the ready, and, it was visually obvious to both Jesse and Cornelius, that the gun's hammers were both cocked, and, it could further be expected that the gun was also in the loaded and ready to fire position. So, the two showed their hands, open and free of any firearms or sharp knives, and, beckoned the resident to lower his aim and to be a little more favorable to converse on the subject matter at hand.

"What might your name be?" Queried Jesse.

The resident responded. "Never mind the introductions, please just state your business if you will, and, do please hold your horses."

Jesse was the first to speak. "I am Jesse Keith, son of Alexander Keith, and, this is Cornelius Bond, both of Warrick County, who, have heard of your holdings, of some such artifact which may have been owned and used by old Abe himself, whilst he lived here in Spencer County, afore he moved on out further west to Illinois, and, we both may very well be most interested in the possible acquirement and purchase of such artifact, by name, as, we have so heard, by word of mouth from some close relatives of ours, that you hereby hold in your very possession such an axe, that very well may have been owned and even used by Abe himself, and, am interested in what you plan to do with such artifact at this time or if it even be for sale, by barter, trade, or outright cash on the barrel head sum."

The resident came out on the porch with two hounds bounding out to the fence to confront Cornelius and Jesse, the resident lowered his gun to the ready position, moved to the steps at the edge of the porch, and said. "If'n you all are interested in such an article which I may or may not have to show, you all must first show some of your money, then I may or may not show you such an article which I may or may not have directly in my possession."

Cornelius spoke up. "How much money do you want to see shown?"

"How much do you have?" The resident came back with.

Cornelius again spoke up. "Twenty dollars in cash on the barrel head sum."

The resident responded. "Twenty dollars ain't a-gonna get me to show you all shit!"

"What or how much are you looking to be shown up front before anyone can see the artifact that you say that you may or may not be ahold of?" Jesse asked.

"Well, twenty dollars ain't a-gonna get it, it would be more likely to be in the range somewhere between three to five hundred dollars." The resident came back with.

Cornelius again responded. "Well, neighbor, we are obviously not the folks that you want to talk to about such an article of interest, because we are just a couple poor folks from Warrick County that earn our living from hard work and gain our bread by the sweat of our brow, so, we may as well head on back down the road, and, ride out on the same horse that we rode in on." And, with that said, Cornelius wheeled his horse around 180 degrees as if to depart.

"Hold your horses, hold your horses there, I may have been too hasty in mentioning such a price just off the top of my head, because, I honestly do not know what the final full value of such an article to be, as I have never heard anyone else in these parts that has similar, that is, if I were in possession of such, or if I could even lay my hands on it, so, how much money would you all be willing to pay for such an article?." The resident came back with.

Cornelius again wheeled his horse around another 180 degrees, and asked. "Well, just how much money would we have to show, just to get you to show, so as to prove up what we have to see what you have?"

"I would say that you all should be able to show at least fifty dollars between the two of you, before I would even think of showing you what it is that I may or may not have to offer." The resident responded.

Cornelius spoke up. "I have twenty, like I said before." And, he held out his money for show.

Jesse added on. "I also have twenty." And Jesse also held out his money for show.

"Well, I have never, in the recent past, shown any artifact which may or may not be in my possession, for any less than fifty dollars at any one time." The resident came back with.

"Well, that is what we have, and that is what we can show, so, it is up to you to decide whether or not that you would accept that for the show on your part." Cornelius said.

"OK, so, tie your horses there at the fence gate, and come on around back of the cabin where maybe we can do some business, and, do not mind the dogs, as they be friendly." The resident said.

Cornelius and Jesse then dismounted and tied their horse up by wrapping the horse's reins around the fence railing, then, after the resident called his dogs off, since they did not want to follow him, they then entered in through the gate, and, followed the resident around the cabin, with the resident still carrying his gun at the ready position.

"What might your name be?" Jesse asked.

"I am just Simpson, no more and no less, and, I own and run the local grist mill." He said.

Well, just Simpson, let's see what you have." Jesse responded.

Simpson walked on around the cabin and came over nearby to the woodpile, picked up an axe which had been left lying on a chopping block, and responded. "Here it is, this is it, take a look and tell me what you think." He said.

Jesse looked at the axe, then looked at Cornelius, then asked. "Simpson, you tell me that you have been using this axe, the same as you report to have been used by young Abe himself?"

Simpson responded. "Sir, it is but a working tool, and if not used on occasion, it would do nothing but rust away." With that said, Simpson picked up the axe, and handed it to Jesse.

Jesse took the axe, looked it over, and handed it by the handle to Cornelius, which in turn took a little closer look.

Simpson added. "If you look closely, you will see the initials "AL" cut into the handle up near the head of the axe, and, if you look even a little more closely, you will see the initials "AL" scratched on the base of the shoulder of the head just back of the eye."

Cornelius and Jesse continued to examine the axe a little more closely, as the dogs sniffed their leather leggings and tried to lick their hands.

Cornelius spoke first. "Now, Simpson, you say, that this may very well be the axe that young Abe used to cut fence railings, railroad cross ties, and logs for cabins?"

"That is the story I is a-tellin'." Simpson said.

Cornelius came back with. "Well, Simpson, if that is the case, why is it, that the handle is more modern, and even has a new look to it, as anyone of sound mind, could easily decipher on their own, to figure out."

Simpson responded. "Well, sir, if I may remind you, what you see, is, a working tool, no more and no less, and, must be maintained accordingly, so, the handle of the axe, may have been replaced an unknown total number of times, as there is no legal recording requirement of such, but with each change, I might add, the initials

"AL" were cut into and put on the handle, at the same and exact position as was the original as was found years ago, and every time it was ever changed out, with almost a religious zeal by the previous owners or holders, and, you can see that with your own eyes, right there, where I showed you, I might add."
Jesse then said, and, also asked. "Simpson, I saw the "AL" marking on the bottom of the shoulder just behind the eye of the handle, on the head of the axe, but, I also see some numbers on the side of the head of the axe, just above the "4-1/2" poundage mark, that says "54", which means that this particular axe head was forged in the year of 1854. Now, Simpson, we all know that Abe left these parts and went on to Illinois with his family back in the late 1830's. So, it would only follow, that the head of the axe had to have been replaced sometime after Abe left this part of the country by quite a few years or so. What do you have to say about that?"
Again, Simpson responded. "Well, it is just like I told you all before. An axe is no more and no less than a working tool and likewise, has to be maintained accordingly. The head may very well have been replaced, but the marking of Abe's initials as "AL" on the base of the shoulder was scratched on and put at the same place as was the original, and, the same holds true for the handle, as previously mentioned, but, yet, I again remind you, that there neither was, nor is to date, any legal recording requirement of such, either for the handle or the head for that matter."
Cornelius interrupted. "Simpson, I see here and now, and forthwith, that neither I, nor Jesse here, even if we put our funds together, have enough cash money on hand to even think of purchasing this fine historical article of which you may or may not be in possession of, depending upon whether or not it is in use in your very hands doing the work with which it was intended and designed to do, and, whether or not you decide to do it or not."
Simpson then asked. "Well, if you don't have the money now, is there some chance that you could come up with a little more on into some near future return?"
"Well, Simpson, we will just have to wait and see on that point, but, if so, or when, we would just have to get back to you at the time, but for now, you are the one and only proud owner and holder of this historical artifact." Cornelius said. With that, Cornelius handed the axe back over to Simpson.
At that point, Jesse jumped in. "Wait, wait, Cornelius, we had the money to show, and Simpson had the axe to show back, but Simpson

has not said whether or not that he would take the forty dollars that we put up for our show for the show of his axe. What do you say, Simpson, would you take the forty dollars flat out, cash on the barrel head sum?"

Simpson responded. "Well, I do not see how in the world, that I could take any less than I had mentioned early on. Too, I know, that such a historical artifact as what you have seen here today, should bring much more, and, may be worth more than even I think it to be. Just as Cornelius said, you all obviously do not have the necessary funds at hand to even consider such a purchase, even with the pooling of your funds, so, the answer is no, as I could not accept such a paltry sum for such an important artifact."

Cornelius spoke up. "So, Jesse, that is it, that is your answer, and, Simpson here, knows what it is that he knows, and, he is an upstanding man, a man upright, standing on his own hind legs, a man who knows the worth his worth, a man of his word no less, an educated man who knows how to count and cipher, a man who will go down in history as part of his destiny, a man who will be remembered for his remembrance, and, we are but pitiful poor witnesses to so much as a little part of it all. So, we now hereby thank you Simpson, for allowing us to view this precious artifact, of which, I might add, that if it were mine, I would think twice before I left it out in the weather, even if you felt that it did feel more at home near the wood pile, and, I would most likely recommend that it be taken into the cabin for security, and put it near by the fireplace when it was not in use, for the very honor and just to protect the very sanctity of such a sacred object."

Cornelius then turned to Jesse and said. "I think our business is over and closed for the day, Jesse, and, I think we ought to head for home to at least arrive before dark."

Simpson jumped in at that point. "Well, you all do need to water your horses before you leave, I'll get a bucket of water from the spring and then you all can be on your way."

Cornelius and Jesse headed back around the cabin toward their horses tied at the fence with the dogs trailing close behind, going through the gate but not allowing the dogs to get out near the horses as they were already skittish from the dogs presence.

Simpson came shortly thereafter, wagging a bucket of water, which he offered up to Cornelius over the fence to water his horse by, which Cornelius did do, and, afterward, he passed the bucket to Jesse, who also gave some for his horse to drink, then, Jesse gave the bucket back to Simpson who was on the other side of the fence with the dogs, with their tails a-wagging.

Cornelius and Jesse, tightened up the cinches on their saddles, untied the horses reins from the fence rail, then mounted up to depart.

"It was more than just a pleasure to get to know you Simpson, if anything, it was more than just a blessing, to say the least." Cornelius said.

"Yes, I would say the same Simpson, or, just Simpson, just to add on to that also." Jesse added.

Simpson responded. "Well, I am sorry that we could not do business, however, I would appreciate it, if you would pass on to any others, as to the important historical artifact which I may or may not hold in my possession, however, please do not overemphasize that I do indeed have it in my possession, as I do not want any neer-do-wells a-coming and a-looking for an easy sneaky take of such an article in the dark on night, if you know what I mean."

"I understand fully, and we will be most discreet in advising anyone who may come looking for such as what it is you may or may not have just to protect your family's safety on into the near future." Cornelius said.

Jesse added. "Simpson, you don't have to worry about me telling anyone about what it is you may or may not have, I'll just say that you may or may not have it, because, you may very well sell it off in the next few days for a veritable fortune for all I know."

Simpson added on. "Well, thanks for stopping by, please know that you are welcome anytime into the future, if you change your minds about the aforementioned article and eventually come up with a little more money between the two of you. By the way, did I mention that this bucket here is the very one and same bucket that Abe's family left hanging at their well, when they headed out to Illinois, back in '37? What would you suppose something like that would be worth in this day and time?"

Both Cornelius and Jesse, looked at one another and just shrugged their shoulders, said that neither one had a clue, and bid Simpson a goodbye, tipped their hats, wheeled their horses around and rode off back toward home in Warrick County.

After riding a little while, Jesse turned to Cornelius, and said. "Damn, Cornelius, you just took over the whole conversation back there, you didn't even think to ask him what it was that he wanted for the danged bucket. We just might have had enough money between the two of us to buy it, and, there is no telling what that thing would

be worth on into the future. Do you think maybe we might turn around and go back just to see what he would take for an offer?"
Cornelius looked at Jesse and just shook his head, but did not respond, and just rode on toward home.
Jesse, took Cornelius's cue, did not mention any of it further, and, decided to himself, that if there was any kind of deal to be made on into the future, he would most likely have to make it himself, because, he assumed, that Cornelius was just to stingy with his money. And, with that, the two, rode on back home, not talking much more between themselves.
With that, the dreamer stirred some, looked at the clock, took note that it was just a dream, then, rolled over, and went back to sleep.

THE RINGERLESS DING-A-LING

The dream began with the clanging of the alarm clock, but once shut off, and reset, the dream resumed with full intensity.

"May this congressional investigatory committee assigned to assess, access and to successfully investigate the soon to be mentioned matter, please come to some borderline condition which borders on some sort of worded order, in this, the most knowledgeable modern world of the 1850's." The Chairman called for.

The Chairman went on. "We are gathered here, today, but, may also be here again tomorrow, if we want to double our pay, that is, with these especially selected most honorable committee members and a couple of volunteers who were thrown in on the side at the last minute, including a couple of wannabees, but yet no unmentionables identified yet to date, to make the proper investigation for the grave and grievous determination as to some of the reported occurrences of which and of what happened many, many, years ago, before our time, right at about five score or more years or so, to be exact, more or less, except for a little procrastination levied up, here and there, and, in some cases, perhaps even more than some time than was seen even previous, if the truth were fully known, to finally try or make some attempt to settle some unanswered questions and to possibly find some final solutions to that long unmentionable problem of the mention of some in-landish or out-landish conspiracy of sorts concerning either this and that, which yet divides us all one way or another, even in this most modern day and time, in the here and now, now and then, here and there. And, with no more and no little than that, I hereby turn the meeting over to our selected Speaker of choice in order to announce and lay down the low down before you as to this committee's obligations accordingly for the interim at this time, and, with no more than that, as an introduction, I will now go order the pizza and heartwarming drinks for your late working lunch a little later. So…..! Here's…..! Johnny…..!" I mean, every family has someone in it by the name of John! For God's sake.

The Speaker then stood up on his hind legs, came forward, looked over the group and took over the podium to boot, and began before someone else could begin the beguine or whatever, whichever. "We are gathered here on this day, ten decades of years or more in some cases, to make a determined determination to find some softer answers to some very uneasy hard unanswered questions concerning even the very mention of some conspiracy of a most hallowed national natural icon, of sorts, as to how, that it was that it all came about, who it was that was, that was directly or indirectly involved or who was instrumental that brought it all about, whichever, also, as to what it was that happened in the interim, up to and including where we are today, so, in a nut shell, to answer the who, what, when, where, and how, with a couple of why's thrown in just for good measure and to make for some good interesting reading with the mention of the conspiracy thing thrown in at the very beginning, but, a little on the side, on this, the one hundredth anniversary, give or take a few years, one way or another, taking procrastination into consideration, of the original first set-up or mockup of the now so-called Liberty Bell as it has begun to be called, less than previous or a little more than just recently in our most more recent past, that is."

"Get to the point Mister Speaker and/or tenured cozy quasi committee member." One of the more junior members yelled out, apparently trying to form up some form of distraction at the mention of some conspiracy. "We want to know why we are here and why this committee and its actions and findings have so been assigned a

CONFIDENTIAL classified status, with the "what you see or hear here stays here" conditions, as if it is like it's a Las Vegas convention or something, which it actually closely resembles considering the members present for the quorum." He bellowed out loud.

"I'm getting to it, I'm getting to it." Retorted the Speaker. "Besides, I have the podium, and, order has been called for, and, you sir, are out of order with that order, according to the official Robert's Rules of Order, here and now, in the when, so, shut your mouth Ralph and take my tip to dip into another sip or nip, and to zip your lip before I clip your whip or I'll have to rip your yip in the interim, without permission granted, kind sir."

"Said comment from the wannabee more senior committee member and known habitual convention goer has done been strictly struck from the record sir, especially his added mention of Las Vegas, whatever or wherever that may be, certainly not anywhere in this the fine great modern State of Pensylviania." Added in the Scribe, purposely throwing up his hands and acting like he was more than just purposely animated, by making wide sweeps of "X's" in the air, with his turkey feathered quill pen held tightly in his hand high up over his head in an awkward position as if he had the jerks, spasms, or some nervous tic or bared tickled nerve with which he was afflicted, affected or effected with or by, whichever.

The Speaker continued. "Just to bring you all up to date, way back, years and years ago, back in the year of 1749, the Superintendents of the Pensylvania State House all finally got together and established a place for the hanging of a celebratory bell, but, because of either an acute or chronic outbreak of procrastination within that august group, it was not until too much later on, well into 1751, that the House and, the Pennsylvania Assembly issued an order for some sort of Bell to be hung and rung for the young, on the fiftieth anniversary of William Penn's 1701 Charter of Privileges which was not now obviously to happen because of the aforementioned procrastination within the glorious State of Pensylvania, as it is solely named on to this day. Then, in 1752, a certain Isaac Norris, along with two other certains by name of Tom Leech and Ed Warner, with another certain called Isaac being the Assembly Speaker and Chairman of the Pensylvania State House Superintendents, with very little yelling, issued an order for the selling of and purchase of a telling pelling bell, through their selected so-called agent Robert Charles, over the pond in London, no less, for the monetary over the counter purchase of such a bell, slick as a whistle it was, to be founded by the Lester and Pack foundry of London, and, in the fine print of the instructions, it was also specifically written in to be added onto the front side as you normally look at a bell if you know which side is the front side that is, so as to be handily etched or sketched on the right side of it as follows….."

" Let the Bell be cast by the best Workmen & examined carefully before it is Shipped with the following words well shaped in large letters round in viz. "By order of the Assembly of the Province of Pensylvania for the State house in the City of Philada 1752", and underneath, "Proclaim Liberty thro' all the Land to all the Inhabitants thereof. - Levit. XXV.10"

The Speaker then proceeded on. "Knowing this, this committee, has been so duly assigned, to make the determination and to uncover any unknown or otherwise known covered up facts or matters at hand of any hands on or off the matter, concerning the very touchy feely subject of the suspected conspiracy of the so called Liberty Bell itself, so named, I might mention at this time, as was such name was assigned much later on, by about eighty years later or so after initial production, actually, if the truth were ever known, by the American anti-slavery Abolitionists movement in the early 1830's, soon after King William the IV of England abolished slavery in all of its colonies in 1833, and, the Abolitionists thought amongst themselves, that everyone else, including the newly established 13 States of the United States at that time, should do the same and also follow suit, just to stay up to date, and to be a little more in fashion with the rest of the world at that time, so to speak."

"So, there you have it. We are called to make some sense of the nonsensical, to open the gate to invest in an investigation and take the view to interview those who have some known firsthand knowledge or information of what has happened previously and afore, before any more of all of them or those directly or indirectly involved, may finally bite the dust, or, make their final journey to the great beyond wherever that may be, or, wherever they may go, that is, if they can even remember, as they may very well have a chronic or acute case of the Alzheimer's, bless their soul if they so have been so diagnosed, and may not fully know what it was that they were involved with, in the first place, and, if not, whether or not that we can even get them to truthfully talk about it anymore, just short of and without putting any of them on the water board, but strike the mention of that from the record, that , and add in that we may recommend them to the water board, I might add, just to keep the end solution to be more than solvent and to prevent any further piracy of some conspiracy."

The Speaker went on. "We are to determine to make the determinations, and to timely set up specific time lines, as to whether or not, the proper governmental contract terminology was sufficient early on in the 1750's for such a significant projected project, whether there was or were more than one bidder on the project at the time, and, whether or not the lowest bidder was selected in the process, or, if there were preferred contractors with the appropriate money in hand from their lobbyists at hand, and, to investigate, the English manufacturers of the bell, being, at the time, under the rule of King George the II, was somehow purposely deficient in the design for some or whatever reason, the metallic makeup, the melting of the mix of the brass, or the temperature of the pouring and casting, and whether or not that the cooling and the tempering of the metal of the bell was limited to all accepted metallurgical limits, and as to the why that the foundry changed its name shortly after the deficiency of design made itself apparent."

The Speaker went on. "We are to determine, whether or not, that the method of portability and transport was adequate and sufficient from the manufacturers storage area to the dock area, with the hoisting, loading and handling onto the boat of transport was within reasonable and contractual long shore man limits, and, whether or not that the hold storage, along with any recurrences of the securance of any of the on board shipments, and, whether or not, that it, all or any, met the present common maritime recommended measures for conditions present, as, to who or whom all was or were on board at the time, who or whom all had access to the bell during the ship's trip over, over the Western Ocean, as it was known to be in this day and time, or, from there to here that is, and, whether the uploading on and the unloading off of the bell upon reaching our shore either by the Harbor Captain or by the ship's Captain himself and his crew members at hand, were properly operating under and within the rules of the International Union of Operating Engineers Crane Operations and Hoisting Guidelines, and to include whether or not everyone stayed out from under the load and out from under the "Y" of the hoisting sheaves and ropes, and, whether or not that the ropes so used had their annual testing accomplished by a third party licensed inspection entity with international rigging certifications both there and here."

The Speaker went on. "At this point in the time line, we are to investigate specifically, whether or not, there was any official acceptance whatsoever, with appropriate quality control documentation which included any testing of the bell onsite, either at the manufacturer's location, or, immediately prior to such acceptance from the manufacturer onsite, or, from the transporter, at our Port of Entry, and whether or not the Port Authority somehow was directly or indirectly involved in the matter or has any record of the transaction, and, if any local members of the International Dockworkers Unions as either Long-shoremen or Short-shoremen, but not to arbitrarily leave out any just plain old shoremen arguably found to be in the middle of either, if any, or, maybe to include even some so-called Stevedores including their wannabees out there stevedoring part time on the side just to make ends meet, who were or may be somehow directly or indirectly involved, whether or not they knew how to lash cargo down and tie proper knots like trained and tested boy scouts at a convention or a camp out for a much needed merit badge, or were properly instructed in how to use shivs, shims, shams or pry-bars, were or were not properly trained in the most up to date ergonomic material lifting standards according to OSHA standards, and, to include, whether or not, any of them or those involved had any previous training whatsoever or any certifications whatsoever in the handling of any specific hazardous materials."

The Speaker was then interrupted by another junior member. "Mr. speaker, mind that you are remanded to remember that we are all mindful, that we are here and now, in the mid 1800's, a hundred years or so hence, now not under the rule anymore of anyone in England, even today by Queen Victoria herself even, even though we still like her on her face book and we would tell her that even to her fair face, but we are here and now trying to look back more than a hundred years or so toward this set of most historical events under the rule of various magistrates in or out of direct authority who had the proper jurisdiction at the time, for or before us, any one of which, could have been in some sort of conspiracy to somehow make the Liberty Bell into something less than what it has come to be, so where would any of us elect to start such an inquiry."

"Point taken, accepted for record, but noted to be only considered as common knowledge as we all know, you have to start somewhere." Replied the Speaker.

"Common knowledge accepted, with historical rule rejected, for the interjected adjudicated record so recorded for the record, as, the recorded record has to start recording somewhere." Added the Scribe.

The Speaker went on. "In addition, we are to determine, whether or not, that the method of transport was adequate and sufficient from the docking area at the Port of Entry, by the then known available wagon equipment which carried the more than two thousand pound Bell, or for those not able to understand large numbers, a twenty hundred pound bell, from the dock area to the Pennsylvania State House according to the official procedures outlined in the Teamsters Union guidebook including all bylines, not to dis-include any local business agent decrees, or contracting coordinator orders or assumptions, which streets, avenues or boulevards that the so laden crew took to get from there to here, and, whether or not there were any pot holes major or minor cracks or uneven bricks, speed bumps, or ongoing contracted update of any such equinanimous infrastructure, or any bridge limits to be considered to be found, along the way, whichever way they went, and, too, not to forget to mention, whether or not there were any witnesses or conspirators to all of this, along the way, here or there."

The Speaker was interrupted again by another junior member. "You are aware, sir, that most of those, who have any of the known common knowledge that you are looking for whatsoever, or, of any of the aforementioned innuendo, have moved out of town, went west on out to the frontier regions, took the next boat out and went back to wherever they came from in the first place, or, if they stayed in place, are either already dead and buried or near on their deathbed at this time awaiting a soon reaping by the grim reaper himself, do you not?"

The Speaker replied. "Point so taken for the record, which assignment predisposes the committee to further make immediate and most fervent search of any of the known records or of those so recording such concerning the assigned matters at hand."

The scribe replied. "Committee assigned to search known signs of records, entered in as part of permanent record of the records as bound to be hounded out, rounded out and sounded out, as to be found around down town or around town."

The Speaker went on. "We are then to determine, why it fell that the bell first cracked in the dell upon first ringing, or, whether it was already cracked to begin with, or, if not, whether or not the danged dangling mangled dapper clapper was used or not used properly or improperly, whichever, or, if used at all, or, if not, whether a danged ramming whamming hammer was used, either inside or outside, at the top or bottom, and, who all was present at the time and who can even remember such activity after so many years have gone by to date and to the most recent present."

Another junior member interjected. "You tell me, you are looking for a hammer man or a clapper banger, a hundred years or so, back in the year 1751 or 1752? Anyone alive today from that time would now have to be almost 120 years old at least if they were a day, and, even if they were, you somehow, now, expect them to tell us, honestly, that they were the one who was responsible for the crack up of that century, even if we could get them to admit such, without any water boarding?"

The Speaker responded. "The Record, it is the record that we are looking for, the record of such, the record of which, the record of "it", whatever be the definition "it", that may come to be some time on into the future, no more, no less, to determine the whether or not of such a possibility of such old unrecorded record and to record it for the new recorded record without the mention of the word conspiracy, with a small "c" that is, and, if none is found, or, if found, to be used most sparingly."

The Scribe added. "Recorded for the record of such, or, the possibility of which, the record of which, or, the possibility of such, with no mention of the "c" word if at all possible, otherwise unrecorded accordingly."

The Speaker went on. "We are then to determine, whether or not or why it was, that the Captain of the Ship called the Hibernian, whatever his name was, who absolutely refused to take the Bell back on board, perhaps in order to cover his ass, to protect his own skin, or to perhaps to protect his contract of insurance with the Lloyd's of London somehow, and also, about those personages, who too soon, and out of the ordinary, just up and showed up, out of the wood work, and came to offer up too much help way too soon, I might add, for some contracted repair to the bell, and promise of work, as if they knew something that no one else knew at the time, and, as to why they would ever in their right minds make such an offer to repair something so unrepairable in the first place, when they were not qualified and really did not have the necessary capability for such work, and, who was it, that made the decision to authorize or allow them to attempt to make such a repair in the first place, then, why it was, that they decided to up and change the metallurgical formula and makeup of the bell, and, why it was that it was found to be totally unacceptable upon first test after pouring, and, why they were allowed to even have a second go at it and another chance to correct their first mistakes, to the extent of them even being allowed to recast the entire bell a second time around, then, how it was, that the danged thing eventually cracked again, after the fact, then, even after some additional repair, by unknown person or persons, that the bell was even allowed to be rung again and again, on and on, year after year, occasion after occasion, doing more and more irreparable damage, and further, to determine who it was in authority that allowed these decisions to have even be ever made in the first place."

Another previously mentioned junior member again interrupted. "Sir, you know, damn well, that this committee is headed down the road to destruction at more than ninety miles an hour, which is, to date, an unheard of break neck speed almost equivalent to the speed of sound itself, so, you know, you are the leader of a committee veritably bent upon self-destruction onto and near on into our very future of which, at no less than the speed of light, I might add, so, you should consider the committee members input and makeup, that if any of us are to ever seek re-election, that we should most likely come about, forthwith, with a most positive recommendation concerning the aforementioned assignments, with no mention of any conspiracy, God forbid."

The Speaker replied. "Point taken on positive recommendations concerning re-elections so recorded for the record, and, again, no mention to be made of the "c" word, if at all plausibly possible."

The Scribe added. "So entered in record, all committee members positively recommended for re-election by further committee recommendation as an additional matter of record with no mention as to the direction said committee is headed."

The Speaker went on. "We are then to determine, why it was, that an order was promulgated for the same flailing failing floundering founder to be allowed to order up for the same foundry in London to make another similar second replica of the previously flawed tolled bell, of the same size and weight, and, whether or not, that someone, somewhere, and somehow, some one or some two or more, whether they got together or not, all but got the two danged manufactured or re-manufactured bells mixed up between one another somehow, as, both were requested of the same manufacturer, that had all but previously provided the first, and, as was common at the time, with another possible mix-up as to which one was which when they were hauled off to Allentown during the great War of Independence, which was later called the Revolutionary War, because it sounded a little better, and, which one was the one which was sold off to a church which was later burned down, then moved to some College named Villanova, which, in Latin, means New Settlement, and as to when which of it all came about, and who it was that was in charge of these Chinese fire drills, and who in proper authority could have or would have allowed such things to happen in the first place just to get their names on their next year's ballot most likely for re-election purposes or to bring some additional money in for their campaign."

Then, one of the more senior junior committee members stood up took the floor, and being totally out of order, yelled out. "This assignment is not what it's cracked up to be. And, I get the idea and the painful impression that we are hereby given the assignment to try to crack open or crack down on some old political crackers in order to cover some cracks in some old politician's ass because of some add-on legislation to some bill that most likely had no merit in the first place but was voted on at the last minute with no line by line, line out veto authority. I say that, because I have here in my hand, a handwritten copy of the official records handed down where the danged bell was all broken up, re-melted and re-cast, right here in town, with some very peculiar denotations, such as, whether or not there was a hung clapper to begin with, whether it was flared, fluted or flanged, or whether it was actually a fairly fluted flapper, or, possibly, even a wedged winged whanger, or a danged dangling dinger, as, no one at the time reported exactly how it was that the bell was first rang at all. Or, how it was that it was ever rung in the first place, as it may have very well been whacked with hand held whapper hammer for all we know, and, I should mention that the hand written note as was passed down, did not even get an honorable mention from the local historical society. So, someone has to investigate things like this, which could lead anyone anywhere at anytime."

"Order, Order, you sir, are out of order, we will have order here, or I will order the announcements and pronouncements tabled until such order again presides over the presidium, so, put a hold on your told and close your pie hole before you have to dole out a tax to pay your toll to meet you goal." Countered the Speaker while politely speaking from behind the prodigious padded podified platformed podium.

"Said comment by the interrupting yahoo in the back has done been already struck on down from the record, sir, except for the no mention by the historical society." Yelled back the Scribe, who again made some more very animated wide sweeps with his turkey feathered quill pen, most probably and more than likely, in order just to draw a little more attention to himself and to his official office at that moment in time.

The Speaker went on. "So as, to bring you all up to date, in speaking of the Liberty Bell itself, the Bell itself was to be hung in the belfry of the State House after the bats were run out, that is, and to be ringed, rang or rung from then on, whichever, for the purpose, to call any known modified bonified sober legislators to office, or on other important occasions, like the birthdays of former presidents or the deaths of other important politicians or great leaders, or, for some other equal consideration. However, nothing worked out for those folks as was planned in their laid out plan, and, the bell itself sorely failed in its attempt to do it's assigned job, and, I might add, not on just one specific occasion, but on several ongoing occasions, here and yon, with more than one historian telling us, time and again, that they consistently continued to attempt banging and clanging on a dangling mangled hanging bad boy bell, and, therefore, we are here today, to try to find some remedy to answer those many unanswered questions which were apparently ignored by the better part of our predecessors for one reason or another during their time. This being a most insurmountable problem and undaunted task as so assigned, with most unmentionable historical problems too hurtful to even speak upon, except for that of the conspiracy part, but yet, to try to answer questions that have too long gone unanswered, in order to add some finality to the matter at hand, once and for all for all future historians to record for the recorded record."

A junior member yelled out, or whooped and hollered, from the back of the room. "Get to the making of the motions part please, before a motion is made to make a commotion with no recant required for a second in the requiem."

The Speaker responded. "I again remind you, if order does not continue to prevail, that I will have no other recourse except to remand the Chair back to the Chairman, so, you had better look out because there is no pouting doubt that he has clout in a rout, even if he does flout his gout about.

"Order to prevail about without rout, so we'll have order on the border." Yelled the Scribe.

The Speaker, then, stepped back, leaned forward, and then made his first motion. "I hereby make the motion to establish appropriate sub-committees for each of the appropriate selected aforementioned investigations."

"Here, here, I second such recommendation and motion." Stated the representative from Scranton.

"Motion is carried without election of an objection." Replied the Scribe.

The Speaker then made his second motion. "I hereby make the motion to gain the authority to contract out any appropriate investigations."

"Here, here, I second such recommendation and motion." Stated the representative from Canton.

"Motion is carried with no beckoning or reckoning objection." Replied the Scribe.

The Speaker made his third motion. "I hereby make the motion to allow the sub-committee members to have control over the directions of the various contractors of the various investigations."

"Here, here, I second such recommendation and motion." Stated the representative from Reading.

"Motion is carried and ferried without wearied objection." Replied the Scribe

The Speaker then made his fourth motion. "I hereby make the motion to allow the contractors to establish needed sub-contractors in order to more fully carry out such assigned investigations."

"Here, here, I second such recommendation and notion of any motion." Stated the representative from Allentown.

"Motion is carried without any dereliction of duty of any objection whatsoever." Replied the Scribe.

The Speaker then made his fifth motion. "I hereby make the motion to allow the sub-committees to have control over the expenses of the contractors and the contractors to have control over the expenses of the sub-contractors in order to fund, finance and furbish their necessary needs in order to more fully carry out the investigations."

"Here, here, I so beckon the second such recommendation and motion." Stated the representative from Pittsburgh.

"Motion is carried, without any mention of any other objection." Stated the Scribe.

The Speaker then made his sixth motion. "I hereby make a motion to establish a sub-committee to investigate the original manufacturer of the Bell, in England, through contractors to reduce and sub-contractors to de-duce the potential for probable manufacturing problems found at the funded foundry.

"Here, here, I wholly second such recommendation and motion." Stated the Chairman.

"Motion is carried, without any or whatever holy objection whenever." Replied the Scribe.

The Speaker then made his seventh motion. "I hereby make a motion to allow payment and re-imbursement of any purported expenses entailed during or for such investigation to be assigned special status for the allowance of passage without review of the finance committee and that the Speaker and the Chairman be provided no less than more than any of any other two committee members for the same time expended complete with travel expenses and heretofore unmentioned per-diem expense account items to be included but not to be included for the final record.

"Here, here, I second such recommendation and motion wherever as needed." Stated the Chairman.

"Motion is carried." Replied the Scribe. "But, Sir, no objection heard or intended, however, the question arises, according to the most recent publication of the Roberts Rules of Order, as to whether or not, that the Chairman may second a second recommendation one after another, or, two times in a row, double lipping on the double dipping part, with the notion of a local motion which causes no little commotion, or, if accepted, why we have to pay you and or him double, just, because he or you just happen to be the manner of men or of the man in charge."

The Speaker then said. "Bear in mind, that the Scribe may be conned into being confused by the confessing of the confusion, but please remember, and, we are all reminded, that we are but an investigatory committee, so appointed as such, under the authority of the Congress itself of this so called sovereign State, to make such assigned investigations, and, to report our findings, if any, back again to the

Congress itself, but to stop and hold short of, of making any final conclusions, if any, that we may or may not find in the interim of such investigation, which, may or may not include any of the aforementioned double dipping as both Committee members and Sub-Committee members along with the assignment as Contractors or Sub-Contractors who may enjoy the same double dipping privileges accordingly, which are all in line with and according to previous recommendations with all seconds recorded. So, with that we, the assigned committee may please allow the Chairman to second the last two local motions and to let the assigned investigation to begin, with no further discussion or any mention, for that matter, whatsoever, for the record, as to the method of pay or re-imbursement allowances for expenses or per diem? With, of course, any previous or further mention of double dipping to be forever stricken from the record of this committee's record accordingly."

The Scribe added. "Recommended recommendation recommended for the record with no mention of the unmentionables to be entered or to be mentioned further after the fact with struck feature to be activated by the escape key."

The speaker continued on, and, then made his eighth motion. "I hereby make a motion to allow the Committee members, to also be allowed to have membership on any of the assigned Sub-Committees so as to have authority of cloture in the selection and assignment of Contractors or Sub-Contractors, and, in addition, to have the authority to assign themselves as prompted, as either as a Contractor or Sub-Contractor for any subject matter at hand, and, further, that the Contractors and or Sub-Contractors may also be assigned and have full membership as Committee and or Sub-Committee members in order to have authority of closure, purposely so, so as to simplify the process of the proceedings in order to reduce the overall cost of such an investigation and the tremendous cost of contractor cross training."

"Here, here, I second such recommendation and motion especially for even the mention of reducing the costs, which anyone and everyone as tax payers would want us to consider in the first place and at first hand." Stated the Chairman.

"Motion is carried, without any objection on the part of any present sitting or standing member, I might add, so that the ones that are on the in can stay on the in, whether they are on the real in or not at the time." Replied the Scribe.

The speaker then made his ninth motion. "I hereby, make a motion, to allow the Scribe, to sit in on as assigned on any Committee, or Sub-Committee as full member, or, as Contractor or Sub-Contractor assignment for all meetings or missions so as to be able to recoup some of the time lost from his other endeavors in which he could so be engaged in, in order to just make ends meet or set aside some monetary gain for his ultimate re-election bid.

"Here, here, I second such a most gracious recommendation and motion with little or no consideration on my behalf, I might add." Stated the Chairman.

"Motion is carried, without any objection especially on my part either whatsoever." Replied the Scribe, and, with that, he wrote the Chairman a note of thanks which was also noted to be shredded either earlier or immediately prior to a little later.

And, with that, the Speaker formally handed the chair back over to the Chairman, gave up the gavel, and went and sat down with a frown, and, the Chairman brought his glass of the drink of his choice to the podium.

The Chairman began. "To reiterate the address and to digress just a little, or some, as, we, at present, have representatives, from Scranton, Canton, Reading, Allentown, and Pittsburgh, so as, to here and forevermore, are to be known officially by the acronym as the "SCRAP" committee, ready and available for such investigatory assignment of the aforementioned matter of the cracked up Liberty Bell at hand, and, I hereby recommend that the assigned representative Committee members and or those Sub-Committee members, to assign additional Contractors and Sub-Contractors to make investigation and to them and themselves or their Contractors or Sub-Contractors to journey half way around the world, to the isle of England itself, if need be, to determine the answers to our unanswered questions concerning the manufacture of the Liberty Bell in that realm, and, the representative Committee members or Sub-Committee members to assign Contractors or Sub-Contractors to make the necessary trips to England for the investigation of the transport of said Liberty Bell, with the up loading and on loading in England, the treacherous transport over the Western Sea, and the downloading, offloading or the unloading of the said Bell at the Port in Philadelphia, and, the representative Committee members or Sub-Committee members to assign Contractors or Sub-Contractors to make the necessary trips and investigations, concerning the investigation of the transport from the Port of acceptance from aboard ship in England to the loading and transportation and unloading of the Bell from the ship at Port and the transportation from the ship at the dock to the Pennsylvania State House at Philadelphia. And when, after first test ring and a failure occurred, when attempting to return said ringerless item to the place of its birth, why the Captain refused to take it back on board. And also, to find out why, that some local yokel wannabee bell makers jumped to the chance to make the folks in England to look bad, and to take it upon themselves to try to fix the unfixable. And, as to why another bad boy bell was ordered from the previous bad boy bell maker with another bad billed billing yet to be balanced, and, whether or not they all got mixed up somehow over in Allentown when they were all hauled off and hid during the War of Independence, and then, which one it was, was up and sold to some church for some unknown reason, which was later sent or passed on to some college over in the new village, and, which one is which, and which one is the one we have today, here and now and which one is there and now, and, which one is here and now. With that, I have spoken openly, albeit brokenly, so, with that, I turn the gavel and the podium back over to the Speaker." And, with that, the Chairman chose to sit down on his chair with what was left of his drink yet held tightly in hand, motioning for the Speaker to get a move on and get a little get up in his get-a-long.

The Speaker finished his drink, then again stood, approached the bench and took the podium by hand, and said. "I make the motion, that the aforementioned assignments of Committees and Sub-Committees be solely assigned and that they be invested with the power and authority of this august body and that the required finances for any expenses of any of the Committees, Sub-Committees, Contractors or Sub-Contractors be so covered by this Committee according to such financial constraints such as those concerning the re-election of said Committee members of which funds may be shaved off, shafted, shifted, shared, shuttled, or so allotted for such individual Committee member needs or whatever purposes accordingly, within their district and within campaign limitations of course, but not shockingly, shamefully, sheepishly, shadily, shoddily, shiftily or shabbily, so as not to appear in any fit, form or fashion as a shystering or sheltering activity, to be so directed by the Chairman and or the Speaker aforementioned for the benefit of those attending in order to provide some form of a perk to encourage future so-called Committee members to serve or volunteer for such said Committee or Sub-Committee appointments and membership on or into the future if not for their re-election purposes in the interim or the beforehand or after the fact."

"Here, here, I second the Speakers's motion without emotion or commotion, not fool heartedly but full heartedly." Said the Chairman.

"The motion must then be more than fully carried and recorded accordingly minus the mention of any further unmentionables." Responded the Scribe.

The Speaker then announced. "With that, no more and no less, I pass the gavel and the podium back over to the Chairman.

The Chairman got up out of his chair, filled his glass once more, then again re-took the podium with glass in hand and stated. "It is now, our august assignment, here in the month of June, to first and foremost do our duty, before we go on vacation again, to remember to refrain ourselves from the most common offered freebies, such as family vacations in the Bahama Islands in the east, or, the Sandwich Islands in the west, or, any specially paid for under the table or on the side speech assignments, inside or outside deals on the side or in between, or any promise for slush funds to be provided from any of the known or unknown deep pocket money bag carrying lobbyists, and for us to remember our mission, which is to begin the process to determine the determination of our immediate prior and most previous predecessors, to say what they would have wanted us to say, as they were there then, or, as if they were here now, in the flesh before and amongst us, hearing what it was that they had to say, as if it was within their power to testify before us and on their own behalf."

The Chairman went on. "Therefore, I make the motion to disallow in any of the proceedings, any and all of the bad "Sn" words, such as snafu, snag, snaky, snarl, snare, sneaky, sneer, snicker, snide, snippy, snobby, snotty, or snobby, just to mention a few of those, and, the same for the bad "Dr" words, such as, drab, drag, drama, drat, dreary, dribble, drizzly, drop, drudge, drugged, drunk, and for the purpose, just to mention a few of those also for clarity. Too, limit the use os he "Cr" words too, such as crab, cracker, crank, crap, crash, crawl, crawfish, crazy, creepy, crime, croak, crook, crucify, cruel or cry."

"Here, here, I more than second the Chairman's motion, here and now." The Speaker responded.

"The motion is carried here and now for the commission of the omissions." The Scribe chimed in. "Also, for everyone's information, off the record, the pizza with drinks has been delivered, so, for the record, someone needs to make a motion to proceed with a recess to the proceedings, followed with a second notion for a solution to the local motion."

The Chairman then stated. "I hereby make the motion to recess the proceedings and for the Scribe to so refrain from any further scripting of the script or recording for the record."

"Here, here, I more than second the Chairman's motion." Yelled the Speaker.

"Motion is carried." The Scribe added. "And, the proceeding process is now in decent process of recess." With that, the Scribe dropped his quill pen onto his desk with a loud whack and threw his hands and arms up into the air, mostly just for the show of it all.

The group then broke up and set up the tables for a get-together for a pizza lunch, passing bottles of various wine drinks with glasses, and boxes of various types of pizza back and forth and began their "paid for by the tax payers" provided working luncheon.

The delegate from Scranton was the first who could not wait patiently to speak. "Being it, that we are now, "off the record", and being at lunch, as it is, it has come to light, dawned upon, or occurred to me, being from Scranton, that I am the most senior delegate to this most august Committee of five members meeting here, and, I have duly noted, that the most senior three of us, are the Scranton "S", Canton "C" and Reading "R" representatives, just happen to be re-elected Republicans, while the other two, the Allentown "A" and Pittsburgh "P" representatives of the group, just happen to be the very most junior of the group, I might add, also, that they just happen to also be first term Democrats. I find it somewhat offensive and detrimental for the Committee to become known as the "SCRAP" Committee for the Liberty Bell project. It would seem to me, with me being in the "S" portion of the acronym SCRAP. It does not have a good sound to it, it does not ring true, it does not clang my clapper, or, bing my bang, but, no pun intended here whatsoever, yet, when all is said and done, it does absolutely nothing for me or my reputation and it does not bang either my bell or my bing, however you want to say it, in any shape, form or fashion, if you know what I mean, and, I feel, down deep in my heart, that, I need to hereby immediately resign my position as the most senior Committee member, because, I get the feeling that there is some yet unidentified subterraneous underground mob controlled personal paranoid plot against my very campaign for re-election. As, I only first accepted the assignment after being talked into taking a position on the Committee after a few too many drinks, and, I now feel, that any time spent on said Committee definitely takes away from the time that I could spend campaigning for my said re-election."

He went on. "However, I might just mention, if I do so resign, the Committee will become to be called, according to the then said seniority, the CRAP Committee for the Liberty Bell project. And, I might also mention, that that acronym does not carry a very good connotation either for anyone attending. However, knowing that the next most senior member that could be appointed would be from Sharon, just south of Erie, and, if that were caused to happen or occurred, the Committee would then be known as the CRAPS Committee for the Liberty Bell project. This all no little disturbs me to all hell and back again, as, I feel that there is some hidden subterfuge movement afloat, that has all but damned us all to the assigned task at hand. I mean, you all just think about it for a moment, how would the paparazzi and the liberal media present this information on the printed page with your name in the same sentence or the paragraph that names the who, who is behind it all?"

The delegate from Scranton went on. "It may also be wrong or mistaken to assume, that the next appointed member would be from Sharon, instead of further north at Erie, and, as, the Erie representative, was elected two hours and fifteen minutes prior when his opponent conceded to the confirmed election of the representative from Sharon, so, if the Cranston representative would so also resign his position, the Committee would then become to be known as the RAPE Committee for the Liberty Bell Project. Which, connotation, I would fully agree, has even more worse definite negative vibes, up the ying-yang and back again, for any of the aforementioned members, whether Republican or Democrat. Too, if it is held, that there are to be assigned the fully five membership of the Committee to establish a quorum, then, I might add, that the next most senior representative to be assigned membership would be the representative from Darby, down southeast near and by Philadelphia, which, would then make the Committee to be known as the RAPED Committee for the Liberty Bell Project, which, I might add, has no known positive connotations whatsoever either, for any foreseeable movement or motion ahead for any of the Committee member futures."

"Here, here." Said the Chairman, after taking another big long swig of the appropriately distributed and apportioned celebetory wine. "We are at a so called working lunch, we are not at one another's throats in a re-election bid, yet, we are only discussing the disgusting assignments as were handed down to us by the Committee assignment Committee as delegated by the delegates handily at hand. However, I so note, that the so called assignments are somewhat less than so noted, so, I recommend that the assigned members of the Committee, take their assignments with a grain of salt, and disregard the disregard-able and immerse themselves in the immersable, and, let us all go on from here on from the get go."

The Speaker feeling that he was in the position that he had to make some comment, added, after shoveling down some pizza and washing it down with a little or a lot more wine swigging. "I have the same feeling concerning the feelings of the most senior Committee member, and too, as the Chairman for the group for that matter as to whatever it was that he had to say. But, to add on to that, I also would like the Committee to know, that, I, as a full-fledged voting member of the Committee, that, I would not like to have my name connected in any method either, in any form or fashion, with the

SCRAP, CRAP, CRAPS, or, CRAPED RAPE or RAPED denotation of said Committee as is denigrates and designates the Committee to being something less than what it was ever meant to be in the first place, or more, than it was to meant to be in the second place either early on at the get go or later on either. However, either way you want to shake it out, I agree with the Senior Scranton member that this committee is either bogus, or, that we have become part and parcel of some contrary hoax, that may very well cost us and our representative positions, on into the very near future, come our next election time, so, I need more information before I proceed with any more of the preceding proceedings that have proceeded afore."

The most junior member from Pittsburgh, finished his slice of pizza, took a big sip or a big gulp of his Cabernet Sauvignon, and rose up to speak, or, further address the most august group which was now officially out of session, but, if it were, it was to be out of order for any in the session or to comment or to make any further innuendo, but, he went on with it, anyway. "If, it was up to me, I would recommend that the Committee at large, would remain so and as such, without any further challenge, or change whatsoever, so as, to complete the assigned assignment for the Committee as a whole and on behalf of the Congress itself, remaining within the group, or congregation at hand, to make the ultimate final decision with all so-called discernment of what was right for the appropriate decision making processes in the matters at hand, and, to take the bull by the horns, if you will, and to make hard decisions for the un-decided to end it all, and to force the reader to read the un-readable, and to not mention the un-mentionable in the process of the proceedings, and, I stand on that and would make such recommendation when the Committee goes back into session, either that, or, I do not get any free advertisement, concessions or extra pay on the side, just as the other junior members were offered as a guarantee, for making such a recommendation in the first place in order to get a motion and a second so as to get the order to get it on the record, or, we do not get any donations from the lobbyists for our re-elections."

The Chairman, took note of the dangerous statement of the innocent as a lamb junior member, and, now made comment, after finishing another piece of pizza and after downing just a little less than another very large glass of wine. "We are not here to re-address the re-dress, or to re-address the address, as, we are here, for the purpose of solving soluble solutions only, and, that is to determine the truths of both the un-muttered and muttered matters, or, of the metered matters at hand, I mean, with little or no imposition of our positions, with the deciding determined by the decision making process of this august Committee, and, to also determine, whether or not, that those previous, applied the same rules to their game, as do we, and, if not, why not, so as to level the playing field, and whether or not that we are here today, to further determine whether or not that they made such determinations or as to whether or not that they did what they said they did, or, if it was even doable at the time, with or without any so called conspiracy."

The Speaker then raised himself up to make comment. "This Committee is headed up and headed out and about, by our Chairman, who just happens to be a Republican, and me, as Speaker, who just happens to be a Democrat, and we are doing everything in our power, to be or at least appear to be, more than just non-partisan, by, being generally non-voting, but do hold the authority to vote in the event that any tie-breaker would ever be needed to sway the vote the way it was that we wanted it to go in the first place, and, we are also authorized, to participate in any discussions in any position of authority as so chosen and accepted, so, I would propose, that the Committee members present, including the Chairman and myself as Speaker, would venture to gain upgraded classified clearances with proper background checks accordingly, to bump it up another notch, to at least the level of SECRET with all or any mention of any or all acronyms be stricken, struck, or perhaps blacked out, blocked out, or even to the extent of being torn out of the official record if need be."

The Scribe yelled out from behind a large glass of wine and a big hunk of pizza. "I can do that, it is do-able, consider it done did already as that is one thing that I am really good at."

The Chairman then stood up and came back with the following comment. "Not to completely compete with the Speaker, but, I am reminded, that this Committee, in retrospect, is supposed to be transparent with its investigations and findings, with all openness for all concerned, but to put a classified higher classification on any of the matters at hand, would be against all principles of free and open discussion of the facts with respect to the Constitutional Amendment on the Freedom of Speech or the right to public records, but as

Committee members appointed by Congress, we may not fully partake of that so called Freedom, as we are required to abide by and to hold to the proceedings according to the Roberts Rules of Order, and, any particular thing that we may say, could be construed or could cause any of the Committee's findings to be construed as less than genuine, which, in turn, could also entangle each of us into the old unmentionable conspiracy, at any time on into the future or at another, on line and on time, and, I might add, no representative present or any of their potential future replacements, would want to have such a question of some problem to come back to haunt any of them, with quotes a-coming back to back, come re-election time or yelled out publically, especially during any of their campaigns. So, stick that up in your starched bonnet, let it cross your brain a little, and think on it a moment and I am sure that you will not want any of such entered into the official record when the Committee resumes. However, I do note, that if the most senior Chairman who is from Rochester, and I, as a second senior, who hail from Elizabethtown, would be added in to form up a more accurate acronym for the Committee, it would then be the "RESCRAP" Committee for the Liberty Bell project, and, if the most senior delegate from Scranton resign Sir, the Committee would then be accronymed as the RECRAP Committee for the Liberty Bell project. Which would require adding the delegate from Erie, but, if the Canton delegate resigned his most august position, then, the Committee would be the RERAPE Committee, so, anyway it is cut, there is no way out for any of us, and, right now, I am confused to the point of not knowing whether to shit, go blind, or wind my watch."

"It's the drinks Sir, it is the drinks, someone has whiskied the wine, rummed the rhine, slipped the gin in the Savignon, charged the "Chardonnay, clipped the Cabernet, candied the brandy, we are all but rocked to the gills, frocked to the frills, socked to the sills, or rocked to the rills." The Scribe yelled out.

The most senior member from Scranton then interrupted. "Sir, it would even be worse if any word of any of this, or any of it all got out and got into some newspaper, and, any and all of our campaigns would be like a ship sitting dead in the water without a breeze to be had on the horizon. But, say, if you will, just for shits and grins, may I seriously ask, if the Congress of the great State of Pensylvania wanted an honest job done, in the first place, just why is it, or, how is it, that we do not have an "L" member, to be called from the town of Liberty itself, and, an "I" member, to be called from the town of Imperial, and, a "B" member, to be called from the town of Bell Acres, and, an "E" member be called from the town of Eagleville, and, an "R" member to be called from the town of Ringtown, and, a "T" member, to be called from the town of Trooper, and a "Y" member, be called from the town of Yoe, so as and in order to have an absolute first rate unfettered and unquestionable accronymned "LIBERTY" Committee representation primarily from the get-go, early on, and, at the out-set, if you follow my drift, and, if you all do not consider that when you all go back into the formal Committee session, then I propose that I will immediately officially and formally resign my position as most senior member of the Committee, and then, you all can go to your so self-chosen "CRAP" or "RECRAP" next designation, for all I care and so go on from there."

The Committee member from Canton came up out of his chair like a shot, and said. "I too will resign my position on the Committee if this thing is ignored and not turned round about, and then you all can go as a "RAP" Committee until you get the next dumb ass eligible junior member from Erie to then come to be known as the "RAPE" or "RERAPE" Committee, or whatever, and to eventually move on forward with your membership from Darby to become the "RAPED" or the "RERAPED" Committee for Liberty Bell project. Anyway, another or any other way, on any day, I say nay, and will even refuse my pay, as, I want no part of any of it and refuse to have my good name attached to it any further whatsoever if that of what is going on continues further.

By now, the Committee was in a crazy concocted commotion. This one was saying that, and, that one was saying this, all in a blithering bleary blaze of a buzz. One says that it all calls for another drink, while the other says more drinks are called for, while another puts in a call for some more puts and calls. Then, the arguments started about who would be senior if so-and-so resigned, then, who would be next, and, what would happen if they all resigned. With, someone else saying that that would be the best thing to happen if such a happenstance had to happen at all, then, almost in unison, they all started calling in their name for resignation one by one and one after the other, from the so called Congressionally assigned Committee, except for the Chairman and the Speaker who sat in stunned silence up to that point.

"Here, here." The Chairman said, then stood up and called for some order, even though the Committee was not in session, and stated. "OK, then, I perceive and agree, that there is possibly and most likely some clandestine movement afloat and some definite "conspiracy" against either some or all of us here today, and, apparently, we have all been "set up" by some persons in authority yet unknown, so, let us set up a plan to "turn the tables" on who ever or whomever "them" is, if you will, whoever or whomever they may be found to eventually be or to be eventually found. I see it here and in the present as it is nothing more or less than poor politics with convertibly vetted vendettas, and, we have to call it what it is. So, let us establish the actions necessary and for the sake of any further discussion or argument to add to the confusion. Let us establish some preventative measures to put into place as we go along. With that in mind, I make the recommendation to go back into session here and now, and today, to make the one and final recommendation for this Committee to cut to the chase, to come to immediate and complete conclusions on the matters at hand with no further procrastination, and to record for the record the report for Congress, that this committee has so fully investigated the matters at hand as so assigned, and thereby state our findings as being the same as was found by our founding fathers who founded all of this fair afore us without one iota of an exception on or to any of the given matters, so as, to settle the matter once and for all and to disband the Committee and to stand down as soon as possible if not immediately thereafter, before any of this bull shit ever hit the fan or gets out, and, to purposefully misspell our names, to also render our signatures unreadable on all documentation by writing our names with our left hands, unless one of us is left handed, then you should use your other hand, and to even go so far as to even misspell the names of our represented areas or to swear up and down and claim that we were from somewhere else, for whatever reason we so chose, just to throw off any attempt to pin anything on any of us in the near future until such time that we can identify the conspirators and to deal with them accordingly in the same fashion that they so tried to deal with us. Or, in other words, say the hearsay was just what was heard, and, the nay say was never said. After all, I mean, it is a downright rotten shame that in this day and time, that Liberty cannot ring true and is not what it is all cracked up to be."

He went on. "In addition, I might add, while you all were doing all of this disgusted discussing, I have been studying the map of our fine

State and this is my finding. For instance, even though I am from Rochester, I can also say that I am from Freedom, which is nearby and also, since I have close family there, a second cousin who also owns property there, it being near to my home town, and, the Speaker although from Elizabethtown, can claim he is from Bellaire, as, that is where he told me that his wife was from along with her family, and besides, it is just up or down the road from where he is from now, and, you Sir, the most senior member on the Committee from Scranton, can truthfully say that you really hail from Old Forge, as I remember you saying that your father was once forced to work at the forge there with little pay and long hours, and the member from Canton can safely say that he is from either Liberty or Liberty Corner, or both, just because they are in close vicinity to one another and both being well within his district, and, both or either are more than willing, I am sure, to have him claim such representation, and they would certainly not argue against him by him saying it, and the member from Reading, can say that he is either from Angelica or State Hill, because both are also in his district and only a stone's throw from either, one of which has an angelic sound and the other has a State connotation, with the Allentown representative saying that he is really from Bethlehem, which has a good ring to it, and even sounds biblical and somewhat holy, and, finally the Pittsburgh member can say that he is really from Jefferson, of which no one can argue politically any better and most representatives would wish that they could say that they were from there and are most jealous that they are not. You will note, and agree, that there are good connotations in all of these selections and nothing negative whatsoever that can be said about any of these localities as none reportedly are harboring any known bank robbers or horse thieves at this time, that I heard of, I might add, and, the resulting acronym OLABJ, or, if the Speaker and I are included, the FBOLABJ acronym means absolutely nothing except to us and will be the only acronym so published for the record, if any, to protect us all and to prevent further split of our august group as the Liberty Bell was so split." With that, the Chairman turned the discussion over to the Speaker with but a nod and a wave of the hand.

The Chairman came forth, walked up, and took the podium. "I, first call this Committee back to full order, here and now, and, heretofore and after fore, and, I offer to you, the findings, of this august body as a Congressionally assigned Committee, that we do find and have found, after full and impartial non-partisan Committee investigation, found, from the first to the last, that the findings are found to be the same as those found previous by our very founders, with no chance of change from as such as what is so previously historically recorded and as which it was that was previously freely found to be fairly and fundamentally founded with no findings of any sort of conspiracy whatsoever in any shape, form or fashion, whatsoever, and hereby suspend any and all rules of order, and, in addition, I now turn this unrecorded and unregulated matter back over to the Speaker." With that, the Chairman sat down, or plopped down.

"Here, here, hear here, all rules are suspended, hung out to dry they are, no objections to rejecting elected dejected adjectives, and open the floodgates to any and all hearsay, and play hide the dog in the dialogue." Yelled out the Scribe.

The Speaker then stood up on his hind legs. "Here, here, I make the non-motion to accept the non-findings as unfounded, with no exception whatsoever for the unrecorded non-record."

The senior committee member from Scranton, then added. "I hereby second the non-motion on no less than behalf of the Committee at large which is reportedly unseated."

The Scribe added. "Non-motion is unrecorded as non-accepted and non-seconded without further ado, with no mention of any of the previous unmentionables and all previous motions and seconds to be unrecorded as only numbered motions and seconds for the total unrecorded record unnumbered but unrecalled as one, two and or maybe a three, just for good measure."

The Scribe went on. "That, being less than what could be interpreted, means that, for the non-record, that the unrecorded motions and non-seconds of the non-recommendations for the non-investigations stand as unassigned, and, are unrecorded as Yes, Yes, Yes, Yes, Yes, Yes, with a final Yes to all of the other Yeses."

The Speaker then made one final motion. "I now make the additional non-motion, that this non-Committee non-business be closed forever, and, that the non-Committee is hereby forever and ever more disbanded, and this non-meeting is now all but closed and adjourned, with no known official record whatsoever of its disappointments of its appointments or even of its non-existence."

"Here, here, I non-second the non-motion so uncalled for." Yelled out the Chariman.

The Scribe added on. "Non-Meeting so adjourned, with no further non-motions, non-record so closed and that is the end of that, except to fill out the official form for the Superintendent of the House. So, without further discussion of the matter at hand, I will complete the report for the non-Committee and deliver it post haste to the Superintendent, immediately upon our adjournment."

"Non-Meeting closed." Added the Chairman, and, with that, everyone cleaned up their pizza mess, straightened up their chairs, wiped the tables off, took the trash out and left the place as if no one had ever been there, and, without further word between themselves.

Filed Failed Findings:

Beginning of Report: "The freely funded failed findings, of this august body justly appointed as a Pensylvania State Congressionally assigned Committee, say, every one and all, that we do find and have found, after full and impartial non-partisan Committee investigations, found the findings, from the very first to the very last as wholly holy reported, that the findings are found to be the very self and same as those found previous by our very previous founders who found it all out in the first place, with no chance of change from as such as what, and as to what is, and was so previously historically recorded, and as to which it was, that was previously fully found, to be more than just fairly and most freely fundamentally founded. With that said, we, the aforementioned assigned Committee members, so swear to (on a two foot high stack of Bibles), and, so assign our very signatures as evidence of such Committee agreement." **End of Report.**

REPORT FOR FILE RECORD

Entry No: _1025_

Dated: _JUNE 1851 Session_

Committee For The: _LIBERTY BELL 100TH ANNIVERSARY INSTIGATION INVESTIGATION_

Representatives: **Location Represented:**

1. Callin Al Dummasers   Freadum, PA
2. Bill E. Aker   Bell Aired, ditto on the PA by the way
3. Ive Haddit   Idled Forges, ditto, samo-samo
4. Raley Teedoff   La'Berte Corners, ditto toitall
5. Stel Pistoff   Level Hills, ditto backtoya
6. Ranglin Douts   Batheleham, ditto agin
7. Aut Ceider   Jafarsun, dittotoo
8. O. Pen Mindt   (None: Scribe), PA at large more or less
9. Iam M. Muneto-Alofit
10. (None: Speaker), ditto toitall
11. Annymous reported only as PRESENT
12. Pard Lee Rathold   None: Chairman), ditto it with it

Shortly thereafter, two of the more senior State Representatives were walking toward one another in the House hallway, when the first stopped the second on the side and opened a very quiet and whispered conversation.

"Have you seen it yet? Have you seen the report of findings of the Liberty Bell Committee? Or, have you heard anything at all about them delivering their written findings to the Superintendent of the House?" Queried the first co-conspirator.

"I haven't seen or heard anything reportable. What do you know about it all? Queried the second co-conspirator.

"Personally, I for one, think that they have somehow got it all figured out. But the main problem is, that I do not know just how much that they know, how deep it will go, or if any of our names are, would be, or will be attached to any of it, if and when any of it or all of it ever

comes to light anytime on into the future." The first co-conspirator said.
The second co-conspirator responded. "Don't worry about it. If and when names and dates start to be mentioned, that will be the time to go on the offensive and set up some personal attack on each and every one of the assigned Committee members as liars, cheats, and neer-do-wells or Johnnie-come-latelies."
"Just how would you propose to do something like that? If you attack the Liberty Bell Committee, it could be construed that you may very well be attacking the historical aspect of the Liberty Bell itself. I think you better re-think that thought." Responded the first co-conspirator.
The second co-conspirator took it all up another notch, and was almost heard audibly to have said. "We can get together and charge them all, or one by one, with dereliction of their duty! There is no way that they could have concluded such an investigation in such a short time, even with a few well heeled, deep pocketed well paid lobbyists helping them out on the side! Either that, or, someone on our side has sold us all out behind our backs, because the ones we got assigned to the Committee were reported to be too dumb-ass to figure anything like that out. But here, refresh my mind as to why we wanted to appoint such a Committee and assign them such a project in the first place?"
The first co-conspirator, stepped back, then, stepped even closer, and whispered. "We needed the negative publicity of anything that they were to find wrong with the historical aspect of the Liberty Bell itself, so, that we could have our cohorts rail against them as being all but un-American come election time and to sway the public's opinion, to get the public to talk about something specific, so that the rest of us would be a shoo-in with little or no competition to face come next election time. Now, we have just all but lost that leverage and it may all come back to haunt us."
In response, the second co-conspirator said. "Well, just keep smiling and keep kissing babies and laugh off any negative comments against us as being nonsense and just say that any comment on the Liberty Bell would be nothing short of bellicose."
He had no sooner said that, when the tower bell began to ring, and, continued to ring, nonstop. Someone, was ringing or banging on the bell that wasn't supposed to be either banged on or rang. As the bell continued to ring, everyone soon realized that someone amongst them, was purposely trying to do even more damage to what was left

of the poor broken and re-bolted shell of a bell. But, nevertheless, the bell continued to ring and ring. Everyone by now, was seen running up and down the halls, trying to account for any missing representatives so as to have someone to place the blame when the next investigation began, all having their watches out, note pads and pencils at the ready and handy, in order to claim their cohorts as witnesses, and, in order to be able to say, that they were not directly involved and had several witnesses, just in case they saw or heard something that they were to be accused of on into the future.

Then, the dreamer awoke, somewhat unsettled, fumbling, mumbling, and trying to get the alarm on the clock turned off once again before he became even more fully awake.

THE BIRDS (in a mixed up concoction)

The dreamer, not being well read, or up-to-date on most daily protocol, aimlessly dreamed of things yet unconsidered by most.

As best as I can recollect, it all started early one Spring, after talking with a good friend. I had been asked by him, if I had put my bird bath out yet, and, I said no, but was not really looking forward to some of the problems that I have had over the past few years. He asked what the problems were exactly, and, I expressed, that the algae bloom and growth in the bird bath was primarily the main problem, with me having to clean it out no less than once a week, and, more than that during the hotter weather. He said that he had experienced the same problem, but, that he took the action of adding about a quarter cup of bleach daily to the water when he filled his bird bath, and, that the bleach helped to control the algae bloom. It seemed to be a new idea to me at the time, so, I decided that I would try it.

Now, the weather was still chilly, especially overnight, but there were quite a number of birds out and about, so, I decided to get an early start on the season, and, go ahead and put out the bird bath. It was clean and dry from where I had put it out last fall, so, I rolled it out of the garage, because it was almost too heavy to pick up, but, I was still able to lift it up on its pedestal near the rose bushes which were starting to leave out. I started out, by first filling the bird bath with a hose, and then, getting a half cup of bleach, pouring it into the water in the bird bath and stirring it around as little just to mix it up. I mean, if a quarter cup works for my friend, then a half cup could only work twice as good for me. I was looking forward to never having to clean out the bird bath again, any time into the near future, I hoped. I mean, I could always cut back if need be.

As the Spring days warmed, I continued my daily routine, of pouring a half cup of bleach into the bird bath when I changed the water, especially when the birds messed in the water, otherwise, I would just add some water to top it off, and, add another quarter cup of bleach to the water, as the bleach seemed to evaporate faster than the water in the heat of the day, and, it had a clean swimming pool smelt to it, which, could only mean that it was good, too, the birds seemed to love it, as, they kept coming for their daily bath.

Previously, in other years, I had come to learn the habits of most of the birds who frequented my bird bath. The Sparrows, or Wrens, never really got into the water, but sat on the edge of the bird bath and flapped their wings. The Red Birds, would land on the edge of the bird bath, then just jump into the water, but would jump out just as fast, as if the water was too cold for them to really take a bath in. The Blue Jays, would do the same thing, but mostly had more fun by running all of the other birds off when they frequented the bath. It was the Black Birds, who seemed to really take full advantage of the bath, landing, bouncing around on the edge of the bird bath, then jumping into the water and flapping their wings, then, jumping out, then back again, into the water all the while spraying water out of the bird bath like a fountain spray. They seemed to enjoy the bath of all the birds frequenting the water, and took full advantage of my clean bird bath, and, I felt proud to accommodate them.

As the weeks went by, I continued my routine of adding bleach when necessary, changing the water when necessary, still enjoying the various birds which frequented the bath. I noticed after a few weeks, that the Black Birds seemed not to come around as much as they did earlier in the Spring, and now, there were some dark brownish mottled birds which took their place bathing daily in my bird bath, with fewer and fewer black birds coming around daily, I thought perhaps, that the darker brown birds could possibly be young Starlings. I observed, sometime along before Summer officially began, that the dark brown birds, or, the young Starlings, were now getting fewer and fewer with their visitations, and, were replaced by some lighter brown birds, of a kind which I did not readily recollect having ever seen in previous years. I mentioned this to my friend, but

he just threw it off by saying, that he had seen the same thing year after year, as different birds have different migratory routes and times that they pass through our area, and, he seemed to be a little more educated than I was, so, I just took his word for it at the time.
As summer broke, hot and humid, I was so proud of my bird bath, as, I had not had to clean it out even once. No algae bloom, or growth, not even a trace of algae could be seen in my bird bath. I had my friend to thank for his idea, and, I did just that on the very next time that I saw him, and, he said that he was only trying to be a good neighbor, and, not to think anything further about it, and, that I did not have to get him a present or anything for his house for his services as; he felt that it was only a neighborly kind of thing to do.
I continued my daily routine, adding water when necessary, changing water when necessary, and, always being mindful of adding that quarter cup of bleach or more to the birdbath on a daily basis. Too, since I was using the hose to water my vegetable garden on dry days, I now changed my routine to having a bucket of water by the garage, which I filled daily from the spigot, and, added the bleach daily, and then, just topped off the bird bath on an as needed basis. This seemed to work for me at the time, and, I just went with the change in my routine.
A month or so, into Summer, I observed that the Sparrows, or Wrens, as they are called, matured, with most of them now having whitish breasts, I noticed too, that the lighter brown birds had most likely flown further North for the Summer, and were becoming replaced by a few almost whitish birds with some mottling, of which type, I do not recollect having ever seen before. I mentioned this to my friend, and, he said that he had seen the darker and lighter brownish birds, but had never seen, to his recollection, any of the whitish birds, and he came over to my house purposely to see them. He hadn't been over at my house an hour before the whitish birds showed up. He said, that he never seen anything like it before, and, he had brought his bird book, and, tried to look them up in the book, but couldn't find anything that even resembled what they looked like. He said that this could be something new, or maybe even peculiar, or then, maybe not, but it might be of some importance, and, he recommended that I call the State Fish and Game Department to tell them about it, just to see what they would say.
Well, after his visit, I got busy with other things, and did not get around right away, to calling the State Fish and Game people. However, when I did, after I finally got their telephone number and

actually got to talk to a real person, after going through punching numbers for a half-hour or so, a lady came on the phone, and, while explaining the purpose of my call about the peculiar birds, I could tell that she did not seem particularly interested, as, she said, finally, that it was not their Department that handled such matters, and, she referred me to the Department of Wild Life. I asked for their number, and, after a wait, listening to music on the phone, the lady finally came back on the phone and gave me a similar number to call, and, I thanked her for her time, and, said my good byes. Well, I had went this far, so far, so, I called the Department of Wild Life, and, after a similar routine of punching numbers, and, after another half hour or so, I finally got to talk to a real person. This time, I got a guy to talk to, and, I felt a little easier this time, explaining the looks of these birds which I had never seen before. He seemed genuinely interested, he took my name, address, telephone number, and said that someone from the Department would be in touch with me within the next couple of weeks, then, he hung up his phone in the middle of me asking him a question.

Well, I didn't call anymore, and, about three weeks had gone by, with me continuing my routine, which was now working out quite well, as, I had went halfway through the Summer, and, had not cleaned out my bird bath because of algae. I felt good about it. My friend had given me advice of the best nature, and, even though I had thanked him, I felt a little more than obligated to do something for him because of it, but couldn't think of anything to do at the time. I told him about the Department of Wild Life promised visit, and, invited him over when and if they ever showed up, and, he said that he would come over, and just to call him, when they did.

Well, no more than a day or two later, here shows up two people, dressed in uniform, with badges and nameplates and identification, with 9mm semi-automatic pistols strapped to their hips. A man and a woman, if you will, traveling in a State vehicle, with official State license plates. They politely introduced themselves, and, asked me if I would just bring them up to date on my initial report, which I did, to the best of my ability. I told them about the whitish bird that I had never seen before in the last fifteen to twenty years of my retirement of bird watching, and, having a bird bath just out back of my house. They said that they had a routine questionnaire that they would appreciate it if I would help them to complete, and, I agreed that I would help, but, most of the ones which I did not have a ready answer and the better part of them, I had to just say that I did not know, one way or the other.

After the questionnaire, they asked if they could possibly set up a schedule to come out and observe the peculiar birds. I told them, that all they had to do was to come into my kitchen, look out the kitchen window, and, observe to their hearts content. They advised me, that that was not in their bailiwick, or, in other words, that that was not their job, and, that someone duly assigned from their Department would be out for such an observing purpose. I asked when that might be, and, they responded, that it would most likely be in the next few weeks, as, they had a schedule to keep. With that, they just up and left in their official State licensed vehicle.

I called my friend, and told him about the visit. He complained that I had not called him, as he had told me that he wanted to be there. I explained, that the two State people only completed a questionnaire and then left without even looking at the peculiar birds. But, he said, that he would still have wanted to have been there. I promised him, that when the State observer shows up in the next few weeks, that I will surely call him and have him over.

A couple more weeks go by, and, I continue my routine, which is now working out quite well, if I may say so myself, I now have a system, and it is working, and, I do not have to clean out the bird bath. I feel right proud that I have not had even a slight problem with any sign of algae bloom.

When the phone rang, I was in the bath room, and couldn't immediately get the call, and, it went to messaging, and, I had to call the lady back at the number that she left. I couldn't believe my luck that the call went through to her without going through the punching numbers routine. I even mentioned this to her and told her that I appreciated her call. She asked me to bring her up to date on the issue at hand, and, I reiterated everything about the peculiar birds that I could readily recollect, then, she told me that she wanted to set up an observation visit by a team of the Department's Biologists. I told her that I was retired, and, at home, and, the visit could be at their convenience. She seemed to be appreciative of that. She said that she was in possession of the questionnaire which I had helped to complete, and, she hoped that the visit would be enlightening. She told me that they would call a day or two prior to the observation visit, dependent upon the weather of course, she said. I told her that I understood and that I appreciated the early warning of their arrival.

I called my friend, told him about the up and coming observation visit, and he said that he would be available, if he was not ailing, as, he said that he had not been feeling all that well of late. I promised him that I would definitely give him a call, whether or not he was up to coming over for the official State visit.

I sat by the window, in quiet expectation, and, sure enough, the birds were still showing up for their daily bird bath, and they were all mostly white with some light brown mottling here and there with some of the younger birds.

The days seemed to fly by, and then, the phone ringing, with the State Department of Wild Life on the other end, telling me that they would be out for an initial observation and survey of the issue at hand. I called my friend, told him about the three days, he said he was up to coming over and act as a witness if I needed such. I told him that I appreciated it, and he said, I mean, what are friends for, except to stand by one another in time of need.

The third day, my friend came over early, just after breakfast and we set up with a hot cup of coffee by the kitchen window, looking out onto the patio and the bird bath between the patio and the garden, I told him that I had just now changed the water, so, that the State Department of Wild Life people could see how well I kept the bird bath and how concerned I was about wild life conservation. Before we finished our cup of coffee, a couple of the whitish birds made their debut. My friend mentioned, that the birds had the same mannerisms as black birds, and, perhaps they could be related somehow.

We had been watching for only about a half hour or so, when my door bell rang and when I went to answer it, there was the team of three Department of Wild Life personnel, all dressed up in uniform, with badges, name tags, and all three were armed with what appeared to be semi-automatic hand guns. I invited them in, and they introduced themselves to me and my friend. I led them into the kitchen, where I told them that my friend and I had been observing the peculiar birds for the morning, and, had already seen a couple at the bird bath. I told them, that we observed the birds from the kitchen window, so as, not to scare them away, as, the birds were somewhat flighty. The lady with them remarked that she found most birds flighty, generally. They said that they were all Biologists, and the lady added that she had done her Master's thesis on the domestication of some wild life. A couple of the whitish birds landed on the bird bath, and, interrupted our conversation, and, naturally, they got the attention of the Biologists. The older man with the team asked if that was the peculiar bird which I had previously reported. I said that it was, and, with that, he pulled out his camera, and started to take photos of the birds at the bird bath through the kitchen window. Too, and almost simultaneously, the lady Biologist pulled out her camera, and began to take photos also.

I asked them if they had ever seen any birds like that before, and, they said no. My friend mentioned that he could not find any birds that looked like that in his latest edition of Birds of North America. The three Biologist just watched the birds with no further comment.

The lady Biologist was the first to make some comment, which was, that she said that this situation needed further study, and, that she would recommend that to her superior. I asked, what further study could include. She said that they needed a monitor set up, with a motion detector, which could activate a camera, which could take photos in real time, and, transmit them via satellite to their office for recording. She asked me if I had any objection to them setting up a camera, possibly mounted on the garage, for such purpose. I said no, that I would have no objection whatsoever, as I was a lifelong card carrying conservationist and would do whatever was necessary to assist them in their endeavor. The said that they appreciated people like me and that the world needed more with that kind of attitude or outlook for nature and wild life in general.

The team had only been at my house about an hour, had observed possibly eight or nine of the peculiar birds, and, told me that a crew of technicians would probably call me for a visit within a week or so, and, that they would set up the equipment necessary to accomplish their goal of maintaining a watch of the peculiar birds. With that, my friend and I bid them goodbye, and they were on their way to some other mission I supposed as being just as important. My friend and I talked about the 21st century technical capability, and, he said that I should have asked if such satellite transmitting equipment that they planned to set up on the garage would in any way cause any problems with my television reception. I said that I had cable TV and could not see it effecting that in any way, however, I told him that I would ask the technicians when they came by to set it all up next week. My friend made me promise to call him when they came out, which I did, and he headed home.

I continued my daily routine with the bird bath, now looking after it with even greater fervor, as, I felt that something big was to come from all of this, and, that I felt good to be part of it all. I could even see myself as even a better wild life conservationist that what I thought myself to be previous to the present happenstance.

The technician crew called the following week and told me that they would be out the very next day, as, bad weather was rolling in and they wanted to get this job up and running as soon as possible, as, they said that there was some urgency brought down upon them from the head of their department, bringing a sense of importance which they had not seen previously. I told them that I would be at home, since I was retired, and they said that they would be there early in the morning as the job would take the better part of the day, with the testing that was required. I called my friend and told him, and, he said that he would be over early and for me to put the coffee on as it could be an exciting day.

Morning came and my friend came over, at about the same time that the technicians arrived in a van. Them were in uniform, had identification and badges and all, but I noted that that they were not toting hand guns. I asked them why, and they said that they were not with the enforcement group, and, that they were not so authorized. I led them out to my garage and showed them the bird bath, and, they said that they had been fully briefed on what needed to be done, and, that they would appreciate it if I would just let them do their job, as, they had a dead line to meet in order to accomplish what all had been assigned them. So, me and my friend left them to their work and went back inside the house, had another cup of coffee and watched them work from the kitchen window.

Before noon, one of the technicians knocked on my back door, which I answered, and he advised that their job was complete, and, that all the equipment was in place and had been tested. My friend reminded me to ask them about the TV reception. I asked if their transmitting system would cause any kind of problem with radio or TV reception, and they assured me and my friend that it was not likely and that they had never had any problems previous, except perhaps with the motion sensor, as, it was very sensitive and focused on the bird bath, which could also be activated at night, and, when doing so, it makes a whirring or whizzing sound which I might notice, but other than that, there should be no concern, however, I should notify them if we have a storm with lightning striking nearby, as it may cause the system to go offline, but, other than that, no problem. I asked them what was to happen next, and, they said that they had no idea, and, that it was anyone's guess, so, we let it go at that, and, they gathered up their tools and left the property.

A week or so went by, and, I noticed that at first, the whirring and whizzing somewhat frightened the birds as they would land and immediately take off again, like doing a touch and go kind of thing, but then, after a couple days, the birds got used to the noise and continued their old habits with no change noted by me. I continued my routine of changing the water when needed, adding bleach as needed, or just adding a little water and bleach as needed, with no further to do.

A week went by, and, my friend called to ask me how things were going. Copasetic, I told him, and, he wanted to know exactly what copasetic meant, or if it was some foreign language, which I told him that it was all A-OK, thumbs up, all systems operating, and, that we were cooking on the front burner. He assured me that he more than fully understood, but to let him know if there were any updates or changes, or, any new visitors around and about. I assured him that I would call and let him know.

About a week and a half went by, and, the telephone rang, with the lady Biologist on the other end, asking me if I would be obliged to have her, her supervisor, and his manager, the whole kit and caboodle chain of command, to show up at my house on the morrow. I told her that that would be fine and she said that they would be out sometime shortly before lunch. I told her that I would be looking forward to seeing her again. I then called my friend to update him and he said that he would be over, and, to put on a pot of coffee, which, I said that I would, just to accommodate him.

Morning came, my friend came over, and, we awaited the visitors from the Department of Wild Life. We had only had one cup of coffee when they arrived. They came to the front door, and, I invited them in, and, they introduced themselves to me and my friend, then, they asked if there had been any bird activity over the morning, as, they said that during their travel, that they could not see the ongoing transmissions which came into their office compound. I told them only normal activity, with nothing unusual.

The manager, the top of their chain of command, then spoke. He said, that there had been much speculation as to what the birds were, some, in the department thought that perhaps they had been blown into the area by a recent hurricane, as, similar birds had been sighted near the Brazilian and Argentine border, and, may have flown north only to get caught up in the winds of the hurricane, then, some others within their department said that they thought the birds were albino, however, upon close up color photos, not one of the birds photographed, had pink eyes, so, that idea was scuttled. The third idea, was, that the birds were of some new variety, perhaps even a new genus, or, maybe even involved with a skipping of generations to evolve into some new species. He went on to explain, that the magnitude of their findings, had already caught the attention of not only the Federal Government, but, even internationally, as many of the photos had already been shared on the internet. He said, that there were some far flung reports, of similar birds, one from Russia, and, one from the Netherlands, but none as clear and conclusive as were the birds monitored for the past few weeks right here in my back yard, and, documented, he added. The Governor is aware and is excited about it all, as he is a devout conservationist, and, has requested that if indeed that the birds are of some new species or genus, that they be named after him, and, also after the local wherein they were first observed.

Both me and my friend were speechless. I really did not know what to say. I was dumbfounded. My friend could only shrug his shoulders. I did not comprehend it all, at all.

The manager added, that it was his director's orders, to set up an observation center on my property, if I would cooperate with such activity, as, it would entail a constant observation team of at least three biologists or other scientists, visiting on a daily basis. He said that the plan was for them to set up a camouflaged man lift situated above the birdbath area, and perhaps a porta-potty to be set up for the folks to relieve themselves if necessary. The operation could take up to a month, that is, if the birds continued to come to the bird bath area, and, could last until they decide to migrate when cooler weather came in the Fall. I told him that I would cooperate fully, that I was also a devout conservationist, and that if it was in the interest of science, that I was ready to serve my community, State, and Nation, if need be, and that our community represented everything good about our good Country, and, he could count on me and my friend to assist in any way for the betterment of the good. He said that he appreciated that response, and that with the urgency of the matter at hand, that if it was OK with me, that they could start as early as tomorrow. Me, being took up in all of the excitement, agreed fully, and invited him and his cohorts to have at it and go for it, with gusto. With that, they all left the property and me and my friend tried to filter out what all was to take place on into the near future.

The next day dawned bright, and, shortly after breakfast, a truck, towing a man lift, backed into my driveway. I went outside to watch their setting up of the equipment. Shortly thereafter, a pickup truck rolled up with a porta-potty which was set out on my front lawn next to the driveway. The man lift had hardly been set up, when the first crew arrived. Three people, to whom I attempted to introduce myself to, did not seem particularly interested in who I was or what I represented. They said, that they were assigned the project, and, that there would be a different crew every four hours for the next week or so, people coming and going, climbing into the man lift, being raised up above the bird bath, with cameras, videos, sound retrieving devices, which went on every morning and every day after lunch, and, neither me or my friend ever saw the same person twice during this time. In between times, and, in between people, there were people climbing trees, looking in the bushes, hunting for the nests of the birds, but, as far as I heard, to no avail, which was even more puzzling to the observation crews and their immediate supervisors. I never did hear how that all came about.

The first part of the second week, the lady Biologist again showed up at my house, amongst all of the other commotion, and told me that they were planning a capture of some of the birds in order to try to get a sample of their DNA to determine if they were of some new strain of bird, and, to possibly observe them in a more controlled environment. I told her that I was OK with that but did ask as to what all of the capture thing entailed. She told me, that they would position a catch net, near the bird bath, and when a couple of the birds arrived, that they would fire the net with blank shotgun shells, the net would envelope the birds, and, the birds would then be caught by hand, put into cages, and taken away for further study. I told her that I was OK with that and advised her that if I could be of any assistance, to please just let me know. She said that she would, but, the technicians seemed to know what they were doing and had the mission well in hand.

The next day, the net people showed up, set up their capture net, and within the first hour, had fired off their net and caught three birds. They said, that they really got lucky, and, had caught one male and two females. Then, they set up their capture net again, and early on in the afternoon, fired off another volley of shots and caught two more. The next day, was the same, but caught only four altogether all day. The third day, they only caught two. I asked them just how many birds they needed to catch, in order to make their study. They told me that they should have at least a dozen or so as that is what the order said that had been handed down to them.

My friend and I, continued to observe the activity, and, between times, I continued to do my routine, adding water to the bird bath when needed, or changing when needed, and, adding bleach to keep the algae growth down.

Everything continued for about two more weeks, and, all in all, probably forty to fifty people had been seen to come and go. The net capturing crew was there every day, and they had captured twenty to thirty birds, all being whitish, with some mottling. Me and my friend got a couple close up looks at some of the birds after they had been caged and they appeared as normal as any other bird that I have seen around and about my birdbath. My friend said the same thing.

Another week went by and the lady Biologist again appeared at my door. She said that she wanted to thank me, and to provide me with a letter of thanks and recognition from the head of the State Department of Wild Life. She read me the letter, then, gave it to me and said that I could have it framed if I wanted to, and, even hang it on the wall in my den if I so choose. She went on to tell me, that the study was now of such magnitude, that it was up to be federally funded by a million dollar grant and was scheduled to be studied by several Universities within the State. Also, that it most likely would be written up and published in several of the nature publications which should gain even more international interest. She said, that the department's work had been now assigned mission status, which meant that funding for additional work on the project would be guaranteed for the foreseeable future. She personally thanked me for my assistance and the allowance of all of the scientists who took part and came and went on my property. I asked her just how much such a study would normally cost. She said, that that was not of her concern, as, she was a scientist, and not an accountant or politician.

I called my friend just to update him and to tell him about the lady's visit. He said that he would come over in order to hear all about it first hand, and, wanted to see the letter. When he came over, we talked about all of the various things that had taken place, and, he says, that he has been thinking about everything, and, he thinks that he has gotten some things all figured out, he then asks me, about me and my routine about putting bleach in the bird bath water. He says, he wanted to know, just how I got to the point of adding the amounts of bleach that I added, he asked. Well, I says, you told me first, last Spring, in order to kill the algae bloom, to add bleach to the bird bath, I says. Yes, but, he says, I told you to add a quarter cup of bleach, and here you told me you were adding a half-cup of bleach, and, if the water was clear, you added in a little more, or, you changed the water and then you added in another fresh half-cup of bleach instead of a quarter cup. He then says. Don't you see what could have been happening? He says, that by adding that much bleach to the water, that it could have been bleaching out the black birds feathers, first turning them brown, then lighter brown, then mottled brown and white and then finally to white as the Summer bore on. What if the State puts two and two together? He says. What if they find out that those white birds are just bleached out black birds? He says. What if they come to think that you purposely hoodwinked them? He says. What if they decide to take you to court and make you reimburse the State and pay for all of their hoaxed scientific studies? He says. What if the DNA study results prove up that they are all really black birds? He says. What if they hatch some of the white birds eggs in captivity and they all come freshly hatched out black birds? He says. By this time, he is somewhat excited and appears to be perplexed.

Hold on, hold on, I says. Don't you think that all of this has already crossed my mind, but with all of the ongoing activity, not to mention the interest that it has generated, it has taken on a life of its own, and, now, it is like a snowball rolling down hill, gaining both mass and momentum. Look here, look at what I done built for some observations by all of the folks that have stopped by and have asked me if they could just take a look, having seen all the reports on the internet, and, wanting to see all of it for real, and, the biggest thing of it all, the real kicker, is this, look at this jar, that I taped a note on for donations. In the last three days alone, I have counted no less than thirty-seven people, who have come to see for themselves, and, every one of them has donated, and, of last count, there was almost a hundred and fifty dollars in the jar. Too, over the next three days, I have scheduled appointments for another twenty-three, and, no telling what they will donate. I have even been giving a tour of the site, showing the bird bath, the observation area where the man lift platform was, and, even pointed out where the porta-potty was. Where this one sat, where that one sat, where this one stood, where the Director of the Department of Wild Life stood, I mean, this is nothing less than a money maker, which could help us supplement our social security, and, most of the donations are cash, with only about ten to fifteen percent being checks. So, what do you say about them apples, dear friend. Besides, with this many government entities, no one of them would go so far as to say that it was all wrong, why, they would rather claim they found a new species, then, up and claim that society let it become endangered, then, even extinct

God forbid, before any one of them would make a contrary peep or even a muffled utterance.

My friend looked at the donation jar, a gallon clear glass dill pickle jar half filled with money, mostly ones, but some tens and a couple twenties, a simple container converted to a cash receptacle for business purposes. Then, he looked at the observation booth that I had built with five port holes for observation and for picture taking, complete with a bench for resting, then, he looked at my tour notes, about what I said when and where, and, then, he finally opened up. He says. You know, we have to keep this just between the two of us, because if any of what we talked about ever gets out, we could wind up having to pay the preacher, if you know what I mean.

The meeting of my friend and I was then abruptly interrupted by three members of the society for the prevention of cruelty to animals from Missouri, and, they seemed to be delighted that my friend and I were devout conservationists, with membership, and, even with magazines that I had gotten from the library so as to be shown on a shelf in the booth. They were even more delighted while in the observation booth, to witness the bathing of two of the peculiar white birds, and, they too, took photos, one after another, until the birds departed and up until two other folks from Ohio showed up for their own look see. I noted that all three did donate ready cash in the gallon dill pickle jar. My friend also noted the donation, and, we just looked at one another and smiled.

A nice ending to a most unusual dream of confusion which became matter-of-fact with some less than straight forward results.

UNCOVERING THE COVERED UP COVER UP

The dreamer hated those working dreams, I mean, it is enough to work on a daily basis, without having to ever even work in your dreams, I mean, it is like doing unpaid overtime, without even an offer of any extra time off to compensate, much less a bonus. However, workers on the job, can be crude in comment, language and character, so, may the reader beware.

Keith sat there, head down, seemingly down and dejected, or, maybe, just plain confused. He was sitting on the walkway and had his legs

hanging down in the electrical vault, looking at the entanglement of control wires, some with prepped ends and some just raw cut, with none bundled that he could see. "None of these wires are color coded, all of them are all white or off white, depending on their age.. It's like two different companies did this, maybe more from the looks of it, two or more totally different worlds, coming together at this point in time, right here in this vault, it is more than just a mess, it's a "WAG" as to which one is which, I'm telling ya'." He said.
"What the hell is a WAG? Bobby asked.
"Anybody's Wild Ass Guess, and, it couldn't get any worse than this." Keith responded. "There are WAG's, P-WAG's, and, E-WAG's, WAGS are just plain everyday guesses, while P-WAG's are professional, and, E-WAG's are Expert. It's like answers, regular everyday answers usually cost you fifty cents, while professional answers cost you a dollar, and expert answers can cost you two dollars or more. Anyway, after all is said and done, it still couldn't get any worse than this."
Bobby responded. "Oh yes it could, you could be a bonafied Union member here in the plant, or, it could be hotter, or, it could be raining, or, that vault could be full of rain water with a water moccasin or two in it, along with a couple dozen brown recluse spiders floatin' around on top, or, some of those wires could be live with some of those wires a-arcin', and you don't know which ones it is yet, or, the water could even be real pizen."
"Pizen? What the hell is pizen, anyway?" Keith asked.
"Poison, that has gone from good to bad, with creepy crawly radioactive microbial germs that I brought back from Chernobyl, that carry death dealin' viruses with a DNA yet unbeknownst to mankind, capable of wiping out the population of this entire planet in less than a week or two, that is what real pizen is." Bobby responded.
Keith, looking like he was trying to ignore Bobby's definition of real pizen, looked back over his shoulder at Bobby and said. "Bobby, did you read in the morning paper where that poor plastic surgeon that done went and hung himself?"
"No, I didn't see anything in this morning's paper about it, I don't read the obituaries, unless I hear that someone I know has died, so, all I ever read is the comics, the funny paper, just to start my day off with a smile. So, what was the obituary write-up all about?" Bobby asked.
"Bobby, there was no obituary, it is supposed to be a damn stupid joke." Keith remarked.

Bobby responded. "Well, I don't get it if it was a joke, and, I didn't read anything about it or hear anything about it, and, like I said, I don't normally read the obituaries unless I hear that someone that I know done went up and died off."

"Forget it Bobby, you're right, you didn't get it." Looking down into the vault Keith remarked. "This hole just might have a couple brown recluser's down in there some where's, maybe we should get some kind of insect spray before we do anything else. Not to change the subject, again, but, did I ever tell you about the time that my wife left me?"

Bobby did respond. "No, Keith, I don't recollect, that you ever told me anything about that, I didn't know that she ever did, but if she did, I could understand it, knowing you and your attitude and outlook on life."

Keith went on. "Well, she did, she left me, and, I was not proud of it at the time, in fact, I was really down hearted, if you know what I mean. Did you know, that I had to go so far as to promise to buy her a brand new pair of flame resistant work coveralls, just to get her to come back home. Then, when she found out that the coveralls weren't Karhardts, she told me, that, if she had known it a-first,that she wouldn't have ever come back at all. Isn't that a typical woman's attitude, or what, or not?"

"Maybe you should have thrown in a new pair of work boots, a new pair of leather gloves along with a pair of safety glasses, a respirator and some knee pads." Bobby responded.

"No, her company would've got her most of that stuff, and she would have had to have been respirator tested, and with all of her hot air, she probably wouldn't have passed the test. Anyway, had I even offered any of that, she would have probably wanted a new pair of light tan suede leather Red Wings with lightweight composite synthetic safety-toes, and, she would have wanted the gloves to have been goatskin and only have been made in America, by union labor no less. You don't know that woman, Bobby, like I do."

"Sounds like my kind of woman." Bobby responded.

Keith returned. "Did I ever tell you how we ever met?"

Bobby looked around to make sure no one was listening, then, responded. "No, Keith, I don't think that you ever brought that up in any of our conversations before. So, tell me, I'm just sittin' here on this five gallon bucket, with my ass on pins and needles, just waitin' for your answer, so, just how did you both, the two of you, you and her or her and you, just how did you all meet?"

"Well." Keith started. "Well, it all started out just innocent enough. I went on the computer down at the library, and joined up on that a-Harmoney web-site, and, I made the mistake of puttin' a picture of myself, and, my phone number along with how much money I made year before last, and within a week, I had one hunnert and seventy three women callin' me at all hours of the day and night, I even had some Princess from Nigeria wantin' to marry me, she said that her husband had died and she needed to get married real quick in order to get her millions of dollars inheritance. That one, I had the good sense not to contact more than two or three times. The first thing I did, was, I got me a ten foot pole, just to keep them all at a distance, then I got me a hickory club, just to beat 'em offen me if or when I had to. I finally had to get my telephone turned off, get a new track phone, and, by the time I got back down to the library to get myself canceled off of that a-Harmoney web-site, I noticed that I had run up my total of women to four hunnert and thirty-five, which, made me feel good, but I didn't need the trouble that I could see a-brewin', so, I just gave it all up. So, I ran an ad in the newspaper for a man a-wantin' a good woman."

Bobby looked back at Keith and said. "You ran an ad? In the newspaper? What did you say?"

"Yea, I ran an ad, I worded it real good too, I thought. It said... "Wanted, a good strong woman, who don't have a bunch of rug rats, curtain climbers, or crumb crushers, who knows how to cook and sew, how to do farmin' chores before breakfast, who knows how to make good bakin' powder buttermilk biscuits before sun-up, who can keep a clean kitchen and bedroom, barn and chicken house, who takes a bath at least every couple of weeks, and, who has a nice boat, and, I did mention that either inboard or outboard motors was OK. I said to please make sure to send a good picture of the boat, and, she did, and, that is how we got together, and, even today, I still think that it was a damn nice boat, if you ask me, as, I've been running that thing to fishin' holes all over the state for the last six years, and, it has always brought me back home to the dock."

Bobby responded. "Keith, I don't believe any of that for even a minute. You are so full of bull shit, if I must say so myself."

Keith responded. "No, no, no, I'm serious as a heart attack about all that relation stuff, I'll give you a good example, just to prove it. For instance, did I ever tell you, or mention out loud, that my first cousin on my mother's side, whose uncle, the brother to my mother's aunt, had a cousin to or of his mother's side of the family, whose daughter, technically a second or third cousin passed down to me, I think, if I think about it, who went to one of those there hair and nail salons, where all they do is gossip about one another, and, especially about the ones who are not there at the time. Well, anyway, she heard the story, about this other teenage girl, maybe, all but eighteen at the time, who actually lives right here in this community amongst us, right here in the same town that we both live in, with you and I no less, that is, that goes out on dates with different boys, and, she would not go the the same place with any two of them, ever, for instance, with one particular boy, she would only go to McDonals with, then, the other boy, she would only go to Dairy King with, then, the other boy, she would only go to Hardy's with, and, the other boy she would only go to Windy's with, or, wherever, each one was different and she didn't crisscross them any, and any one of them didn't know about any of the others."

He went on. "Then, she would only kiss and smooch with one of the boys, then, the other, she would only hug and embrace, then, one other, she would only hold hands, and the other one, she would only go on walks with, and the other, she would only play around with him, and the other, he would be the one she let him rub up against her, then another, even yet, that would be the only one for her to let him feel her up, and another, she would only do something else, and another something else, on and on, or whatever. She segmented and compartmentalized them just like President Clanton did, or, said that he did or didn't do, according to his definition of "is" or "did" or, whatever. So, what do you think of a girl like that? Have you ever heard of such?"

Bobby responded. "Well, Keith, maybe, just maybe, she was just checking them all out, you know, trying to determine which one would be the best father for their children, the best one to make a home with, the one that had the best job, or, the one that was the best lookin', that kind of thing, I mean, for all I know, she might even be related to me, and, that might be why you are telling me about it all. But then, when you really think about it, ain't we all that way, to some extent or another?"

"Well, I don't know for sure, but, I don't think so, at least I don't think that I am that way. I personally think that she knew damn well what she was doing, or, is a-doing, and, a-doing it all on a-purpose, for whatever reasons she so chose to choose at the time. I think, probably, most likely, maybe, it was just to get her jollies off, but then, on the other hand, nobody has ever come up saying that she ever had a hard time getting a date yet."

Bobby, sitting nearby on a five-gallon bucket turned upside down, was just shaking his head and was starring off into the blue beyond, past the plumes of steam from the reactors, acting like he was trying to think, then he responded. "Keith, back to our problem in the here and now with this vault and wire thing. Do you think maybe we better call boss Darv, I mean, he's the only one amongst us all who is smart enough to figure something like this out, you know, that he is somewhat educated, and, he seems to know most everything that is goin' on out here since he sees the whole picture, I mean, that is why he has the job he has. Or, better yet, maybe I could go get him if you want me to, just say the word." Bobby said.

Keith nodded in the affirmative, and, with that, Bobby jumped up off of the five gallon bucket and left the work area on his way to attempt to find boss Darv, not wanting to wait for another short story coming from or out of Keith.

Before Bobby had the time to return, here comes an out-sourced contract Safety Engineer stopping by the worksite just to ask Keith if everything was OK, and, Keith just kind of off handedly mentioned that he had a problem with the no-color coding of the control wires with white and off white color coding of more or less than half of them, because they were all white to some degree or another, and, added that it was more than like a problem from hell itself, as, there were at least a couple a- hundred or so control wires coming in on the left side, and about the same number coming in from the right side by estimate or guestimate, whatever, with nothing even mentioned on the schematic as to the no-color code of either or how they all were to be connected up or terminated in the vault.

"Somehow, I am not really surprised. By the way, my name is Gene, what's yours?" He said.

"I'm Keith, that is, if you have a need to know." He responded.

"What company are you with? What union you with? Is the power on? Are the wires energized? Are the panels all locked out? Who has the lockout keys? Do they all have the proper tags if they don't have locks? Have you traced the conduits back to their origin? By the way, where is your work permit, isn't it supposed to be posted somewhere here? Are those the right gloves for your job? Do you have a high voltage flash suit on site? Why don't you have it on? Is it fire proof or just fire resistant? Have you been trained in Confined Space entry? Where is your Hole Watch? Where is your supplied air breathing tank and respirator? Have you been respirator fit tested? Is your Hole Watch Air Tank trained? Who is your assigned

Supervisor? Where is your buddy? This job site has a required buddy system; didn't you get any of that information during your safety orientation before you started to work? How long have you worked here in the plant? What are you? Are you just an Apprentice, a neophyte or what? Why don't you have your badge hooked up proper on your coveralls? Are those coveralls flame resistant, oh, I'm sorry, I already asked that. Is that hard hat you are wearing approved for electrical work?" The Safety Engineer both emphatically asked and exclaimed.

Keith responded. "Well, I am a "what", I guess, and, I was, at one time in my life, both a neophyte and an apprentice. Once, I remember, while I was working my way through high school, I was an apprentice on a fishing boat out of Mobile, Alabama, livin' down by the Gulf Shores area, in a condo I was, and, I started out on the fishin' boat as an Apprentice Baiter, then, after a few months, I did very well in my work, did a good job, and, got promoted to Assistant Baiter, then, after a couple more months at sea, or, maybe a year or so, I was promoted to Junior Baiter, and, after a couple years, I got myself promoted to being Senior or Lead Baiter, and, right before I graduated from high school, I finally made it, after another year to become a Master Baiter. But, I let that job go, because I actually never got a good handle on it, and now, here I am, here and today, I is as I is, working for the Tele-Masters Communications Company."

He went on. The company I work for is non-union, and, we are downright proud to be proud of it, and, everything here in this vault is dead as four o'clock, The conduit on the left, goes back to vault number seven by way of cable tray thirty-five-A, which is not connected to anything yet as far as I can see at the other end, except some hot air, but should be, when the switchgear is ready to be set in, and, the conduit on the right wyes out twice on cable trays number twenty-two B and C, and trays nineteen D and E, to the control panels at bumper pump stations Charlie-7 and Echo 5. Those, are all locked out, although the wires are not connected over there yet either, and, there is no power yet wired in to the switchgear, or the pump stations, but, just in case of a lightning strike, or the fall of a crane boom coming down on us along with some extraneous energized wires, caused by none other than an act of God Himself, so, we are in good shape with that, and there is no high voltage here, these are all control wires, so there is no need for a flash suit, and, the vault is not classified as either a permit or non-permit Confined Space because it is too small to get my fat ass into, so, I do not need breathing air, and, my buddy went to get our foreman to come and have a look at the problem, and, the permits are right here, down in the vault, out of the weather. Here, let me get it for you, and, just to check, did you get all of that which I mentioned aforesaid for your daily report?"

Over his shoulder, Keith saw Darv and Bobby coming back and said. "Hey guys, we got us a live wire Safety guy here by the name of Gene who can ask more questions than anyone I've met lately, other than my wife when I come home too late, so, maybe you all can help me answer some of the ones that I have so far avoided or neglected to answer."

With that, Keith got the permits and gave them to Gene the Safety Engineer to look at. Gene, took them out of their plastic sleeve and was looking them over when Bobby and boss Darv came up the steps to the work site. Bobby had sort of briefed Darv about the problem, in his own way, about the connector wire problem within the vault, and Darv went over to the vault area and looked into the vault where Keith was sitting.

Darv then acknowledged the Safety Engineer and introduced himself. The Safety Engineer introduced himself as Gene with his company called "Safety Coordinators 'R' Us" and said that his company was kind of a girl Friday kind of business, that he was more than just officially trained with both OSHA 30-hour Construction and OSHA 30-hour General Industry Training, including his DOE 40-hour training from a nuclear plant that he worked at, just so everyone understood that he just didn't have only an OSHA 10-hour training, and, explaining that he was providing temporary contract safety over-site at a moment's notice, with his Company's motto of "You Call Us & We Haul Ass", which was also on the back of his 9-mile orange colored sweat shirt and which was also visible through his yellow net safety vest with a back-up sticker on his hard hat which showed a caricature of the south end of a kickin' ass in a hustle headed north, and, a-draggin' along a "Safety First" sign behind itself, all of which was covered up partly by a dust cloud. He went on to say, that he even considered going for the additional training for becoming an OSHA Instructor as they seemed to have more steady work, but, he thought that it was totally cost prohibitive, with but few fleeting moments of pleasure, and, the positions were absolutely ridiculous, and, he added, not really much different than sex.

Darv then said. "I think I remember you from the Electro-Precipitation project here last year. Didn't you work with Wagman Electric on their way up for their set up?" He asked.

"Yea, I've worked for most of the companies on the projects here at one time or another, I go out the gate with one company one day and come back in with another the next, but I've never worked for your Tele-Masters Communications Company, here yet. But, we would be glad to if you ever need some good professional safety oversight." He said.

"By the way, weren't you one of the ones with your company who had an ongoing problem with not being able to pass your drug tests on your pre-entry piss tests?"

"Same company, but not me, I've never had any question on my integrity, I've always been clean as a hounds tooth and have never missed a day's work, I'm proud to say, but, we did have a few older retired guys, who were out here working part time to supplement their retirement, who were medicated up to the gills, and, they had some "false negative" or "false positives" kind of problems here and there, but nothing of a serious nature that I ever heard about." He responded.

Then, the Safety man looked down again at Keith, and said. "Hey, what is that insect crawling there in the upper right corner of the vault?"

Keith looked, saw the insect, and, jumped up in one movement to get his legs out of the vault and yelled. "Damn, I didn't see that thing. I think it's one of them damn recluse spiders." Then, he began stomping the thing to death, squashing the thing to smithereens, would have been a better explanation.

The Safety man said. "Now, see here, that is all but "at risk behavior", no different than having your boots untied, steppin' on your shoe string, falling down and breaking you neck, you could have been bitten, and then, that would have been an OSHA recordable injury because he would have had to have gotten a prescription, and maybe even a lost time accident if he couldn't have worked. This type of thing is what we are tryin' to correct. Attitude and awareness is what we are trying to preach. It is the "what if" scenario, where it is what could have happened could have happened. Don't you all see that?"

Keith responded. "Maybe it was a HoBo spider, or, maybe it was something else for all I know, anyway, it is dead and I killed it, and, I even feel bad about getting all excited about it."

Gene responded. "Well, that is a good example as to why I am out here and assigned the job I have and how I go about preventin'
accidents on a daily basis. That is what I am good at and I do it well if I say so myself."

"Well, thank you for that, Gene, anyway, do we have some kind of a problem here, with this job, or what?" Darv asked.

The Safety Engineer looked at Darv, then at Keith, and then at Bobby, then, back to Darv, and said. "We, don't have a problem, you all have the problem, this area is not barricaded in accordance with plant requirement, in order to keep someone from stepping off into that open hole there, breaking their legs or even their neck, and I have no choice but to write you up for allowing the exposure of such a dangerous open hazard, and I have no choice, but to close this job down until the situation is corrected, but, I won't write you all up for the Brown Recluse problem, because, obviously, Keith corrected that at the time, although he should have seen it earlier on than what he did, and, you have to admit, that he was at risk for that thing biting him before he got his leg out of that vault. But, I am not running you all out the gate over the infraction, I'll leave that up to the company Superintendent."

Keith interrupted. "This is not a "hole", Mister Gene, Safety guy, it is a "vault", so don't put it down on your report as a "hole", because if you say it is a "hole", then you are insinuating that we might need a "hole watch", as if it were classified as some sort of a confined space, and, I already told you that it is not big enough, deep enough, wide enough or open enough, to be classified as such, whether permit or non-permit required, at most, as it is, it is a no permit required vault, dumb ass."

"What's the identifier on your vault there?" Gene asked, but not fully ignoring Keith's dumb ass remark. "Did the dumb ass having his feet hanging down inside it know what it was before he saw the Recluse?"

Keith looked down on the side of the vault lid, then replied. "This is vault R-127, but I don't think you will find it put on the master plan yet, because it is still considered under construction and in the process of yet being finally fabricated, and has not yet been signed off by operations and maintenance or released to production, or, otherwise assigned any particular functional requirements."

The Safety Engineer was writing as Keith, Darv and Bobby looked on. Gene then added. "Darv, you know that I will also have to advise the area plant Superintendent and the Bull Steward who has oversight for this area."

Darv responded. "That's fine, we have no problem with that, however, we have barricade tape right here on site, and, we can have this area barricaded within a few minutes or so, so, you will have to also write it up on your write up that the situation was all but corrected immediately."

Hearing Darv's comment, Bobby jumped up off of his five gallon bucket again and grabbed the role of yellow "Hazard – Keep Out", barricade tape. He said. "I'm on it! I'm on it! I'm on it like stink on shit! It is all but done already!" Then, he tied one end off on an I-beam, or, then again, maybe it was an H-beam, and, began barricading the area, climbing in and out and around the superstructure, and, in the process, he asked Gene if he would kindly step out of his way, as, he was in the process of trying to do his job and to get the violation abated.

Darv stepped back with Gene while Bobby barricaded himself and Keith in around the vault. Darv then asked. "You said that you would be required to notify the area plant Superintendent, and, I have no problem with that, but, on second thought, why would you have to notify the Bull Steward, as, we are non-union, and, all of our workers on site are all classified as "Technicians", so where do you get your requirements for that?" Darv asked.

"It's no more or no less than just common protocol, and, I just do what I am told." Gene responded, then, he stepped away from the area and called on his handie-talkie radio, first appearing to be calling the Superintendent, then secondly, to also be appearing to call the Bull Steward, by just listening to his end of the conversations.

Then, Gene came back up the steps to the worksite, and, briefed Darv. He began by saying. "Darv, your company really needs to get your personnel enrolled in some health and fitness program. Both Keith and Bobby here apparently have obvious needs in that respect. Can you see that, or, do you understand or know what I mean?"

Keith heard Gene's comment and responded first, with. "Hey, Mister Gene the Safety guy, looks like the pan calling the kettle black here, just look at your own beer belly a-hangin' out over your belt, I mean, I at least play golf to stay in shape."

Bobby backed Keith up by saying. "Yea, and on a regular basis, sometimes every day, I play pool to stay in shape, what do you think of that?"

Gene, the Safety guy just shrugged his shoulders, and said. "Well, all I can do is recommend and advise, it is up to you all to carry the ball on down field from here on."

The Superintendent must have been nearby, because no sooner than Gene had made his call, here he was, climbing up the steps to the work area. "Mornin' Darv. What have you all got going on here? Oh, hi Gene, you done found some more problems? "

Darv acknowledged the Superintendent's arrival, Gene saluted him, and, then stepped over to the superintendent and said. "Well, Bruce, it's like this. I had to write the job up here for not being barricaded, but, Bobby here, took care of that, although I almost wrote him up for not being tied off in the process of barricading, or, maybe he still is taking care of that, so, I will have to report in my write-up that the infraction and situation was corrected following soon after the time of the findings."

"Report that the situation was corrected at the time of findings and make sure to use the word "immediately" with no mention of a hole." Bobby added.

"I like to hear things like that, and, I wish I could hear more like it throughout the work site." Bruce responded.

Gene looked back at Keith, who was now, again, sitting with his legs again dangling down in the vault, and said. "Keith, I know you from somewhere, but I can't quite place it. What do you do when you aren't working out here?"

Keith responded. "Well, I'm a golfer, and a shooter, mostly, just to get my mind off of the work out here."

Gene then responded. "That's probably where I know you from. I shoot down at the Pyramid range when I have the extra time and the extra money or sometimes when they offer free shells for skeet practice."

Keith added. "Yea, I think I may have seen you down there at one time or another. I've acted as range officer there more or less on a regular basis. Come on down, I'm usually there on Tuesday nights."

Bobby chimed in. "I'm down there on Thursdays and we usually have hot seasoned salsa and ranch flavored tortilla chips with hot melted cheese that you would die for, but you won't see that on Keith's night, because he is tighter than the bark on a tree."

Keith looked around, rolled his eyes, but didn't say anything further.

"OK, Keith, Bobby, Darv and Bruce, I may see you then, sometime on into the near future for one thing or another, anyway, good luck with your problems as you may encounter them, you know, that a problem is only another door to an another opportunity. Well, with that, my part of the job is done here, so, I will take my leave, and leave you all's future problems for someone else to solve." Gene said, as he bid everyone a good bye and headed down the steps, leaving the work site.

Darv called out behind him as he left, and said. "Gene, it will always be a good day when we see you out here, your presence is like a fresh bouquet of flowers out here on a dreary job site."

"What kind of future problems do you suppose he is referring to Darv?" Bruce asked, after Gene had left.

"Well, Bruce, it appears here, that maybe two different companies, maybe even more, pulled these bundles of control wires from opposite ends, with both ends junctioned out here in this here vault, but, there are no identifiers showing which wires are which. That means, every single pair of these non-colored wires will need be traced back to their origin prior to connection. This is the kind of thing that couldn't get any worse, and, that is why I put my best two Technicians to work here, Keith and Bobby, because they always have the right answers and know how to solve these type of problems on a daily basis." Darv said.

Bobby responded. "Oh, it could be worse, what if the wires were all different colors on each end?"

Keith responded. "It would be the same, no different, the problem would be the same, or, in your words, samo samo, dumb ass."

"Don't dumb ass me, Keith, I know where yer' comin' from and where ya' got yer' skeletons hid away in yer' damned closet." Bobby said.

Bruce looked over in the vault from behind the barricade tape, then said. "You know, this is not what I would call just a normal problem, but, I am sure that someone from either engineering, planning, maintenance or operations can be of help and I am also sure, that they can solve it for you, or, if not, they know who to pass it on to, so, let me call them and get them on site to take a look. Maintenance has some oversight and Operations can provide some support and guidance for you in your predicaments, and, the planning department can get engineering to maybe get a better lay-out and set-up for you." With that, he turned around, bid the group good bye, pulled out his radio, walked down the stairs, and made a couple quick contact calls, and, was gone for good, out of further earshot.

In the meantime, before anyone had time to go take a piss, here comes the Assistant Junior Bull Steward purposely stomping up the steps to the vault area, yelling out. "Who's in charge here? Who's your union rep? What's your problem? Why was I called out here?"

Darv met him at the top of the steps. "Hi Claude, there's no problem here, the Safety Rep wrote us up for not barricading, but, we took care of it, and, it is settled. Bruce was here and is on-line trying to getting us some company assistance in some of the other matters."

Claude responded. "Darv, you know, you would have much less trouble out here, if you all were unionized and had some legal above board proper official employee representation, don't you know that, haven't you not yet come to that realization or conclusion?"

"Claude, it's like we all speak different languages, or we are in a miss-speak mode, like if I say, JU-CEE-DAT-MON-WOKIN-DONA-SRET-WIDA-SACH-IN-EESHAN, you would say. "What did you say?" And, I would say… DIDJU-CEE-DA-MAN-WAKIN-DONDA-STRET WIDA-SAK-IN-ES-HAN, and, you s again "What did you say?" and, I would say. DID YOU SEE THAT MAN WALKING DOWN THE STREET WITH A SACK IN HIS HAND, and, THEN, you would finally get it, you get the inflection, you get the meaning, you get the language. It is like that. Whether I say it in another language, or, whether I say it in miss-speak, you don't understand it until it comes to you and you finally get it. It is the same way between the different unions and the technicians, one does not understand the other, because they all speak different languages, or have different meanings for different terms and words and they talk at one another rather than to one another, but, in the beginning, they do not communicate with one another."

Claude responded. "That is so much bullshit, and, I know bullshit when I hear it, when I see it, when I smell it, however and but, just for the record, I have never tasted it or felt it for that matter, but I know when it is real and up in your face."

Darv responded. "Claude, no offense meant, but, you and I have known one another for years, and, you know, that our company has never been unionized, and, never will be, as we have no need whatsoever for any union, as we pay more than what union wages would pay for the same work. If the fact of the matter were truly known, we pay better than most any of the unions that you represent out here on the job. We make wire-up end terminal connections only. We do not pull wires or climb poles, which is in the electrician's bailiwick, we don't operate equipment, all we do is come in, work our magic, and make sure everything runs when someone hits the button or throws the switch, all on a letter contract and only paid for hour by hour on an as needed basis, to deliver a service as a sub-contractor, most usually under some union contractor, I might mention. You know, back in the fifties, unions represented more than fifty percent of the work force, yet, today, they represent less than ten percent, there is a simple reason for that, and you could research it if you so choose."

Claude, seemingly ignoring Darv at first, then looked over into the barricaded area, and looked down in the vault area, then, responded to Darv. "Well, Darv, it's like this. I was here, when the unionized company pulled that batch of wires into the vault on the right, and, I was here when the another unionized company pulled that batch of wires into the vault on the left, and, both of them were hard cast union in agreement by vote, and, they did their job as it was contracted and, they both finished their job in fine form in accordance with that contract at the time. However, you, I am sure, will eventually learn the names and the games of those two companies, sooner or later, but, because, you are not union as you say, and, never will be, again as you say, however, you most likely will never come to know why they had to do what they did, why it was done in such a fashion, why it was so required of them, why you got the contract to put on the so-called finishing touches, why it all will never come to fruition, why it will never work, or, even the why of your problem here now, or even, why you and your company will be blamed for the eventual failure sometime on into the distant future, when the job is finalized, if it ever is, for that matter."

Darv responded smiling. "Claude, it is always good to see you. You are such a cheerful soul, and, I am so happy that you had the time to stop by. Now, I know why they call you "Easy Ely". You are so like just a ray of sunshine bursting through the gray overcast clouds, out here on the job site. I hope to see you again the next time that we are here or out and about. Just look out for, THAT MAN YOU MIGHT SEE WALKING DOWN THE STREET WITH A SACK IN HIS HAND."

With that, Claude, with a dumb look on his face, wheeled around on his heels and headed down the steps and out of the work area without further word, except for an arm wave for so much as a good bye with a good riddance thrown in on the side.

He no sooner left, and, again before anyone could go take a piss, than, Darv got a call on his cell phone to someone or somebody. "Are you sure?" Darv was overheard to have said. Then, he mumbled something else that no one heard. After the phone call, Darv came back to the work area and announced that we were to immediately get a welder, a union welder if you will, or, maybe an equivalent union boilermaker welder, to close up all hatches, covers, tops and plates, to tack weld them all shut on each corner, including the switch gear and switch plates, finish the shift, give the work site a final inspection and provide a check out report to the contractor, exit the worksite, and,

turn in all badges at the gate. Darv added on for Keith and Bobby to also report to the company's shop in the morning for reassignment on another job, as, this job was complete, done up, finished, over, and finalized for and into the foreseeable future, and, it wasn't even lunch time yet. With that, Darv indicated that he was headed back to the shop.
Keith and Bobby complied to the best of their abilities. And, after the union welder showed up, they provided him with a proper work permit, signed off on an authorization for him to do his job, set up a fire watch for him, and directed him to tack weld the vault, any and all of the other openings, switch gear, plates and/or covers, and after shielding themselves from his arc, they stayed with him to make sure everything was secured, then Bobby and Keith headed out to the gate to turn in their badges and to make good their exit according to assigned plan. Another day, on the job, with everything all screwed up (whoops) all covered up and behind them.
On their way out to the gate, Keith asked Bobby. "Bobby, did you ever read that book "Katcher out in the Rye", written by some shirt tail kin of President Kannedy?"
"Yea, I think we had to read it in high school, but I don't remember much about it now. I don't remember that there was really all that much to it." Bobby responded.
Keith came back with. "That's it Bobby, that's it. That's what it's all about. There was not much to it. That book was one of the most ridiculous pieces of literature, if you could even call it that, that I have ever read, one of the worst, mostly no good for nothin', worthless, it was stupid, it was ignorant, it was a total waste of time, no plot whatsoever, where ever, nothing, some damn made up story about some damn made up guy, who was some damn piece of shit, a worthless shit even, who had no job, no income, wouldn't work, paid to go to school by his no clue whatsoever parents no less, and then the stupid shit ups and fails out of school because he didn't apply himself to his studies because he filled his stupid mind with some more stupid shit, or maybe girls, I can't remember which. Which, when you think about it all. It is about the same with the work out here in the plant. Don't you see that Bobby?"
Bobby was walking and looking straight ahead as if he knew where he was going. "No, Keith, I don't remember much about that book, I must have just read at it instead of really reading it. But I don't get what you're driving at."
Keith said. "See that is what I am talking about, that is the way it

really is, that is what it is all about. Sometimes, the girl will kiss you goodnight, then, other times, she will kiss some other guy goodnight, but, you will never know about the other guy, unless you are out there in the dark, a-hidin' and a-watchin', but then, if you are, you're not with the girl, so, there is very little salvation in a-knowin' what is happening out there somewhere in the dark recesses of the plant management mind, or, that of the union mind, for that matter. Even though you are in the dark and fed bullshit like they feed mushrooms in a dark cave, you can still learn shit that will rattle your brains, you know what I mean Bobby?"

Bobby just shook his head as he was turning in his and Keith's badge to the security guard, with the security guard asking Keith why he couldn't do it himself. "I don't know, I haven't had my brains rattled more than a couple times yet today." He said.

"Because, he has shit for brains, and, as a result he ain't got sense that God gave a goose. Hells bells! He can't even pound sand down a rat hole, or, pour piss out of a boot. Even if the instructions were written on the heel. Mostly, because he is blind in one eye, and, can't see much out of the other, and, to tell the truth, I'm not much better. When we are out on the job, it is like the blind leading the blind." Bobby responded.

"I see that you know him well enough. And, I can see just how you can even answer for him. You probably even do his work most of the time out there in the plant, if the truth were known." The security guard said.

Keith just rolled his eyes, opened his lunch box so the security guard could inspect it, and went on out through the turnstile with Bobby trailing along behind, maybe they would just have lunch in their truck before they went back to the shop. That was probably the smartest thing that he thought of all day, as, the truck had air conditioning. So, that was it, just another typical day at work in the plant and the trip back to the shop.

Six months passed by. Darv, Keith and Bobby had left their former employ, and, had started up their own company. They named it "Electric Techs", and, they had just received notice that they were the low bidder on their first contract at the plant. Upon arrival, they completed the orientation training, then, were escorted to the worksite by a new plant representative. Upon arrival at the worksite, the plant rep briefed them on the job at hand, filled out and approved their work permit with Darv signing the acceptance of the conditions and location. The plant rep then explained what was required of them.

"Here, we have an electric vault, I have noted that it was tack welded shut on all four corners, so, the first thing that you have to do is to get a welder to cut it open for you. Inside, you will find several bundles of wires, the wires need to be separated and identified according to this schematic that I have provided as part of the work permit. The job is estimated to take three personnel at least nine or ten days to accomplish. This is your assignment. Welcome aboard, and, good luck. By the way, do work safe." And, with that he left the worksite. Darv looked at Keith, Keith looked at Bobby, and, Bobby looked back at Darv. "Well, let's get to work. You all get the worksite barricaded and I'll go get us a welder."

The dreamer was glad to have awakened from this dream, at least to end the nights work. And, he queried himself, why not dream up a vacation dream, or a cruise dream, or a traveling dream, or why not have a beach with a palm tree or two with a gentle sea breeze, just thrown in on the side of the dream, or better yet, why not a little more excitement or have some shoot-em up adventure in a dream, instead of what plant workers know to be the way things really are anyway, after all, work dreams only raise the question of which reality is which, or, what the benefit of it all is, or was, in the past, or possibly what it could be some time on into the future, once you have awakened, that is, if you ever come to know the definition of "is", or "did", or whatever. Either way, neither you nor anyone else ever will get paid for any of it, at all, or ever come out even with the amount of labor expended. Damn, the dreamer just thought, why couldn't it have been one of those union dreams, maybe the Bull Steward's written complaint to the Superintendent could have gotten some of us some back pay.

Herein lays the secret to the managing of politics at work and still getting some work done in the process, and, getting paid for it in the long run, that is, if the readers were even reading or listening even a little bit to a story that did not even have a semblance or a glimpse of a plot and was probably one of the worst shit pieces of writing that they have ever read, and, even come to wonder why they had even considered to start it in the first place or finish it off in the second place. So there! A crude good morning to you too.

THE LAST FAST TALKING ANGEL

Fred, had his suspicions up. He had seen someone, most likely a culprit no less, who seemed to be following him home from the tavern, not just on occasion, but more than once, over the past month, and, he decided to take the law into his own hands, and, find out for himself, just who this wannabe culprit was, and, to bring this following to a head, and, to end it once and for all, even if he had to knock the guy down and drag him out himself. Mona, his wife, had told him that he was acting paranoid. But, he knew, down deep in his heart, that just because you are paranoid, it doesn't mean that there is not still someone out there hiding behind a bush trying to get you.

Tonight, could be the night. This would be a church night for his wife, she would take the car, and, he could hoof it down to the tavern for a few hands of poker in the back room with a couple of the guys, and, be back home, before she got in from church, just like he has done many times in the past. But, the fact that someone was a-following him, not all of the time, but too many times not to be concerned, was enough, or, maybe even more than enough for him to try to do something about it.

He went out to the shed and hunted up his axe, not to use on the culprit, but to cut himself a walking stick that he could also use for a club of defense if need be. He decided on some second growth hickory, where a hickory tree had been cut down, and, the growth from the roots brought up another sapling, which was the toughest wood that he ever heard anything about. He picked out what he thought was the best of the best, and he cut the sapling out and trimmed it up with his axe. A mighty fine walking stick if I say so myself, he thought, and, a finer whoopin' club if need be. He felt good about this maybe being the very night, that he could settle up with whoever had more than just a passing interest in him, maybe the culprit wanted to rob him, or do him harm, or, just to knock him down and take what little money that he made playing cards down at the tavern. Who knows what else the culprit might have in mind, being as persistent as he seemed to have become.

He put the axe away, then, came up to the house, leaned the walking stick up against the house out on the porch, and went in for supper.

Mona his wife, had called him two or three times already, but, he was too busy with his own business at hand.

"Wash up Fred, your supper's on the table." Mona said. "What you doin' out there choppin' wood?" She asked.

"I done got and made me a good walkin' stick." He said, walking back into the kitchen after he had washed his hands.

He and Mona had supper, then, Mona got ready for church, said that she was picking up someone else for service, so, he cleaned up the supper table and washed the dishes for her just to help out some. Shortly thereafter, Mona came back into the kitchen, gave him a hug and a kiss on the cheek, and told him that she loved him, just like she always did, and, he gave her the same and told her that he loved her too, then, Mona headed out toward church, driving herself in the car.

Mona had patience, he thought. She was a school teacher for years, she had to have patience wit all of those kids. Although she was now retired, she still filled in teaching now and then as a substitute. Just like he did, in his own way, he thought, a-filling in now and then at the bar, where he had tended drinkers for years, before he finally gave it all up for retirement. She had heard the kids stories while they were growing up, first hand in school, and, he had heard their parents stories in the bar, the other side of the tales that were told, off and on over the years. He remembered, that he and Mona, used to try to put all of the stories together night after night, before they went to sleep.

As soon as Mona was out of sight on down the road, he straightened things up a bit, turned on a light in the living room, locked up, and headed out himself toward the tavern on foot. He took the hickory walking stick and practiced swinging it back and forth, knocking down some weeds, just to get the feel of it, while taking his shortcut down through the woods.

He made it to the tavern, went to the back room where his friends were, had a couple of drinks, and played several hands of poker, but didn't do all that well, as, he figured that he just about broke even, all in all, as usual, and, watching the time, because he sure wanted to be back home before Mona got in from church service. He estimated the time that he had to leave, then, told the guys that the next hand would be his last, and, after that, he scraped his winnings off of the table, mostly small change, and, headed out the door to go back home. As he came out of the tavern, he noticed that it was just beginning to get dark, so, he decided to hurry up and hoof it on home. He again tried out his walking stick to see just how good it would be as a club while on his way back along the shortcut through the woods, swishing it back and forth through the weeds.

Now, tonight, here and again, while looking back time and again, and watching close, he finally caught sight of the shadowy culprit, a-trailing him again, on his way home, again along the same path, through the woods, the culprit holding off, just far enough behind, but still close enough to watch, while he was making his way, along the pathway, so, he started making up his plan as he went. As he rounded a bend along the wooded path, he ducked down, and, hid himself behind an autumn olive bush, one of the places which he had previously chosen to meet his plan of attack if need be. He held his club tight with both hands as the culprit rounded the bend, then, when he caught up, he pounced, he jumped out from behind the bush with his hickory club held high, and by surprise, he knocked the culprit down in the pathway with only one blow of the club to the culprit's backside. He had aimed for his head, but the club caught on a tree limb and ricocheted into the guys rear end. Then, he jump on him, with arms and legs a-flailin' in the ensuing fight, he finally got the best of the culprit. He struggled to get himself up on top and astride of the culprit, overpowering him, and, pinned the culprit's hands and arms down with the hickory club, while a-holding him on the ground.

"Who are you? What do you want? Why are you followin' me?" Fred demanded.

The culprit yelled back at him. "Get off me, get off me, you are a-hurtin' my arms, I can't breathe!"

"Why you been following me? Why?" Fred demanded. "If you don't tell me, so help me, I'll club you good, up the side of your dumb ass head!" He added.

"Don't hit me again. I'm not out to hurt you any, if anything, I'm tryin' to help you if you only had sense enough to know it!" The culprit said. "So, just let me up, please!"

"Help me? You, helpin' me? I don't need your help! Talk? You want to talk? You can talk right where yer' at! I want to know why you done been followin' me off and on over the last month or so, and, again tonight, why? Why are you doin' this?" Fred yelled in the face of the culprit. "Did my old lady hire you to track me from the tavern for some no good reason?" He added.

The culprit struggled just to breath beneath the weight of Fred sitting on top of him. "I can't hardly breath, please let me up, I'll tell ya', I'll tell ya'!" He said. "I said please, didn't I?"

"Tell me what? What ya' got to tell me except what I want to know?" Fred said.

"OK, OK, whether you believe it or not, I'm your guardian angel! I'm supposed to be a-lookin' out after you, just to make sure you got home OK. OK? So, now you know, the cat is out of the bag. So, let me up! I can't talk down here on the ground like some animal that walks and talks, and crawls on its belly like a reptile!" The culprit said.

Fred backed off some with the pressure of the club on the culprit's arms, but still held him down, still sitting on him, still astride the culprit. "This sounds like some cock and bull story, I've never heard of such in my entire life time! What do you mean you are an angel?"

The culprit responded. "I mean you no harm. If you will just let me up, I promise, I will tell you anything you want to know."

Fred relieved some of the pressure on the culprit, but still held him to the ground. "OK, I'll let you up, but, if you make any funny moves, I'll whoop on you 'til sunrise. I'll club you up one side of yer' head and down the other, and you'll never forget it. Do you understand me? Do you?" He demanded.

Fred pulled back the club, still holding it tightly in both hands, stood up, and, backed off a step or two from the culprit. The culprit sat up, rubbing his arms and hands, then got up, rubbing his backside where the old man had hit him when he had knocked him down. "It's like this." The culprit said. "You done caught me, off my guard, I might say, which means, that you are pretty good, physically that is, for your age. But, I'm caught, I admit it. But, in my own defense, I maintain, that I have your best interest at heart, in my heart that is. I am supposed to be a-lookin' out for you and a-lookin' over you instead of you a-lookin' over me. You may or may not believe me just yet, but, I can prove it all if you just give me a chance or an opportunity. I am, your guardian angel, or, supposed to have been up to now. What I need to know, is, just how can you see me? I am supposed to be invisible to you! Something here is awry with either me or you, because this kind of thing is never supposed to happen, and, I can't say that it has ever happened to me or any of the other angels that I ever heard of, before this. So, just how can you see me? How do you go about it?" He added on and asked..

"I can see ya' outta' the corner of me good eye as if yer' a-movin' shadow." Fred said.

The culprit leaned forward, again rubbing his backside, but the old man drew back the club, so, the culprit backed up a little on the path. "Honest to god, the culprit said, I don't know what went wrong, or maybe something went right, I don't know either, but if you can see me, something is definitely different, which may be good, or, may be right, between the two of us, but you have me at an odds and under threat, so, I may as well tell you whatever you want to know." The culprit said.

"Are you really an honest to God angel?" Fred asked.

"Well, yes, I guess that I am." The angel responded.

"How come you don't have wings? You seem to have bones and muscles and sinews, you don't otherwise look like any angel that I ever imagined!" Fred said.

"Is there somewhere we could go and just sit down and talk and maybe get a cup of coffee? Maybe where it is a little more light. It is starting to get dark out here and its getting a little chilly, and, I'm cold from wallowing around down there on the cold ground." The culprit both asked and said.

Fred felt that he had gained control and had some power over the culprit, half-way considered that he could over power him again if he had to, after all, the culprit was not a very big guy, although he appeared young, it didn't appear that he was much of a fighter. He felt that if there was any further danger that he could handle it, so, he told the culprit to lead the way on down the path, and, he would follow and tell him when to turn right of left, all the time following along behind the culprit with the hickory club held high and at the ready position to pound the shit out of the guy if he had to. Besides, his wife Mona would be headed home from church shortly, and, he sure wanted to beat her home.

They arrived at the house, and, Fred told the culprit, to go ahead and open the door and showed him the way into the house and into the kitchen, all the while, holding the hickory club at the ready position. He told the culprit to sit down at the table, and, he put on a pot of coffee, then sat down at the opposite end of the table, across from the culprit, still with the hickory club at the ready.

"What's yer' name?" Fred asked. And, he noticed that the culprit was coming in better focus.

The culprit-alias-angel responded. "I am not sure that I ever had a name. I am not sure that any of the other angels have names either. At least I never knew any that had names, and, none of them ever called me by any name. They just yell "hey you" or nod their head at me and I get their message to come or go."

"Where do you come from?" Fred asked.

"I'm not rightly sure of that either. I have some ideas, but other than that, I haven't had any of the other angels ever tell me any more than what it is that I have come to know. In some respects, I am like you, you are from here, and, I am from here too." The angel said.

"You have the appearance of being made out of flesh and blood, skin and all, is that the whole of you, or, what else might you be put together with? You got bones and sinews?" Fred added.

Meanwhile, the coffee was percolating on the stove.

"Well, on one hand, I can be like flesh and blood, when and if I so want, that is, if the occasion ever calls for it, I guess. I feel more comfortable that way, or, on more important occasions, I can choose to be seen or not to be seen, however, I mostly choose not to be seen usually, but, can change a little, somewhat like a chameleon, if you can imagine how they do that, depending upon the circumstance, since that is what mostly alters cases, without respect to any facts of any matter. Not too much different than when you humans commune with one another on a daily basis, or, in a dream at night in your sleep. Not too much different, overall." The culprit-now-tuning-angel said.

"Please do not speak in riddles. I never did like riddles in school. Mostly because I never liked school either. I have a need to know! Just answer my questions! How old are you anyway? You don't look old enough to even be dry behind your ears!" Fred said.

"Well, that is another thing that I do not rightly know, right now, as, I have never paid all that much attention to the time of things and all, as, I have to compare my age with everything else that has happened that I can remember, or maybe even try to think about." The now, more self-proclaimed angel and wannabe former culprit responded.

OK, so, what are some of the earliest memories that you can recall, just spit it out, say, as an example?" Fred queried again.

"Well, honest to god, I do remember early on, all of those slimy creatures and wild animals roaming hither and yon, from one end of the earth to the other, about the same time as it was summer time almost everywhere in the world at the same time." The so called angel now questioning his culprit status answered.

"Well, so far, I have determined that you mostly don't answer questions very well. You don't say god with a capital "G" like I would expect an angel to do, of all people, which is almost sacrilegious if you ask me, almost like you are not really sure that the old man upstairs is really a-watchin' what you do. Too, you seem surprised that I have the upper hand, hickory club and all. However, If you are a guardian angel, you sure ain't very good at it! Either that, or, you have fallen down on the job or need to be retrained in your occupation. Or, do you even have a job?" Fred asked.

"You keep changing the subject. You're a-bouncin' around in your questions worse than I am in my answers. I can only answer of what I know." The wannabe angel trying to put the culprit tag behind him pleaded.

The coffee had quit percolating, so, Fred got up, got a couple cups, poured two cups of coffee and sat them on the table, and, sat out some sugar and cream, with a couple spoons. Then, he sat down again across the table, still holding the hickory stick, and, resumed the conversation.

"I'm just asking questions of my interest in tryin' to prove you up to me to what you say you is. Again, do you have a job or not?" Fred re-asked. Then, he noticed that the culprit was in a little more than full focus, and, could see him well in the lamp light.

"Well, yes, I guess that everyone and everything has some job or another, no matter how large or how small, even humans, even other living things. My job, I guess, is that of being a guard, that is why I am in the guardian angels kind of business thing of weights and balances, debits and credits, ups and downs, and ins and outs. To oversee, to watch, or, for instance, as an example, to serve and protect. This is not really dis-similar to your human police officers or military requirements." The exclaiming wannabe angel and possible former culprit explained.

"What exactly do you guard? What do you guard against? What is your purpose of being a guard in the first place? Why are you supposed to be guarding me?" Fred questioned more than once with more than one question.

"I guard all of the prisoners. It just happens, that your wife has prayed nightly for angels to come and escort you safely home from the tavern. I am your answer to her prayers and your wellbeing is my answer. Some nights, it has been me, while other nights, it has been some other angel, probably one that you didn't or couldn't see. At least, I never heard of any of them getting' hit with a hickory stick!" The curt, proclaimed angel now rejecting the culprit title, responded curtly.

"Prisoners? What prisoners? What prisoners do you so guard? What prisoners are you talkin' about?" Fred spluttered.

"Sorry to break it to you badly, but, all the forms of life are prisoners here on earth. I guard the lives of all living things, as, all living things have been placed here in this prison, of which I, along with all of the other angels, oversee, watch, keep to the best of our ability, and, sometimes, even enjoy." The now more convincing sounding angel explained, along with a lesser look as a culprit.

"Prison? Of what prison do you speak? Where is this so called prison? Do you work there?" Fred again spluttered.

"This prison earth. To explain, again, since you didn't get it the first time. The earth itself, is a prison, it is my prison, and, it is your prison, just as it is for all other forms of life, they are all imprisoned herein, or, to soften it a little for you, you could say, perhaps to be more politically correct, the living things are stored here, however, it is with no chance of escape for any of them, or you, or me, for that matter, although of late, there are some nations spending a lot of money trying to get out of outer space, however, they really have no place to go if they ever escape in the first place, and, they would never live long enough to get where they were trying to go in the second place. So, therefore, there is not much hope in their trying to escape in the third place, except to just say that they tried." The now more politically correct so-called angel with a culprit background responded.

"Exactly, what do you mean, by the earth here being a prison, or some kind of storages, and, what has this got to do with you being a guardian angel, or, a guard, over all of the life forms? Or, a little more down to earth and more personal, what's it with you, a-followin' me home at night from the tavern? What has this got to do with that?" Fred queried again.

"Well." The now recognized wannabe angel with culprit status in question then said. "You asked me about my age. I told you of what I could first remember. That old memory was before I ever had a memory of the first humans. For instance. on one hand, I remember, at first, when the first humans came along, I thought that they were ugly, for the most part, but, as time went by, they got prettier, but, they didn't get any nicer, or neither did they all get along with one another, for one reason or another, whichever, and this form of life got harder and harder to guard, you just couldn't deal with any of them, because, you never quite knew what any one of them was going to do next. They eventually became totally unpredictable in all respects, especially the females. So, my job, just as all of the other guardian angels jobs, became harder and more difficult in the process. But, on the other hand, bein' pretty has become a thing of the past, and, now, most humans look like that they got hit with an ugly stick, or, a pump handle, that got stole by some vandal, or, maybe some, more than once." He apparently attempted to try to explain in his own way.

"You know, you do not answer the questions well, that you are asked. You ramble, you are not focused, and, damn if you are not even a-distractin' me! I would expect an angel to be on his toes and be in tip top shape both physically and mentally. Too, I would expect an angel to be a little better in the explanations of things. You never did answer me as to why you don't have or never had wings. I have a big problem with all of that, and, I am at my wits end in trying to get any information out of you. You are worse than some criminal at some interrogation where some detective has already advised that anything they say can and will be used against them in a court of law, and then, they still go on, like you are a-goin' on, and a-spillin' their guts, just to say that they spoke their mind at the time." Fred said.

Fred then got up from his chair, still holding the hickory stick at the ready position. Poured a couple more cups of coffee, and sat back down to resume the conversation. Noticing, that the culprit could be seen as plain as day, and almost as if he was human, even.

"Well, I will be the first to admit, that, I'm sure not on my toes in this case. Anyway, whether I am or not in other cases, I am what I am and I do what I do. But, if you don't mind, I would like to say, that there is some question whether or not that I actually have a mind, like some of you humans." The now more believable angel and recovering culpriholic guardian said somewhat defiantly.

"There you go again, talkin' more gobble-de-gook nonsense. But, now, let me get this straight for once, before we go any further." Fred said. "You are here, you say, to guard life forms that none of which has any chance of escape whatsoever. All forms of life, which, is contained, within the confines of this planet earth a-floatin' round and about this solar system, which has no hope whatsoever, of ever being able to go to another planet in some other distant solar system, so as, to propagate life in some other environment than that of which we all are so contained, stored, or imprisoned. That type of guard duty, in my opinion, any fool could do, it would seem to be easy, a so-called slam-dunk, under any set of facts or circumstances, would it not?"

"I think that you have it right, in a nutshell, if you will, and, you could even get the blue ribbon for hitting the nail right on the head after you grabbed the brass ring." The angel responded. "That is partly the reason that we do not have to do any more than that it is that we do, other than watch, which, in some respects, can even be a fun thing to do, if you could so imagine it. Although, some of the more personal things that we oversee, especially some of the interactions between the males and the females, I personally, have to even hide my eyes, once in a while, or, maybe sometimes." The explaining angel and somewhat certifiably recovered culpriholic tried to explain.

"You don't talk much like I think that an angel would talk. What other proof do you provide that you are really an angel, and, not some looney bird loose from the care of some insane asylum or psycho-sanitarium? Tell me something that I don't know, that might prove you up a little better." Fred both asked and said.

"Well, for one thing, and apparently, with respect to you, I am no more than a talking head, for whatever reason besides just talking, which I am not supposed to do under any circumstance. On one hand, I will probably get into some kind of trouble for it, or that, sooner or later, when my superiors hear of it all, I'll probably get thrown into some other prison in some other galaxy. Otherwise, either way, I couldn't be any worse off than what I am, yet, on the other hand, I am relatively sure, that I am somewhat safe, as, angels never talk, otherwise, for whatever reason, I never figured it all out myself, it is just the way we are, or, they are, as, for example, the plants never talk, other life forms do not talk, only humans do, but, well, maybe some or a few of the other animals have some communication methods of sorts, but otherwise, they never say and tell, or play that game as well, with anyone, with themselves, or, with humans otherwise. So, my superiors would have only heard it from one of those Irish a-wantin' wind at their back, or maybe you, or, maybe your cohorts, or, maybe even your wife when she is a-prayin' for you to just get home safe from the tavern, and, I think that I could deal with that, if and when it ever happened again sometime on into the future." The now somewhat put down, dejected and despondent appearing angel responded with a little less of a snitch of culprit status in the mind of Fred.

Fred countered. "Well, I asked you for some proof about you bein' a real angel or not, and, you give me some cock and bull story about not talking, which doesn't' make any sense whatsoever to me, and then, had the gall to not answer another question, then, just threw in some other baloney on one side, along with some of the other things that you just happened to throw in on the other side, included some stuff in and excluded some other stuff out. Anyway, you may not want to tell me any more for one reason or another, whichever, but, all in all, you have peaked my interest in you, however, I am more interested in your direct interests with the humans and me with my tavern hopping habit in particular. So, what is that particular interest?"

The now self-called angel and somewhat culprit denying guardian, appeared to think, then, responded. "Well, the human bunch, in particular, the ones who have become total fools, worldwide, just for past time, because they have no other reason, have loved themselves into generally all but becoming overpopulated, it is worse than almost like an infestation of both lice, mites and fleas on an itchy raw mangy dog, as, it could not get any worse if they had of planned it somehow. Today, they totally take up too much of my time, and all of the other guardian angels time, I might add, and that stresses not only me, but all of the other angels trying to maintain their guard as well. The humans have this damned inborn tendency, to be rebellious and to fight amongst themselves almost for past time, they always have, and, they always will, and, that is why they are here in the first place if not even for the second place thrown in just for shits and grins."

He went on. "If I remember right, they were rebellious, from even before they stood up on their hind legs in the recent or distant past, and yet, in more recent years, have now developed an arsenal of ingenious weaponry of no less than that of a damned dangerous nature. Now, I, along with the other angels, have our own arsenal to use in retaliation. We have the lightning storms, we have earthquakes, we have volcanoes, we have tornadoes, we have the wind, which, I might say, that I like the best, expect when those Irish pray for wind to always be at their backs, as, that takes up totally too many angels to take care of with respect to time. Then, we have fires, we have cyclones and hurricanes, we have tsunamis and floods, we have droughts, we have pestilence, we have plagues and epidemics, we have those viruses that keep a-changin', we have that kind of physical power, but, it don't make the humans to be good, or, any better for that matter, no matter how much that we try in testing our natural weaponry out on them, trying to gain their attention or try to make them behave like you know they should. They just wait out the passage of the drought, or the rainstorm, or, whatever, then oil up their weapons, reload, gang-up, and start their dumb ass conflicts all over again, between themselves even, for god's sake, if they don't have anyone else to fight with, especially the males. And, usually, in their process, they damage the environment all to hell and back, more so, than the global warming thing." The now more confirming sounding angel and culprit thingy denying guardian said.

"Global warming?" The Irish, with a wind at their backs? Are you sure it just wasn't just their farts? The old man queried. "But now, besides that, it would be interesting to know something about, that is, if you ever existed during such an episode. The global warming thing, not the Irish fart thing. Say, if you did, what would be the history of it?" Fred said. "Hold that thought." He added.

Fred then got up from the table, told the explaining angel to sit tight, got them both a cup of coffee, sat the cups on the table, then resumed the discussion. Fred noted, that the culprit was now plain as anything, and, he had no problem seeing the whole of the culprit, for what he was.

The now self-proclaimed guardian angel without culprit status answered. "I have, and, I was there, in the middle of it all, I was on it like stink on shit, on more than one occasion, if I remember right. But, as it happened, there were none of the humans that recorded any of the happenings, mostly, because they did not write it up like they do today, or, pass any such information on to their politicians, for that matter, or, maybe, they just didn't pay that much attention to what was happening around them at the time, as, most of them were all caught up fightin' with their wives, and then using that as a reason for a-walkin' out only to fight amongst themselves down at the pub, then they all got together and went to the next town over, then it all went to hell in a hand basket from there. Anyways, most, or, some, or, maybe even all, if I can remember right about the global warming's, as there were more than just one. They were all, now that I think about it, at the end of one or another or most or all of the ice ages, whichever. Actually, at that time, compared to today, there were really not that many humans that we had to put up with, I mean that we still had to guard them, but, compared to now, the summer times were easy. Although, personally, I never did think that there were enough of us angels to go around in the first place in order to getting the job done that we were assigned to do, not then, and, not now, and on into the future for sure." The now more reasonable sounding angel said without reference to previous cupriholic activities.

"How in the hell did you ever get to be an angel? Surely not because the writer just finally gave up and up and gave you that title or just tacked it on at the end of the previous paragraph. You don't have, in my mind, what it takes to handle the job of what I think the job of an angel would be. I sure wouldn't hire you, not even at today's minimum wages in Illinois." Fred said.

The now more fully recovered culpriholic-but-not-yet-fully-named-to-full-angel-status, still trying to hold his own, before Fred's onslaught of questioning, continued. "Well, to tell you the truth, as, I am sure you would find it out sooner or later, I was with the bunch of angels that got the boot and was put out of heaven itself by the old man up topside at the time. The angels that were booted out, including me, I have to say, were all rebellious, just like everything else on the face of the earth happens to be rebellious, mostly the humans, I put all the blame on them, I might say, in my observation, that is just the way it is, just the way I see it. But, to give them some credit where credit is due, it was not just the humans who were rebellious from their beginning, most all of all of the other living things on the face of the earth were or is or will be rebellious, in one form or another at one time or another. Even the plants, just think about the noxious weeds, or, consider the bamboo, or, the honeysuckle vine, or sugar cane, plants that will try to take over their area and everything in it, totally, or, the animals, the bears, lions and tigers, not to mention all of the poisonous snakes a-slitherin' out and about, those things still give some of the angels, including me, the heebie-jeebies to this day. I mean, it don't stop there. Just think about the weather that you would be better off not thinking about. That is why everything is here, it has been put here, put in its place, and, under our guard, the angels that is, so as to never be able to leave the place. Everything on the face of the earth is rebellious for god's sake."

"There you go again." Fred said. "There you go, you don't even have enough respect to put a capital "G" in god. That is borderline sacrilegious, if I don't say so myself. You need to be more careful, the big man upstairs might have big ears, or, at least you need to be a little more politically correct in this day and time. I can begin to see the rebellious streak in even you. And, I might even go so far as to say, that if it were true, that you got your dumb ass booted out of heaven, then, it must have been your own damn fault. You should consider yourself lucky that you didn't get sent to hell in a hand basket, and, a-shakin hands with Dante down there."

"Been there, done that, and I am back again. So, OK, OK, I already told you that I am what I am, or, what I is, whatever the definition of "is" is. Anyway, would you mind, if I just stood up? My legs are almost cramping the shit out of me." The now apparently fully recovered culpriholic and now a little more accepted guardian angel said.

Fred ignored the culpriholic, alias angel, alias pseudo-angel, or alias dumb ass, whichever, or whatever the guy thought himself or called himself to be, and asked. "Back to the global warming thing. What kinds of things happened during those times? But, hold that thought."

Fred got up and got him and the angel another cup of coffee, then, sat back down to listen to the angel's explanation of things.

The now alias angel looked down, rubbed his legs to keep them from cramping, then responded. "Well, you don't need a geologist, or a meteorologist with a doctorate to tell you that the severity of all aspects of the weather increased in those days. The winds became greater in velocity, as the storms clouds went to higher altitudes and latitudes, the deluges of rain were followed by extended droughts, the deserts expanded, crops were destroyed, both humans and animals experienced starvation, with heat waves in the winter and snows in the summer, many life forms became sick, or even died off and became extinct. The only survivors, to speak of, were the ones along the coasts of the oceans, seas, and lakes, where island or lake effect weather prevailed, which included most of the peninsulas, where, because of the size of the land mass or, it caused or brought about its own weather. Most of those areas were inundated from time to time because of the severe weather; however, the humans in those coastal areas seemed to survive much better than those poor bastards who were inland."

"Is this somethin' that I need to be concerned about? Do you think me and my old lady would have to move some where's else? If that's the case, I probably wouldn't fix up the house. Would I have to come out of retirement or would Mona have to take some other job? Is it a-comin' soon, or, is this somethin' that I could hold off on until I situated and get myself in better straits?" Fred said.

Before the more or less now confirmed angel in Fred's mind, could answer, Mona's car pulled up in the driveway, distracting their conversation, and, Fred said. "That's Mona, you have to meet her, I want her to meet you. She will be so surprised."

Fred got up to go from the kitchen toward the living room where Mona came in the front door. But she got to the door before him and burst in saying. "Fred, you are not going to believe what I heard at church tonight!"

Fred interrupted. "Well, before you tell me that, I have something to tell you that is more important and someone for you to meet, someone who has impressed me somewhat. Hurry. Come in the kitchen." He said.

Mona followed Fred into the kitchen. Fred said. "Mona, I want you to meet someone who……"

But, Mona, interrupted him by saying. "Eugene, what in the world are you doing here? Did you walk away again? Are you out on a weekend pass? Where is your mother and father?"

Fred hesitated, then stuttered. "Mona, what are you talkin' about, I was just about to introduce you to this here...."

Mona interrupted again. "Fred, I know who this is. This is Eugene, I had him in my class years ago at school, when he still went to school, that is. Eugene has a bad case of Attention Deficit Disorder, why, he could have been the poster child for ADD, but he could never sit or even ever hold still enough for the photo-shoot. He's never been able to remember anything for more than three minutes after it was said, whether he said it or not, as, his short term interest span, shorted out a long time ago. Then, she turned her attention to Eugene and said. "Eugene, look at me. Does your mother and father know you are out here?" She asked.

"I don't know where mom and dad are." Eugene answered.

Mona continued. "Well, let me call them. They may want you to come home right away."

Fred appeared perplexed to say the least, and he tried to get a word in edgewise while Mona was going for the phone. But, declined to say anything further, being all but bewildered at what Mona had said. He first looked at Mona, then, he would look at Eugene, or, the angel, or, the culprit, whichever, then, he would look back again, then, decided the best thing he could do under the circumstance was to sit back down at the table across from Eugene and hold onto his hickory stick and to have another sip of coffee, and just wait out what was going to happen next.

Mona was looking up a number in the phone directory and trying to dial at the same time. She finished dialing, then, she began talking on the phone. "Yes, she said, this is Mona, I was trying to reach you, I was wondering if you knew that Eugene was over at our house. You didn't. Well, that figures, and well, he is, he is here now. Yes, he is here, sitting at the table with Fred. What? You have had the Sheriff out looking for him since this afternoon? Well, he is right here a-sittin' at our table and a-drinkin' coffee. You say he shouldn't have caffeine? Well, too late now. Do you want to come pick him up? No? You want the Sheriff to come pick him up? You will give them a call and tell them. OK, we will just stand by here, until they come. Yes, it has been a hectic day all in all. I know what you must be going through. Yes, I remember Eugene from school. Yes, he was a good boy, and, he always seemed to try hard to learn. I think he did very well under the circumstances. You say, he has walked away from the sanitarium a number of times. I didn't know that, I hadn't heard anything about it, except maybe someone at church might have mentioned it at one time or another, but, I didn't pay much attention to it all at the time. OK, we will just stand by here, and, I may give you a call back after the Sheriff arrives.

Fred was listening intently to Mona's conversation on the phone, and looking at Eugene who was now holding his head down halfway between his knees. "So." Fred said. "Your name is really Eugene. You told me before that you didn't even know your own name, so, now you do. You are not really an angel are you? You led me on. You put me on. You really played me out for a fool, didn't you? You think you are hot stuff, don't you? Well, you might have thought that you had me fooled a little, but, I knew it all the time, that you were not what you claimed to be. Hells bells, Eugene, you don't have any wings! Besides that, I can see you clear as a bell!"

In little or no time, the Sheriff's car pulled up in the driveway, and the deputies came in, introduced themselves, and talked with Eugene and with Fred and Mona, then, they took Eugene with them, and put him in the back seat of their car. Coming back in, one of the deputies thanked Mona and Fred for their patience, and told them that they would sure take good care of Eugene, as they remembered him from his escapades a-previous, as, they had been keeping a record on all of his occasional departures from the sanitarium.

After they left with Eugene, Mona sat down at the table, and turned to Fred, and said. "Fred, you must have the patience of an angel to have put up with Eugene until I got home. I am so proud of you!"

Fred went over and got himself another cup of coffee, got one for Mona, then, sat down at the kitchen table. Then said. "Well, Mona, sometimes, you just have to do what you have to do. But, I have one question of you, or, maybe two or threee, depends on how you count. Do you suppose, or, is there any way whatsoever, that, somehow, in some manner, that Eugene could maybe, or, maybe in some fashion, even really be some type of an angel put out here amongst us all for some unknown purpose, and in some kind of weird disguise?"

Mona looked at him, across from the table, then said. "Fred, he was sure not an angel when I had him in class at school, but to answer your questions fairly, on one hand, I don't think so, but then, like I have always said, that anything, anything is possible, but then, my gut feeling is, that it would have to take some mighty powerful disguise to hide Eugene's a-being an angel. Besides, like I heard you say to him, Eugene doesn't have wings, now, does he? But then, on the other hand I am not sure how he keeps getting out of the sanitarium on more than what I would call a regular basis, at any time that he so wants, with all of the security guards that they have out there."

THE PATIENT WITH PATIENCE

The patient came out of his unconsciousness, somewhat groggy, as if he had been asleep for too long a time. He had been awakened by a pulsating sound which caused him to wonder as to what it was. At first, he was somewhat startled, he tried to look around all about himself, but quickly came to the realization that he could not see, no matter how hard he tried to look, and, it scared him even more. He was blind as a bat, he thought. He attempted to cry out, but, he had not the capability, as, his voice was mute. He squirmed but could not move, which concerned him greatly. He tried to determine if there was anything which he could identify with any of his senses, but everything was coming up zero. His hearing was still in check he determined, but, not really all that good either, as, he could only hear the muffled noises all appearing as if to be some distance from him. There was no particular sound that he could readily identify as to what it actually was, even with his straining. He persisted in trying to open his eyes, time and time again. Perhaps if someone, anyone, were out there somewhere, they could see him trying to signal them in some manner, by the blink of his eye, but to no avail, as, everything was always dark, each and every time. He listened to the rhythmic pulsating noises and reasoned that they must be coming from some type of pump. He wondered what its purpose was, but, could not readily reason it out. Off and on, he again heard confusing gurgling and rumbling sounds. He thought, again, perhaps it was his stomach or bowels that were making those most embarrassing sounds. He hoped that no one was around and about to hear such pitiful physical emanations. Now and then, he heard running water which he identified readily, as it made him want to pee. He tried to feel himself, but his hands would not readily move, and, he had little feeling in any of his body parts, as, he couldn't even distinguish between his fingers or his toes. He tried again, more forcefully, to move, but found the attempts to be most difficult, as if, his entire body was being restrained in some manner or another. He tried time and time again, to just move different parts of his body a little, but it was with so much, or, too much effort. Too, he realized that he was so weak he could hardly even move his legs. He felt lethargic. He considered that he was all doped up perhaps on some medications. He tried to move his hands and arms to feel about his body for any restraints, but could not feel any, or, perhaps, he just had no feeling in his hands. He evaluated his restraint system. His restraints, as he could best identify them, felt as if he had a heavy weight bearing down on him, yet, he could not discern any particular pressure point against his body, such as belts, as it seemed that the restraint system, whatever it was, was all over his body, holding him in place by some method of total restraint. But why?

He strained with his reasoning, thinking, at first, that he surely must thereby be under some type of extreme nursing care, most likely in some sort of Intensive Care Unit at some hospital. He hoped that it was a good hospital, he thought. But, he questioned, why would he possibly be in a hospital or an ICU bed in the first place? What could have happened to him to bring such a thing about? He questioned himself first, then, tried answering his own questions by exercising his own reasoning with what part of his brains that were functioning. Partial brains are better than none, he thought, or, leftover brains, whichever it might be, he thought. He must have surely been in some sort of bad accident or severe health related event, and, now, was being restrained in some manner, where he was, without the ability for any abrupt movement of any of his body parts whatsoever, for some purpose. He must be pretty busted up to be in such a predicament, he thought. He tried again to open his eyes to see, but again and again, could only perceive darkness. No improvement to date, he thought. Yet, in spite of it all, he still strained with all of his might, just to try to see something, hear something, taste something, smell something, feel something, anything. Time and again, he tried to cry out for help, but could not utter a sound. He must have been blinded as a result of some sort of accident, he reasoned. Restrained and blinded as he was, with little or no capability of response, in any manner. Definitely not a good position to be in for anyone, anywhere, at any time, he thought, and, most likely, if the truth were to be known, nothing good could come from any of it for anyone to report. However, he did note, that he was not feeling any pain in any part of his body, that could be a good sign. However, on the other hand, that may not mean much, he thought, because, if he was in an ICU, the doctors had already most likely loaded him up on pain killers along with the sedation medicines, all mixed together like a cocktail, dripped in most likely with his intravenous feeding, of which he must surely be hooked up some extent in order to provide his meds.

He again and again tried to form his thoughts, even to the point of trying to converse with himself, in an attempt to try to evaluate his situation even more. He realized, that, he could hear, but all of the noises that he heard were more than just muffled, and yet, none of them appearing to be nearby. Obviously, he had lost his vision and he had also lost some but not all of his hearing, he reasoned. He also reasoned to himself that the rhythmic pulsating noise must be coming from some sort of respirator or resuscitator. But, why should he be on a resuscitator or a respirator? He questioned his memory. He remembered, sometime in the past, as having previously signed a legally binding "Do Not Resuscitate" document, some years ago, when he had written out his Will. So, why would he now have been provided some type of resuscitator or respirator, and, for what reason? What would be the purpose of that? He asked of himself, with no reasonable answer following.

Yet, he continued in his efforts to reason. If he was on a resuscitator, or some type of respirator, it must be only to sustain life in some manner as a result of some temporary injury of which he could readily recover. So, with that reasoning, he felt somewhat better. Perhaps he had been in some sort of car accident, or had experienced a fall of some type. If he didn't have his vision, perhaps he had been hit in the back of his head, as that is where the vision part of the brain is, he thought. Maybe he had been robbed, and, some culprit had hit him in the back of the head with a baseball bat before they took his money. Perhaps he had a heart attack, depleting his brain of the needed blood flow, or, maybe he just had a stroke, but, all of his reasoning only brought about more questions. He had absolutely no memory of anything having happened to him. Short term memory loss, along with selective long term memory loss, that's most likely it, he thought that is what is wrong with him. He continued to try to reason with himself. If it was, that he had been in an accident, it must have surely been put in the newspapers, or, if it had been bad enough, it would have even been announced on the television news. Ha! His name would have been in the newspaper and on television! But then, he realized at that time, that he could not even think of what his name was. That, hit him hard. Uh Oh! That would mean that another part of his potentially damaged brain was in complete dysfunction mode other than just the vision problem. Not good. Not good, in any respects, he thought.

Other thoughts flowed through his mind. Perhaps, he thought, he might try to figure out how to communicate in some way when he heard those peculiar muffled noises more near about. He waited patiently, and lay very quietly, but no noises came during his wait. Then, in the interim, he must have went back to sleep, or, perhaps, became unconscious again, possibly due to his medications kicking in.

Shortly thereafter, it seemed, he again awoke, or, again came out of his unconsciousness, still somewhat groggy, he thought. He now definitely heard more muffled noises, as if people were talking to one another near his very presence. He purposely lay very still so that he could listen. Yes! It was someone talking, one with a special high pitched muffled voice, and, the other with a lower voice which was more muffled than the first, both of which, he had heard on many past immediate previous occasions. He strained his ears to hear but could not make out any of the words between the two voices. Yes! They were definitely voices and he rejoiced in it all. He was thrilled, just to be able to identify voices. However, the voices came and went, sounding at first, as if they were from some distance, then, closer yet, then again more distant. Muffled noises sounding like voices mostly, but none understandable, yet, identified by him as being definitely voices of real people. Well, he had that figured out, finally. When he heard the voices near, he would blink to try to send some signal, he tried to squirm, he tried to move his arms and legs, he tried to call out or at least give out a sound, to try to communicate by any method, but, no response came, or, no one indicated any type of response, as far as he could tell. Although, it was possible, that, the noises and voices may have only been from the television or radio, he reasoned, and, that was why he gained no response. But now, the next problem was, to try to continue to communicate somehow with those voices each and every time that they were in the near vicinity, and, if they were those of real people, perhaps they might see his attempts to communicate, and respond in some manner, on into the future.

He continued to squirm and again tried to move his arms and legs but it was by now almost too much of an effort to even try. He tried to stretch, to change his position, but definitely knew now, as he had figured it all out, that he was being restrained in some manner unbeknownst to him which totally prevented him from doing what it was that he wanted to do or to move in a way that he wanted to move. His restraint, most likely was there in order to prevent him from hurting himself in some way, or, to help his body heal, he reasoned. He could move some, but not quickly, and, he could move his arms and legs somewhat, which was an improvement from what he could remember when he had tried before. That in itself, was reassuring, but not enough to be able to communicate his consciousness somehow to any of those around and about, apparently.

His thoughts turned again to what it was that was making the now more soothing rhythmic pulsating sounds. It definitely sounded like some kind of pump. Most likely, it must surely be some kind of a resuscitator or respirator, he thought again. But, what kind? He had visited other family members temporarily housed in ICU's in the past and was familiar with most types of respirators but could not figure out how it was providing him the sustenance of oxygen. He wondered why he remembered that, and, too, what was the purpose of it at all? That would be part of his long term memory coming back, only indicating some partial loss. He felt better about even thinking about it. However, the thought left him no sooner than he had thought it.

His attention now was more acute, and, he felt the better for it. He reasoned, that, he surely must have on some kind of face mask, in order to provide the needed oxygen for his body. But, he did not feel anything such as an oxygen mask to be pressing against his face. He tried with great effort, and, finally moved his hand up near his face but could not feel any covering his nose or mouth. Perhaps, he had no feeling in his face or hands, or, he thought that perhaps he could be in some kind of an oxygen tent, or, maybe in something like an "Iron Lung", like the polio patients of years ago were put in. Maybe, that's it! Maybe he has something like polio! He has trouble moving his arms and legs and maybe that is why he is on this respirator thing, just to help him breathe, he reasoned to himself. Well, maybe or maybe not, he thought, polio has all but been eradicated almost all over the world. Maybe instead, he had a stroke and was paralyzed, either partially or even perhaps totally. The thought of that did not set well with him. That would explain not being able to feel anything, including pain, he thought. Or, maybe he had some kind of reaction, like a reaction to sea food, or, maybe came he had into contact with some sort of poisonous spray, or, maybe he is in anaphylactic shock. Maybe he had a heart attack that caused him to have lost oxygen circulation to his brain. Or, maybe he had been hit in the back of his head with a golf ball, as, the part of the brain that controls vision is in the back of the head. Ha! Long term memory coming back little by little he thought, as, he remembered thinking something like that some time previous, and, he felt better about that. That would certainly answer that problem, he thought, whichever the cause might be. Maybe that is all that it is and nothing more, he further reasoned. He felt better, just thinking about it all. His mind continued to race from one thought to another, but then, he tired, and, he again lost consciousness, or, maybe, he just went back to sleep, or, perhaps the meds were taking effect, again.

He awoke, again, seemingly, shortly thereafter, as if he had not gotten his nap out, and, yet again, to that consoling pumping noise that the respirator was making. It was becoming more and more familiar and friendly now, and sometimes, even soothing to his very soul. Sometimes, it was louder, and, sometimes it was faster. Right now, it was definitely faster, and, he was evidently being bounced around some for some unknown reason. Perhaps that was all of what it was that woke him up, he thought. The nurses must be moving his bed, or, he has been put on a gurney to take him somewhere, he thought. Where was he being taken? He tried to signal them, he blinked, he squirmed, he tried to kick his leg and wave his arms, but all to no avail, again. After a while, the rustling noises subsided and the movement stopped, and the pumping noise again slowed. Perhaps he had been in some sort of stress, and they gave him some therapy or some different type of medication, he thought. Again, he could hear muffled noises that sounded like voices, but could not hear them over the pumping of the respirator, then, he heard what he thought was the news being broadcast on television, which was followed by what sounded like singing, but, again, he could not make out what was being said, since the words were more than what anyone in their right mind would call more than just muffled. He reveled in his realization that he was able to identify more and more about his surroundings through nothing more than what he could hear.

New thoughts now crossed his mind in one manner or another. He had more and more feelings as compared to what he had remembered of recent, but as of yet, there was little or no strength yet to be realized in his muscles. Movement of any manner, whether it was his arms or legs, or, even trying to turn his head, any movement at all, was more than difficult to say the least, and very tiring almost to the point of exhaustion. He wondered what kind of sedative that the doctors had put him on, and reasoned that it was most likely some type of pain reliever, no doubt, most probably, morphine, which has the capability of deadening the senses. Ha! More long term memory coming to light! He tried to feel both arms and both legs, just to assure himself that he was all still on one piece. He satisfied himself with that thought, and, somewhat, he felt better and a little more assured of some type of recovery lay out there somewhere in his future. Still, wonderment and questions passed through his brain bouncing from one possible realization to another. He mentally examined himself further, to try to develop his senses, but, he then realized, that, he still could not smell anything, or, taste anything, for that matter. He could feel, but not all over, he could not see at all, he could hear some, albeit partially, but not anything in particular that he could yet readily identify.

His mind turned again to the method or type of sedation. Maybe that is what makes him come and go from being awake and conscious, to and fro, of going back to sleep or going into unconsciousness. Maybe the physicians are giving him too much of the stuff, whatever it might be, or, maybe there is some reckless nurse on the job with her mind being somewhere else. Maybe, they are giving him a super strength placebo, allowing him to awaken, followed by strong morphine, which would put him to sleep, just to see if any of it could make some difference or if his body could somehow distinguish between the two, being bounced from sedation to full awareness, perhaps they were doing this, just to exercise his body and brain in some fashion. He reasoned, that, too much sedation could do more harm sometimes than good, he thought. However, he felt no pain that he noticed, whether he was awake or asleep, and, that was more than some relief to him, as, he had yet to figure out exactly what was wrong with him or what his problem was. But then, who can ever remember that they had pain in their sleep, unless it woke them up when it was in process? He again slumped back into unconsciousness, or, fell asleep, having tired himself out from all of his thinking, questioning and reasoning.

He awoke once again, to the now even more friendly and familiar sound of the respirator pumping along with some more of the gurgling sounds which he had become accustomed to, and which he now reasoned to be some sort of oxygenator which bubbled up oxygen through water to hydrate the respirator system to which he was attached. He wondered just how much of that pure oxygen that his lungs could sustain over a long period of time, and yet retain his health, not to mention his very sanity. He tried to reason as to just how many days had passed. Too many he thought, but, he could not yet number them. Ah Ha! He realized that he had no concept of time! And, he realized that counting was even a problem which he had not yet even considered. Why, it crossed his mind that he couldn't even think of how to count to ten. Maybe he was in a coma, either voluntary, or because of the medicine, or, perhaps, coming and going in and out of some physician induced comatic state. Perhaps the physicians had it all figured out as to what it was that he needed. He again came to the realization with respect to the time thing, that he had no concept whatsoever of what day it was, or, what time of day it was, even what month or year that it was. Partial or selective long term memory loss, he thought, that is what it is. That part of his brain was not functioning well, the thought. He reasoned that his situation was similar to blind people who get their days and nights mixed up. That thought, reminded him to again strain to see. He opened his eyes, but could not see anything. Everything about him was extreme darkness, no glow, no shadows, nothing! He then realized, that he never remembered ever seeing anything other than the darkness of which he was held and restrained within. So, just how could he even consider that he should otherwise be able to see and have good vision? Again, hope was, that his vision would somehow improve, like his selective long term memory could come and go or improve, he thought.

Those continuing thoughts, reverted to who it was that he was. He then realized, that he again remembered that he could not even remember his name. He tried to go through the A-B-C's to try to decipher his name somehow, but could not even remember his A-B-C's. Uh Oh! He thought, that is a bad realization. That means that his brain could be more damaged than what it was and worse than he first thought. What could have happened to him to have caused such damages? Maybe it was a bad heart attack, or, maybe he didn't get enough blood or oxygen to his brain. He tried to remember what if was that he was worked at in the past, but could not think of anything in particular. He tried to think whether he was a plumber, a carpenter, an electrician, a lawyer, maybe a schoolteacher, or, a pilot, or, maybe he was a doctor, maybe that is why they were trying to save him and bring him back into the world of the living, or, maybe he was a politician of some importance whose vote was needed on some bill on capitol hill. Maybe that is why he was on the respirator; trying to be saved for some purpose, perhaps, he was someone very much needed and of some importance to the world at large. His range of thoughts also puzzled him, as; it only confirmed the possibility of some sustained brain damage from some unidentified source with no evaluation as to its severity. These type thoughts did not make him feel better at all, he thought.

The familiar and consoling sounds of the pumping respirator, although peaceful, at times actually kept him awake, then, at other times, it caused him to be able to go to sleep. Sometimes, it caused him to be distracted, then at other times, it actually helped him to think. Either way, it was something that he adjudged to now be more than acceptable, which meant that there was some potential future for him yet, out there somewhere in the world. But, on the other hand, this was no way to live for any extended length of time, for anyone, he thought. He wondered if he was messing on himself and that some nurse had to clean him up but that he couldn't feel it, or, maybe he had a catheter which was not emplaced properly that needed some kind of manipulation. He reasoned, that he was no doubt surely being fed intravenously in some manner and wondered if they gave him breakfast in the morning and dinner in the evening. Ha! There is time element coming back into his brain! Yet, he wondered if he could possibly tell the difference between the two. He was so full of wonderment, yet, he was vexed. Here he was, blind as a bat, could not move his body parts, except that is, with some extreme effort. Could not taste, smell or feel very well, but, overall, and comparatively, he was feeling better about himself as time went by. As a positive thought, he reasoned within himself, that he was now, at this time, stronger than in some time immediately previous, within the remnants of his partial and selective memory, although, he could not particularly tell just how long that was, because he yet had no further concept of time whatsoever. His thoughts bounced from one thing to another and back again like a ping pong ball. He strained and worked to try to train himself to listen even more intently than he had when he remembered to have first awoken. He could hear his own heartbeat sometimes, but not always, because that ever familiar respirator pump drowned out most of all the other sounds.

He began to strain to hear more and more of the sounds which he could more readily identify. Those sounds, some of which sounded like voices, came and went. The voices, if they were truly that, seemed to have little or no emphasis one way or another, neither prose nor poetry. Ha! Good thought, he thought. But, he couldn't think as to what the difference was between the two. Then, sometimes the voices were just there when they were, and, not there at another time when they weren't. This didn't make any sense to him at all. Sometimes the voices were low, more like whispers, like the wind, or maybe a fan, on and off, coming and going, then, at other times, the voices were more audible but never intelligible by any means. Yet, no matter how hard he strained, with no specific words like doctor, nurse, bed, day, night, TV, hot, cold, which could be expected to have been heard by someone like him in the ICU, he heard naught, or, nothing for that matter for those who do not know what naught is. Even more puzzling, was the regularity of the gurgling noises. Perhaps it could be the bubbles in the oxygenator tube, or, maybe it was his passing of gas, or, most likely, he reasoned, it was the resuscitator attached to the respirator. If it was the passing of gas, it would certainly be no little embarrassing to him, even in his condition, or, perhaps, on the other hand, it could be some siphon where the nurses would try to get the phlegm or mucus out of his throat to prevent him from getting pneumonia, or maybe, that was what it was, maybe he had pneumonia! As, that would explain the respirator!

Pneumonia could be bad, he thought to himself. He had heard that the best place to get pneumonia was in the hospital, along with several other incurable diseases. He did not need any of that, he thought. He figured that he was in enough trouble the way that it was. But Ha! Again! There is that selective long term memory, making a strong comes back, he thought. He was more than all but delighted with himself. He again returned to his listening. It seemed that his thoughts were now to the point of drowning out what he was trying to listen for. So, he agreed with himself, to try not to think too much, any more than what was absolutely necessary, so as to hear a little more of the world that was going on around and about him. He tried to listen to the possible entrance of a nurse, or a doctor, or, a family visitor. Which brought him to the realization, that he did not know who it was that would be visiting him. He then came to the realization that he did not even know how old he was. Was he in school? Did he have a girl friend? Was he married? Did he have a family of his own? What did he do for a living? Was he a professional person? Was he unemployed, or, was he a workaholic?

Now, it had gotten to the point of where it was the questions, not the reasoning or the attempt at any thinking that was drowning out all of the other sounds of which he was trying to listen for. While he was purposely trying to lay still, trying not to move around except for comfort sake, since any movement was very tiring and very difficult still with all of the pressures of the restraints, he realized, that comfort was a definite feeling, and, that he was also getting more feeling in his toes and fingers, although other parts of his body did not feel like they had any of it yet circulated to their parts. He could now move his hand up to his face and feel his face, and, he could also feel his hand at the same time. Hey! Now, if nothing else, that is some progress, he reasoned, as, he had not previously experienced such feelings. He felt better about himself, overall, and felt somewhat more assured of some potential recovery sometime on into the future. Then, unconsciousness or sleep came over him like a shadow, again.

He awoke, again, to that now more familiar and acceptable pumping sound of the respirator. He thought that that sound, almost had a loving sound to its rhythm. The very next thought that crossed his mind was that since the point of his first memory, he realized that he had not dreamed about anything that he could readily remember. That did not set very well with him, as, that also implied the possibility of some other type of brain damage in some other part of his brain. He tried to sort out his various thoughts and go over them all, at least one more time. So, here he was, and, most likely had been for some time, most likely in an ICU, in some hospital, who knows where, being kept alive by a respirator, restrained from any movement in his bed, yet, still having all of his limbs attached, but, so far, not having much of a memory of much of anything, not knowing anything of himself, even of his very own name, or, any memory of much of anything for that matter as to any of his previous activities. Perhaps, he thought to himself, once, when he awakens, maybe seeing a relative, or, an old friend, or his pet, or something, maybe something, someday, will jog his memory and it will all come back to him as if in a flood. That would be difficult to contain, he thought, maybe they would just feed those memories to him a little at a time, so as not to overwhelm him so much. Perhaps, they would just show him one photo at a time, until such time as he could contemplate more. The doctors and nurses would know best, he assured himself, and, he thought to return to again attempting to listen more intently and perhaps learn a little more. Selective memory that was what it was, with the selecting only that which pertained directly to his condition. His remembering of only certain things, some specific things here, some general things there, spotty yet, but still memories of things. Perhaps, other memories would return too, hopefully sometime on into his near future.

Again, returning to listening intently, he tried to identify what it was that he was listening to. Once, he heard what he thought was music. Different notes of sounds bouncing all around him. Then, it dawned upon him. Hey! He had a memory of at least something as to what music was! Now, that was progress, he thought. Now, he was even more assured that if one more memory could return, albeit a recent one, perhaps others would follow with some long term hopeful recovery in sight on into the future. Thinking of sight, he again opened his eyes and again strained to see something, anything, but yet, nothing came into view and darkness still prevailed. The thought again passed through his brain, that he most likely had damage to the back of his head where the vision sensors are housed. He could not even imagine seeing something, which caused him some additional despair, because, not being able to imagine seeing something, could also indicate additional brain damage to those vision sensors and memory centers. One good thought, followed by one bad thought, he thought. Good news followed by bad news, which one do you want first. That was the last thing that he remembered, as he again lapsed back into his unconscious world, or, perhaps, just went back to sleep again.

He was yet awakened, again, by some intense shaking, some vibrations, with a definite increased pressure on his body restraint system. He was yet being moved again, he knew it, he could feel it, he thought, and wondered where they, whoever they were, were moving him now. He definitely felt as if he was being restrained even more than what he had become somewhat accustomed to in his previous condition. The pressure on him was now more than just what could be considered as overbearing. He pushed back against it with his entire might; he used the pressure of his legs and arms, which were stronger now than previous, as he remembered, but yet useless and of little use against such an overall pressure. He felt his head being encompassed by a band and being held in a tightened position. Uh Oh, he thought, the doctors have taken him to an operating room, restrained his head for the much needed brain surgery. This could be it, either, the beginning, or, the end, he thought, depending on the severity of the brain damage. This must surely mean, that his thoughts of having brain damage were most likely more severe than he had realized and that surgery was now deemed to be the only option left to save him. If that were not the case, they would have left him to heal up on his own, back in the confines of the ICU. He realized that he had actually not really made all that much progress toward recovery, however, even being able to remember that, he believed that it was progress in his own mind, but, apparently, the doctors were not going to leave well enough alone, and now he was going into major neurosurgery for sure. He hoped that they had a good team set up for the surgery. He knew enough about surgery to know that the doctors would be administering a sedative shortly, and, again, his thinking would probably stop along with him again going into some form of unconscious with a wakeup call in some recovery room. That is, if he made it. If he didn't make it, he had no idea in hell where he would awaken. He tried to make some contact with them, with anyone, trying every signal that he could think of, he tried to blink his eyes, he tried to shake his arms and legs, he squirmed, but all to no avail, as, no one paid any attention to his attempts at communications with them, whoever they were, whatsoever. He was almost insulted at being ignored, because, he just knew that someone should have noticed his signaling.

He took notice, that, the pressure on his head had been increased even more, as if the doctors were trying to cram a too small a cap onto his head, to hold it in place for the surgery, he supposed, and, now, they were in the process of even restraining his body more, to the point where he could not even move his arms. He was now secured and restrained to the point where he could only move his legs a little, with a little wiggle here and a little wiggle there. He thought that maybe the tight squeezing of his head would drain all of the blood from his brain and he would pass out and lose consciousness and do more damage in the long run, but, so far, that was a no go, and, he was all the more awake and more alert than ever, even to the point of feeling uncomfortable but not yet to the point of being in any pain, which he realized, that even pain was a feeling too, but he did not welcome that feeling like the opposite feeling of being more than what you could consider as being comfortable. He tried to open his eyes but could not, as, apparently; the doctors had put some kind of mask or band over his eyes because he felt the pressure of it and over and onto his face to the point where he could not even turn his head one way or another, even though he tried.

Suddenly, the pressure on his head and upper body was released, then, the pressure slipped down over his hip and legs. He realized that he was suddenly free of any pressure on his upper torso whatsoever. Then, just as suddenly, his legs were relieved of the pressure, and, he threw his arms up and kicked his legs. He could move! He was suddenly free from all of his restraints! He opened his eyes for a split second as in a blink, but was struck with such a blinding light that it was painful to him. The light was so bright, that he had to squeeze his eyes tight shut, but could still see the glow of it through his eyelids, which even hurt. When he purposely blinked his eyes to try to see, he got glimpses of what he thought looked like a giant, he supposed, with the giant all dressed in blue clothing, and, another giant, beside him, all dressed in white, as he blinked his eyes, enduring the pain, but ever trying to see. He realized, that he must certainly be dying, and, he was now entering into that bright light of heaven itself, just as others before him, had entered into that recorded historic warm and bright white light of the afterlife. That light, which was so bright that it could not so much as be looked upon. He felt the inner need within himself, a yearning, directing him, telling him, drawing him, that he should let go, and, peaceably go toward that great white holy light.

Suddenly, and just as abruptly, he felt as if he was being suspended upside down, strung up and held up by his legs as he was, as if being held upside down for some purpose by this giant dressed in blue colored clothing so surrounded by that great bright white light. He then felt a pain on his butt, as if he had been slapped, of all things, by the giant, and he again waved his arms and kicked his legs, and cried out to this heavenly world as if in some form of acceptance or defiance of it all. He realized that by his own noise, that, he finally had a voice, albeit finally upon his entrance into heaven!

He heard the giant in the blue clothing say something. "Congratulations, Stephanie, you have a healthy baby boy!" The noise of the giant's voice was so loud he felt the pain of it, but, he could not make out what he had said and the booming voice even made his ears ring.

He could feel the giant handling his body like a doll baby, then, felt the severing of the intravenous feeder source and the tying of it off. He could get only a glimpse of the giant now and then and the other giants with and around about him, all because of the intense bright white light which otherwise prohibited him from even opening his eyes to take a look, except for just a quick glimpse or two. Then, the other giant in white clothing wrapped him up into something soft, then squirted something into his eyes which made him blink and caused everything to be blurry to his newly found vision. Most likely, to help him transcend into that great bright white light toward heaven a little better, he thought.

He then felt himself being laid upon another giant's warm and inviting bosom. He felt her arms wrap gently around him, holding him ever so softly. Most likely for him to be carried into that great bright white light of heaven, he thought. Then, with his ear laid tightly against her bare breast, his eyes held ever so tightly shut, with her shielding him from that great bright light, he again heard that sweet consoling sound of that familiar soothing sound of the respirator pump, that loving friendly sound, that he had come to know so well, and, he went off again, into unconsciousness with a most peaceful sleep, knowing deep within himself, that he must have finally been allowed to be held and carried so gently through the gates of heaven itself.

DOCKER YING YANG   (which showed which side he was on of either side of any matter)

The dream began, full of on-again, off-again conflicts, similar to a convoluted argument between someone by the name of Ying and Yang themselves, but just between the two of them
…
"So, you tink you know Docker Ying Yang? Well, I know Docker Ying Yang velly velly well, betta over most, and, not only, I tell you some ting about Docker Ying Yang, make you wonder whole bunch after dark when daylight go out, even after daylight saving time change, so you read and you know what clazy tings oder older folks dream about, when sleepin' not so sound."

"Sometime, Docker Ying Yang velly velly bad man, he bad, so bad no good in him anywhere anyhow, total rotten, bottom of barrel kind of scum, snake belly in Deaf Valley low down, felon with a capital F arraigned and found guilty as charge, full of greedy vice only to satisfy self wif ill-gotten gain on weekend even wif no let up, wif a gotta get even mind-set just like guy wif criminal mind wif capital C."

"No, no, Docker Ying Yang velly velly good man, he do all good, everywhere, all time, he stand straight up forward, upright, walkin' tall, on hind leg, him no talk with fork tongue, he got full respec' in community vote, he full of character wif capital C, anyway you look at him up or down on Monday when work day begin on green light."

"Sometime, Docker Ying Yang, loose it at get go, he all talk wif big mouf, act like he know all, like brain scramble, he full of hot air, he all wind, he blow off steam like he have diarrhea of mouf, he spill all beans and guts down sewer after late night too much to drink, you could nick-name him gabby wif capital G."

"No, no, Docker Ying Yang all close mouf, tight lip, all clam up, you not pry word out of him, from between his teef, working between his lip, wif new Chinese crow bar on Sunday morning after church."

"Sometime, you see Docker Ying Yang out about during day, go for walk, enjoy sun shine, smell fresh air, pick flower, sit by lake, get sun tan, enjoy life, wif wife."

"No, no, you never see Docker Ying Yang out during day, only at night, like vampire, he watch stars, he enjoy cool evening breezes, have cool drinks on veranda, he relax in casual pajamas and have friends over even on Tuesday evening, enjoying same bad habits, wif wife serving drinks."

"All the time, Docker Ying Yang velly hard worker, you see him everywhere you go, coming, going, doing whatever at all time, he busy body, he all in over-drive over all time, he everywhere just like stink in dairy farm barn yard."

"No, no, Docker Ying Yang lost, nowhere be found, as if he done disappear, like ghost shadow in wispy dissipate fog, he just long gone, little or no notice, no tell anyone or anybody, he both absent in mind and body, not even Johnny Come Lately show up on his behalf."

"Sometime, Docker Ying Yang have good basic reason for all he do, very logic kind of guy, he velly predictable day in and day out, know what to do next in all case, he of sound mind wif capital M."

"No, no, Docker Ying Yang full of one excuse good as other, know no way to do, like he lit the fuse but it went out, like he brain freeze on ice cream, he no have even drop of common sense, his idea machine all lock up like French sabot shoe in machine cog gear on 12 hour workday shift in France for underage worker on Sunday."

"Sometime, Docker Ying Yang full of success, all go his way, he in right place at right time, his boat come in and he at dock on time, only mistake he make is not staying awake twenty-four-seven, if he put money in, stock go up, if he take money out, stock go down, even on rainy Wednesday afternoon at four thirty."

"No, no, Docker Ying Yang total failure, never make it even in America, make same mistake over and over and expect different result every time, if easy street freeway open with empty four lane, danged if he no take bypass with bumper to bumper go to work traffic and he done get in slow lane."

"Sometime Docker Ying Yang work hard, is busy as bee, go nonstop, hell bent for leather or rabbit fur, going hundred mile an hour in downtown traffic like Chinese fire drill, everywhere he go he run in hard sweat with blood pressure high, he work day in and day out, sleep velly little, even on weekend, he go in hard rush from daylight to dark wif no family time to speak of."

"No, no, Docker Ying Yang let everyone else work instead, he never lift finger, he like tub who forever sit on own bottom, lazy as old hound dog not turn over to scratch flea, he even dead in water, laid up some like he sleepy pie eyed, his get up and go has got up and went, he lazy ass, he so lazy he forget to tell time, he lazy, wif capital L."

"Sometime, Docker Ying Yang full of compromise by negotiation, he help find solution no one else see, he build new bridge and get agreement where all sides happy and content, he have answers wif capital A, he make velly good politician, if but given chance first of week."

"No, no, Docker Ying Yang very cause of friction, he not know definition of word compromise, he cause new argument where none exist before, he set bridge on fire from both end and everyone get ass burned while wait in bumper to bumper traffic."

"Sometime, Docker Ying Yang have positive nature, he on top of world, he feel good, he full of spitz and spitzerinctum, have positive mind, good outlook on all, he first one out of race gate wif hard bit in mouf, and race belong to him from first turn on."

"No, no, Docker Ying Yang negative on all he come in contact wif, he never see bright side, his sky always gray and all wrong, like he have too much caffeine at night before going to bed, one sorry SOB with capital S."

"Sometime, Docker Ying Yang, put off, he procrastinate, he never finish anything he start, he go in wrong door and come out wrong door wif no open door policy, he waste of time, big time wif capital T or W, whichever."

"No, no, Docker Ying Yang Johnny on spot, he do what he say, he deliver project on time every time, and under budget, he have job done before ink dry on contrak by end of week."

"Sometime, Docker Ying Yang argumentative, frowning, wanting to fuss, has bad karma all way to bone, all way home, no Feng Shui around him, he aggravated to the gills, need little to touch or torch him off, he have short fuse, he bad medicine wif capital M."

"No, no, Docker Ying Yang forever smiling, agreeable, have positive outlook on life, kind of guy you want your sister marry, his glass full up, he no fail inkblot test, he spread happy all over wif capital H."

"Sometime, Docker Ying Yang hit on all four cylinder, never make mistake, right on time every time, he like mechanic with right size wrench on Thursday afternoon in certified repair shop."

"No, no, Docker Ying Yang other name is Mister Mistake, he full of error, he not know which answer which, his brain turn total jelly, he not know which way up, he lose all contact with reality on day in and day out basis, big time."

"Sometime, Docker Ying Yang have good advice, he right on target, he know which way to go, he know what to do, he like wizard with magic wand wif up to date road map to never never land."

"No, no, Docker Ying Yang advice come from hell, bottom up delivery of upside down pizza, he say all to suit purpose or just to sound good at time, he have belly full of manure and some come out his mouf at time of delivery."

"Sometime, Docker Ying Yang act smart, when he like that, he think good, he have answer to question not even asked yet, his brain sharp as razor, he have new answer to old question, his mind like new blade on old plow pulled by fresh horse."

"No, no, Docker Ying Yang act complete ignorant, downright stupid wif capital S, you not know he even smart enough to pound sand down rat hole, dumb-ass wif capital D, no can pour water out of boot even with instruction written on heel."

"Sometime, Docker Ying Yang have good habit, do right thing at right time, he wait overnight to make serious decision on matter, he wear habit like nun, he admired by peer, he regular as Big Ben clock at noon or midnight."

"No, no, Docker Ying Yang have velly bad habit day in and day out, he not decide or weigh opinion or option, he not ask for advice, but if he do he not use it, he run head on into trouble wif capital T by middle of week."

"Sometime Docker Ying Yang one lucky dude, he win all time at no effort, he play poker, he win, he play crap, he win, he play roulette, he win, he no loose at game on call and dealer hate to see him coming to sit at table."

"No, no, Dockey Ying Yang, most unlucky guy on block, he so unlucky he believe it better to have bad luck from no luck at all, he drop his lucky penney in gutter at age five, he unlucky wif capital U even on weekend."

"Sometime, Docker Ying Yang a boozer wif capital B, he be a rum dumb whiskey head, an albino wino, and he have beer belly hanging over belt from outside in, he make stagger Lee look stone cold sober even on holiday."

"No, no, Docker Ying Yang sober as judge, he teetotaler, alcohol never touch his lip, he never set foot in road house or Pub when open for business, he even run for politic, hug woman and kiss baby on tour."

"Sometime, Docker Ying Yang strong, you see him, you not want mess with him, he carry big stick, muscleman wif capital M, you walk on opposite side of street, he get lee way, he not afraid of dark."

"No, no, Docker Ying Yang total pansy, he weak, he all dried up and waste away, he disgrace to human race, everyone kick sand in his face on beach, he willy nilly with yellow streak up back from get go, even on Saturday."

"Sometime, Docker Ying Yang know no wrong, on right side, good side up, straight as arrow, pure as fresh blown snow, and white as virgin wool wif capital V or maybe W, whichever."

"No, no, Docker Ying yang liar with capital L, no truf in him, he tell cock and bull story, he mislead you to hell and back just for fun, no good side to him even on Sunday morning."

"Sometime, Docker Ying Yang, all business, in five hunert dollar hickey freemin twin breasted suit wif briefcase, wif updated laptop computer, ready go to meeting to make decision on important matter, solid as brick laid by union bricklayer on Monday morning."

"No, no, Docker Ying Yang know little of business, he believe trade same as trade off, he believe GNP means Generally Nobody Pays, he believe foreign trade required be done in foreign language wif bank account off shore in Bimini."

"Sometime, Docker Ying Yang all up, feel oats, prance around on hind leg, dance to tune, he energetic with capital E, bounce around like football on Monday night."

"No, no, Docker Ying Yang down and out, drag butt, lethargic, no energy to speak of, wasted, like he all laid out in wait for undertaker to show up on Friday for embalming schedule."

"Sometimes, Docker Ying Yang, act like old friend, buddy-buddy kind of guy, he first to introduce self, ask what he can do for you, he even warm up to total stranger, he so pleasant he qualify as tour guide at disneylan."

"No, no, Docker Ying Yang strange, act like he never seen you before, wonder who you are, or where you come from, he no care for you or horse you rode in on, he isolate self and avoid contact like cur dog with sore claw at ASPCA dog pound."

"Sometime, Docker Ying Yang tell of his extensive education, he got AS, BS, MS and Ph'd, and some study beyond what he got at Ivy League school, he have extensive resume' and long curriculum vitae, but he no brag or ever put down lower educated peer."

"No, no, Docker Ying Yang have little or no education at all, what he got is diploma mill paper, paid for in cash, wif no homework required, over internet from Baloney or Bullshit University with capital B or B or U, whichever."

"Sometime, Docker Ying Yang say, love and hate same emotion but only positive or negative, like magnet, love be positive and attract while hate be negative and repel."

"No, no, Docker Ying Yang say love answer to all worlds' ills, say hate is cause of war, he no cut slack between two and he admit he have both experience on his record."

"Sometime, Docker Ying Yang most happy married man around town, married to same girl almost all life, she happy in love since high school, he not be able to wait get home from work to see her, she all but pee down leg in wait for him arrive."

"No, no, Docker Ying Yang never marry, he live lonely single life, go out night club by club to get lonely off mind when he not doing companion search on internet dating web site, he not sleep well because he dream of one night stand relationship, he one sorry Charlie kind of guy wif capital C."

"Sometime, Docker Ying Yang think he politician, he think run for office is piece of cake, he so ignorant he think voter elect candidate, he never hear of bought and paid for electoral college already been put in big businessman pocket, he like to hear himself talk even when no one listen."

"No, no, Docker Ying Yang velly good politician, he always look out for poor man and middle man too, he even lower tax on rich man, so rich man can give more money to poor man so rich man have even greater tax write off to use money to buy new boat and poor man can buy new shoes and diapers for baby."

"Sometime, Docker Ying Yang, sad, he so sad he sorry, you see him, he make you want to cry, he a mess, he borrow trouble and not pay back, he have to get better just to tink of suicide."

"No, no, Docker Ying Yang always in upbeat good mood, he happy, he in trills-ville all time, like he on laughing gas or maybe he smoke too much loco weed, if you around him, he make you want to be like him, even on Wednesday."

"Sometime Docker Ying Yang, tink he on one side or other, but you never know which side he on at any time, and, just about time you tink you know for sure which side he really on, he done flip flop to other side like dang fish out of water, like surprise, surprise, on you, wif capital S."

"No, no, Docker Ying yang solid in his mind, he straight forward all time, he full of wisdom wif capital W, he go out of way to be positive in all, ask him what he tink and he give you story from book of knowledge, he all up front wif no hidy hidy."

"Sometime, Docker Ying Yang, full of vanity, he have ego like blow up balloon, he like I, my, me, mine, take me, drive me, show me time, all time, wif capital T."

"No, no, Docker Ying yang humble wif capital H, he always look out for all, not his-self anytime, he go out of way to do favor. He put his place second to all he meet on street, even on Tuesday morning."

"Sometime, Docker Ying Yang act like he have no experience, he believe one year experience ten times in row equal ten year of experience, he have no concept wif capital C."

"No, no, Docker Ying Yang velly experienced kind of guy, know history of needs of puts and calls, and know of required meets and bounds, in and out, up, down, and sideways when commodities stock market open in Chicago Monday morning on daylight savings time."

"Sometime, Docker Ying Yang, leader in all, he talk, all listen, he make decision all agree, he show all what need be done on daily basis, he idea man wif capital I, all look up to him in respect and he look out for all."

"No, no, Docker Ying Yang not know which way to go on any day of week, he indecisive, he can no make decision on own, one turn good as another, he dumbass wif capital D."

"Sometime, Docker Ying Yang velly good golfer, he par most hole, sometime he get birdie, he know which club and ball to use when in all case "

"No, no, Docker Ying Yang doffer, he lie on card, act like he not know how to count, he put down number of choice, he not know difference between niblick or mashie, beater, weed eater, or whanger banger, he bummer at drive, pitch, chip and putt, he not even have cart driver license at public club."

"Sometime Docker Ying Yang, have good excuse for all that happen, he always have good reason for what he do at any time, everyone buy off on what he say and no question or sign statement."

"No, no, Docker Ying Yang just have one excuse after one more, he believe excuse is better than lie, but he even lie about it, he say he here, but he really be somewhere else at time of happening."
"Sometime, Docker Ying Yang, make one mistake after next, and not know difference, he think everyone have same problem so it OK in his mind."

"No, no, Docker Ying Yang never make mistake, he Mister correct on all issue, his mind like steel trap closed on chicken eating scraggley coyote leg, he decide which way to go and make way for new idea wif capital I."

"Sometime, Docker Ying Yang Clazy, clazy as loon, clazy as bed bug, his mind floating loose around behind him like balloon behind motor scooter, he loose goose and loose cannon all rolled up in one."

"No, no, Docker Ying Yang logic as geometry or algebra, he got mind sharp as tack about him twenty-four seven week day or week end, whichever, and his mind click and clack back on track with no lack of knack, even on Thursday."

"When all said and done, eventually at the end, sometimes, Docker Ying Yang, says that he is up but he be down, and sometimes, he knows that he is down but he says that he is up, and invariably, he never knows the difference between the two, sometimes he is forward and he is really backward, and he has no clue of that either, sometimes he is hot and sometimes he is cold, and never seems to know the difference between the two except if he notes that he either has too many or not enough clothes on at the time, sometime he says he is on the ins and he really is on the outs, sometimes he gets so mixed up on which he is supposed to be on any given day or moment in time, he makes a mess of himself wif a capital M or H, and everyone else around him, in the process, and, it just adds to the confusion for both Ying and Yang to argue a little more about it even on Friday afternoon at quitting time."

At this time, at first, the dreamer, could not decide, whether he had been awake, fell asleep and then began dreaming, or, had been asleep, dreaming and then awoke, and, had to just wait around and see what was going to happen next. So, the dreamer gave up on it all and finally and fully awoke but was then unable to remember the aforementioned order statements concerning the good Doctor Ying or the bad Doctor Yang, or, were they the other way around, hopefully, you will do much better with it all when you dream about it the second time around.

THE BRAIN GAME

I sat in the waiting room, just chatting away with the office clerk, waiting patiently until it was my time for being called in to see the referred physician. I sorted through my medical reports, I sorted my letters of response and some of my papers, one by one, page by page, attempting to make some sense of what it was that I wanted to say and just how and when I should say it, running it over and over in my mind, as, to what I should or should not present and when I should or should not present it, until, I got to the point of saying to myself, that it was what it was, it is what it is, and, there was nothing else that I could make of it for myself, so, that was where I left it.
In no less than five minutes off of my appointment time, I was called, and, entered into the doctor's office. I did not understand it at the time, as to the why of it all, but, I was a little taken aback and surprised that the referred doctor was a woman. "Good morning, Ma'am, I am Kelly, here for my ten o'clock appointment." I said.
She responded. "Is that Kelley with an "e-y", or Kelly with a just plain "y"?" She asked.
"With just a plain "y". I said.

"So, just plain "y" Kelly it is." She said. "So, brief me here, Kelly with a just plain "y", I see here in your reports that were you were referred to me by both of your personal physicians, and I will withhold the question until later as to how it has come about that you have two personal physicians putting out reports on you, so, let's get

on with the purpose of your appointment. What is your concern, or, what are a couple, a few, or, perhaps some of your concerns?"
"I've just been referred, to you, here, as I see it, to get my brain examined. I'm having terrible pains in my head, I'm taking daily doses of over-the-counter pain medication, but have not yet progressed to prescription pain relievers, because, I do not want to get hooked on that kind of medicine, so, I go with the O-T-C a few or more times daily on an as needed basis. I think that my problem is caused by me having so much pressure on my brain because, as I see it, my memory tank is stuck on open, with everything going in and nothing coming out, causing an overpressure, along with the pump of my non-stop thinking which causes me no little pain within my skull and it has now progressed to the point of it even keeping we awake at night. But, my main problem, which I believe to be the root cause, is, that I have come by a great humongous secret which is stuck up somewhere's in the middle of my brain, of which I cannot tell anyone else of, and, the pressure of that alone I believe to be the basis of my problems." I said.

"From a one to a ten, what would you say your pain level is?" She asked.

"It is about ten times what a sinus headache could cause, and, I would say that it is at least a seven and maybe even an eight on an hour by hour day in and day out basis, with a nine off and on now and then, and sometimes with a ten which even wakes me up at night." I said.

"Is it ongoing, day in and day out, or, does it just come and go now and then?" She asked.

"I thought that I had already answered that, but to add on to it, it is never ending, even when I try to sleep." I said.

She sat back in her chair, and said. "Well, Kelly, with a just plain "y", I am not a Psychiatrist, I am not a Psychologist, I do not take my patients brains out and play with them, although I have been unduly accused of such activity in the past on more than one occasion. I am a neurologist, and a surgeon, and, I determine how some, but usually only a few here and there, of the wires between the neurons are connected up in the old brain box, and, sometimes I have to clip some of those wires, and re-wire a junction box, or wire in a throw switch.

Now and then, or, once in a while, I have to do an entire panel board with a couple hundred breakers, which is usually when I have to connect up the spinal cord nerves, which in itself, is not much different than a goodly trained union electrician would do, no more, no less, matching up wires. However, as an immediate priority, it is, all about the money, so, as a side line, I also cut peoples water off, take their meter out, and withhold their deposit, that is, when they don't pay their bills a-pronto. So, up front, I need three hundred and fifty-five dollars and sixty-three cents for your scheduled two hour appointment, or some proof of some good insurance before we proceed further."

"I have my Medicare insurance and Supplemental plan information presently on file with your office lady, so, that part should not be problem. So, where do I, or, where do we go from here?" I said and asked almost in the same sentence, but not quite.

She responded. "Well, with that aside, please do tell me, what else is it that brings you here, why do you feel you need my special attention, tell me what the problem is, if any, or, what you think the problem is. So, do tell me, bring me up to date, tell me your story, spit it all out, dump it on me, tell me your concerns, help me help you get some of the burden off of your shoulders, open up and tell me why you think that I can be of some help to you in some fashion or another. Give it to me with both barrels, let me have it, spill your guts, cut to the chase, don't beat around the bush, hit me up aside my head with it, let me have it all lumped into one big sentence, if you think you can."

I started to start, but stopped, then started again, but, stopped again, thinking as to just how I could answer all of those commands and questions in just one sentence, but, I knew I had to try, but in order to save my mysterious humongous secret for some later date, I just said. "I told you, that I have discovered a most mysterious humongous secret, and, it is so secret, that I can't tell anyone in the whole wide world right now, and the pressure of that alone, on my brain, has now mounted to the point of overpressure like in a sunken submarine, which causes me no little pain, which O-T-C pain medication does not abate, I might add, and, in addition, it is most frightening to me that I know something that no one else knows, or no one else but me has figured out to this day, it is like someone knowing where Jimmy

Hoffa is buried and how he got himself snuffed out and who done it, and, if some scrupulous person ever found out what I have come to know, I am sure, no doubt in my mind, that they would stop at nothing and may even resort to torture just to get it out of me, or, on the other hand, maybe Jimmy Hoffa had a secret like I have and someone else found out about it, which, no doubt, just thinking about that even causes me greater pain, and, that is really scary, mostly because I have always had a low pain threshold in the first place as far back as I can remember along with secretly wanting to be a big rig over-the-road truck driver." I said.

"That's it? That is all there is? Perhaps, you must mean, that you have figured out a new theory or some new idea or premise that has not yet been patented, published or copyrighted. Is that what you mean? That would be more like something that some common everyday University professor would be more concerned with much more than a world famous neurosurgeon like me would be." She added.

I responded. "Well, what got me here, was, that both of my primary physicians felt that as a result of that and a few other things that I said, and, a couple of things that I didn't say, and, some of the things that I wouldn't say, along with some things that I just couldn't say, along with the fact that that my brain seemed to have developed some otherwise unexplained exceptional method of looking at things and figuring things out that both physicians thought might be of some interest to you or to some aspect of the science of man himself, of which you may be acquainted and had the connections to pick up and run with, but in the process, figuring out a secret otherwise unknown to anyone else the world over, has caused me to be miserable with the pain of it all inside my brain and because of the over pressure it has placed within my skull. Which, is my problem encapsulated into the one sentence that you so requested and I did the best job that I could do with what I had to work with at the time with regard to fit, form and fashion. However, I want you to know, up front, that I am not yet quite ready because of it all to donate my brain to science anytime soon in the near future." I said, all in one breathless breath.

"OK, you have a two hour appointment, so, let's get it on, and start talking. I want to hear your story about how all of this came about, perhaps that will give me some insight into what I need to ask you next." She said. "And, by the way, I respect your candor with respect to your secret, and, I don't blame you for not telling me or anyone else, as, I would feel the same way under the same circumstances even with the pain and all, I would probably be mixing up and popping multiple Tylenols and Advils on an hour by hour basis. And, I just might mention, for your information, women, generally, have more secrets than men, overall, and, generally, they are also better, and they are also better at keeping their better secrets, again, overall. I should also say that that is really no secret anyway, by the way." She said.

She went on. "Just so you understand, I have worked on many memory problems. I have seen multiple first-in and first-out, and, last-in and last-out problems. I have also seen quite a number of first-in and last-out problems, and, a few last-in and first out problems, of which I find that any one of them can be just as bad as the other, depending upon the circumstances, and, everyone knows that circumstances can alter cases. Seventy-five percent of the problems usually solve themselves, with no help from me, and, the other half is where I make some hard earned cash by altering a few of those circumstances before someone makes a case. So, in addition to my former requests, what are your circumstances and what cases could they possibly alter?" She asked, adding on.

Well, I thought about what she was saying, on one hand, I thought maybe I didn't fully understand exactly what she was trying to say, on the other hand, I doubted if I could get the full story out within two hours, but, on the third hand, maybe I could, and, maybe I could get some answers to some unanswered questions that I had thought up back in the back of my mind, so, on the fourth hand, I decided to try to shorten up my story a little where I could as I went along, primarily so as to not be accused of nattering the readers along with a couple of those cranky editors at the New York Times Human Interests desk, or the Boston Globe's Department of Eternal Affairs, should they every be called on the carpet because of it all, so, I started, but trying not to just blurt it all out in one breath.

"Well, it is like this, on one hand, if I had of come by a precious gem or a gold bar of some great value, not knowing the origin thereof whatsoever, I would perhaps think that maybe, or, perhaps, someone might very well have stolen it and hid it out, or, in some emergency, they cast it away to prevent being caught with it, or, on the other hand, perhaps someone else had honestly lost it, and, one or either, or, perhaps even neither, or, perhaps even both, unknowingly between the two of these two previous parties, knew of the true origin whether it was right, wrong or something in between, but, not I, in no way would know either or neither of the other, whichever. So, by the same token, or the third hand, I know not, as I found it, whether my secret has been stolen by some persons a-previous and with criminal intent, then cast away, or hidden away for some time out of sight and out of mind, until some nefarious crime was long forgotten, and then misplaced sometime later, by one of those persons of a criminal mind, or on the fourth hand, perhaps, having been even lost somehow by them, or, otherwise, honestly lost by some honest person of good repute, but with the question in the back of my mind, as to why no public search was ever reported, or, why has no inquiry of such has ever been put out on the nightly news or reported in the New York Times editorial pages, the Boston Globe or even in any of their advertisements. Then, the secret that I have found, like the gold bar or the precious gem, if I ever said that I had such a thing in my possession, in the first place, in either case, surely those or others of well advanced ill repute, even including those reportedly of good intent as nothing more than but a front, could seek me out to seize it and get it from me in one way or another, then, either way, if it were only the honest person and I, we would then be at a complete loss, and the criminals would have more than what could be called a free total gain. Either way, because of such announcement, I would not be in any enviable position in anyone's consideration, and, in our society as it is today, my very life, including those in my close family nit, could quite possibly even be in some great grave danger. Yet, the added on further problem of where it was lost, not also being where it was found, perplexes me to no end just for the knowing of it all, and which brings about the great mystery part of it which swells the pressure in my head even more, and, causing me even greater pain as I even think about it now, as such thought crosses my swollen brain, and, that's about all that I can say about it all in one breath." I said.

She looked at me quizzically, then, said. "Your problem has a conundrumish perplexing puzzle within a mysterious enigma which has a hidden meaning written all over it from the get-a-long get-go, that is, if the get-up-and-go, has not already got-up-and-left without even saying one goodbye."

I responded with. "Yes, I know, and, you know that I didn't make up or write any or either one of those words, because my spelling is piss poor, and, my command of the English language is even worse, why, if you do your research like you should, you will find that even my two primary personal physicians left most of those very words out of their reports, mostly on purpose I would surmise, if I were a surmising kind of person."

"OK." She said. "The first report from your first personal physician, says here, that you so very eloquently refused to tell what this great mysterious humongous secret of yours was all about, and, I would suppose, that you may so choose not to tell me what it is either, under the circumstances, because your second personal physician said the same thing but in even fewer words. But, I can proceed with that, if that is part of the inevitable. However, I would encourage you to somehow share this great mysterious humongous secret of yours with someone. Someone, or anyone, that you have come to feel that you could more than just fully trust, and, here is the why of that. Think about this. If something happened to you, for instance, if you were in a car wreck and up and got yourself killed off and was completely dead as four o'clock in the morning, this great mysterious humongous secret of yours would go to the great beyond and to a very cold grave with you, and the world with all of its civilizations down through the future centuries ahead, may very well be at a great loss for never having the occasion of ever knowing it at all."

She went on. "The second report goes on to say, that I have here in front of me from the second physician, also says that you have a very great pressure on your skull because of your brain activity regarding this great mysterious humongous secret, spelled out the same way that I spelled it out here and now and not too dissimilar from the first personal physician, but again as I mention in fewer words, overall. Both reports indicate a serious problem with your brain of which I have been referred to evaluate, and so requested herein their reports by both of your first and second personal physicians. Are you aware, or, have you been briefed of the similar sameness of both of these diagnoses from the two different physicians in question?"

"That is part of the great burden that I bear, and partly the reason that I am here today." I said. "However, this is only page three or four of my story, and, I may not be ready for a "tell all" of that great mysterious humongous secret until at least page five or six just ahead, just to let the little cat out of the big bag or the big cat out of the little bag, for some of the more picky readers and to advise them that if they ever want to find anything out further, that they have no recourse except to read on and get themselves up to date on the forthcoming low down." I added, somewhat pompous-assed which made me feel bad, in the first place, and, a little guilty for even mentioning it to the readers in the second place.

"That is fine with me." She said. "But by the initial acceptance of your referral from these two physicians, along with the very basis of your acceptance of those referrals indicates that you would be more than willing for me to slice your bloody rotten flesh open, hammer, chisel and saw my way into and through your bony skull, then, poke around inside a little into your gray matter with nothing more than a plastic coffee stir stick, and, perform the delicate microscopic surgery on your very brains neurons, and even have the liberty to take out some of the unused or non-working parts, bits and pieces and throw them away with the Friday morning's trash. Yet, you still imply that you would not trust me enough to tell me of this great mysterious humongous secret of yours. This is not my first rodeo or my last dog and pony show. Now, just so you know, I have been to a couple county fairs, and witnessed a couple of goat roping's, in addition, I have seen some cold hard facts raked over the coals, and have lived through worse, and, I am reasonably sure, somewhere back in my own mind, that I will live through this, but, when push comes to shove, I do not need a need to know order from a court of law in order to do my job, so, let us move that small problem on along and kick that can on down the road."

She then sat back and re-read the two reports, frowning now and then, three times that I counted, then, smiling a couple of times, that I saw, then, scowled once after she had rolled her eyes twice, with her mouth dropping open only once that I noticed down on toward the end.

She then leaned forward in her chair behind her desk, and, began. "Now, Kelly, it says here in your report from your first referring physician, that you have a mind like unto a V-8 engine, which, I fully understand, as, it is more powerful than a V-6 or a straight fuel injected I-4 even with a turbo-blower. However, according to the report, it seems, that you are misfiring on cylinder number five, and, off and on firing on cylinder number three, but, cylinder number two and seven seem to try to make up for the loss of power by firing off on both the compression stroke and the exhaust stroke, with those two acting more like a two cycle rather than a four cycle engine. This, sounds to me, in my opinion, as if you might just need a goodly trained engine mechanic rather than a world renowned brain surgeon like me. As I remember it, from my high school years in auto mechanic shop, the four cycle engine function is, Intake, Compression, Power and Exhaust, in that order. It has always been so, ever since the four cycle internal combustion engines were invented, except for the two cycles however, of which I do not yet fully understand just how they work as I can never seem to get my weed eater started. So, as I see it, you have six goodly functioning cylinders operating on the four cycle principle, and, a couple that seem to be operating on the two cycle principle, which brings about a rough idle and some loss of power and undue engine wear and tear which can cause unheard of costly maintenance problems, overheating and pressure in the crankcase, not to mention some affiliated transmission problems. I understand that. That is most likely why you are here if the truth were ever known. Now, as I see it, the inherent problem here is this, when this principle is applied to your brain, it is more akin to a computer that is looping, where, one question leads to another and as the answers flow forth, eventually returning to the original question, this causes overheating and overpressure that also causes undue and unbelievable pressure within your skull, to the point of you having terrible episodes of migraine headaches, with some thinking that they might even have some abnormal growth, concussion event or some similar ailment causing such painful internal pressure. I have had similar patients with your problem before. I know exactly what to do. Rest assured that you are not the first to have such a common problem. It is called in medical circles, Brain Under Labored Load, or by the more common acronym, B-U-L-L."

She went on. "So, let's take the B-U-L-L by the horns and get to the point. Many have come and gone before you, but, to put it into the few words and very bluntly, I will try my best to break it to you easy, and, that is this. The only answer for your condition is to have an immediate brain transplant as soon as possible! I will put you on the candidate list for your brain transplant, and, when I get notification of a proper donor, I will notify you, and, you can come in for the surgery. It should not last long, and, you should be out of the hospital within a day or two, no worse for the wear, but not quite qualifying for outpatient status under Medicare or Medicaid. However, I must advise you, as your personal world renowned neurosurgeon, that over the last six and one-half years, that 1.68% of the brain transplant recipients, which even in this modern time has yet to be perfected, have some report of partial or temporary paralysis along with possible nerve damage which can also cause a speech impediment and a nervous twitch here or there. This is usually associated with the re-connecting of the nerve fibers in the spinal cord just under the Medulla Oblongata, which we surgeons call the gray matter abysmal pit, however, I also should say, personally, that none of my patients, that I can remember, or can even think to mention, over the last thirty years or so, have ever reported any such problems, much less having any of them even mentioning or even remembering such and none to date have reported any particular memory loss, I should add, if I could add." She said.

I was no little taken aback. "Brain transplant!" I all but yelled out. "I didn't option either in or out for any kind or type of brain transplant! I didn't even know that that was one of the optional options! I mean, what if the donor of the incoming brain had something mentally wrong with him, or, some disease, then, after the transplant, I would have it would I not? Are all of those incoming brains on your list checked for defect by some State registered quality control group before they get put up for donorship?" I asked.

"Well, Kelly, it couldn't get any worse, or, it wouldn't be any worse, in the worse sense, in any or either case, with all of that internal pressure within your skull along with the pain that you complain of, or, than that of which you are operating with now, now would it?" She both said and asked.

"What about other options?" I asked. "What about troubleshooting the ignition system, or, the fuel injectors, how about the coil or the regulator, what if I just needed a new battery, what about putting in a new ignition switch, or, what about replacing that high cost computer chip for the fuel injection and automatic shifting, how about replacing the compensator, or, maybe the Ji-jippa-rod just jumped out of the

Johnson Box, and knocked the Pflamagator loose, what about any or all of that as a possibility? Wouldn't those things be something to check out first before you go slap-jacking and transplanting brains a-willy-nilly?" I also asked.

She responded. "Well, Kelly, I am only comparing your problem with a great multitude of similar patients which I have seen over the last thirty years or so, and, I could nickel and dime you to death over all of this like a back yard shade tree small town bad engine mechanic without enough of the right tools with no certifications or warranties, but, to save your life and for you to be of some benefit to society in general on into your feel good future, in your condition, you have all but got down in your get-a-long, and are all but down and out and really only have the one option left in the bag of neurological tricks. But please, don't feel bad. This is not uncommon in any respect. Everyone thinks that their problem is the only one like it in the whole wide world, but, the truth of the matter is, there are more people out there in the world rattling away in their cages, both day and night, thinking that they are the world's shakers and movers, with most of them thinking that they have the same problems that you have, some, even more than you could imagine or more than you could shake a crooked stick at on Saturday night at a snipe hunting contest."

She hesitated, then, went on. "However, to set aside, allay and abate your worries and concerns, concerning a brain transplant, it has become more or less common for such an operation in this day and time, but to fully insure your total recovery, we do recommend that you record your memories, family information, sexual preferences, financial information, telephone numbers, computer passwords, names of both friends and enemies, photos are good in that case, just so that you can tell what your differences are later on, and the like, then, after your transplant, you can play the recordings back to yourself and bring your new brain up to speed early on, so that you can function normally in society as a whole, right off of the bat and to know where to go home to and know which key fits which car and just who you are sleeping with on a regular basis. By the same token, consider this; after all, you will still have the same body, the same spirit, the same soul, the same tanning parlor tan, the same hair stylist, and so forth, so, none of that will be changed in any way. Only your driver, your engine, your brain, will be changed out. Too, you can even record your great mysterious humongous secret and then recover it after the transplant, and, nothing much would ever be lost in the process."

"OK, OK, let me think about this just a danged New Jersey minute. On the one hand, if I told you my great mysterious humongous secret that my brain has figured out, and, by doing so, it possibly relieved me of some of or a little of the tremendous pressure on my skull, which in turn, relieved me of some of my great pain, would you still recommend that I still have to have the brain transplant?" I queried.

She looked at me, then said. "Well, Kelly, that would most likely depend upon exactly what the secret was, and how much pressure was relieved in the process of or by the telling of it. However, I must remind you, that doctor-patient information is protected by both federal and State laws and I may not divulge any information of any conversation between us with any other third party entity, other than your other primary physicians, neither the public in general, nor those in your very private matters, which includes the New York Times and Boston Globe, for that matter, except that is, with your signed agreement along with your Power of Attorney and Personal Representative assignment, or signed over Guradianship for any future Probate Court matters. Didn't both of your personal physicians also advise you of that? Did they not provide you with a yippy HIPPAY form?"

"Well, yes and no, but, if they did, I didn't remember then or don't remember now, although I do remember signing off on a bunch of documents that I didn't completely read, but, I thought that the form was a Yappy Hippy, and, I don't remember signing a release of information or anything else at all concerning neither the New York Times or the Boston Globe either." I said.

She went back to reviewing the reports from the referring physicians. "I see here, that you had a CAT scan of your skull, but, it did not show anything. Not that you did not have anything up there, inside your skull, that is, it is not that, it is, that there did not appear to be anything abnormal that they could record, but, that test could not measure the tremendous pressure you must have on your skull, so, that information is still hiding or hanging out there somewhere in the unknown. Too, I do note here, that neither of the reports say, that everything about your brain was normal. That is what we call a minor void in the world's professional medical practiceer's. This is no different in your case whatsoever. There seems to be a more than a significant void of information regarding whether or not that your referring physicians found any further semblance of normalcy as they did not record it as such here in the recorded section of the record. That is not a bad sign, in and of itself or by itself. However, it raises more than one red flag that most world renowned brain neurosurgeons like myself would normally want to take a second, third or maybe even a fourth look at, while there was a fifth setting out and open on the desk along with a couple of clean glasses. Depending, that is, on how good your insurance was or is, whichever, however, I might add. Now, I do note and I see, that your second personal physician recommended both a Sonogram and an MRI, but he neglected to write the order for them. Did he or you have some problem with the Sonogram and MRI test recommendation?" She asked.

"Well, the CAT Scan cost me so damned much money because Medicare didn't hardly pay anything, and my Supplemental insurance only paid for part of it, but, I was never told which part, and, I thought that the Sonogram and MRI most likely wouldn't show anything additional, so, I opted out of that option on my own, just short of ignoring my physicians recommendations." I said. "I mean, they showed me the slices of my brain, laid out like raw T-bone steaks on a meat cutters platter, front to back, top to bottom, back and forth, hither and yon, and, there did not appear to be anything that I could see that some other test would or could have shown better. I mean, if there is nothing there, there is nothing there, do you know what I mean?" I said.

"I understand very well." She said. "The cost of medicine and medical procedures has all but gone through the roof and skyrocketed over the last few years, for no known reason, or, for no reason that I know of other than to pad the pockets of some pretty petty pediatricians. However, brain transplants are not one of them on the Medicare auditor's hit list. Those costs have fairly leveled out over the last few years, and, most insurance companies are more than happy to pay the entire cost of the transplant, without any copay whatsoever, if that is one of your fears or concerns." She added.

"Well, in your opinion, otherwise, but not necessarily negating the brain transplant thing, are there other options, or, would you recommend that I get a second opinion?" I both said and asked.

"I fully understand your concerns." She said. "Like I said before, I have had many patients over the last thirty years or so, that have appeared to have the same diagnosis with the same prognosis that you have. Some, have opted out at the time and went home to live an all work and no play makes Jack a dull boy kind of life. Some went for the surgery and it changed their life Hollywood style albeit a little short of what you could call dramatically. For example, why, I remember, one young man, who just happened to get himself transplanted with some young teenage girls brain, and, when he was released, he danced all of the way out of the hospital and went out to pick flowers and sing songs, then got all emotional about his possible acne and a couple zits, and sat on a park bench and cried about it all, all the while trying to cover themup with some Dollar Store makeup, and, on his follow up visit, he insisted that he wanted to have a most peculiar sexual operation of which I had to decline but referred him to a local renowned sexy sexologist. Then, in another case, I remember the young lady who got a brain from one of the Hell's Angels motorcycle gang, who had been in a most unfortunate motorcycle accident, if you could believe it, bless his soul, and, all she wanted to do when she got out of the hospital was to buy a big hog Harley on a seven year term and go riding on a curvy road along the ocean with the wind in her face and her hair a-blowing in the breeze all while fully dressed in oiled down leathers and flying colors. When I saw her later, for a follow up appointment, she told me, that she had learned, that, a happy motorcyclist, is one who can still smile with bugs in their teeth and that she had already gotten a tattoo or two which she was so proud of, especially the one on her hiney, or, maybe it was just above it. To solve any of your concerns, and, to bring it to a head, with no pun intended otherwise, you are already at the location of your second opinion, as you were referred by your previous two personal physicians for this opinion, so, the buck stops here and this is the officially accepted cash crash site." She added.

"Do I have a choice, if I opt for the brain transplant, to get what I want, like the women who go in for artificial insemination who get to pick out the father of their child?" I asked.

"Well, generally, brain transplanting doesn't work just like that. It is usually set up on a first come and first served basis in that matter. If a brain becomes available, we call you, and you come a-running **post-haste in a hurry**, because brains, as a rule, do not preserve well, so, it is generally a slam bam, thank you ma'am, yank it out, cram it and jam it in, kind of thing, or a hurry up and get 'er done job as you would be more familiar with, then, we all then just sit back a little, or back off a little, and just take a wait and see attitude, to see how far it will all go downhill from there." She said.

"OK, I think that I understand the process, however, just what happens to my brain after it is taken out? I asked.

She responded. "Kelly, your brain will go to the next available person on the donor-candidate call list, as a listed recipient, the way it all works is, that you also automatically go on the donor list as a donor. It is as simple as that, and, that is just the way the system is set up, somewhat of a medical shuffle with you in the middle, and somewhat of a make work kind of thing for us neurosurgeons, just for us to have a way to keep our heads above the water, along with some more regular monthly income and related investment portfolios, if you will, and, I might also add, without us all having to pay union dues.

"Wait just a minute." I said. "If I underwent the brain transplant, would that not mean, that whoever, or, whomever, was the recipient of my brain, would also be the recipient of my great mysterious humongous secret? Would it not? And, would they not also have the same tremendous pressure on their skull?" I fired off both questions at the same time expecting at least one good answer between the two, to be on target.

"What you surmise would be true in all aspects and respects, most likely, and respectively. Then, there would be two people on the face of the earth sharing your mysterious humongous secret but perhaps the other person could withstand the pressure and find it more accommodating and accepting than what is your experience, and, in some cases, they may not even realize that such a secret ever existed, or, would otherwise ignore it if they ever realized it." She said.

"Would that not also mean, that I would not have the secret secure anymore, that someone else would have the secret, isn't that how it would pan out, eventually, when it crossed their mind and they thought about what I used to think about with the looping thing you called B-U-L-L going on inside my fragile skull?" I asked.

"True again." She said. "But, that is all part of the problem solving of the solving of your problem. Remember, for every action, there is a reaction, which is a most peculiar law unto itself, but, in your case, it just happens to also be the better part of the end result forthcoming, so, that would be a secondary purpose for your primary recording of your interests as I mentioned a-prior or a-previous."

"OK, OK, back to my prior previous question. Would it be necessary, or even recommended, that if I told my great mysterious humongous secret, and by doing so, it perhaps relieved some of the great pressure that it puts on my present brain, and thereby reduced the great associated pains somewhat, would I then not even so much as require the brain transplant thing? Or, maybe, even, what if we could figure out which half of my brain that the secret is on and only transplant that half, in that way, I could keep my secret, could I not?" I asked.

She responded. "Again, Kelly, it is totally dependent upon your great mysterious humongous secret, whatever it may be in your mind as to just how much of the pressure and pain could be relieved in the process of blowing it off like a cheap rented steam-jenny along with the obvious spilling of your guts on the matter at hand. On the half brain thing, there are very few half brained people on the donor lists, unfortunately. Most of the half brained people only want to supplement and top off what they already have. Also, replacing only half of your brain may only reduce the pain and pressure by an equal amount for the other half, and would not completely correct your problem."

I came right back at her, with. "I don't understand or fully see the connection of the great mysterious humongous secret as being dependent upon whether or not that I had the brain transplant. Something either here or there, or somewhere in the middle, is amiss, or, I have missed something in my misunderstanding of the requirements for such an operation in the first place if the overall pressure along with the pain could be relieved in some fit, form or fashion somehow otherwise." I said.

She responded. "Well, Kelly, it is only by your own ingenuity, that you have figured it all out and have come to know that you readily really need a new brain. But, to shed a little light on that, remember, your brain is the engine that motivates you, your brain is your driver, it gets you up and gets you going. Now, an automobile engine can be rebuilt, or, overhauled, or, even a new engine can be ordered out and installed with new heads, carburetor shackles, muffler baffles, dual tail pipes and all chromed up from one end to the other. However, science has not yet advanced to the point of being able to build a new brain engine from scratch, so, as neurosurgeons, we can only replace those brain engines, or, tune them up sometimes somewhat to extend their usefulness. To put it bluntly to you, I cannot give you a different engine and implant the same memory that you have in your old engine, as, that is something you would have to do yourself as was previously mentioned twice already now, just in case any of the readers who have gotten this far in the story may have missed it. Too, what you surmise, it is true, that is, that whoever or whomever, would get your brain as the next in line transplant, would also get your thoughts, your memory, and your feelings, along with the pressure and possibly some or all of the pain. There is no other way around it. Is it a problem? Why sure it is. Can we do anything about it? Why no, not at this time with neuroscience being what it is in this day and time. But, it solves your particular problem both in the short term and the long run, and, that is the best that modern medical neurological practice can do for you at this time with respect to your never ending and ongoing problem which solves the form and fashion thing, but, it still leaves the fit thing on the table. I can always replace your brain with a smaller one, but, if it is a larger on to be put in, I may have to do some fancy dancy trimming here and there along with the cram and jam it thingy."

I came right back at her with some statements along with a couple questions. "OK, OK, let me advise you of my mysterious humongous secret, if you will, let me, please, let the cat out of the bag, and then, you determine, whether or not, that it qualifies me, or, disqualifies me for the brain transplant thing as to just how much pressure on my skull that could be relieved and also see just how much pain could also be relieved in the process." I said.

"OK." She said. "Spit it all out and get it over with, show it to me, lay it out on the line, bounce it off the wall!"

I took a couple deep breaths, and then went on. "So, here it is in a nutshell with no pun intended. My great mysterious humongous secret is this; everything on the face of the earth, exists and is ongoing between two different merging alternate, paralleled or mirrored Universes, the first is found and dwelt in, normally, as, in my case, in my waking hours, and the second, is when I am asleep and supposedly dwelling in what I call my dream world, however, in each, my soul, or, my spirit is the same, they, or it, is active in both the alternate or paralleled and mirrored Universes especially when they merge or coalesce at some various junction points, as, it is written, the spirit or soul of man never sleeps, It is, as if it is on steroids, and sometimes, during the night or while my body is asleep in the first alternate or paralleled mirrored Universe, my spirit gets tired of sitting or lying around and waiting for my body to awaken, and, it just takes off on its own and wanders around in the other alternate or paralleled mirrored Universe, sometimes the activities, allow my memories from that second Universe to be brought back as remembrances into the first Universe, especially from the parts that have merged or have coalesced. Too, in most cases, there is an equivalent amount of activity or trouble that I as a person can get into in either the awake first Universe or the second asleep Universe which I have so named in order for me just to help me keep a-track of the two, personally, when it crosses my mind. Especially when lost keys, telephone or TV remote are involved." I said.

"Is that it? That's all there is to it? Or, is there more?" She asked, seriously, as if it were only one serious question with three different potential answers.

"That's about it, and, I feel already, more than just relieved, that a tremendous amount of pressure has been relieved from within my skull, which I am sure that you could measure, if you had some technical medical method, and, I can tell that most or at least much of the pain is also already gone a-by-by, and, has certainly been more than just relieved already, somewhat suddenly, I might add, and my brain within my skull, being also relieved of the pressure, hasn't felt this good in years, that I can even remember, and, really, right now, I don't feel the least bit loopy with your B-U-L-L thingy anymore, as, I can't think of a single further question that I need to have answered at this time." I said.

"Well, surprise, surprise, it all lies before your very eyes." She said. "You just might be interested to know, that the Aborigines in Australia, believe the same damn thing in general to that so-called secret of yours of which you have just related to me in no less than your one full breathless breath. They done figured something like that all out hundreds of years ago, if not even more, and, have come to believe, that the spirit of man leaves the body and goes a-wandering around and about the world at will when the physical body goes to sleep. This is nothing new, this was discovered centuries ago, as, it has been recorded in the history of their findings and beliefs, and, is on record as having been believed by them for hundreds if not even thousands of years. I should mention, however, that there is no record of any of them ever having any recorded pressure on their skulls or having any ensuing or on-going headache pain accordingly by any of them believing in such a thing that I ever read about in the medical journals. Although, I might add that they do not mention the merging alternate or paralleled mirrored Universes things as you do, so, you may be able to record that information for a patent and even copyright that portion of your so-called secret with the Library of Congress, why, you may even get an ISBN number to go along with it all if you do it electronically and want to wait for it all."

"You are telling me, that there are others in the world that has come to believe some of the same things that I believe, these things that have caused me so much pain from this great pressure on my skull and endangered my very lifestyle because of just thinking about these things as they crossed my brain? I mean, you would not believe the number of relationships that have been ditched because of it all and the questions that it has all brought about, not to mention the raised eyebrows and the eyes rolling thing that it has caused." I both asked and said in the same breath.

"Absolutely, with no ifs, ands, buts or maybes, baby." She said. "Now, perhaps, if you will, please advise me, as, to just how you came about having the two primary physicians, as both Medicare and Medicaid disallows such, even with Supplemental coverage, however, I mean, I do have two different and distinct reports on your condition, one from each, and do not understand how each or one or the other, or, either for that matter, all came about." She said, somewhat also asking.

I tried to explain. "Well, it is like this, one of the physicians is from the primary or my first awake Universe, and, the second one, is from my second asleep Universe, I think, but, I am not fully sure at this time as to which one is which. I did not choose the same physician in both universes. However, I have no exacting explanation as to how I got the doctor from the second Universe to get a report back into the first Universe, or perhaps, it is one of those vice-a-versa kind of things, as, on one hand, if I am now present in the second asleep Universe, then the other report came from the first awake Universe, but, on the other hand, if I am now in the first awake Universe, then, the other report was transported over from the second asleep Universe, or, whichever, according to whichever Universe that I am in at present or perhaps I am in the merged part where both are represented albeit partially, although I can't explain the co-pay process between the two. Either way, I have no partiality on the partiality thing, as that is another problem in itself of which I readily have no ready answer at the ready. And, I am now totally baffled, and, mixed up as dog poop from the dog walk park from the get go, as to which Universe is which at any given moment in time along with which one that I am in, unless that I may just be in both of them at the same time, right now, like I said a-previous, maybe I'm in the merged part with my car keys stuck in one of the other unmerged parts. So, I feel that I am in no position to make any major financial purchases, make any sort of marital, or sex change operation decisions at this time." I said. "Or, operate complicated equipment, run machinery or volunteer to be someone's designated driver, even if I take one-a-day vitamins twice daily." I added on.

"I think that that is probably the wisest thing for you to do or not do, whichever you so choose to decide upon, to all aforementioned, at this time and place, whichever it might be for you. I might add, that I am not married either in this Universe, or the other that I know of, but do have some friends that I have now come to doubt as to where they are at, along with a few financial problems now and then, of which I am not sure as to just what is either the primary or secondary cause. But, all in all, besides all of that, I am so thankful that we were able to solve your problem and relieve the pressure and reduce your pain, I mean, that is why I am here in the first place, according to the

Hippocratic or the hypocritic oath, whichever, however, the thing of which Universe that you are in at any given time is something you will have to work out for yourself on your own. Run a few tests and try to evaluate it yourself, make some notes, I mean, you can save a lot of money in the long run. Go to your local library and check out some of the self-help and do-it-yourself books. In this day and time, you do not have to be a rocket scientist, all you have to do is go on the internet to find what you want to know, after all, I have never yet seen google come up with a blank page on any topic. Too, I hear that they now have a new book out called "An Idiots Guide to Do-It-Yourself Brain Surgery", which, I already have on order through Amazon Books dot com. I could pass it on to you after I read it if you would be interested." She said.

She went on. "But, please tell me, how did you come to choose two different primary physicians in the two different dimensions who were able to provide both of your referrals?" She asked.

"Well, I didn't choose the same physician in the different dimensions, because, I wanted a quasi-second opinion, without an initial referral. However, both apparently came to the same similar conclusion as to what my problem was early on, and, provided me with an immediate referral, which, in turn, brought me to your office for a secondary evaluation." I said.

Without further ado, or additional questions, she concluded. "In the meanwhile, and, back to reality, you have more than just exceeded your two hour limit, and, you will have to address this with the clerk before you leave, as, you owe another Sixty-five dollars and seventeen cents according to my calculations, otherwise, she will not push the button under her desk on the right side in order to unlock the exit door until you belly up to the bar and pay your bill." She said.

Then, I bounced up, without another further word, without so much as even a thank you, I just got up on my hind legs, put one foot in front of the other, walked out of her office, and left, thinking to myself that this doctor's appointment was worth every penny that I spent over and above my insurance co-pay no matter which Universe that I was in at this time, and, whether or not that they were merged, coalesced or just messing around with the other just trying to confuse me. I now could care less, however, I did wonder after I paid my bill, as to whether or not, perchance, that one payment could be credited against the debit into the other, for tax purposes, just in case I was in both of them at the same time. I realized then, at that time, as it crossed my mind, that in either dimension, it is all about the money.

While walking home, It crossed my mind as to the Jimmy Hoffa thing, as if to which universe he was in at the time of his disappearance, and then I wondered, whether a person could be alive in one dimension and dead in the other, or, vice-a-versa, then, my thoughts turned to Elvis Presley, I mean, Elvis has been seen just about everywhere since he departed one or the other dimensions, and, what about that Amelia Earhart disappearing thing? How come she has never been seen again, or, what about all of those alien abduction reports on file at the Area 51 UFO headquarters? But then, that got me to thinking about myself and my own problems again, wondering about some of the chances that I had been taking willy-nilly without regard to my betterment or my wellbeing for that matter, not to mention some of those experimental pain killers that I had taken in the past like Elvis did. I was most likely one of the lucky ones who survived it all.

It was about this time that I woke up with a another terrible headache and more than just a great pressure on my skull, just trying to figure out which dimension that I was now in along with wondering what the Aborigines in Australia took for headaches years ago while looking in the medicine cabinet to see what pain relievers were left, wherever I was now.

THE SPY THAT CAME DOWN WITH A COLD

The young Lieutenant was on his way to reporting to the Confederate Company Commander after the Commander's Chief Runner had advised him that the Commander wanted to see him immediately, so, the Lieutenant headed out toward the Commander's tent. He had a good idea, that he knew what it was all about, already, as, two of his sharp Privates within the Company, had captured what they believed to be, of all things, a northern spy, and, the spy was now being prepared, or, softened up so to speak, for the first phase of his interrogation. The Lieutenant had arrived early, and stood outside the Commander's tent, until one of the two guards advised the Commander as to just who it was that was to be reporting to him. The guard came out of the Commander's tent and held the flap open, saluted the Lieutenant, thereby, signaling for the young Lieutenant to enter in.

The young Lieutenant entered into the tent, and said. "Lieutenant Brockman reporting as ordered, Sir." He said, while standing at attention before the Confederate Company Commander.
Major Marshall acknowledged his presence, and said that he was to be at ease as easily as he could be, then, he began. "I understand that a couple of your Company's finest, a couple of your troops, have done up and nabbed what they have identified forthrightly to be a dirty no good northern spy, working down here amongst us. Please tell me, why do you think that you have come into such luck of having captured such a prize? Are you two-thirds Irish or something?"

"Well Sir, of that I know not, one way or another, or the other." The young Lieutenant began. "However, the man reportedly speaks with a foreign tongue and with a dialect of some undetermined origin. He speaks of such things as "The Civil War", instead of "The Northern Aggression", and not "The War Between The States", too, he is of a draftable or conscriptable age for military service, whether it be Union or Confederate, yet he claims to be affiliated with neither, without a "nor" after-mentioned. In addition, he appears to be smarter than what he looks, that is, if his looks have anything to say about it."

Without further ado, the Major stated. "Lieutenant, I am hereby relieving you of your duty with respect to the captured alleged suspected spy detail. None of your other duties are relieved however, however, I am relieved that you are however relieved, as, I would expect you to be too, with some relief, however."

The young Lieutenant responded in somewhat of a complaint. "Sir, I have performed my service always, to the point of almost forever, have accomplished all of my duties with courage and honor, not to mention the due diligence that I just threw in on the back side and up front. Besides, I have never ever even once disobeyed the orders to obey the orders. If I may ask. Will this relief, in any way shape, form or fashion, go against my record of service in any way, anyway? I mean, I am one of those chosen few from my dear sweet home Alabama, I have served you well in both way down south in the steamy hot Mississippi delta, and now, here, way up north by Memphis, in cold Tennessee, hot or cold when need be, on tap, but have yet to ever have been called Lieutenant luke warm by any of which I have been so affiliated."

"No, no, not at all, not at all, no it don't, and, and don't tell me it doesn't, so, don't you worry a minute about it, even if it did, does or did not do." The Major replied. "I see it this way Lieutenant, it is so much more general than that, but please don't say anything about that to the General, as, the very word Lieutenant, and I remember how hard it was even to pronounce it, or, to spell it for that matter, when I was one, that is, is more than just too long of a word, and, it is more than too hard to spell for the common man, for that matter, when you think about it, and besides that, the word contains three distinct syllables, so, I am hereby passing this extra duty on to Captain White, as, the word Captain is easier to spell, overall at the outset, and, from the get go, and, the word Captain only contains two syllables, and is spelled the same way in both the Army and the Navy, and, thereby, more than used overall, besides, the word Lieutenant has already been used entirely too much in this story already, and, if it be continued to be used, it might take up too much space totally, and make the overall story too long, which any respectable editor would ding me for, along with the making of a too long a sentence in the process. I am sure that you would understand that. By the same token, but not to ding you unfairly, your name, Brockman, contains two full syllables, whereas, Captain Whites' name only has one syllable, so in order to meet the General's standing order to reduce paper for correspondence, and to go to more word of mouth communication, not to mention the estimated measured energy consumption along with those bad boy carbon emissions, I am hereby ordering the change, forthright for the fortnight. That's it in a nut shell, no more, no less. So, that is all, Lieutenant. Thank you for your service to date. By the way, on your way out, and, in your free time, see if you can try to see if you can find out why the morning Enquirer newspaper has been being delivered at no less than what I would call more than just erratic times, slung here and yon, for a hide and hunt, sometimes before dawn, at dawn or after dawn, sometimes even when

I am gone to breakfast or after. See if you can find out why that is happening to me, for me, if you would be so kind, just to make sure that it is not some insidious part of some failed future battle plan which I do not need to be as part of my retirement career package." He added.

The young Lieutenant saluted the Major, and said that he would make the necessary inquire about the Enquirer, duly do some more due diligence, and concentrate on his assigned duty, then, he about faced, or, reverse turned and faced the other way, away from the presence of the Commander, somewhat backwards in some respects, but not backwardly so, and certainly not walking backward, but so thus, departed the Commanders tent, and thought firstly to himself, that maybe the word Commander could be considered as too long too, as it contains three syllables and eight letters, but, he thought secondly that maybe it would be best not to point that out to the Commander at this time. As he departed the Commanders tent, he recognized and saluted the recognized Captain White, who had just reported in to the Commander's guards at his tent. Then, the Lieutenant went on his way to get where he was going and to do his assigned duty, to the best of his ability, within the parameters of his contract agreement, without any omission of his commission.

The senior guard then advised the Commander that Captain White was awaiting patiently outside, around and about, and, was so instructed by the Major to hurry up and usher him in post haste, or, in other more shorter words, right away, or "do it now!". Captain White, as he was called, then entered the Commander's tent.

"Captain White reporting as the Commander has so ordered, with everything within the border in order, Sir." He said.

The Commander began. "Captain White, as you may have heard, a couple of outstanding Privates, over in Lieutenant Brockman's Company, who appear to be out standing in their field, were, overnight, no less, more than outstanding in their field, and caught what they have every reason to believe to be, a northern spy from the north, no more or no less. If found to be so, they are then to be commended and are in line for further commendation with an upgrade in their accommodations, so, I am now assigning you with the extra duty of overseeing the interrogation of the spy in question in the accompaniment of the Adjutant General, although he is called that, he is not a real General, generally, so to speak. You and he, or the two of you, with you being technically the one in charge, but are both assigned to question him, the spy that is, but, do not call it an interrogation, as, that is totally too long a word for this story, so, just call it a preview or a review of the circumstances, but then, circumstances may be a too long a word considering the circumstances, so, only use it with discretion accordingly. Anyway, if nothing else, just call it a question and answer period, period."

He went on. "So, with that in mind, I have here, directions for you, from the Battalion Commander no less, ten cards, held out here in my left hand, before your very eyes, with questions on them, on each card that is, that need be addressed, but, that may be the wrong word, as, I don't mean for you to address the cards, I mean for you to get some answers. It is your job, therefore, for you to be there with whomever, or whoever you should also choose to assist you in getting these questions answered, in addition to the Adjutant General, that is, although, he is not yet adjudged to be a judge, jury and executioner, although, he has the capability and the authority to do any one or either or all, for all I know. So, I now pass these cards to you at this moment in time. You are now in charge of these cards, those just passed from my left hand to your left hand, left handedly, but, not under the table. I might also mention, just for the sake of mentioning, that the information mentioned on these cards, and, the answers, when mentioned, and if can be determined; will be of an unmentionable classified nature at this time. On the front of each card, you will see a question, and, when you ask the questions of the alleged captured no good for nothing northern spy, you are to write his answer, or, his response, what it was that he said, and, how he said it, verbatim, on the back side of the card, as, it would be difficult to write it on the front, since that is where the question is, and, once completed, you and the Adjutant General being the only ones who have the answers to the assigned questions, although I have some answers myself already, especially when I know what the questions are up front, or ahead of time. You are then, to bring all of the cards back to me, so, that I can forward the questions with answers, on up to the Battalion Commander, who, then, I would suppose, would send them on up to the Regimental Commander, who then, in turn, would send them on up to the Division Commander, where, I am sure, if not sooner or later, the cards, with both the questions and answers, will, sooner or later, be lost in the passage to one level or the other, or in some other paper work somewhere in the shuffle along the way. But disregard the last remark, as that was just off of the cuff, or just off of the top of my head, so to speak." He said.

The Captain asked. "Sir, if I may ask, what was it that made the Privates that caught the guy think that the prisoner was, or, is a spy?" The Major responded. "The Privates, as was reported to me, were on guard during the night, and caught him in the early hours, sometime, just before dawn, running around the camp, as if he was counting the tents, counting the horses, counting the guns stacked up, and, he is not a member of our Quartermaster or any of our Supply details." He said.

The Captain nodded his head and accepted the special assignment of this extra duty with robust fervor. Telling the Commander that he was proud to have the opportunity to serve and to provide service of such nature for the betterment of the southern endeavor, and, that he considered that it was all part of his job from the get-go, that he had always been trained to always be on the top of and to get to the bottom of things as they came to be, and that the Commander had picked the right man for the job, and, that he personally had always had an eye out for a spy, especially those no good dirty low down good for nothing northern spies, and that this particular spy did not have a chance in hell of ever withholding out even a little smiget of information if and when he ever got through with him, and, that if he so tried, or even acted like it, that he would be one sorry Charlie, and, that he would get the answers to the questions even if it took six months of beating them out of the dirty no good for nothing northern albeit alleged spy on a daily basis, even if he had to go to the threat of water boarding, but only if absolutely necessary under the circumstances. And, even though that he had said "that" too many times already, he would totally dismiss that, as that was just the way he talked about things like that.

The Commander then added. "Don't refer to the spy as a spy, any more than what is absolutely necessary, just call him a common prisoner for now, for, I am sure, under the circumstances, that you understand." The Commander then dismissed the Captain, and, the Captain said "Yes Sir", spelled with capital letters, then he saluted the Commander after the Commander had said. "Dismissed." Also spelled with a capital letter as the first letter of the word.

213

The Captain left the tent, and so as, to save space, to refer to the same method of departure that the previous Lieutenant aforementioned had done and in the same manner with the same results in one of the previous paragraphs which referenced the departed Lieutenant aforementioned although he was not really departed, as, it is just an awkward way of wording to say it that way. Just so as to save some a little space here and there, maybe, and, just to explain it all a little better, or, to make it all a little more clearer for the reader to absorb, that is, if they were following the sentence like they should have been doing in the first place.

The Captain, then went into a herky-jerky hurry, post haste, quarter trot as it was, first on, going on his way to the tent of the Adjutant General, and thereby requesting his immediate assistance in the questioning of a so-called prisoner, saying, and almost yelling it all out loud, enough for anyone within earshot, to have heard even if they weren't listening, and, also explained the circumstances to him whilst on the their journey to the tent whence the alleged northern spy was being held chained to a stake in the ground. But, also told him, that the Major did not want anyone else to know any of the information, of that of which the spy was a suspected spy and to even keep it to himself without saying anything about it to anyone else. The Adjutant General assured the Captain that he understood what he was attempting or trying to say, perfectly.

The Captain, had the ten cards of questions securely in hand, left hand that is, which was where he had received them in the first place. So, when he and the Adjutant General arrived at the tent which contained the allege spy, he moved the sinister questions from his left hand, so as, to make himself more dexterous, moved the questions to his right hand. At this time, the two privates, out in front of, and guarding the very tent which contained the spy, came to attention and saluted the Captain and the Adjutant General.

"I am Captain White, and, I am here along with the Adjutant General in tow, to question the prisoner." He said to the guards. With that, the guards completed their salute, and, opened the tent flaps and held them back for the Captain and the Adjutant General to enter. Then, the Captain and the Adjutant General started to enter the entrance, but hesitated in order to make an entranced entrance. He felt, in his own mind, that some words, just had a need, or, actually deserved to be used more than once, once in a while, before they got all worn out in the process, although he thought that words used just once in a while would not wear out as soon as long as if they were said quickly.

However, before the Captain and Adjutant General could enter into the tent, one of the guards, stepped in front of them or him, whichever one was the first in line, and said. "Sirs, I should warn or advise you both, that the prisoner speaks with a foreign tongue of which we know not, the sounds of which are peculiar to both me and all of the other guards, partly sounding like a criss-cross, or, halfway, or somewhere there in between, between a southern and northern tongue of that foreign language we have all come to know, or, have called Kentuckian."

"Kentuckian?" The Captain said. "I don't reckon I ever heard anyone speak that foreign language anywhere in these parts, here about, around about, or here and there from kingdom come. Now, here, between the two of you, you recognized the problem first, so you, the senior guard, you depart now, and go throughout the Company, tent by tent if you have to, and, you may even have to go throughout the Battalion even if need be, and question round and about if anyone speaks or understands, or, can translate the foreign tongue of this Kentuckian language of which you speak along with the assorted dialects. So, step and fetch it, or, hurry on now, get up and go, and, we will await your imminent return when and if you ever plan to make a quick comeback."

The Captain and the Adjutant General stood outside the tent for a few moments. The Captain asked the Adjutant General. "Do you know anything about Kentuckians?" He asked.

"Well, I know that there is a difference between Northern Kentuckians, and, Southern Kentuckians, Eastern Kentuckians and Western Kentuckians, and, I remember, that one or the other can't read writing, while the other can't write reading, but, for the life of me, I don't remember exactly which one is which." The Adjutant General said.

With that, as they had no other alternative, the Captain and the Adjutant General finally entered the tent and sat down with the alleged northern spy, not exactly with, as it was more than somewhat across from. The spy looked somewhat normal in most respects, in their opinion, as opposed to him looking somewhat abnormal, with the Captain and Adjutant General nodding back and forth between the two of them, in silent agreement, but, not at or toward the alleged spy, and, yet trying not to catch his eye. The spy looked to be more than well fed. He was young, but not too young. He was old, but not too old. He was tall, but not too tall. He was not exactly what the Captain expected or had envisioned an alleged spy to look like if he had ever encountered one, even though this was the first one that he had ever seen or heard of for that matter. So, the three of them just sat there, in the tent, not saying anything, awaiting the translator, or, translators, or, someone who could speak a little of this foreign language called Kentuckian, with no telling the number of dialects that it could possibly contain. It seemed like it took forever and a day, but, finally, the guard arrived with two fellow Privates in tow, just behind, and, following him, and he brought them in, and, introduced them to the Captain and the Adjutant General.

"Sirs, I have here, the only ones in the total of our entire Battalion who has ever heard of the language of Kentuckian with its assorted dialects, all of those of these who have heard it spoken at one time or another, and who at one time or another, has tried to make a trade or barter with someone who they thought spoke the tongue. The first one, a formerly accused horse thief, charged and arraigned but never yet found guilty, who admits to trying to deal with a Kentuckian, but who was not successful at the time, as he freely admits that it was all but an impossibility, hence, the one and same Private has now been put in charge of our horses, but only because he understands horses, and, the second one, one, whose second cousin came within a hair's breadth of almost marrying a Kentuckian at a previously arranged shot gun wedding, right before he up and run off out of gunshot range and took to the hills, completely run off he did, hence, he is now one of our private Privates. Between the two of them, perhaps, they may be of some assistance to you in your endeavor." And, with that, the guard returned to his posted position on the outside, near the exterior of the tent, leaving the two pre-mentioned Privates with the Captain, the Adjutant General and the alleged no good for nothing northern spy.

The Captain then spoke to the prisoner, or, the so called accused alleged northern spy, now, one and same as far as he was concerned, but only mentioning the former and not the latter. He began his spiel. "I am Confederate Captain White, but, I shouldn't have to tell you that, since you see me in the here and now in my grey uniform, with my rank so evidently exposed on the frontispiece of my uniform here, so, I should not have to tell you that, and, that should go unsaid, so disregard that I ever said it in the first place. I have to tell you, that you have the right to remain silent, however, I should also advise you, that we will do anything in our power to make sure that you don't, too, anything that you may say, may be used against you, which, we will make sure of one way or another that it is, and, at one time or another, you will be afforded representation of any of the trumped up charges that we so choose to bring against you, however, that so-called representation will be of our choosing and of not of yours, I should also advise."

With that forewarned and forearmed statements, the Captain turned to the two Privates or so-called translators who were to make some attempt to communicate with this alleged spy who was, or is, believed to speak the foreign language of Kentuckian, although yet of some uncertain dialect.

The Captain looked at the first card and read the question. He realized that the very first question contained the word "spy", and did not know how to ask the question without saying the word, but then, there it was, the word was there, so, he thought that he would just have to go with it, so, he then turned to the Privates, and said. "Ask the prisoner; say to him, if you can get it across to him. Ask him in his tongue. Do you still work as a spy?" He was said to have asked.
The two Privates looked at one another, acting like they were trying to decide who was going to say something first. Then, one of them nodded and started to speak to the prisoner. "Ya'll frum Kaintuck? Watcha callin' hanger? Is yousa low startin' wage part-time beginner spy or you all a-workin' full time with insurance, benefits, bonuses, a retirement package and a bail out with a golden parachute to hang by when and if the great conflict is over?" The one Private asked.
The alleged spy responded. "That sounds like one of those "do you still beat your wife" questions."

"Just answer the question." The Private said somewhat flatly.

"No." The alleged spy said.

The Private came back at him. "No? No what? The question what was asked, is one of those "which one" questions, no matter what dialect of Kentuckian which or what of you speak. So, again, which, which one is it, is it the first which one, or, the second which one?"
"No." The alleged spy said. "It is actually, more than one of those "either-or", or a "neither-nor" questions. Either I answer it, or, I don't. It's either way or neither way. It ain't a-gonna' be one way or the other, ever."

The Private turned to the Captain and the Adjutant General and said. "Sirs, the prisoner is being more than what I would call dilatory. I don't think he's a-gonna answer the question, even under torture, if you want my private opinion as a Private."

"Hold that thought, Private. I think that he just did. But, give me a minute here as I have to finish writing out my notes." The Captain said, as he was writing out the response to the question on the back of the first card, just as he was instructed to do by the Major. By this time, the card was full up to the edges with his notes being duly recorded as he was so ordered to do.

The Adjutant General leaned over to the Captain and said under his breath. "Captain, I think that this cracker is going to be one tough nut to crack, if you ask me."

The Captain put the first question card with the recorded answers written on the back in his jacket pocket and then looked at the second question card and read the next question to himself. He then turned to the Private and said. "Private, ask the prisoner, if he is from around here, or, does he hail from somewhere's else."

The Private looked at the prisoner again, and said. "Is yousa total local hokey yokel, or, is yousa one of those stradlin' and gaumin' traipsin' travelers?"

The spy looked up and said. "I'm from hear abouts, but I've been to Louisville, Knoxville, Nashville, Pittsburg, Rexburg, Vicksburg, Reno, Fargo, Buffalo, Winslow, Sarasota, Minnesota, Monterey, Santa Fe, Little Rock, Black Rock, Sioux City, Dodge City, I mean, I might sound like a local, but I have just about been everywhere."
The Captain was scribbling like mad on the back side of the second

card. "Wait, wait." He asked. "How do you spell Minnesota? Is is one "n" and two "s's" or is it two "n's" and one "s"?

"It's two "n's" and one "s"." The prisoner said. "Do you want me to write it down for you?" He added.

The Adjutant General leaned over and whispered to the Captain. "I remember now, I remember. This guy is most likely from Southern Kentucky. He can most likely write reading, but, most likely, he won't be able to read writing. You write it down and ask him to read it, just to prove it up."

The Captain held the card in front of the prisoner and asked him to read the writing on the card and pointed to the word "Minnesota", and, asked the prisoner to sign the card.

The prisoner responded. "I ain't signin' nothin' for nobody, for all I know, that could be some kind of confession or some admission of guilt. You ain't a-gonna trick me. You is talkin' to someone who has been to a couple County Fairs, and seen a goat ropin', why, I even seen a tattooed lady once, way up north in Bowling Green." He said.

The Adjutant General again leaned over to the Captain and said. "See, I told you, that proves it. The guy is definitely from Southern Kentucky, no doubt about it, one way or another."

The Captain was still scribbling all of the names of the places where the prisoner had said that he had been, and, at the end edge of the card, the Captain added "Southern Kentucky" and finally added "Bowling Green" to the list.

The period of questioning and answering went on into the wee hours of the early morning, until, finally, the prisoner appeared to have broken down completely.

"Look." The prisoner said. "This is the way it is. It is what it is. Now, I know, that you all have a job to do, and, you appear to do it well, but, so do I. I am in my own right and I know it. I don't appreciate going through this rigamarole night after night. I have some papers to deliver, and, your Regimental Commander, is really getting pissed, about not getting his morning paper on time."

"You are the paper boy? You are the one who delivers the Enquirer?" The Captain asked. Somewhat surprised.

"Yes, I am the one and only deliverer of the Enquirer newspaper, brought every morning to your camp in the rain, sleet or snow, just to keep you all in the know." He said.

With that, the Captain immediately closed out the interrogation, or, the question and answer session as was previously assigned. He then dismissed the two Privates and the two guards outside the tent, then, released the prisoner and allowed the newly identified paper boy to depart.

The Captain and the Adjutant General left the interrogation tent, and walked toward the cook's tent to have a cup of coffee and maybe even an early breakfast. Upon arrival at the cook's tent, they observed that the Regimental Commander and Lieutenant Brockman were already having breakfast, so, the Captain and the Adjutant General joined them for breakfast.

"Do you have a report for me?" The Major asked the Captain as he sipped his coffee.

The Captain responded. "Well, yes Sir, but it may not be what you were quite looking for. You see, it seems, that it was the paper boy, as he was, who was suspected as being a spy, as, he was mistakenly caught by a couple of the guards in the early morning hours, while he was out and about delivering his papers throughout the Regiment's encampment, they seemed to think that he was counting the tents throughout the encampment."

The Lieutenant added. "Yea, and, not only that, but it seems as if the guards with some of the different Companies have really been messing around with him some to no end, and, apparently, that is the why, of your paper not being delivered every day, on time, at the same time."
"I can understand that. I can see that. Pass the word down, to leave him alone. I need to keep up on the daily news, and, I don't want that messed up anymore." The Major said.

The Adjutant General, leaned over to the Captain, and whispered, "I think, that I have made a terrible mistake, I think, that I got myself mixed up somewhat, and, that the prisoner at the interrogation, was actually a Northern Kentuckian, as opposed to a Southern Kentuckian, and, although he mentioned Bowling Green, I think, that he just said that to throw us off, and, that he might be really from up around Paducah." He said.

The Captain did not acknowledge the Adjutant General's comment, as, no one else seemed to have heard it at the time.
Then, they all continued to enjoy their breakfast.

Meanwhile, the paper boy was out and about, doing his job, delivering the morning Enquirer, and, on the side, he was busy counting, counting the horses, counting the number of guns racked up in front of the tents, busy counting the tents and multiplying the number times 4 soldiers each and thereby adding up the total number of troops, then, counting the number of cannon, counting the number of wagons, counting the number of whatever, counting, counting, counting.

Just then, a couple of guards showed up, while he was counting the number of horses the second time around, and started to question him, and, then, the story started all over again for the next day. The guards, obviously had not yet got the word passed down to them.
It did not look much like, that this paper boy was going to get much sleep again this morning, and, to make things worse, he even felt like he was coming down with a cold (sic).

ALIENS UNAWARES

I am passing on to you, a dream of an intervention, which took place, in Mitchell, Indiana, home of both Gus Grissom, the Astronaut, and, Sam Bass, the bandit, without as much as a glimmer of a playful pundit of the good and bad, or, the best and worst.

Now, as it all first came to be about, every equipment operator at the Mitchell, IN, power plant job, was letting everyone else know, that everything was shutting down at noon, because of the heat of the hot August 108 degree heat. Everyone was saying that they were meeting at Davy's Dive on the west side of town for a cold drink.

I was operating a scraper, an earth mover if you will, but, I moving a coal pile, to make way for a two hundred coal train car drop from Gillette, Wyoming. Low sulfur coal from out west, which was the future, as, the power plants would not have to install scrubbers, to eliminate the sulfur or sulfur dioxide emissions, which would have been costly, and a cost which would have to be passed on to the consumers who would raise hell. All the while, running in dust, breathing in black coal dust, which dust which should have been meant for energy production, or, black lung cases on into the future. But even with my mind wandering, all I came back to was imagining a frosty mug of cold beer on the bar in front of me.

The heat was beyond belief. Radiant heat from above, or, overhead, direct from the sun, added to the heat from the reflected heat reflected from the ground, with the added heat from the hot engines on the equipment from the operations, and the heat from the metal itself, working on hot black coal, which was just short of self-ignition, spontaneous combustion, it was called, the coal was smoking, and, the smoking coal was so hot that it was making the rubber on the tires of the earth mover start to melt and smell, along with the high humidity at more than 90 percent, the overall heat was more than what anyone could call unbearable, along with the choking dust as thick as a dense black fog, from operations of the scrapers and the tractors, but yet again, my mind wandering back to that image of a frosty mug of cold beer. I mean, after all is said and done, I have always thought, that I would rather have a bottle in front of me, than have a frontal lobotomy.

So, management decided, in their infinite wisdom, to shut down our operations at noon. Although most of us started our shift at six in the morning, we would still be cutting our pay by two hours each day of

operations, but yet, no one was heard of, who were arguing against such a decision coming from upper management.
All morning, at every stop for water, there was a call for the ceasing of operations and a regroup at Davy's Dive at the west edge of town, for a cool drink, which, sounded more than just good to me at the time, as, the cheese on my baloney and cheese sandwich I had for lunch was probably already melted into the bread.
So, noon came, with the work shutdown, and, we all began to move our scrapers in to the secured safe area and began the shut down for the day. It just happened, by the time of it all, that I was the first to park my 27 yard Terex scraper at the fueling station and shut it down for the day and got the signal from the timekeeper that my day was done and that my time was in and recorded for the day for my pay. That was all I needed to check out after refueling.
I headed up and headed out, got in my pickup, and made tracks for Davy's Dive, on the north- side of the big town of Mitchell on the road toward Bedford.
I just happened to be, the first to arrive at Davy's Dive And, upon entry, I observed an old man at the right end of the bar, and a woman sitting over at the other end of the bar, so, I chose the safest point of entry, and I sat down next to the man. I mean, what would you have done in the same situation under the same circumstances? I mean, I didn't know her from Adam, or Eve, for that matter, and, besides, I was what most folks who did not know me, would be hard put not to call me a married man at the time.
I noticed, that the old man's hands were gnarled, indicating hard labor work, hard wrinkles on his dark sun damaged face, with the breaking apart of the dried skin on his knuckles, and, his curly grey hair pushing out from underneath his ball cap, and, that he did not have a drink in front of him at the bar, yet. I also, took notice of the woman at the other end, or, the west end of the bar, who had been apparently served previous, as, she had a drink in front of her, of which she was in the process of a-sipping.
I heard the bartender come out of an office behind the bar and say....
"I'm Davy, what'll you have?"
"I'll have a light draft, Davy." I responded.
"I'll have the same." The old man added.
Davy added. "We have a seventy-five cent special on our draft beer on tap for veterans, ladies and seniors. I know one of you looks old enough, but if you are a veteran too, you get another quarter off yer' mug."

The old man just looked up, but didn't say anything. I said. "Well, Davey, maybe I should get in on at least one of those specials, because I was in the Marine Corps, got three fourths of the way around the world, and got tired of getting shot at in Lebanon real quick."

Davy went to the middle of the bar, pulled two mugs from the freezer, and drew the drafts in the now frost covered mugs, then, slid them both down the bar to me and the old man. I passed the one to the old man, and commandeered the other for myself, cooling my hot hands on the frosty mug.

The woman at the other end of the bar spoke up. "Davy, you could get a lot more women in ther during the day, if you made your specials to include a glass or two of wine."

Davy did not respond, but did nod, just to show that he heard her.

Trying to initiate some small talk, I turned to and asked the old man. "Pap, are you a workin' man, or have you done up and totally retired yet?"

He replied. "Well, I still work some, now and then, when work is available or some need needs to be filled."

"Well, what do you do for a living?" I asked.

"Oh, this and that." He replied.

I saw an entry now to start a good conversation with the old man. Although, I thought maybe I had been a little hasty about thinking that I had and entry here, so, I countered and asked him. "Where do you do this and that, now and then?"

"Oh, here and there, He replied. And now, went on to sipping his beer from his frosted glass and looking straight ahead without moving his head one way or another.

I then confirmed my thought that what I had considered an entry to some small talk conversation with the old man was probably going downhill from here on out, so, I went to sipping on my own cold beer.

"I'll have another." Said the woman, from down at the other end of the bar. And, the bartender responded to her order, said "Thank you Clara", and then returned to the middle of the bar and started wiping and drying glasses.

"You all believe in aliens?" The old man said quietly, without as much as moving his lips. It kind of startled me, for him to start saying anything, because I had him all figured out already to be the kind of person that only answered prodding questions.

"What kind of aliens?" I asked. "Do you mean the kind that comes across the border looking for work to be able to feed their families from down in Mexico?"

Davy, the bartender, left his work area and came over to in front of us to polish his mugs when he heard the old man ask me about aliens.

"I've had a few that I suspected as being aliens in here, off and on." Davy said.

The old man looked up at Davy from his beer, and said. "No, I mean do you believe in aliens like in those movies like Man in Black, or the Star War shows, or like the watchers in that Noah's Arc movie."

Davy responded first, with. "Oh, I don't know, I just thought that those kinds of things were resulted from someone's over active imagination."

I added. "Personally, I have never seen any myself, but I did work with a guy one time down in Evansville, that swears up and down that he had been abducted by aliens when he was just a kid, and claims to this day, that that is why he does crazy things and has bad dreams, fits and bad spells."

The old man turned back to his beer and said, kind of under his breath. "What about ghosts and goblins? What about devils and demons? What about spirits and apparitions? What about souls and angels? How about a will-o-the-wisp or a booger or two? Or, poltergeists and apparitions, thrown in on the side? Do you all believe in any of them kinds of things?" He asked.

Davy just stood there, behind the bar, drying a mug and looking at the old man, with a kind of dumb ass stupefied look on his face.

Since it didn't look like Davy was going to say anything, I responded. "Well, personally, I have never seen anything of that nature that I can readily think of, however, I have known a couple folks in my life time that claims to have seen a ghost, and another who claims that he saw an angel up in the clouds with flutterin' wings, but me, personally, I just can't offer any testimony one way or another, although I do feel more like there could be than couldn't be, if I had to choose one way or another."

Davy then chimed in with. "Well, Pap, I have seen a few honky-tonk angels who have wandered in here off and on." And, he turned his head down toward the woman at the other end of the bar.

The woman must have overheard him and caught his glance, because she responded immediately with. "Don't be includin' me in with that bunch of yahoos, Davy, if you want me to continue my business with ya', 'cause, I only while away my time in here in the cool, awaitin' to get my kids from school and just biddin' my time and a-waitin' for my husband to get off work, so's I can fix him a warm lovin' supper, so, don't any of you ever think I'm one of them honky-tonk kind of girls." And, with that said, she got off of the bar stool and went over to the juke box and was looking at the selections to see what she could play.

Davy said. "Don't pay a mind to Clara, she is a regular in here, and she doesn't mean to be abrupt, that is just her way. By the way, Pap, what's your name?" Davy asked.

"I am but one." He said.

"No, I mean what is your name?" Davy came back with.

"That's me, that's what I am called, that's what I answer to, always have, always will." The old man responded.

Davey looked at the old man quizzically, but did not pursue the question further.

The old man took another sip of his beer and said. "You know, that angels are mentioned in the

Bible and other historical documents, don't you? You have heard of Gabriel and Lucifer, haven't you? I mean, didn't either of you ever go to church or Sunday school, or even read the Bible at home, or, anything historical?"

Davy kind of struck back with. "Well, yes, I know enough about the Bible where it mentions angels, and, I know that Gabriel and Cupid were good angels, and too, that Lucifer the devil was one of the bad angels, and, that some angels are supposed to be messengers between God and man, but I've never seen one in my lifetime yet, so, for all I know, it may be just a bedtime story, either that, or I have never had to have any messages delivered by any of them on my behalf that I know of." Davy said.

"Me too, or me neither, whatever or whichever." I said. "And, although I do believe that most of the Bible must be true to some extent or another, although I question some of the interpretations I have been privy to hear about, but, that doesn't mean that I must believe in angels doing anything personal for me, maybe they do what they do for other people who have greater needs, and so far have left me alone, I guess, but, I just never thought much more than that about all of that kind of thing."

The old man looked up again from his beer and said. "Well; the first thing is, that God Almighty, Himself, named those angels that you mentioned, except for Cupid, as, the Romans named him and a bunch of other cherubs, on a take-off from the Greeks naming all their gods, but, what if I told you that all of them, the whole kit and kaboodle, the whole bunch, all, any or either, the whole gang, them, theirs and those for that matter, even that bunch of Greek gods, as being one in all and all in one and are all the same inside and out?"

"The whole bunch of what's all the same, the Angels?" Davy asked.

"Ghosts, goblins, aliens, specters, boogers, will-o-the-wisps, devils, apparitions, souls, angels, that list of Greek gods, all of those things, they are all the same, with no difference between any of them, except maybe where they work, just like where you all work today, everyone has someplace different to work here and they have someplace different to work there." The old man said. "Besides, like I said, they are recorded in history in all religions, whether it be in the Egyptian hieroglyphics in their temples or in the Old or New Testament, the Koran, Hamarabbi's basalt pillar chiseling's, Gilgamish's markings, or, even some of the Hindu writings, big bubba Buddha's sayings, or, even in the old Egyptian wall picture carvings, or even, more recently found, in those ancient French cave art scratching's.

Davy struck back with. "Pap, angels are supposed to be good, devils are supposed to be bad, ghosts don't do much but scare people, how can they be all the same?"

"They are, they are, and, in addition to being the same, they are all around and about us all the time, both day and night, all of them working in their respective endeavors, no different than you in the here and now, like shift work, they are always there in the forever there and then, and, mostly just standin' around and watchin', that is, if you ever even get a glimpse of them. Your only hope is, that there are two-thirds of them good and only one-third of them being bad, at any given time, but, the bad news is, that they are all like your Marines, the Devil Dogs, as they are known, that is, that they are mean and they don't mind dying, but that is mostly only because they know that they will never die, but, they dearly love a good fight. Too, just like humans, some of the good ones, do bad things sometimes, and, some of the bad ones, do good things once in a while." The old man said.

The old man went on. "The problem with them, is this, that you never see them, except for just a glimpse once in a great while, if you are so lucky. What you do see, is what they do, what comes about, what happens. But, you can never figure them out. They are like the sinister-dexterous thing where their right hand doesn't know what their left hand is doing, and, both hands are a-goin' all the time. Sometimes, if you are really cognizant, and looking for it, you can see

the results of what they did and how it all came about, but it's like they already have been there and done that, and now, you just realized it, or, you never know what they will do next. That kind of thing."
Davy had a quizzical look on his face, and, the thought crossed my brain that I had just sat down beside an old man who was probably crazy as a loon and needed some sort of psychological rehabilitation or better yet some psychiatric care for at least six months or so, or, maybe even more. I looked at Davy, rolled my eyes, and, he picked up my queue, and put his head down, indicating that he most likely thought the same, and, was all but ready to give up on the matter at hand. I looked down the bar at the lady and she looked like she was in deep concentration about something, then, I looked at Davy again, and he was the same. I wondered if I had missed something or had misconstrued some of the stuff that I had heard.
I asked. "Just how, can all of those things be the same?" And, I looked at the old man a little more intently, mostly just to get a better look at just who I was talking to, and, maybe just who was doing the talking.
Davy responded too. "Yea, Pap, just how can all of those alien things, like you said, like in the Man in Black and Star War movies, or those "watchers" in that Noah Arc movie, all be the same?"
"Yea, Pap, how could something be both something good and something evil be the same at the same time?" I asked.
The old man took a sip of his beer, then looked up toward the ceiling, not looking at me or Davy, and said. "Good and evil are the same, there are no differences between them, or, between the two, whichever, no matter if you call them by good names or bad names, it is what it is at any given time, and they are what they are. What is important, is, that, they is what they is in this day and time, even with the new definition of what "is" is."
Davy sputtered. "Pap, good and evil is as different as daylight and dark, there is no way that either of them could ever be considered the same, I'm sorry to contradict you, but, that is plumb hog wash, and, I am also really sorry that I so disagree with you, but, I have seen a lot of bad, and, I have seen some little good here and there, and I know that I have seen more bad than good over the years, and, I know the difference between the two, whether you do, or not, or whether or not that you will admit it."
The old man took another sip of his beer, and then said. "Well, consider this, you would not know if something was good or not, unless you had a comparison with something bad, and you would not

recognize something bad, unless you had a comparison of it with something good. Too, when any of you see something bad happen, you are compelled to try to correct it with something you call good, or try to change the bad behavior. For example, if you look back into history, you see things that those folks back in some time gone by, which was considered to be good in that time, but, today, you all see it as being something bad, like and such as, the doctors years ago thought it was a good treatment to cut and bleed people when they had a fever, like they did old George Washington, which we now know to be nonsense today, and, if you look closely enough, you can also see things that they at one time considered to have been bad, like and such as, the simple tomato, which was thought to be poisonous for ages, but today, we know that they are full of vitamins, to actually be good, in this day and time, but, they didn't know it at the time then, and it took years and generations to pass for civilization to come to know which it was and for recorded history itself to eventually bear it all out. If you took the time, and did the research, you could find case after case down through history that has gone from one to the other and even back again in some instances."
I said. "Pap, a little more proof on that would shine, how about a more personal specific example of good and bad, for this modern day and time?"
The old man looked up from his beer and said. "It's like this, better to explain all of it to you, as, you all have a saying, for your Marines in military service, that they are, "your best friend or your worst enemy", sometimes, even at the same time, take that to the bank, and, you will see that any of this aforementioned so called Angels could be good up to a point, but, if you mess with them or cross them, or, you do not do what they want you to do, or, you do not do what they request for you to do, or what they think that you should have done, or, when you do or not do what they expect of you, or if you choose to do nothing when you know you should really do something, they can absolutely turn against you and do you a job that you will never ever forget in your life time, worse than anything you ever saw in the Man in Black or Star War movies, and, thereby of which could be considered early on as bad but later on as good some time on in your future viewpoint. It is like this. It is like a coin, which has both a heads and a tails, which some folks bet on or choose to call to see who goes first and who goes last. Good and evil is like a coin, one is only on the flip side of the other. Or, like love and hate, which is another example of another two sided coin, as, one is same as the

other turned the other way around or turned inside out, or, another example, even pain and pleasure. For, there is nothing more painful, or so full of anguish, as, the loving of someone who does not love you, or that of a lost loved child. However, humans see as their only recompense, to first hate themselves for being so damned foolish, and then, turning that damned hate toward some other thing or person, to at least gain some little satisfaction in order for them to eventually feel good about it all to some degree."

I thought of my own personal predicament with that little bit of insight, with me, loving someone who did not love me, and, even having children with them, only to find out too late, that they did not love me or even wanted my children either, and, could only love themselves, and, wondering which days of that marriage could have been considered good, as, most of it I now considered to have been bad from the start, although, I blindly thought it to be good at the outset, until something flipped the coin and I came to the realization of what I now know today. I found myself looking up at the ceiling.

Now, Clara, unbeknownst to me, because I had been so intent on the old man's talking, had heard enough of the conversation to have become more than just interested, so, she had moved her drink and position on down the bar, shuffling just to my left on the barstool next to me, which I had just realized, with the old man, just to my right on another barstool, and, Davy, the bartender just on the other side of the bar, with me in my mind, just trying to put everyone in their proper place, with me feeling somewhat uncomfortable in mine, being sandwiched in like I was, all but in the middle.

The old man went on without interruption. "Here, let me prove it to you. For, all of your understandings, which, can begat realizations which can begat further understanding, and, on and on, back and forth, forever and again. So, listen up and hear this, as an example, I can show you, or, explain to you all, how these alien things are organized, in both number and name, so that, you may gain some further understanding, that is, if you ever become so interested or ever come to believe in or of them. Do you have a calculator?" He asked, as he looked at Davy.

"I have one in the office, let me go get it." He said, and Davey swung around on his heels, left the bar for his office area just to the left, just behind the bar, then returned just as quickly, across from us, laying the calculator out before us on the bar.

"It's like this." The old man started. "Just like it says in the Bible's New Testament, where it was so recorded, that Jesus Himself, said, that he could have called up 10,000 angels for his defense, to come to his aid, if he had so chosen, or would have wanted to at the time. But, he chose not to do so, so as, to further fulfil the prophecies of that Old Testament. So, there must be some magic in this peculiar number of 10,000, with respect to the organization of angels, or to some prophecy, or, from some ancient wisdom, so, just how do you think those 10,000 angels would have been organized?"

Davy, from behind the bar, responded first. "Well, from a business management view, they should have a leader or manager, with a board of directors, and, a board of directors with a president and at least a couple vice-presidents or more thrown in just to make a good mix."

"What about a military mix?" The old man asked.

Davy responded. "From a military view, I have no experience in that, having not been in the military, so, I can't be of any help along that line, although, I think that they could similarly be organized, somehow."

I spoke up. "Well, I was in the Marines, and, I know how they are organized, so, what are you saying, that angels are organized like the military as we know it today?"

The old man then looked at me, and said. "Maybe, just maybe, it is the other way around, as, the military and business is organized, similar to how the angels are organized, instead of vice-a-versa." Then, he looked again, down at his beer. He continued. "So, I ask you again, if, 10,000 angels were organized, just how do you think such an organization would look like?" He asked.

Now, I responded. "Well, if the whole organization would be like the military, they would be split up into Divisions, Regiments, Battalions, Companies, and Squads, if it was anything like the Marines." I said.

"Exactly." The old man said. "Any organization of 10,000 of anything or anyone, would be similar to the organizations of today, if it was meant for us to fully understand it and how such an organization could work. So, here it is, all laid out for you, as a prophecy if you will. The group of 10,000 angels is first divided into four groups, for the purpose of covering the four winds, the four corners of the earth itself, and, the directions of North Pole winds, the South Pole winds, the East Wind which brings typhoons and cyclones in the eastern hemisphere, and the West wind which brings hurricanes in the western hemisphere, which, for no other reason, than, it just gives them someplace to start and stop so as to stay within their jurisdictions and boundaries. With Captains as commanders of the four winds, if you will, then, the heads of these four groups, or the Captains, must need be named, and, I for one, have come to know their secret names, so, please, very carefully, take the time to remember this if you will, for it is important, if you ever want to make any attempt try to communicate with them on any occasion on into the future, for any purpose whatsoever, to call them on or to call them off, but, I need to tell you now, that trying to talk to them, is like ten or fifteen people trying to order at the same time at Mcdonals, they may hear you or not, and, what you get when you get to the head of the line, what you get may not be what you ordered, so, you need to call them out by their names for them to respond to any request or for them to deliver any message, and, they in turn will also come to know you by name, and, may on occasion, call for you on the wind, that is, if you are listening, listen like you are listening for the wind to say something, or listening for the lapping of the ocean waves coming ashore to advise you, or, listening for the distant thunder to warn you, you may or may not hear them."

The old man hesitated here, then, went on. "Personally, I have only heard them speak a couple of times, but, I soon got over trying to talk to them, not that they don't hear you, maybe they do, then, maybe they don't, or, maybe they are just not listening at the time, you may never know for sure, but never expect any of them to ever remember anything personal on your behalf, because they all seem to have short term memory problems, just remember, they do not talk much, like I said, or really, mostly not at all, as, they are mostly gawkers and watchers and doers who exist only to live in the moment, so, remember again, that they are definitely not talkers, not gabby kind of guys, so, if you hear voices, other than your name a-whistling on the wind, while you are at the seashore during a thunderstorm, you can rest assured that it is definitely not any of them. But remember this also, do not, under any circumstances, I say, do not, piss any of these guys off, as, they do not take kindly to it very well, as it seems that their work is kind of a personal thing with them, and, there is no predicting or no telling how they would respond, when or where that response would take place, or, who would be effected or affected, whichever."

He hesitated again, took a sip of his beer, then, went on. "So, now comes the important part, you have to remember their names, it is most important. So, hear this. The East head is Binyamin, and he is the senior commander in charge of the four, with, the North head being Notemin, the West head is Yomin, and the South head is

Bharto, so much for their names. If you were not listening intently, you are probably already up a flooded shit creek without a paddle in in a leaking canoe, with the wind a-howling and in the middle of a thunderstorm. So, back to the numbers, how much is 10,000 minus the four heads? " He asked. "Use your calculator there Mister barkeep." He added.

Davy responded. "10,000 minus the four leaders would leave 9,996."

"Divide that in fours." The old man said.

"That would be 2,499 each." Davy responded.

The old man continued. "Well, how many secondary commanders or Lieutenants would it take to make all of the remainder of the four groups to all but come out equal?"

Davy responded. "Well, I could take one for each of the four which would leave a group of 2,498, which would simplify the organization, but, that would be a lot of personnel to be overseen for one head in any organization." He said.

The old man interrupted. "Well, try this, if you will, for, I will give it to you head on, so that you don't have to waste your good time calculating it all out and waste the rest of the afternoon. Try 17 secondary heads under the four leaders, and put that into your calculator."

Davy, poked at the calculator. "Well, let's see, 2499, minus 17 secondary leaders, would be 2,482." He said.

Again, the old man interrupted. "Now, divide that by the 17 leaders." He said.

Davy, began poking at his calculator again. "That would be 2,482 divided by 17, which would be 146." He said.

The old man all but became livid. "That's it, that's it, now, you've got it! That is how a band of 10,000 Angels is organized. Each Captain is over 17 Lieutenants, who are over each company of 146 Angels which could further be broken down into two groups of 73 Angels each, who have a second in command leader such as a First Sergeant each, which would allow two First Sergeants under each Lieutenant, for each group of 146 or one for each groups of 73, and 73 minus the First Sergeant would be 72, and, the groups could be so divided further as needed, for example, they could be divided into two groups of 36 each, or three groups of 24 each, or four groups of 18 each, or, six groups of 12 each, or eight groups of 9 each, or twelve groups of 6 each, or eighteen groups of 4 each, or twenty four groups of 3 each, or, 36 groups of 2 each, so, that would be the most flexible grouping for any band of Angels to be organized into for the greatest

effectiveness or any potential assignment where a specific need of a particular number would be needed to go to someone's defense or to go into an all-out battle and combat on someone's behalf, or, I remind you, they could gang up and come against even you for that matter. And, you will admit, that, it would have taken you the rest of the day to figure it all out, even with your calculator, if you had the time." The old man said.
Davy, coming to his own defense, countered. "Yes, but, I could have eventually figured it all out with no input whatsoever from you, but I had no need or notion to even think about such a thing until you came into this bar with all of your ranting's. Besides, maybe you figured it all out on a calculator somewhere else, at some other bar, and sometime previous, and just wanted something to start some conversation with, for all we know, and, are just now telling us about it for some unbeknownst reason, and, if the truth were known, it may not mean anything at all now or anytime on into the future, or, forever for that matter."
"Rantings, you call it, rantings, and, not meaning anything, FOREVER? Well, I will tell you this, young man. The calculations of how Angels are organized, is only one proof of what it is that I know about, not to mention their names, of which, I am so delegated and obligated to pass this on to your generation now at this day and time, here in this particular place, for it has come time for you and your generation to come to know and consider such for the future salvation of all mankind if you all are ever to continue to even exist on the face of this Earth. The earth, has become overpopulated, there are not enough guardian angels to go around in this day and time. That is one reason why there is so much trouble throughout the world. These guys need help. They need all of the assistance that they can get. They need it now, and, they need it from you all." He said.
"Why us, or, better yet, why anyone, for that matter, in the here and now needs to know any of this?" Davey asked.
"Because, between the four of us here, the three of you, have the necessary connections in your world, now chosen to communicate this information further on into the future and can even pass it on to the next generation where someone somewhere at some time can pick it up and make a run with it."
Clara spoke up. "Who in the coming generation would listen to any of this? They know everything they need to know, none of them can spell, but they all know how to get on the internet, they know how to tweeter, they know how to get on the faces book, and, all they want to

do is to play video games and piddle their time away a-texting their friends, a-takin' selfies with their smart phones, and, they don't even want to learn how to write in cursive?" She both asked and said.

"Yea." I said. "Who in the world really even cares about anything like this day in time today? Or, for that matter, on into our future?"

The old man did not answer, he took a sip of beer, sat the half full glass down, shrugged his shoulders as if excusing himself, and, without saying anything further, or even looking back at any of us, for that matter, headed back toward the rest room toward the back of the bar, albeit, in a huff.

When the old man was out of ear shot, Davey asked in almost a whisper to me and Clara. "What do you all think about the old man's rantings? Is he for real or not?"

Clara responded first. "Well, for one thing, what he was talking about, can sure enough get you to thinking on a completely different level than what most people call normal in this day and time."

"Yea." I said. "I had no considerations or ideas for anything other than a cold beer when I came in here a little while ago, but then, I remember what my father used to say. He always asked me. "You know what I think?." He would say. And, I would say, No, Pap, what do you think? Then, he would say. "I think, that nobody really gives a shit what I think, that is what I think." And, he would end it with that."

Davey put his head down, put both hands on the bar, and said. "I do not think, that I have ever, in all of my days, tending bar, that I have ever, ever, had anyone like that old man, show up in here. In one respect, he seems sensible, but in another respect, he seems absolutely crazy as a loon, but, the numbers that he came up with all add up, which, most likely, if the truth were known, he had most probably calculated out previous, just to start some conversation or to call up something controversial. I specifically noticed that he didn't give me his name when I asked him."

Clara responded. "Oh yes he did, he did indeed give you his name!"

Davey responded. "When I asked him what his name was, he said that I am but one, which makes no sense to me whatsoever."

"He said, that his name was Butwon, his name is Butwon, he said, to quote him directly, "I am Butwon". You need to pick your ears out Davey, I heard him say it clear as a bell all the way from the other end of the bar down there." Clara said.

"I did not understand what he said that way." Davy said.

"I didn't either." I added on.

"Well, that is what I heard, whether you all heard it or not, his name is "Butwon"." Clara said. "What were the other names? "Bartow"? I've been in Bartow, Florida, maybe it was named for that Angel, and the "Yankton", South Dakota one, although I've never been there, I heard about it, and, the other one, "Napoleon", himself, maybe he was an alien, and their leader most likely named after "Bennington", Vermont." She added.

"I didn't hear him say any of those names like that, I way heard him say their names was, that "Barrow", like Barrow, Alaska, not "Bartow", and that "Binghamton", New York one, the leader, or the "Yerington", Nevada one or was it "Yo-Man"" like you're yellin' for someone, but then, none of them would be yelling for a man if they were yelling for Angels, and, that "Nottingham", England one, that one figures, being from the East." I said.

Davy responded. "This is absolutely crazy, I did not hear what you heard, and Clara did not hear what you or I heard, I definitely heard the old man call their leader "Birmingham", like from Alabama, and the other one, "Barstow", like from Barstow, California, out in the Mojave desert, and "Norman", like after Norman, Oklahoma, and that one named "Woman", that doesn't make sense to me at all, because I thought all of the Angels were males, so, I think know what I heard, and you all say what you thought you heard, but, the three of us all heard three different things, on every count, and, I was listening intently, I mean, I am a bartender, and, it has taken me years, but, I have learned how to listen to a patron, I know what I heard and it sure as hell was not what you two heard."

Clara spoke up. "Maybe that is the way it is supposed to be. Maybe what he is saying or what he said when you try to tell someone else, that they hear something that you didn't really say or mean, like that game they played in school about passing messages, where the end message is totally different than what was started out after going from person to person. On the other hand, if you think about it, we three have been talkin' about it and in the process we have been calling out their names, and you know what the old man said about calling out their names, that if you did, maybe not having a good reason, you have to look out for all hell to break loose."

We all just sat and stood there for a minute or so, just looking at one another, but not saying anything, yet, we all were fully engaged in our thoughts, up to a point, as, I for one, admit to having a limit, especially after a couple of beers.

Davey raised his head and looked at me, and said. "Hey, the old man has been back in the rest room for some time, could you go back to kind of check on him to make sure nothing has happened to the old man? Maybe our arguing with him got his blood pressure up and he just might have stroked out back there or maybe even had a heart attack, for God's sake, he looked to be up in age you know."

"Sure." I said. "I'll go check." And, I slipped off of the barstool and headed for the rest room in the back.

When I got back to the men's room, I found no one, nothing, I found nobody, I even looked in the stalls behind the swinging doors, and still, I found nothing. Then, I came back out, and went back up to the bar.

"He's not back there." I said, flat out to Davey.

"What do you mean, he's not back there?" Davey responded.

"That's what I said, there is nobody back there in the men's restroom." I said.

Davey looked at me, then, he looked at Clara and said. "Clara, maybe he went into the ladies room by mistake, would you mind going back to check to see if he is in there, I mean, he may very well have had a stroke or a heart attack or something, he might be laying back there dying, for all we know, really, there is no telling, please go check, will you?."

Clara did not respond, she just slipped off of her seat and walked back toward the ladies room, and, I heard the door open, heard her yell "Hello in there." Then, I heard the door close, which, I noted, that I had not heard either a-previous, that is, when the old man had went back to the restroom.

Shortly thereafter, Clara came out of the rest room area and walked back up to the bar area and said. "There is nobody in the ladies room."

Davey then said. "Look, you both sit right here, and let me go take a look, maybe he realized that he had went into the wrong restroom and then went back to the other between the time you both were checking." And, with that, Davey headed back to the restrooms, checking the men's first, then, checking the ladies, and, came back up to the bar, with me hearing the doors open and close on both. Then, Davy came back to the bar area.

"Did both of you see him go back to the restroom?" Davey asked me and Clara.

"Yea, I definitely saw him head that way." I said.

Clara, shaking her head up and down, while trying not to shake her

glass, also responded in the positive.
"He didn't go out the front door by any chance?" Davey asked.
"No, no way, he would have had to walk back right by us if he did, I mean, we are right here at the end of the bar for God's sake." I responded.
Clara added on. "Any of us would have seen him if he would have come back out, Davey, I was sittin' sideways on the barstool just like I am now, and I would have been lookin' right at him if he had of went out the front door."
Davey left the bar area and went back to the office behind the bar. I heard him calling 911 and reporting an unusual and suspicious circumstance and requesting an officer come to the bar. Then, Davey came back out from the office and asked. "Are you both sure that you saw the old man go back to the restroom and not come back out, or, maybe fake us out and up and go out the front door?"
Both Clara and I confirmed that both of us witnessed him going back but neither of us seeing him come out, which, was somewhat confusing to both of us, with both of us taking turns shrugging shoulders and throwing up our hands with Clara even rolling her eyes.
Davey, trying to explain himself, said. "I called 911, because, I have had, at one time or another, on occasion, had patrons hiding or trying to hide somewhere in the bar area for whatever purpose in the past, maybe to burglarize the place later, to steal the whiskey, or whatever, and, I think that this may be one of those occasions, so, just stay alert and pay attention to anything that happens next."
"Well, he left a little less or a little more than half of his beer." I said.
"He didn't even pay for it." Davey responded.
"Well, for that matter, I haven't paid for mine either." Clara added.
"Me neither." I added.
"Clara, did you see the old man come in?" Davy asked.
She replied. "No, I was the only one here, and you served me and went back into your office, but I went to the rest room, and, when I came back out, he was sitting patiently there at the other end of the bar.
"He was sitting there when I came in, I'm sure of that because I chose to sit down beside him." I responded.
Davy added. "I don't remember him coming in. I normally hear the front door open and close, I heard Clara, when she came in, then, I heard you come in, nodding at me, but, I didn't hear him."
"Well, he was here when I first got here, so, he must have come in between the time Clara and me showed up." I said. "I'm sorry, I

said, I take it that your name is Clara, but I did not introduce myself, I am Don, no more or no less." I added.

"Pleased to meet you, Don, no more or no less, is no more or no less your last name or your middle name?" Clara said.

"Yea." Davy added. "Pleased to meet you, Don, no more or no less."

"Same here, Davy." I added, and did not respond further, sometimes, no more or no less is better left unsaid.

By this time, we were up and about, all walking around, all looking around the bar area, glancing under the tables and looking up on the stage, looking behind the curtains, but, not seeing anyone else in the darkened bar. With no other conversation to speak of, we were all kind of surprised, when the policeman arrived at almost straight up at one o'clock.

"Hi Davy, sorry I took so long, there's a bunch of heavy equipment operators down at Patty's Place, just south of town, the whole bunch got a little rowdy and I had to back up the Sheriff down there, so, what's up here?" The police officer said.

Davy responded. "Jasper, we had this old man in here, I would adjudge him to be in his early sixties, gray haired, with one of those "go-to-hell" ball caps, blue jeans and one of those ragged old "catch me if you can" plaid shirts, and, he had a beer, or, part of a beer while we were all talking, and, after we had talked some, he went back to the restroom but he never came out, or came back, or went back out the front door because at least one of us would have seen him. So, he is still in here somewhere, I think maybe hiding, for whatever reason, and, I don't want any more trouble, so, would you mind taking a look-see around."

I added. "He also had on a pair of "shit-kicking" boots." I said

It was now, at this moment in time, it dawned on me, and, my brain came to realize that I had been hoaxed by my very co-workers, telling me they were all going to this place when they went to that other place. A cruel joke played upon me by not only one, but by most of the guys that I worked with. They were all probably laughing about it all now, just as I am coming to that realization. Dumb ass, on me, again. I thought.

The police office went back to the rest room area, looked in both the men's and the women's restrooms, came out, looked at the ceiling, looked under the tables, looked up on the stage, where I supposed that some band would play on weekends, looked behind the drapes on each side, then, came back up to the bar area.

"Nothing back there Davy, and nothing in here. So, what more is there to the story, I have to make a report here don't you know?" He asked.

Davy started. "Well, not much, Jasper, I was in the office, I heard Clara come in, so I came out and served her, then, went back to the office, and, I heard Don here, come in, and, I came out to serve him, him and this old man was sitting here at the end of the bar."

Jasper looked at me and asked. "Any of you know the old man, ever seen him before, or, did you come in with the old man?"

"No to all three questions." I responded. "When I came in, Clara was at the other end of the bar, and the old man was already sitting at this end of the bar, and, I just sat down beside him."

"Samo-Samo." Clara added.

"How long have you all been here, or, what time did you all come in?" Jasper asked.

Clara chimed up first. "I came in right at about noon. The old man was not here when I came in, but after Davy served me, I went to the rest room, and, when I came out, the old man was sitting at this end of the bar, which was some little time before Don here came at about ten minutes or so after noon, or, maybe a quarter or so after."

Davy added. "I did not hear him come in, I didn't hear the door open or close, as I did when both Clara and Don here came in, as, I was back in the office doing paper work."

Jasper interrupted. "Davy, there are no windows in either the men's or women's restroom, and, no back door, and, there is no one in there at this time, there is no one hiding behind the curtains on the stage, and no one hiding under tables or in any of the dark corners, there is no one in this bar except the four of us, unless you have someone stashed back in your office, so, what is it that you want me to do?"

"Well, now that you mention it, just stay right here while I check the office." Davy said, and turned to check his office behind the bar. After a quick check, Davy wheeled back around and said that it was all clear, threw his hands up in the air, and, came back up to the bar.

Jasper asked. "Davy, is this guy a regular, do you know anything of him?"

"No." Davy said. "I have never seen him in here before today."

Jasper asked again. "Don, Clara, do either of you know anything about this guy?"

I shook my head and said. "I have never seen him before in my life until today."

Clara added. "I'm what you call a regular, and, I have never seen him before either."

Jasper continued. "Do any of you know his name, where he came from or where he works?"

Clara spoke up. "He said his name was Butwon, and, I definitely heard him say that."

"That could be either his first or last name." Jasper said.

"I didn't take it that way, that that was his name, as all I heard him say was, that he "was but one", or something like that." Davy added.

Jasper interrupted. "Give me a description of the guy, age, height, weight, how he was dressed, whatever you all can remember."

Davey led off first. "Well I would judge him to be in his late fifties or early sixties, and, he was almost as tall as Don here, I'd say about 6 foot tall, and, weighed about 200 pounds, he was what you would call barrel chested, and, he had on a gray plaid long sleeved shirt and blue jeans."

I added. "He had on ankle high work shoes which were pretty worn out and he had curly gray hair sticking out from under his hat, and, I am sure that he was quite a powerful man in his day, just from the looks of him as he was in pretty good shape for his age, I would judge."

"He had on a ball cap, it wasn't a hat." Clara chimed in, correcting me.

Jasper was writing it all down on his notebook and asked. "What color was the ball cap and did it have any insignia or lettering on it?"

"I didn't notice any insignia, but it was a black ball cap." I said.

"Yea, it was black." Davey added.

Clara chimed in again. "The ball cap had something like something Angels, like the Los Angeles Angels or something like that, something about Angels."

Jasper finished taking his notes and then said. "Now, if I get this right, you all talked with this old man for almost an hour, then, you all saw him get up off of the barstool here, and go back to the rest room, and, none of you saw him come back out from there and go on out the front door. Is that right? I mean, he didn't do something like a basketball player does, by faking, or feinting that he was going one way, then, went another?"

Davy responded. "No, we all were right here when he headed to the restroom. That's it in a nutshell, he was here, for almost an hour, and, as of right now, this very minute, has not left the premises, as far as I know or as far as any of us know, I mean, at least one of us would have seen him go out the front door if that was the way he headed.

After all, the front door is only about ten to twelve feet from this end of the bar where we all were sitting and talking."
Jasper countered. "Do I understand, that you want me to put down in my report, that this particular old man all but vanished right here in and from your bar?"
"Maybe he was transmorgrified." Davey said.
What the hell is transmorgrified, or, whatever, Davey?" Jasper asked.
"Well, I mean, for almost an hour, all the old man talked about was angels, spirits, aliens, ghosts and the like, maybe he was one of them. Maybe he was like Enoch and got took up into heaven and got himself rode off in some invisible golden chariot." Davey said.
"Enoch." Jasper asked. "Was he here too, should I put his name in the report, or, do you have a description on him?"
"No, no." Davey added. "I just used that as some comparison with someone disappearing off of the face of the earth, like in those alien abductions that you read or hear about."
Clara chimed in again. "Do you know what you are sayin' Davey. You are sayin' that we all have done been talkin' to some alien spook for the last hour right here in your bar. Who in the hell, in their right mind, would believe such a cock and bull story. That is almost as bad as some of those abduction stories. On second thought, do you think maybe he intended to abduct us? Hells bells, if I got myself abducted, who would pick up my kids from school, who would pick up my old man from work? I mean, he got himself a DUI and lost his license, now, I've got to take him to work and go get him. I've got no business whatsoever, messing around with these alien Angels, I've got enough trouble in my life right now to last me a lifetime."
I felt downright uncomfortable, even thinking about such a thing, much less talking about something that I knew zilch about, so, I just kept my mouth shut and sipped on my beer, although I felt odd, drinking beer in front of a police officer.
Jasper interrupted our alarm. "Look, all of you, and especially you, Davey, because, I have to write up some report on this call here, and the story would read like nonsense if I wrote it up the way you all have given it to me. So, let me put it this way. Davey, as the proprietor of this bar, you have reported a suspicious person which was also seen by both Don and Clara here, and, I will not say in my report anything about his comings or his goings, how would that be?"
"Fine with me." Davy said. "Maybe that would be best."
"I'm good with that." I added. "That is, if my name is not going to be attached to the report or come up later in some newspaper article."

"Me too." Clara said. "But, I would just as soon you also leave my name out of it altogether, I mean, I have kids here in school and a husband that works right here in Mitchell, and, I don't need any publicity with my name attached to it with the bar and the whole folded up mystery about some old man that is now a missing person."

"I'm not putting that into the report, Clara, about him being a missing person. As far as I know, he is still around here somewhere, and, I might just go looking for him, and, may even find him sometime around and about into the near future, or, he may even show up again sometime, but, as far as I am concerned, the old man is not missing, he is only a suspicious person and can only be reported as such." Jasper clarified.

"OK." Davey said. "Off the record, police report aside, what do you personally make of all this rigmarole, Jasper?"

Jasper looked at Davey, then at me and Clara, and said. "I would not even go so far as to even speculate, as to what it was that took place here this afternoon. Maybe it took place, then, maybe again, maybe it didn't. Who is to know, who is to judge, except, someone reading the report of of it, some time on into the future, that has some clue, unbeknownst to us, who could better figure it all out, and solve the mystery. Anyway, the report will read as I have mentioned, without any speculation as to the suspect's comings and goings or about his whereabouts. Anyway, Davy, pour his beer mug out, because I want to take it in if we have to try to get his fingerprints off of it."

Davey got a napkin, picked up the half full or half empty mug of beer, poured it out in the sink, put the mug in a plastic bag and gave it to Jasper.

I asked Jasper if he was finished with me, and, he said that I was free to go, so, I excused myself, paid for my beer, and also paid for the old man's beer, and, even bought Clara's drink, I thanked Davy for his hospitality, and, headed out toward the other end of town to Patty's Place, to get some get even time with all of my operator buddies who had no doubt hoaxed me earlier on in the day.

By the time that I got through town and down to Patty's place, it appeared that the crowd was breaking up and everyone was heading out and leaving with the Sheriff directing traffic. So, I just drove on by, and, headed on for home, and thought that I would deal with my friends hoax tomorrow back on the job, then my mind floated about and thought about how my life at home was, and, how my children's life was, or would be without me around had I been abducted, or, how my potential ex to be would react, or, what would happen if she got abducted, or, where I would live or work, but then, my mind would come back to what all just happened and that happenstance was heavy on my mind all the way home, and, the first night, I even dreamt about the old man and his ramblings, later on that night in my sleep, I pondered the mystery, with no final solution coming then or even when I awoke. Yet and still, to this day, it is all heavy on my mind, whether it was just a vivid dream that I couldn't forget, or, whether it was real and actually happened as I remembered, but yet, whichever or whether it was either, it still yet stands alone in my undimmed mind in the dreams of my old age. But, at the time, I was still thinking on my way home about all of this bullshit being a possible hoax. Maybe it was two hoaxes in a row. Or maybe it was one hoax after the other hoax, or, maybe, a hoax within a hoax. Or, a hoax of a hoax differentiated. Why, it could even become the hoax of the month, or the year, or maybe of the decade, or, maybe even one of a lifetime. Or, maybe, just something else different to dream about.

THE HORSE SALE

Now, Eugene and Oscar were good but albeit old fashioned farmers, and, between the two of them, as neighbors, they tended some 80 acres of good land with teams of both horses and mules, as, the advent of motorized and mechanized farming had not yet come to full fruition and the technology was not yet affordable to either of them. Between the two of them, they managed, somehow, to continue in their old farming ways by helping one another out, just as good neighbors would do anywhere else in the whole wide world under similar circumstances.

Now, it was Eugene, that first read about the horse auction coming up within two weeks at the Boonville Fairgrounds that first generated his interest of purchasing a horse to add new blood into his present livestock bank. According to the newspaper announcement, anyone who had a horse to sell, could bring it to the auction and sell it and even buy another if they found one of value.

So, it was Eugene, who went over to his neighbor Oscar, and initiated the idea for the two of them to go to the auction.

"Now, Oscar, according to this ad right here in the newspaper, there is going to be a horse auction, a-comin' up in two weeks, right down in Boonville, at the Fairgrounds, where there just might be a horse or two that one of us, or, either one of us, or, both of us, just might add to our livestock which just might benefit out farming endeavors overall." He said.

Oscar responded. "Just let me know when you want to go, and, I'll go with you, and, if you want to buy another horse for your farm, I'll help you pick out a good one, and, if I see something that I think is a bargain, perhaps you could help me out somehow. If need be, we could even pool our money." He said.

"OK, then, two weeks from Saturday, on the nineteenth, we'll head out to Boonville, and, see what is offered, and, if there is something interesting, maybe we might buy us a horse or maybe even two. My father always said, that you can buy anything money can pay for." He said.

"The ad says to bring your own tack." Oscar said.

"All I'm bringin' is a bridle, or maybe a halter, and a rope to tie whatever I bought to the back end of my wagon." Eugene added.

The two weeks passed by quickly, and, the two farmers decided on a plan whereby they joined forces. They agreed to support one another and to help each other make the best and wisest purchase, if they happened to see something that they especially liked. The final agreements were made at the last minute while they were on their way down to the Boonville fairgrounds to see just what there was to offer for purchase.

On the way down, on Eugene's wagon, Eugene asked Oscar, just what he might offer and what he might pay for a new horse. "I might go as much as fifty, maybe even sixty, if need be, to get a good broken mare or stud of breeding age, either, as, I could use either to add to my stock." Oscar said.

"So could I." Eugene responded. "I could go with either, and, I think that it would be the price that would determine whether or not that I would make the purchase, because, I probably would only start out with a twenty-five or thirty dollar bid."

Oscar came back with. "You know Eugene, that there will be big money there. There will be farmers with six to eight times the land that we tend, with hired hands even, that will be bidding on those horses, and, we will have to bide our time in order to get the best deal if we get any chance whatsoever." He said.

"I know, I know, it will be a contest no less just to be able to get a bid in edgewise, but, if we wait until later on, after most of the horses are sold, and they have spent all of their money, perhaps we would gain a better chance for a good purchase." Eugene said.

Oscar responded. "The only problem with that, is, that they will most likely sell the best horses first, and the old swayback nags will come up last. If that is the case, we will lose out from early on." He said.

"OK, OK, so, let's watch the early bids, and, if there is a horse that is within our price range, maybe we'll bid on it, if, for no other reason, than to get the price up, on the other hand, maybe we'll just wait and watch to see who all the real buyers and bidders are." Eugene said.

"Sounds like a plan to me, just remember to bring an extra bridle and some tack, just in case we buy one." Oscar added.

Upon arrival at the fairgrounds, before the auction was to begin, Eugene and Oscar went out to the holding pens to look over the prospective horses which had been brought in for the sale. They could not believe that there were more than forty some odd horses, mules and ponies to choose from. Too, they were all good looking in all respects with only a couple of sway-backs in the whole bunch. They looked at the numbers that had been pinned on the horses and between the two of them, they selected for bid horse numbers 17, 22, 35 and 41. Four horses which met their criteria, two studs and two mares, all of good color and of right age. Any one of the four would be a nice addition to their livestock needs, and, they both agreed on that up front, and then they returned to the sales pen.

They first went to the sign-in table, showed their identification, got their numbers cards, then, they got into a good position in one corner of the show pen, where they had a good view of both the horses and the bidders. They observed that there were more than a couple hundred farmers present for the auction, but agreed, that most likely not all of them would be buyers. They agreed between themselves, that most of them came just to get out of the house on the weekend for some reason or another, and to get a chance to have a drink or two on the side.

The auctioneer took the podium and welcomed the crowd. "Today, we have thirty-seven fine horses, eight mules, and two ponies put up for sale. It is now noon, and, we will continue the auction today, until every one of them has been sold at whatever price they bring! So, with that, let the auction begin and let's get down to business! We have a long way to go and a short time to get there! Bring 'em on out boys!" He yelled.

The auctioneer took his stand, and, the handlers led out the first horse, then, proceeded to show that the horse was broken, by having a rider mount up on the horse and ride him around the show pen. Then, the auctioneer started his spiel.

"OK, now, de sale is on! Now, wadda ya gonna bid, ah gotta good horse, a fine horse, who'll starda bid at a hunnert dolla bid, one hunnert dolla, who gonna gi a bid, now, one hunnert dolla for one fine horse, now, ninedy, who gonna bid a ninedy, a ninedy dolla bid, gimme ninedy now, so, OK, who gonna gi me aighty, aighty dolla bid, who gonna bid an aighty dolla bid, now, les go, dis is wadda we here for, lookin' for da bidder, now, gimme sebendy. Don be a horse whisperer, yell out ya bid, so, we now lookin' for sebendy five dolla bid… who gonna bid sebendy dolla! Le'me hear yer bid now!"

The auctioneer went all the way down to sixty dollars, then, got a run for the bids to climb back up to one hundred and forty dollars at which time horse number 1, was sold.

Someone yelled out from the back. "Is this two for one, or is it buy one and get one free? This is supposed to be a horse sale. What's with the high prices! This ain't New York City, you know. You can lead a horse to water but you can't make him drink, and, you can bring horse buyers to an auction but you can't make'm bid!" Others chimed in with similar remarks.

Evidently, someone in the crowd was upset about the price other than Eugene and Oscar.

The early sales went fast, faster than either Eugene or Oscar could keep track of, as to who it was doing the main bidding. More than a dozen horses had already been sold in the first half hour, and, most of the bids had started at seventy-five dollars or more at the outset, and, most had brought between one hundred and fifty to two hundred dollars per horse. Oscar looked at Eugene and just shook his head. Neither one could believe what they thought to be the exorbitant prices being paid for the horses. Who would have thought that the price of horses would have been driven up so high at a little weekend auction in Boonville.

They watched closely as horse number 17 was led out. He looked good. The auctioneer asked for a bid to start at fifty dollars, but, did not get an early bid, so, he came back to the crowd asking for a forty dollar bid. With that, Eugene held his number card high in the air and yelled "forty here", but, the bidding went within seconds from his

forty to fifty to sixty, and, in a short time was hanging on a hundred dollar bid. Eugene was glad that he had backed off early on, chickened out and had quit bidding. Oscar was glad that he had.
"Well, Oscar, number seventeen is down the hole and on out the gate, and, we didn't even have a chance with that one whatsoever." Eugene said.
"They'll be more, let's just hide and watch. Jusr remember, if you want to make a small fortune trading in horses, start out with a large fortune." Oscar responded.
Someone from the back started yelling again. "If yer sellin' all the broken down nags, at too high a-prices, what the hell are you gonna sell the good horses for?"
"You get what you pay for! Put your money where your mouth is!" The auctioneer yelled back, and, otherwise, ignored the hassle and went on with his business. The handlers brought out horse after horse, and, every one of them brought what Eugene and Oscar thought was a too high price, even the mules, except when two of them were sold as a team.
Oscar nudged Eugene. "Eugene, I know that number 17 horse, that horse belonged to Wylie, and, the guy who bought it was Charlie, and, both of them are gamblers, poker players they are, and, they's both been known to shake them bones for hard earned cash, why, I'll bet you ten dollars to a dime, that one of them owes the other some gambling money, and, this is the way that they are getting about the exchange of owed money."
Eugene just shook his head.
Almost the same way, horses number 22, 35 and 41, were bid for, either by Oscar, Eugene, or, in the case of number 35 by both, because they were so excited and had gotten caught up in the bidding process, however, none of their bids were high enough for either one of them to buy any one of them.
It was almost at the end of the auction, when the handlers led out horse number 47, which was announced by the auctioneer to be the last horse to be auctioned that day. By this time, more than half of the crowd had already left the sales pen and headed out to the local taverns, with a few, having left the auction and led off their purchases with them.
The auctioneer seemed tired out from all of the sales of the day, having spent almost five hours selling off the 46 previous horses. He called for the handlers to circle horse number 47 around, for all to see. The horse was scraggly, he still had bits and pieces of his winter hair

hanging here and there with mud caked chunks hanging under his belly, his hooves were curled up and broken, from not having been trimmed for some time or not having horse shoes. It looked like he had two different colored eyes, either that, or he was blind in one eye and couldn't see out of the other.

Oscar looked at Eugene, and said. "Eugene, the only thing good about that horse is, that he ain't completely swayback yet, maybe he has hay fever, but, we're not adopting horses today, we're here for the buyin'."

"He ain't dead yet either, go look in his mouth and let's see if we want to bid on him. He looks like one of those rescued wild mustangs from Nevada." Eugene said.

Oscar headed down to the pen and asked the handler to look at the horses teeth. The handler brought the horse over to the fence and Oscar reach through the fence and pulled back the horses lips. He looked at the teeth, then, gave Eugene a "thumbs up" as the teeth looked good to him. Then; Eugene started the bid while Oscar returned.

The auctioneer started out at fifty, but did not get a bid, then, he went to forty with no bidders, then, he went to thirty with no bids, but said that he couldn't go any lower than twenty-five, as, in all good conscience he did not want to embarrass the horse any further, and Eugene's hand went up with his numbers card in it and he yelled "twenty-five over here". The auctioneer took the bid and then asked for thirty, but, no other bidders answered, so, the auctioneer asked once, twice and three times rattlin' away for thirty, but, not hearing any other bid, he yelled out "sold for twenty-five dollars to that man holding card number 115, the last horse of the day. And, with that, the last sale of the day, this auction is hereby closed, shut down, and over, if you catch my drift." With that, the auctioneer climbed down from his pedestal and walked out.

Oscar yelled out. "You got him, Eugene, you got him, you got him for twenty-five dollars!"

Eugene replied. "Well, let's go pay for him, then, we'll bridle him up and take him home. I can't believe that we did'nt get one of the other horses that we'd picked out, and, now, we get to go home with the last horse sold at the auction. Oscar, the dang horse may not even make it back home to the farm for all we know."

Eugene paid for the horse, then, took his receipt to the sales pen and gave it to one of the handlers along with the bridle that he had brought. The handler bridled the horse, opened the pen gate and

249

handed over the horse along with Eugene's receipt, and, Eugene and Oscar both led the horse out to Eugene's wagon, where they tied the horse to the back end of the wagon for him to follow them home. On the way home, the pair did not say much, but did look back now and then just to make sure the horse was still back behind the wagon and still walking. Eugene dropped Oscar off at his farm, then, went on home, unhooked his team from the wagon, unharnessed them, then, got the horse that he had bought and turned the three loose in the barnyard so they could get some water at the trough, he fed the three, and, turned them into the barn for the night.

The next morning after breakfast, Eugene went out to the barn to do his chores, let the horses out into the barnyard but took horse number 47 and a couple bars of lye soap with him, and went down to the creek where he tied the horse to a tree limb, then, proceeded to wash the horse down. Afterwards, he took the horse back to the barn where he curried him down and got rid of most of the winter hair, combed out his mane and tail, removing most of the entanglements, then, let the horse out into the barnyard.

Later, that day, Oscar dropped by Eugene's house. "I just thought I'd come over to get a better look at the horse you bought yesterday, Eugene. You know, it was me, who was the first at wanting to buy another horse for my farm. By the way, what did you do with him? Did he live through the night? Where's he at?" Oscar asked.

"He's out there in the barnyard, Oscar, go take a look." Eugene said.

Oscar ventured out to the barnyard to see the horse, but, could not believe his eyes. The horse was not scraggly anymore. His mane and tail were blowing in the breeze. He went back up to the house where Eugene was sitting on the front porch and said. "Eugene, you know, I meant to go to the auction to buy a horse. You know I needed an extra horse. I'll tell you what I'll do, I'll give you thirty dollars right now for that horse, cash on the barrel head. You know, you have always said, that everything you own was for sale at one price or another. What do you say?" Oscar said.

"Let me see the color of your money, Oscar." Eugene responded.

Oscar pulled out his money and showed Eugene the thirty dollars, then, stuck it out to him.

Eugene took the money and said. "You got yourself a deal there Oscar, I'll get a bridle and you can lead him home, but, I want my bridle back. OK?"

Oscar agreed. He took the bridle, went to the barnyard, bridled horse 47 and walked him home. After he got him home, he called the farrier and he came out to Oscars place, filed down the horses hooves and nailed four new shoes on the horse, and, only charged Oscar four dollars for his work. Oscar then got some corn, shelled it out, and fed horse 47, then, turned him loose in his barnyard.

In the meantime, Eugene had too much time to think. He wished that he had not sold horse 47 to Oscar, but, since Oscar was a close friend, and, a good neighbor, he thought that he would do him a good deed. However, by the next morning, more dread had set in, and, by early afternoon, he headed over to Oscar's place to talk to him about the horse. When he got over to Oscar's, he caught sight of horse 47 prancing around in the barnyard. Then he went up to the house. He had a long talk with Oscar, finally getting around to offering Oscar thirty-five dollars for the horse, and agreeing to even reimbursing him for the farrier's work. After a while, Oscar did relent, and let Eugene buy the horse back, and, at the same time, returning he bridle. Eugene then led the horse back home.

The next morning, again after breakfast, Eugene went out to the barn to do his chores, but before turning horse 47 out of his stall, he took his scissors and trimmed up his mane and tail, curried him down, getting rid of almost all traces of his winter hair, and, combed out the remaining tangles in his mane and tail, then, turned him loose in the barnyard.

Meanwhile, Oscar had too much free time on his hands, and, he got to the point of wishing that he had not sold the horse back to Eugene. So, that afternoon, he headed over to Eugene's house but in the process of getting there, he saw horse 47 prancing about in the barnyard, looking good. He just had to get that horse back from Eugene. He went up to the house. Eugene came out, and, Oscar hit him up straight out for a forty dollar cash up front to buy back horse 47. Eugene said that he would have to think about it a little, but, he knew, everything that he had was for sale if the price was right, so, he agreed with Oscar and took his forty dollars. Oscar told him, that he had brought his own bridle this time, and went out to the barnyard, bridled horse 47, and, led him home.

Well, as it happened, the next morning, while Oscar was out doing his chores, there was a horse trader, driving a wagon, who stopped by the farm, saw horse 47 in the barnyard, and, asked Oscar if that particular horse was for sale. Well, Oscar told him that he wasn't, but, the horse trader told him, that he could see himself clear to pay up to fifty dollars for such a fine horse, and, that fifty dollars could go a long way in this day and time, he told Oscar. Oscar thought about it a

little, walked around the barnyard, trying to decide, then, agreed to sell him the horse for the fifty dollars. The horse trader paid Oscar and told him, that he really needed the horse, as, he was in process of selling tickets for a horse raffle, and he would use the horse to fulfill that need. However, he said, he could not pick up the horse until the next day, when he was passing back through. Oscar told him that that was fine with him and that he would hold the horse for him to pick up the next day. The horse trader then went on about his business.
In the meantime. Eugene, had got to thinking, that he really wanted that horse. He had bid on him in the first place, and, had already bought him back from Oscar once and maybe Oscar would sell horse 47 back to him again. So, that afternoon, he went over to Oscar's house, and hailed him down. He hit him up to buy back the horse and said that he would offer him forty-five dollars cash just to get him back. Well, Oscar broke the news to Eugene, that he had sold horse 47 that morning to a horse trader for fifty dollars, and, that the horse trader needed the horse to fulfill a horse raffle that he was holding.
Eugene was shaken. "What do you mean, that you sold our horse? Between the two of us, we were making at least five dollars a day on that horse!" Eugene said.
Oscar responded. "Well, why don't you come over in the morning and we will get horse 47 ready for the horse trader, but, in light of the difference between what the horse trader paid and what you offered, I do feel bad, so, I'll share the profit with you. Here's your twenty-five dollars back that you paid for the horse in the first place, if that will ease your mind about it all." Oscar said.
Eugene took the money, and, agreed to come over the next morning to help get horse 47 ready for the horse trader, then, he went on back home. Later on that evening, Oscar put the horses up in their stalls for the night.
Morning came bright and early. Oscar had breakfast, then, went out to the barn to do his chores. He let his horses out of their stalls, but, when he got to horse 47's stall, he saw the horse lying on the ground. He checked the horse, and found that the horse was dead as four o'clock in the morning. It flashed through his mind as to what he was going to do next, as, he had sold the horse the day previous. Not knowing what else to do, he headed over to Eugene's house to see if he could help him come up with some explanation. Eugene said that, he had to see it all for himself, so, he went back over to Oscar's place to maybe help out some with the problem. They discussed every possible explanation that they could think of, but, between the two of

them, neither could come up with any sensible answers.

They were sitting on the front porch when the horse trader came up the road with his wagon. "I'm here to pick up my horse, Oscar." He yelled out.

Oscar came down from the porch and began his pitiful story. "Well, I don't know how to readily explain it to you, but, I'll just tell you straight out. Your horse died in his stall last night, and, I don't know what to do about it, and, neither does Eugene, my neighbor here. But we had no idea that the horse was anywhere near death in any way, fit, form or fashion." He said.

The horse trader responded. "Well, go get some rope and a couple of pulleys and I'll get my wagon pulled over by the barn and we'll pull the horse out of that stall and you all can help me drag him up and load him on my wagon, and, I'll take him just the way he is. Get some boards to lay up on the back end of the wagon to drag him up on. I'll use my horse to do the pulling."

Both Oscar and Eugene were astounded. Oscar asked first. "You mean, you still want the horse, even if he's stone cold dead? I mean, you said you needed the horse to fulfill your raffle, you can't just go out and raffle off a dead horse!" He exclaimed.

"Sure I can, and, I most certainly will. Now, go get some rope, lace up those pulley, and, open the gate to the barnyard, I'll pull my wagon in and we'll pull that nag out of your barn and load I'll load him up myself if I have to." The horse trader said.

They all proceeded to get ropes and pulleys to haul the dead horse out of the stall in the barn, and leaned boards up on the end of the wagon to scoot the dead horse up on the wagon. The horse was actually easier to load than either Oscar or Eugene thought.

Eugene asked next. "OK, we've helped you load your dead horse up, but, please, do tell me, just what do you plan to tell the person that wins your horse raffle when he finds out that the horse that he has won is now dead as a door nail, and, just what do you plan to do with a dead assed horse?"

"Hell, Eugene, I don't have to tell the guy that wins the raffle anything, except that the horse he won in the raffle just happened to have died last night, which, is the truth before God Almighty Himself, and, what I'll do, after I bend over backwards, is to offer him all of his money back. If he bought more than one ticket, I'll tell him that according to State Law, that I can only refund money on the winning ticket and it has to be filed with the County Clerk." The horse trader said. "Besides, the horse already being dead and all, why, he'll bring at least fifteen to twenty dollars at the glue factory."

After the horse trader had hauled off the dead horse, Eugene said to Oscar. "Oscar, in the morning, after breakfast and chores, I'll pick you up, and, we'll head out to Boonville, to see the auctioneer. I plan to get my money back on the horse one way or another."

Oscar responded. "Dang, Eugene, I thought that we already had gotten our money back already. I mean, we already more than doubled our money on the horse so far with that sale to that horse trader for his raffle."

"Just be ready in the mornin' Oscar. I plan to get my hard earned money back on that horse, and, you are my primary witness to the horse a-dyin', and, when I do, I'll split it with you, that way, plus all the expense we've been out, we will more than triple our money on the horse." Eugene said.

Oscar responded. "Now, Eugene, just what makes you think, that you are going to get your money back on that dead horse?"

"Oscar, we have been out our good time cleaning, currying, trimming mane and even braiding up the tail, not to mention the farrier's charge for new shoes on the horse. Why, that horse was hauled out of the stall and loaded on that wagon with the new horse shoes, never used, on him. If the auctioneer doesn't agree on reimbursement, then, I'll go to the Boonville newspaper and give them my story, and, it will not be pretty. I mean, some farmer brought an almost dead horse to be auctioned, and, the auctioneer was part of it all. He got his ten percent, and, the owner got his money that day. We are the ones, or, me in particular, was the one, who got took, hook, line and sinker. Just be ready when the morning comes." Eugene said.

OOMA AND WOMA

Now, Ooma and Woma, were sisters, close enough as neighbors, to be able to meet and talk on a daily basis and confide in one another on their more intimate personal matters. They met every morning to join together for a peaceful cup of tea, and, some discussion about daily happenings in their cave living environment. They also went out together on a daily basis hunting for berries, nuts, grain and herbs.

"I've had it with this cave, Ooma. I don't like it, I'm ready to move on. I'm ready for an up-grade. I'm ready for a change. I've all but had it with my mate Raa, he can't hunt, he can't fish, he don't have sense enough even to try the gathering of grain when the season comes in. I don't think that he could pound sand down a rat hole if he had an eight pound rock. I have to tell him everything to do and give him instruction for each step. He is a loser with a capital "L" from the word get-go. I cook, I clean, I keep a good cave, respectable, to say the least. I deserve more. I want more. I want a life that I can be excited about or at least get excited about. I want something that others would say that they would also like to have, so, there is nothing secret there. No more and no less. I am ready to leave Raa along with his bad habits and his smelly ass. I keep all my things in that one bag over there by the sleeping mat just in case I have to leave at any moment's notice. But, I just don't know just how to go about it. I don't want him chasing after me, dragging me back to this cave by the hair of my head. I want a complete break. I want to turn it all off. Especially, before we start a family and have children who have to be taken into account for any break up. My wish is, that I would rather that he leave, rather than me, but, if it comes to it, I am ready but not totally prepared yet to do it myself without some help. Do you hear what I'm trying to say?" Woma both said and asked.

"You sound like you have had it. Just how do you plan to go about this break up thing?" Ooma asked.

"I'm not sure just yet. But, I know, in my heart, that I have to do it. The time of it is near, I can feel it. Raa was raised by his mother, and, she provided him with his daily needs, until such time that we moved in here together. I mean, it is like that I came along only to continue to fulfil those needs, and, he is still locked into his old style of life without moving on. Raa ceased to mature as a fifteen year old kid, and he will locked in at that age mentally for years to come. He knows of nothing else. He will never mature. He blatantly refuses to grow up. He will never be what I want him to be. He would never make a good father. I can't change him. So, I don't even want to have children with him. If the truth were to be known, I don't want anything further to do with him either. I don't know what attraction it was that I had for him in the first place. I must have been naïve. I must have surely been operating on over gorged hormones to even make any effort whatsoever to try to select him as a mate early on. I guess, that I was not totally aware of just how large the gene pool was here in our area." Woma said.

Ooma listened to wail of her sister and felt her pain as Woma went on. "Ooma, Raa cannot barter, he hasn't got a clue about how to go about it. Now, Mik, a guy who lives just below us down by the creek, is really good at it. That is how Mik gets me to cook some of the game that he brings in when he takes half after it is cooked. Sometimes, Mik even brings us in some wild grapes or black cherries that he has come across to provide us some benefit. Raa couldn't barter his way out of a hole that he had dug or a paper bag is there was such a thing. If someone ever invents money, Raa will be in deep shit trouble. Mik, the guy I mentioned who lives down by the creek, now, he would survive. I wish I could take some of Mik's moxey and inject it into Raa, but if I did, or, if I could, Raa would probably come down sick for a month or two and then the whole burden of our lives would be in my hands."

Ooma responded. "Well, you remember Bot? My first beau? All he wanted was my naked bod bouncing in bed. He didn't care about what I thought about anything. He didn't care about my feelings on any matter. He never had a job that I ever heard about and he did not know how to work at anything. He was an overgrown kid in disguise. He was like that, in a way, and then, you, of all people, had the gall to take his side of some of our dumb ass arguments, and then, you were appalled and wondered why I ditched him early on. Why, if I remember rightly, you were upset that I cut him off at the pass, even before he ever got to first base with me."

"Well, this is different, Raa and I have been together now for a couple of years. Although there were times that I can think of that were good, mostly, as, it was because of me and what I did rather than the other way around. I'm just sick and tired of being sick and tired about it all." Woma said. "I mean, yes, we have have moved up, we are now up and out of living in the trees, and have moved into the caves, which is a move up in our society somewhat, it is not high society, overall, but, I long so much for the next generational upgrade. I long for a stick and mud hut with a thatched roof, with a door, maybe even with a window, situated on the sunny side of a mountain, I might add, but not in town where the city lights and the crying singing drunks keep you awake at night. Yea, I know, a cave is better than any tree, especially in the winter months, but I am the one who pushed Raa to get us to where we are today, mostly because he fell out of every damn tree that he ever slept in, which, may be part of his problem, come to think of it, but, that is not my fault, and, I feel, that if we both worked together with him helping out a little, we could even have more, but, that I will never see any of it at all with Raa, and, I know it down deep in my heart. I'm more than ready to give it all up. Just to give you an example of what I'm putting up with, I caught two chickens, a hen and a rooster, and planned to have my own eggs and maybe raise a couple more chickens in the process, and, Raa, one day, when he didn't get anything while out hunting, he killed them both, de-feathered them and cooked the both of them for supper. On another occasion, I saved any seeds for planting, and, damned if he didn't go and cook them for breakfast one morning. He has a way about him to undo everything that I try to do."

"Woma, just what do you see as a hope for your future, without Raa, as being any better than what you have now?" Ooma asked.

Woma responded. "Well, on the side, I've been very quietly checking out this guy Mik who I mentioned before. He keeps to himself down by the creek. He doesn't have a cave, so, he built his own out of piled up rocks and used creek mud for mortar. Then, he put up sticks, leaves and moss on the roof to keep the rains out. His place is dry as a bone, and, he always has a fire to keep warm by. Now, Raa is down there on a daily basis, early, asking, or, I should say, bumming Mik up for a few hot coals to start our fire almost every morning, day in and day out. Raa moans, groans, whoops and hollers, and, cusses like a sailor, if there was such a thing, when things don't go like he wants it. Mik don't yell, he is quiet. Mik sometimes brings game or some fish by our cave for me to cook, and, it is always already de-scaled, gutted out and cleaned, and, he then quietly takes his share, never asking for more. Now, that says something for his bartering skills. Raa, on the other hand, never guts out the rabbits or squirrels, or any of the fish that he says that he catches for that matter. I absolutely hate to gut out, clean and descale the fish. Rabbits aren't so bad to skin, but those squirrels are just too much, they are tough to skin and tougher to cook. They all stink from the get-go. Raa always leaves that job up to me. He thinks that that is just part of my duty along with the collecting of nuts, grains and berries. Most of the time, Mik is better at hunting and fishing than Raa. Mik never complains, that I have ever heard. Mik's home made stick cave is close enough to ours that I could hear him snoring if he did, and, Mik never snores. Raa's snoring wakes me up in the middle of the night and then I can't ever get back to sleep. Mik's home made stick cave is inviting, he even has a window to throw out his trash into the creek. It smells good. It is clean. It is the kind of living place that any woman would or could ever want, and, Mik is the kind of man, any woman would want, if she had any sense about herself at all. Besides, Raa picks his nose and scratches his butt. I have never, ever, seen Mik pick his nose. Raa never, ever, takes a bath in the creek, he says the water is too cold. Mik is always in the creek, bare butt naked. I have been bathing in the creek and I know for a fact that the water is not all that cold because I've been in it myself."

Just how do you know, or, better yet, just how have you come to know all of this about Mik and about his homemade stick cave? I mean, I recognize petty private stuff for what it is." Ooma asked.

"Well, I've been down there, during the day, when both Raa and Mik have been out hunting or fishing, but, they never go together that I have ever seen, Raa always goes to find his hunting and fishing buddy from God knows where. I have seen with my own eyes the order that Mik keeps his living area. Then, I look at what I have now, and, there is something definitely missing from my present relationship. Something that I want, something that I need, something different than what I have now. Something more. It is that something, that all women would want if they had any sense about themselves at all. I feel trapped. There are no organizations yet to be found in our society to help someone like me in my predicament. I feel abused. I'm worse than that crazy lady in town who goes up and down the streets yelling "Whip me, beat me, make me write bad checks!" In some cases, she has more going for her than I do." Woma said.

Ooma responded. "OK, so, I do feel your pain, but, again, just how do you propose to go about this separation thing with Raa if it comes to that?"

"Well, I thought about accusing Raa of sleeping with some other woman, some day after he claims to be out hunting or fishing, especially when he comes home empty handed and he is all stinky smelly with beer on his breath. That accusation would both boost his self-esteem and render me the excuse that I needed to end our relationship, albeit temporarily, but, at least enough initially to get out of what I've gotten myself into. I mean, I feel like I am in over my head and would have to stand on a box, if there were such a thing, just to get a good breath of air or see daylight." Woma said.

Ooma countered and asked. "Well, Woma, you just can't walk out of one cave and into another at the drop of a hat. If you did, Raa, or, any man for that matter, would suspect something. Just how do you plan to accomplish such a thing, I mean, it appears to me, that you definitely have a thing for this Mik guy, and, as of right now, you don't have a clue as how to go about getting rid of Raa!"

"I've thought about it. I've thought that maybe on some dark rainy night, that I could get up to go pee, and then wander off someplace, Mik's home made cave in particular being my first choice. Or, claim that I must surely have been walking in my sleep, a little beforehand, just in case I get caught in the process. Or, I could trump up some argument, and, stomp out of the cave mad as a hornet, and, maybe look to Mik to house me up for the night. Or, I could just disappear for a couple of days, and, hide out in Mik's homemade cave, just to wait and see what Raa would do. I've thought of other things, like going back into the trees with those Neanderthals, but, none are simple, or seem to have any quick solution to get out of one relationship and to try to start out on another." Woma added.

Ooma responded. "What happens now, just for shits and grins, what happens, if Raa gets really mad, and confronts Mik with trying to take his mate away, and, a fight ensues between the two of them, and, one of them kills or wounds the other. Are you prepared for the worse? I mean, what if Raa accuses you of infidelity, although nothing yet has happened, but, what if Raa turns and takes his vengeance out on you? You could be hurt, not just physically, but also mentally. Too, you may never be able to have a relationship with Mik, because he saw what happened and then may refuse to interfere, not wanting to touch you with a ten foot pole, or, he may not ever want to have anything to do with you after everything is said and done anyway. I mean, how would it look for you and Mik to be together as neighbors with him being just a few snores length from Raa and, with Raa having to cook for himself and coming to you every morning bumming hot coals? All with Raa within some close clubbing, rock throwing or spear chucking distance of him trying the getting even thing with the you and Mik as primary targets? How are you going to handle that if it came to it? I mean, I have heard of worse on more than just one occasion with some of my close neighbors." Ooma both asked and said.

"I just don't know yet. I'm only surmising. It's all still mixed up in my mind and I can't get it all straight to even think about the consequences of it all just yet." Woma said.

"How about doing some kind of crazy things just to stir up some shit?" Ooma asked.

"Like what?" Woma returned.

"Well, scratch some pictograph of a naked woman on the out of sight back wall of your cave wall, and then, when Raa comes home, accuse him of doing it. Or, what about making up a dummy, made out of vines and weeds, that looks like a woman, and hide it out in the back of the cave, then, act like you came upon it, and, found it, and accuse Raa of making it up to appeal to some his goofy off the wall needs. Or, what about finding a leaf, with some other woman's name scratched on it, just to ask him about, or just to bust him up. If he says in his defense that he can't read or write, blame it on him anyway by saying that she must have wrote it and then gave it to him and he must have took it on high hopes. The simple solution is, is to accuse him, flat out, of ogling and looking at other women. He can't deny that. All men do it to some degree or another at some time or another. It is an accusation of which there is no good answer at hand for the man. If he is ignorant or stupid enough, he won't have an answer to any of it and will only be puzzled about it all, but, it can get you an out to get out, to put some distance between you and him. I would invite you over to my cave, or, our cave, but, as you know, it is much smaller than what you have now, and, you wouldn't have many creature comforts. I mean, my mate Haro is a patient man, but, he likes his privacy. I could take you in for a few days, just to get you the space that you need, but, there is no telling what will happen after that. By the same token, if you have any yearnings for this other guy Mik, you still need to put some space and distance between you and Raa. Or, convince him that he needs to make some space between the two of you, especially if he has any yearnings for you at all. After all, he could change his mind, other men have been known to have done that in the past, you know. Otherwise, you have little choice in the matter." Ooma said.

Woma responded with. "Well, I've thought about following Raa, when he leaves in the morning, just to see what he does and when he is out and about, supposedly out hunting or fishing. The only thing is, is, I don't know what I would do if he ever caught me following him, or, what I would do if I caught him doing something that I don't even want to think of."

"Well, what about the two of us trying to trail him and his so-called hunting and fishing buddies? Just to see where they go and what they do and how they do it, that way, you would have a witness." Ooma both asked and said.

"Do you think that we could really do such a thing and get away with it?" Woma asked.

Ooma responded with. "Well, early on, in our relationship, I followed Haro on some of his rounds, just enough to ask questions of him when he came home, just to see if what he said matched up with what I saw him actually do during the day, and that worked for me."

"So, you think that you and I could do something similar with Raa? I mean, it is kind of scary, to try to spy on someone else, especially someone who you are in a relationship with." Woma said.

"What is his plan for tomorrow?" Ooma asked.

"It is samo-samo every day, day in and day out. Raa gets up when he wakes up, he goes down to Mik's to get some hot coals to come back and start our fire to warm the cave, along with getting a gourd full of water from the creek for me to cook with. Then, after I cook some grain and berries for breakfast, he gathers up his crooked sticks and walnuts, puts them in his bag, dresses up for his hunting or fishing expedition, and, takes off, and, he usually heads out north and up along the creek." Woma answered.

Ooma responded. "You say, that he gathers up his sticks and his walnuts, what kind of sticks does he gather up, what is it with that?" Ooma asked Woma.

Woma responded with. "Well, he has two or three sharp pointed sticks, that I have burned in the fire and sharpened for him, that he says that he uses as a spear for his hunting, then, he has these other sticks, that have a crooked end to them, probably five or six of them, which, he says, that he uses those particular sticks for fishing, for flipping the fish out of the water and onto the bank, which he calls his effort at his method of fishing, or, rousting out a rabbit out of his hole, or, a squirrel out of a hollow tree, and hitting them in their head. Then, he has his bag of walnuts, which he has smoothed down the rough edges on rocks around the fire pit. He says that he uses those to throw at rabbits or squirrels. He is forever making new ones, as, he says he loses the old ones throwing at birds."

Ooma responded. "Well, that is no help, as, Haro has similar sticks, except for the walnut thing. So, OK, let's do this, early in the morning, I will get up and come down here to meet with you, right after my mate Haro takes off and your mate Raa leaves for his hunting and fishing expedition. But, what we will do, is watch him only part way the first day until he is out of sight, just to see which way that he goes, and try to track him from there, then, on the second day, we will set up in that area, and follow him or track him onto his next journey. It may take a few days in order to eventually get to see his ultimate destination, but, it will be worth it all in the long run. That is most likely the best plan to do what it is that you want to do. Are you up to it?" Ooma both said and asked.

"Ok, so, do you think that we could start early in the morning? As, I want to get this thing over and done with as soon as possible. I'm telling you, you don't know just how fed up I am with it all and am at my wits end." Woma said.

"I'll be down here after breakfast, and, I will wait for Raa to leave, then, I'll throw a rock into your cave for you to know that I am hid out and ready, and, you can join me, and, we'll follow Raa out to his daily activity to see just what he does and how he does it, we'll track him down if we have to, one way or another." Ooma said.

Ooma then left the cave, headed for home, with plans to begin the following of Raa on the morrow with Woma.

Morning came early, with a little less than a slight chance of rain. Raa left the cave to journey down to Mik's to get some hot coals in order to start the early morning fire. He returned with a clamshell of hot coals and a gourd full of water. Woma cooked their breakfast in a baked clay bowl, using some of the new clam shells that she had found for spoons. The morning was followed with Raa getting dressed somewhat early and leaving out to hunt and fish with his bag of crooked sticks, along with the three sharp pointed sticks, as, Woma had counted them in his bag the night before but had lost count of just how many crooked stick that were in the bag as she could not yet count that high. Woma observed Raa to head out to the north, along the creek, and, as far as she could see, he continued on up along the creek. It was some time before Ooma tossed a rock into the cave to signal Woma that she was hiding nearby and on the ready for their venture.

Woma yelled out to Ooma. "Ooma, he's already gone. We need to hurry, as, I lost sight of him going out and about north along the creek." She said.

"OK, let's get it on, let's boogie up to where you last seen him, and, let's see if we can track him from there." Woma said.

The two women headed out of the cave and onto the trail to the point of where Woma had last seen Raa, then, the two, tried to track him from there, scanning the ground for any footprints or broken blades of grass.

"What if he catches us following him?" Woma asked.

"We'll just say that we are out looking for nuts, berries or grain, and, we'll ask him if he has seen any." Ooma said.

Sneaking along, bush by bush, trying to follow Raa seemed to be a lost cause, and the time came for both Woma and Ooma to finally agree to give up the chase and head back home, to start again on the morrow from where they left off today. They marked their trail with a broken branch bent toward the last direction that they had found any trail of Raa.

Morning came bright and sunny, and, the day began as always. However, Woma noted that Raa had not brought home any game or fish for the last three days. All that they had to eat were the berries and grain along with a few nuts that Woma had gathered and cooked. But, she bit her tongue and said nothing about it to Raa, dead set in her mind to allowing their situation to run out its ultimate course. After breakfast, Raa gathered up his bag of sticks and his walnuts, and headed out for his daily routine of so-called hunting and fishing. Shortly after Raa had left, Ooma tossed a rock into the cave and Woma called her in, telling her that the coast was clear. The two laid out their plan for the day, gathered up their collecting bags and headed out along Raa's trail. They found their previous markings along the trail, and continued their endeavor of the tracking and following of Raa. They came out along the trail to a wide meadow by the sea, where only short grass grew. It was the place of sheep and goat grazing which kept the grass short. Bushes now came far and few between. Creeping and crawling from bush to bush along the trail, they continued in their effort at tracking Raa and also keeping a sharp eye out for him along the trail ahead of them. There being very few bushes to hide behind in this area, their progress was slowed as was their movements and they became more and more careful in their endeavor. It was Ooma, up in the front of the two, who first spotted Raa and his hunting partners.

Ooma whispered as loud as she could to Woma. "Woma, hide quick, I think I see Raa out in the open out in the short grass."

"Let me crawl up to where you are at." Woma whispered loudly back.

"No, no, hide and don't even move." Ooma said. "The bush I'm behind is too small for both of us to hide behind, besides, there are few bushes here that don't have a snake under them, so, just stay where you are, and, lay down if you have to, but, stay hidden."

"Are you sure that it is Raa?" Woma asked.

"Yes, it's Raa, and, three other men walking on further north in the short grass." Ooma said.

"What are they doing?" Woma asked.

"They walk along, then, they all stop, and, one of the men hits something in the grass with a stick, and then, they all go back to walking on further north. Woma, they all have their backs to me now, so, I am going to crawl on up to the next bush, and you can crawl on up to where I am at now so that you can see, but, be quiet about it." Ooma said.

Ooma moved on up to the next bush and made it without the men seeing her while Woma scrambled on her hands and knees to get up to where she could now see the men out in the meadow.

"Well, they are certainly not fishing out there, so, they must be hunting. What do you suppose that they are hunting for?" Ooma asked.

Woma responded quietly. "I have no idea, I've only went hunting with Raa a couple of times, but, we never came up here this far north where you can feel the sea breezes. Maybe, they are trying to scare rabbits out of their holes." She said.

Ooma whispered frantically as loud as she could. "Woma, Woma, hide, hide, lay down if you have to, the men have turned around and are heading back down the other side of the meadow."

"I see them, I see them, I'm well hidden, just be sure you hide well yourself. You are the one up front, they would see you first before they saw me." Woma said.

Both Ooma and Woma, now observed the men coming back down the meadow, still stopping now and then to allow one of them to hit at something in the grass with their sticks.

Ooma spoke up, a little more loudly now. "Woma, I don't think that you are going to believe this, but, I think that Raa and those other men out there in the meadow in the short grass are not hunting at all, but playing at some sort of a game. I remember coming up here with Haro some time ago, and, there were some other men out there, doing the same thing that Raa and those other three men are doing, and, Haro told me it was some kind of game." She said.

"Game? Game? What kind of game would they be playing out there in the short grass and out in the open? Woma asked.

Ooma responded. "I can't think of the name of it right now, but, I know that it has got to be some sort of game, no doubt in my mind." She said.

The men were closer now, and, Ooma could see them clearly. The men would walk along and hit something with their sticks, then, they all proceeded on along down the meadow walking together. They were so close now, that they could hear them talking and laughing amongst themselves.

Woma could not take it any longer. "I'm coming up where you are so I can see a little better!" She exclaimed.

Ooma responded. "Woma! This bush is not big enough for the two of us, stay where you are!" She said.

"I'm coming up anyway, I got to see more for myself! I'll hide behind you if I have to!" Woma said as she crawled up to where Ooma was.

Ooma whispered. "Look, Woma, they all walk along together for a while, then, they all stop, and, one of them hits something like a rock with their stick. I can see something fly through the air. Then, they all walk along on down the meadow to where the next man stops and hits something with his stick. Then, I see something else fly through the air. I'm telling you, Woma, they are definitely playing some dumb ass game." Ooma said.

Woma responded. "Ooma, I think you are right. And, I think I have seen enough. This is why Raa has not brought home any game or fish now for almost a week. Instead of hunting and fishing, he is out here with some of his buddies, playing some stupid ass game. That is grounds for divorce as far as I am concerned, as, he is neglecting his duty to help feed his family. What if we had kids, why, they would all probably starve to death before Raa ever brought any food home to eat. I don't need to see any more. Let's head back home." She said.

Ooma responded back. "Don't move Woma! The men are now turning back around and going the other way on further north and on further across the meadow. As soon as they all get their backs turned to us, we can move out, until then, stay put and stay hid, and talk more softly." She said.

Shortly thereafter, the men were all but out of sight across the meadow, and Woma and Ooma first crawled, then, crept back along the trail heading back home.

Ooma was the first to speak after they were full out of sight to the men and no longer crouching but walking upright. "Woma, I think that I remember the name of that game that Raa and those men were playing. It is called "Gauf" I think." She said.

"Gauf? Gauf. I've never heard of the game. I know several games that we played growing up, but, I never seen or ever heard of any game like that." Woma said.

"Woma, I think that it is somewhat of a men's only game. That is probably why we have never played it or why we have never heard anything about it." Ooma said.

"Well, from what I have seen today, as far as I am concerned, it is more than just grounds for divorce. So, I'm starting proceedings tomorrow. If I get a good attorney I could come out alright. As far as I am concerned, Raa could go back to living in some damn tree with his entire bag of sticks. Now, I know, that they weren't hunting and trying to chase rabbits out of their holes, and, they weren't hitting rocks. Damn, I just realized that they were hitting those damn walnuts that Raa has been working on and making over the last year or so." Woma said.

"Well, now at least you know that you have got down to the bottom of the truth." Ooma said. "Just how are you going to confront Raa?" She also asked.

"I don't know just yet, this is something that I am going to have to take a step at a time." Woma said. "Gauf, I can't believe that that no good worthless son-of-a-b---- was out playing a game when he came in day in and day out telling me how tired he was from being out hunting and fishing. Damn, Ooma, Mik looks better and better every minute." She added.

Ooma responded. "I don't know about that, Woma, one of those other men sure looked a lot like Mik to me. Maybe he isn't what you think him to be either. I mean, it just didn't look like him, it was a dead ringer for him, unless he has a twin brother hid out somewhere." She said.

"Well, Ooma, don't be so high and mighty, I think, that one of them laughed, walked and talked a lot like your husband Haro does, so, what do you think of that? Can you handle that?" Woma said.

"Damn." Ooma said. "Come to think of it, it did look like Haro. It was most likely him! Damn, damn, damn. Woma, we're both in the same damn boat, and, we are both up shit creek without a paddle!" She added.

Woma responded. "Well, it looks like Raa, Mik and Haro along with someone else that we don't know yet were all out playing "Gauf" when we thought that they were out hunting or fishing, trying to feed their family."

"Haro, as far as I know, has never done anything like this before that I know of." Ooma said.

"Well, it is divorce city for me." Woma said. "In addition to possession of the cave, I'll probably get most of the animal skins, along with most of the gourds, clay bowls and the clam shells. Raa will probably have to continue to provide me with some fish and game to support me for at least six months or so until I can get back on my feet. I'll make sure to ask the Judge for everything, and would probably get more than just half. Why, I could even tell them that I thought that I was pregnant, just to get a little more sympathy." She added.

"I don't know if I could get the same out of Haro." Ooma said. "He would most likely just take off for tim-buck-too and no one, along with me would probably not ever hear from him again. I'm not sure that I want to go through all of the legal bull-shit just to get a few skins and some clay bowls, along with some hot rocks for the fire pit." She added.

"So, you are all the more unsure as to what you will do than I am." Woma said. "You really don't know what you are going to do either, do you? Now, both of our backs are to the wall." Woma also asked and said.

Ooma responded. "Well, I'm not as sure as to what I will do as you are, I mean, Haro has been, up to this time, a good mate, but I would not go so far as to call him husband material. He is always bringing in enough food for the two of us, but, then, on the other hand, I don't know how good of a father he would be. I have some mixed emotions as to just what I should and should not do right now. What if it all escalates to a knock down and drag out fight? We can't call the police to settle the matter because there are no police to call around here as we live too far out. You could yell as loud as you could and it would still not wake them from their naps or cause them to backoff their donut eating. You know, when we were young, when we were all still hanging out and living in the trees, we were really at that time, living below our means, but, when we bought the cave, we suddenly went to just barely living within our means, I mean, it has been just pay day to pay day, barely making ends meet for the last two years. I don't ever see us getting to the point of moving on up in society to ever live in a stick and mud hut with a moss thatched roof like what you talk about that you want." She said.

Then, the two continued to hike on south along the trail not speaking to one another about anything further.

Nearing Woma's cave, Ooma finally spoke up. "Woma, I have an idea. Why don't we just keep quiet about what it is that we found out today and what we know about Raa and Haro, and, each of us ask them what kind of day that they had, and then we will have something that we can compare notes about, so, why don't I come down in the morning, after the men leave for the day, have some tea, and we can talk about what they said and go from there, but, don't act like you even know what they were up to today, just talk and see what they have to say for themselves."

"OK." Woma said. "I'll see you in the morning."

"But." Ooma said. "Not to rain on your parade, or, to put a chink in your plans, I think that I finally figured out just who the fourth man was playing in Raa, Mik and Haro's game. It was none other than the Divorce Court Judge! I remember him from when Haro and I had our first major argument and I was going to file for a separation. I didn't meet him, but, I saw him at the Court House. So, you just might keep that under your bonnet and keep your mouth shut tonight until we can figure out what to do in the morning."

"Damn, Ooma, the marriage gods have turned against us in our time of need! We've done pissed them off royally! It's a man's world after all, isn't it? We don't have a chance in hell of making a comeback! We've had it!" Woma exclaimed.

"Well, after all of this, today, do you still want me to come over tomorrow morning for tea?" Ooma asked.

"You may as well, I'm sure we'll find something to talk about. Maybe we can go out and find some wild strawberries to reset out closer to the cave or try to catch some wild chickens." Woma said.

"So, see you in the morning." Ooma said.

"Yea, see you then, I have to get in and start a fire to cook supper, Raa will be headed home soon." Woma said.

"Yea, I've got the same duty, like they say, "A man's work is from sun to sun, but a woman's work is never done", or, is it?" Ooma said as she waved bye.

THE LAST LEPRECHAUN STANDING

Geneva, somewhat excitedly, met her husband Aaron, at the door, just as he came in from his work.

"Aaron, you are not going to believe who I met at the store today. Of all people, I met that cute couple who just recently moved into that little house down in Happy Hollow." Geneva said. "They are so tiny, or little, or, minute, but they are a glorious couple. They are the "Keel's". His name is Even, and, her name is Julia but she goes by her nickname "Jules". She told me, just listen to this, that, they are the last of the Leprechauns, the last of a dying breed, she said, but that they want to live out the remainder of their lives right here amongst us, in peace. The two of them are so cute, he is not even five feet tall, and she is about a half-a-head less. I met them at the General Store, they had come to town for supplies, and, had come to town in a small two wheeled cart pulled by a little pony which had two goats riding in the back end of it, of all things. She said, that they were just taking the goats out for a ride, just for the fun of it, she said. I thought that that was delightful. I invited her to the ladies garden club party next Wednesday, and, she said that she would be thrilled to attend. I volunteered you and told her, that you would be more than accommodating to go fishing with her husband Even while we went to the ladies garden party. Even, her husband, said to thank you a-forehand for the offer and that he would bring his own bait and his own fishing gear. So, what do you think of that?" Geneva said.

"Well, I guess that I've got part of my week planned out for me, for the most part, anyway." Aaron said.

The days went by and Wednesday came. It was the day for Aaron to go fishing with Even and Geneva to take Jules to the ladies garden club party. It was early in the morning, just after breakfast, when, a little earlier than what was expected, that the sweet little couple, known as Even and Jules Keel showed up at Aaron and Geneva's house. Aaron went out to meet them and invited them in for coffee and homemade donuts. After coffee, and a little chit-chat, Aaron and Even went out to get the fishing gear together and they headed out to a local fishing hole, while Jules and Geneva prepared some cookies for the ladies garden club meeting later on in the morning.

While walking down to the local fishing hole, Aaron noticed that Even was more than just somewhat of a small stature, to say the least. He asked Even straightforward. "Even, I've never had anything to do with Leprechauns, know very little about them, except for some legend kind of stories. Are all of your people as small as you?" He asked.

"Well." Even began. "There are not many in this day and time that I know of that still even exist. All that I ever met, or knew, or, even heard of, for that matter, were all small people. "Wee People", or, "Little People", they were always known as, as far as I ever heard. They were all hard workers, they were, from all that I have ever heard of any of them. Many were taken from Ireland to England and Wales, to work in the coal mines and the tin mines, and, they were suppressed. They were used in the "low coal" mines and the "low roof" tin mines where other miners would have to stoop over and hurt their backs in the process of just getting to the face where the work was. There, they were nicknamed "Tommy Knockers" by the other miners, mostly because they were not allowed to take breaks like the other miners did, and, their hammering and chipping could be heard by the other miners while the other miners were relaxing on their breaks. Other countries had different names for the "Little People". In the early Sandwich Islands, which is now called Hawaii; the "Little People" there are called the "Menehune". In America, the Shoshone Indians called them "the little people". Some countries have good names and some have bad names, depending upon, whether or not that they want to blame something on them at the time. Names like "Gremlins", "Elves", "Goblins", "Trolls", "Ogres", "Gnomes", or, whatever. Sometimes good, sometimes bad, depending upon the connotations, the circumstances or their reactions to them. However, all of the Leprechauns that I ever heard of are small compared to most of the other people around and about. However, calling them names like demons and devils are usually bad, while names like pixies and fairies are usually good, just to make some differences, but then, what is good for some folks, may be bad for others."

Aaron then asked. "Well, I've heard, either by the grape vine, or by stories passed down through the ages, that if you can catch a Leprechaun, you can make him show you or give you his gold. Is that just a story, or is there some truth to it?"

Even responded. "The truth of that matter is this. It is all legend. Nothing more. The "Little People" have no more wealth than anyone else on the face of this earth. The "wealth" that they have, is what they know, what they have learned, how to do things, how to make things, all of which can make for a better life for everyone. This is their "Pot of Gold" to offer the other people in the world. When asked, they freely give of what they know to help all of mankind and their own. So, in that light, or, in that respect, the legend holds and is furthered on even into the present generation." He said.

"What about the wearing of the green?" Aaron asked. "I thought that all of the Leprechauns all wore green, and, here you are dressed in brown. What's with that?" He further asked.

"More legend and stories." Even said. "In the Spring and Summer, generally, we do wear green, but, in the Fall we wear brown, and in the Winter, we wear gray and white combinations. Sometimes, like the festive times of the holidays, we may wear some red. Personally, I wear what I feel like, as long as it is clean at the time and Jules approves of it." He added.

As they arrived at the local fishing hole, Aaron had more questions that he thought about but decided to hold them in the back of his mind for some later time.

"So, what did you bring for bait?" Aaron asked.

Even opened a couple of clamshells, and showed Aaron the worms that were therein. "Worms." Even said. "Worms. Worms that you can slide on a fishing hook without hurting them because they have a hollow gut from one end to the other. Worms that will go so far as to give up their very life to help you catch a fish in order for you to sustain yourself. That is what they were born for, that is what they have lived for, awaiting the time of their ultimate sacrifice to further sustain the life of another living being. For, it is written, there is no greater sacrifice on the face of the earth, than the giving of one's life in order to save another." He added.

"That sounds pretty heavy for a fishing worm to say, if they could but say it." Aaron said.

"You know, Aaron, that, the only reason, that a fish will bite on a worm, is that they can't keep their mouths shut in the first place, and, too, they will always bite off more than they can chew in the second place." Even said.

Aaron responded with. "Even, that sounds like some good advice for most folks not to do."

"You know, Aaron, that if fish ever consulted a good attorney, that he would most likely tell them to always keep their mouths shut." Even said. "We should be so glad that they have never heeded such advice." He added. "You know, there is nothing, absolutely nothing, that you can say, that cannot be misinterpreted, misunderstood, or misconstrued, by someone or anyone else. That is why the authorities tell you, upon an arrest for some made up crime, that anything that you say may, can, or will be used against you. They just don't tell you that to console you. They tell you that because that is one of the cold hard facts of a life of crime, and, you will learn it one way or another, but, usually, in the end, a most difficult lesson to absorb in your mind." He added.

Aaron looked over at Even, then responded. "Been there and done that, and, I have been between a rock and a hard place on more than one occasion, I might add, but, sometimes, it can get real personal when it's at home and your mate is the one that puts you in your place."

Even took a net out of his fishing basket and put it down into the water to soak.

"What's with the net thing there Even?" He asked. I thought you were fishing with hook, line and sinker." He added.

"Well, the net is just in case that the fish aren't biting. Jules made me the net with the work of her own hands, and, the net works wonders when I get tired of not getting a bite with a fish hook. Besides, with a net, you can catch, pick out the ones you want, then, release the remainder. The net doesn't hurt the fish like a hook in the mouth does, and you get to keep only what you want. But, nets are better used from a boat, rather than from shore. When you use nets from the shore, you stir up the mud on the bottom and cloud up the water, then, you have to move on over to clear water. Eventually, you will run out of clear water as you work your way around the lake or the pond. Then, the fishing is all but over. "Even said.

"That makes sense to me." Aaron said.

"You know, Aaron, I really like Tilapia fish, but, they are algae eaters, and, they won't bite on a worm wiggling on a hook. The only way to catch them is with a net. That is why I brought the net. I have to soak it before I use it, because you can't cast out a dry net. It just don't work, as, a dry net will float on the surface of the water and scare away the fish under it. But, a wet net, can be cast, and, it will sink faster, and, the fish don't seem to mind. Too, that is the only foolproof way to catch the Tilapia." Even said.

I guess you gotta' do, what you gotta' do." Aaron added while throwing out another line.

Even baited his hook and passed the worm filled clamshell to Aaron. In no time, Even had a bite, and, had caught his first fish, before Aaron had even baited his hook. Then, by the time that Aaron had even put his line into the water, Even had caught his second fish and had put both of them on a stringer. Then, with Aaron looking on, Even caught his third fish, then he took one of the smaller fish off of the stringer and replaced it with the larger fish.

Aaron saw it and just had to say something. "You know, Even, that changing out a fish on your stringer like you just did, is illegal around here in these parts. I thought I just might mention that, just in case you were not fully aware of the fishing regulations."

Even responded. "Aaron, it is only illegal, when and if you get yourself caught by the Game Warden. It is no different than getting caught with more than your daily limit. Either case, if you do not get caught, then, you must not have done anything wrong in the eyes of the law, because they did not see it. It is in all, just how you look at things and whether or not that they saw it at the time. From the fishes point of view, one is relieved to continue to grow in size, since he was released from capture, while the other accepts his glorious position as becoming food for someone of a higher order, which is no different than the philosophy of the worm." He said.

Aaron was no little puzzled. They continued to fish, then just to make conversation, Aaron asked. "How old are you, now, Even?"

"Aaron, I am ashamed to have to answer that question. Not because it is embarrassing, which, it is, to some extent, but, most other people do not understand the life of the Leprechaun, what it entails, how it came about, what they do, why they do it, and all of that. But, to answer your question truthfully, straight forward, up front, without guile, I am now no less than nigh on close to almost three hundred and fifty years old, or so, give or take a few decades, and, my wife Jules is a just few decades younger, from what she tells me and anyone else that ever asks. She never really says how old she is, she just says that she is younger than me to anyone that asks." He said.

"Three hundred years or more old!" Exclaimed Aaron. "You do not look to be over forty or so! How do you all go about keeping yourself looking so young?" He asked.

"It is what it is. We eat well, exercise, take our vitamins and love life. You have to love life, when the time comes that you fall out of love for life, it is all but over." Even said. "So, how old are you?" He asked.

Aaron responded. "Well, I'm thirty-two, and, my wife Geneva is twenty-nine. But, for the life of me, I really can't believe that you and your wife are that old. I have never heard of anyone who ever lived to be over a hundred!"

"Well, let me try to explain." Even began. "One of the reasons that Leprechauns, or, the "little people" live so long, is for our primary assigned purpose is the monitoring of all of the other living things in this world. It is our glorious assignment, by the Grand Architect of the Universe, and, it is also our obligated job. However, today, in this day and time, it is harder for us to assimilate into the societies throughout the world. In the past, the Leprechauns hid out in the woods. Too, in days gone by, we would live out our life in one area, then, move to another area as a younger couple, never having to move except after a generation or so, and all the while, carrying out the obligations and our assignments. Today, however, with all of the identification requirements the methods that the States and Countries now use are no little problem for us. So, we either leave, totally, or, live out our life in a peaceful place until we finally die of a very, very, old age, hopefully quiet and mostly nondescript. And, without ever signing up for social security." He said.

"What do you mean, "leave, totally", as, opposed to living out your life, and, dying, like most people do?" Aaron asked.

Even responded. "Everyone, on the face of this good earth, has the option of either staying in one place or leaving for somewhere else. It is as simple as that. Some know it, some don't. If the time would come, when our job is done, and there is nothing else for us to do, we will just up and leave from where we are at and go someplace else. That is it. Period."

"I still do not understand what you are saying with respect to the either leaving or living out your life and the dying thing, I don't understand just how you can just up and leave and in doing so it allows you to continue to live on." Aaron said.

Between baiting his hook and putting another fish on his stringer, Even responded. "Did you not up and walk out of your house after coffee and donuts early this morning, did you not go to a shed by your house and get your fishing gear, and did you not walk down here to this fishing hole, and, did you not start fishing?" He asked.

"Sure." Aaron said. "But, what are you saying, that you just up and walk out of this life and to where, to what, to who, when, and how? That is too many questions to answer even in our life time."

"That's it!" Even said. "All you have to do is go out for a walk, and, never come back. Many have done it before, and, before long, most of their acquaintances have made up to that time are all but forgotten about when or why that you did it, except perhaps the fact that you never came back, mostly because those acquaintances were more concerned with their own lives than your life or the lives of others that did the same."

Aaron responded. "Well, obviously, you and your wife have never considered such a possibility since you have done took up residence down there in Happy Hollow."

"Oh, we have talked about it. We have discussed it. We have considered the best time to do such a thing. It is not like that it is a secret or anything between the two of us. Our families left explicit instructions in those matters." Even said.

"So, what's your plan, or, what's your instruction?" Aaron asked.

"Well, as it is appointed, and, we have decided accordingly, that, when we can no longer be of some help to our fellow man, or, when those around us refuse the help that we kindly offer, when other folks come to see us as being either ignorant or stupid, behind the times, or whatever, that we will then take that long and lonely walk. Until then, it is but a waiting game." Even said.

Aaron countered. "Even, you say, that you and your wife, are the last of the last, the end of the end and that you and her have probably seen more than ten generations come and go before me and Geneva were ever born. That would lead me to believe, that all of the others, the other Leprechauns, have already left, have already taken that walk, have given up on their fellow man, either because they would not listen, or, that they did not think that they needed any advice on how to live. Is that the case? Is that what has happened? Is that not your very future too? I mean, I can see it already at my young age, and, I have not collected the wisdom anywhere near your three hundred plus years of age."

Even responded. "In this day and time, most Leprechauns have either assimilated into the societies of the world, or, have went on and taken that great walk. But, it was not always the case. For instance, just to give you an example, the primary Leprechaun trade, early on, was, the lowly task to make shoes by hand, to design shoes, to repair and maintain shoes, for the very purpose of easing the pain of stone bruises on the tender feet of all mankind, with the ultimate goal to help and assist those along the way to greater success in their endeavors and to get where they needed to go on their journeys throughout life. Yet, today, our trade has fallen by the wayside, not needed, daily hand labor has been replaced by machinery, and, our overall benefit to all mankind has lost some of its kindness, it has lost some of its very purpose. Our lives have become no more on the face of this good earth than the worms on our hooks or the fish on our lines, who are now giving of themselves to further other orders of life itself. However, there is a down side, as, when the time comes, if people refuse to fish and hunt to feed themselves, and, want others to feed them instead, then the others will sooner or later become offended and will eventually turn and walk away insulted with disdain in their heart and eventually come to even hate the laziness of their fellow man instead of showing love for one another. Lesser notions, between nations, have actually caused the peoples of those nations to go to war with one another. You are right in your realization that that is where we are at this time, and, the time a-coming for me and Jules to walk away may be on the very morrow, if we but only but knew it." He said.

Aaron was puzzled. "OK, I understand the why, and the when, and maybe even the who, but, the what and where is a little fuzzy, and, I do not get the how settled in my mind, just yet. Could you politely explain to me as to the how of the matter?" He asked.

Even responded. "The how of it all is probably the simplest answer to your question. All you have to do, it to pack up what you need, but not necessarily what you want, which is your first decision, then, walk out of your old life and into your future life on your own hind legs along with those of whom you have come to love if you can convince them to do it with you. If you truly love life, you will have the courage to move on, and then, you will live on, if you do not have the love of life, you will not have the courage to move on, then you will eventually wither and die in the location that you so previously have chosen amongst those whom you have come to love. It is the moving on, the going on to a new life, which have kept the Leprechauns young, compared to their compatriots around and about or in any given country. Yes, you will lose all of your old friends and most of your family members, but, you will gain new friends in the process, and, you will continue to grow, and, the secret of it all is this, if you do it on a more regular basis, you will live longer, and in the end, when that time comes, you will have lived a much richer life overall, and, most likely, dependent upon your journey, may even come to be able to speak more than just one language." He said.

By now, they were both catching a fish and taking one off of their stringer to put a larger fish on, without even a cringe of guilt between either of the two of them.

"Now, Even, life itself, with all of its demands, takes its toll on everyone, and, once you get into your position as people have placed you, I have come to realize that you do not have the time anymore to enjoy the simple things of life. It is a puzzle. It is a conundrum. It is an enigma. But, we are set in our ways, and, cannot come to ever give it all up." Aaron said.

"But only if you chose it to be so." He said. "Accept it for what it is. Life is too short to drink bad wine. Life is too short to live someplace that you do not like. Life is too short to put up with sorry people. Life is too short to live with someone who does not love you. Life is too short not to try to make the best of it while you can and have the energy to do so. Life is too short not to try to do something different. Say it anyway you want, it is all the same, but it is a fact of life itself. On the one hand, you first have to love people, but then, on the other hand, it is meant for some people to be best loved when left alone or avoided, not of your choice, but of their choice." Even responded.

"That reasoning, could lead quite a number of couples to the divorce court." Aaron commented.

"Only, if it were inevitable in the first place, with one or the other, coming to losing their love for life." Even said. "It is all about love. You can take a lifetime just learning how to love. A lot of people can love some things but not all things. It took me years and years before I came to love mosquitos. Now, I see that they too have a purpose, as, they probably pollenate more plants than do the bees. I have learned, that you can put the flowers of Geraniums, Marigolds or Catnip, or, the leaves of Basil, Thyme, or Mint, a little bark of Cinnamon, or a few seeds of Cloves, rub any of them on or about your body and hair, or, put any or all of them in a bag and hang it around your neck like an asafoetida bag that you can also moisten and rub around on your body. Or, you can eat more garlic, but that can cut into your love life. By the same token, it took me a long time to ever come to love snakes, although, I am still a little leary of those crooked little buggars. I mean, they catch the mice and rats and they help to clean up bugs around the outside of the house. I love them even more for staying out of my house. It might also be a different kind of love with them as I love it when they are out of sight or not around and out of mind."

"Do you not love the mice and rats too?" Aaron asked.

"Absolutely, they live their lives out just for the glorious purpose of providing themselves as feed for the snakes and maybe a few cats that are not particularly particular." Even said.

"What about fleas and ticks?" Aaron asked.

"Absolutely, I love them as long as they leave me and my dogs alone, but, I draw a fine line when they come about and start hopping on me. I found that orange juice or lemon juice, or the juice from the skin of such, when rubbed on my dog around the neck back and tail, or, even the Geranium flower rubbed on my dog's hair, will keep both the fleas and ticks away. If you want to spend some money, you can buy Rose Geranium Oil, which will do the same thing. For an outright infestation, I usually take my dog for a swim, and, when all of the fleas get up on his head, I dunk his head under the water, and, viola, all the fleas are gone. The fleas have then met their glorious purpose of becoming food for the local fish. Like I said, some things are better loved when they are not around. Love is all about perspective, how you look at things, how you come to feel about things as you grow in your wisdom of the world." He said.

Aaron looked over at Even and said. "Even, I feel that you are even wiser than your many years. What would it take for you to impart some of the wisdom that you have learned over those years that I could benefit somehow? Huh? What about it? I have always wondered if there was some method of knowing when someone is lying to you. In all of your wisdom from all of your years, how do you ever tell, whether or not, that someone is lying to you, out rightly, even to your face? I mean, how could you ever tell, so that you would know it at the time that it was in progress?"

Even looked back at Aaron and said. "Well, Aaron, you have heard that fishermen, for the most part, tell decent lies, but, you should never bet, if given the chance, that they would not tell an indecent one. I mean, most people have a problem of telling the difference between good fishermen who are bad liars as opposed to bad fishermen who are good liars, and, the bad fishermen who are also bad liars never even come into competition with the other two. Now, when it comes right down to where the rubber meets the road, hunters are always running behind and usually in second place to any of the fishermen. But, people should never expect them to ever quit trying to catch up in the long run. Fishermen are most likely the most professional, the most experienced and the most seasoned of all liars. And, sooner or later, they can be expected to give up fishing go into politics, and start playing golf. Now, here, if you ever read a resume, where someone puts down on paper, that they are an avid fisherman, an avid hunter, and, an avid golfer, you can bet your bottom dollar that they are lying through their teeth."

Aaron then asked. "But what of lies themselves, some of which appear to have a life of their own?"

Even responded. "Lies, like many other living things, have to be fed, watered and tended, on a regular basis if people ever expect them to gain any respect or notoriety whatsoever. Once people learn how to lie, and get the hang of it, most of them can't wait to try it out for real just to see how well it works. If they ever attempt to gain any proficiency whatsoever, to ever attain habitual liar status, they had better have a good memory, coupled up with lots of daily practice for an ever changing audience. The crux of the matter is, for the most part, people do not pay all that much attention to the truth, while, a few lies, passed with a whisper over pursed lips, can gain their close focused attention to no end. The people who learn to phrase their lies as questions are the worst of the worst. As, they hesitate to lie outright, and, their spurious questions, spiced with a little rumor and innuendo, and, in doing so, they are not put down or accused of lying outright, as much that is as they were before. Their biggest problem when caught in a lie, is trying to figure out how to get some of the real truth out without lying too much at all about it. Remember this, a bleached out or faded out black lie, is almost as good as a dyed up white lie. So, trying to hold someone to the truth is almost as hard as holding someone back from a lie."

Aaron then asked. "Just how do you, outrightly, ever come to learn how to tell if someone is blatantly lying to your face?"

Even continued fishing and also continued his spiel. "Anyone can tell a lie, but, everyone needs to realize that it is an art to tell such a lie that is good enough to be completely believed that will even be sworn to by a third party. Generally, the majority of the best lies, come to an abrupt and complete halt, just an inch or two short of the truth, so, for lies to be furthered, to become legend, they need be adjusted, balanced, and mixed in with a few half-truths thrown in for good measure. These types of lies will even cover up a badly told lie. The main difference, between the most common run of the mill type of liar and someone that you could call a professional, is, that the former are usually bad liars because they never mix in much of the real truth into their lies. People that really work at it, and take the time, to learn how to lie, most of them add in a little spice and flavor to their lies, and, either become famous for it for a short time, or, notorious for their remaining lifetime. The better liars, normally contain themselves and hold back until such time that they are reasonably sure as to what the real truth is, and then they adjust up their lies accordingly. I have met some liars, that have gotten to the point of being proud and even bragged about the fact that some of their lies were actually believed and passed on by others."

Aaron then asked. "What about those people who can't ever tell the truth and just tell one lie after the other for no particular reason known to man?"

"Well." Even started. "After those people tell their first lie, their second one will come out of their mouth as if sliding on the grease of the first, and, the third lie, will fly through their teeth and out of their mouth like spit. In these people's mind, one lie, will lead to another, until such time, that they are so numerous, that their early lies will start killing off their later ones, while the remainder will be left to wilt and die of starvation. Now, some liars have lied so much, that they are to the point of you even being able to smell most of them on their breath and you may even see the flicker of the lies in their eyes. The problem of them telling more than one lie is, it is like having more than one clock to tell the time by, and, most people, sooner or later, will begin to doubt one or the other, and, then, finally doubt them both as being in error."

"But, how do you tell if they are really lying as opposed to just stretching the truth?" Aaron asked.

Even went on. "You can tell, sometimes, when some people are lying, when their mouth flops open. But, you should be able to recognize the different types and levels of liars, as, there are the good liars, bad liars, bald faced liars, not to forget to mention those damned liars, as the latter group are forever applying for an upgrade. However, there is little difference between the natural born liars and those who claim to be self-made. You probably have heard that saying that the second liar never has a chance, which, most likely, is why there are so many people out there in the scramble vying up for first place. There are some, who cannot think up their own lies, but, will beg, borrow or steal one from whomever, just to get themselves some relief. Now those called honest liars, are generally more acceptable and palatable than are the dishonest liars, but then, when all is said and done, they both have many of the same things in common that it becomes difficult for the rest of us to tell which one is which. Anyway, you should never ask a known liar for advice, when an unknown one will serve the same purpose. Then, there are those liars which have the knack of embellishing other people's stories, by emplacing themselves into them, then, on the retell, making them somewhat more interesting for the rest of us to enjoy and to pass on to some other unsuspecting party. A particular group of liars, those who are disagreeable, are amongst the worse to encounter the world over. Mostly, because, one liar, telling another liar a lie, considers it no great sin of trespass, because, the second liar never believes the first one, in the first place. I mean, I have even met those who only pretended to be a liar, and, pretended only to lie to other liars, but, when caught at it called the other a hypocrite. Just like the old saying that there is no honor amongst thieves, liars have no shame, but, they can pretend to have it, if need be, and, if they are absolutely required to do so at the time. If you look closely, and listen, sometimes, you can see and hear lies swarming around liars like flies around the stink on a manure pile."

Aaron then said. "What really gets me, is the deceit that liars portray. How do you recognize that?" He also asked.

Even went on, still. "Remember this, and, write it down. If someone will lie to you, they will also steal from you, and, have the gall to then turn around and lie about it, even when they are caught in the process. Deception, is nothing more, than a lie being acted out and covered up by professionals looking to make some money off of it. But then, you should remember too, figures can lie, and, liars can figure, so, go figure. Of all the lies, there is no such thing as an old friendly lie, as, most lies are short lived, except those that some people try to live out their entire life on. It is the trickery and deceit, which work together, to defraud others, in almost everything that is done, which takes much of the fun out of it for the rest of us. By the same token, there is little difference between a liar saying that they are going to do something and then not doing it, or, a liar doing something and then saying that they didn't do it. Either way, they are going to have to lie about it sooner or later. If they knew the truth of the matter, they would understand, that bragging, stretching the truth and exaggerating to extreme, even with their deceit thrown in on the side, is never as believable, as on good solid sounding and forthright bald faced lie."

"Has this not been the way it has been since time began with most people?" Aaron asked.

Even responded. "Well, it was a lie, out rightly, when people were told that the earth was flat, and, it was a lie, when they were told that the sun revolved around the earth, as, those were a couple of rather significant great lies of yesteryear, which was purposely perpetrated upon all of mankind by their leaders, who knew better, but allowed them to be fully believed by most of the populace. So, if history repeats itself, if that is really true, what would you suppose are the great lies of today that are being perpetrated upon mankind? Think about it, when a lie is put into writing, published and provided public appeal, it will become more interesting and more believable by the public when repeated daily on the evening news, and, even to other liars and their peers. After all is said and done. Even when people, or, our leaders, are proven up in public to be liars, the people will still listen to what they have to say, even if they don't believe it."

Aaron continued fishing, but had his mind somewhat shifted now onto many other things.

Even then asked. "Aaron, do you, or, have you, ever played golf?

"Yea, I tried it a couple of times, but couldn't break a hundred. So, I thought that I could never get good at it without an awful lot of practice, which, required time that I didn't have because of my work." Aaron said.

"Did you know, that when Old Tom, along with his golfing buddy Mose, first invented the game as we know it today, some few hundred years ago, around the year 1400, over in Scotland, did you know, that both of them were natural born Leprechauns?" Even asked.

"I had no idea!" Aaron exclaimed.

"Do you know why they invented the game?" Even asked.

"Ok, lay it on me, I'm sure that there was some odd reason to come up with such a game." Aaron said.

Even responded. "Yes, they invented the game of golf, so as to provide the players with a sense of frustration and aggravation that makes the players forget about all of their other frustrations and aggravations, albeit, for a short period of time. Too, they first called it Gawf or Gauf, which was taken from the Dutch game Kolf where they stole the method of the game and took it back to Scotland."

"Yea, I can remember some of that aggravation but I didn't ever hear where the game ever originated from." Aaron said.

Even went on. "Did you also know, that for the most part, that golfers tell little white lies about their game, not only to their wives, and their golfing partners, but also to themselves? And, do you know why?"

"No, I never really thought about it much before. So, why is it?" Aaron asked.

Even responded. "Well, Aaron, it is like this, golf is a game, between the golfer and the course, although some make it to be between the group of golfers themselves, which, is not what the game intended. So, if the game is between the golfer and the course, then, a little lie to two, here or there would not make so much of a difference, as, no one would be hurt by it. And, the course cannot speak to defend itself."

Aaron then asked. "Well, would it not be like you said before, about the fish change out on your stringer, where if no one sees you do it, especially the game warden, then, it is not illegal. Would that not be the same thought pattern?"

"What I am saying is, that there are lies that are so different, that honest people come to feel that it is OK to tell. Not just us fishermen. What it amounts to is, that most people want other people to think more highly of them than what they think of themselves." Even said.

Aaron responded. "Well, damn, I've been there and done that too, but, now that you have explained it all to me, I actually feel better about it all, and, some of my guilt that I have carried along over the years, has been lifted off of my shoulders just a little. It is better than having to go to confession even when you don't have anything to confess. And, you don't feel any guiltier about something that you haven't done yet than anyone else."

"Aaron, I think you finally got it." Even said.

Meanwhile, back at the house, Geneva was serving cookies to the ladies garden club and introducing Julia to the group.

Julia, began, after her introduction, to show the ladies, how to make a net trellis for climbing green beans, pickles, tomatoes, vining clematis or for morning glories. She laid out one string, then, tied knots in the long strings every inch or two, using a small bottle for sizing of the squares in the net, and advised on bottle or can size depending on what the net was to be used for, and, added, that smaller squares would be needed for something like a fishing net, or, a net basket for collecting eggs, or garden produce like tomatoes or peppers. The ladies each laid out their strings, and followed along with Jules in the making of a net trellis, then, a net basket for home use, and a finally, a fishing net for their husbands use. Julia used fossil crinoid stems which had holes in them for weights for her fishing net display and also used them to make a necklace, which the ladies really liked. A couple of ladies decided to just use rocks for weight and had to get Julia to show them where and how to tie in the rocks. Off and on, the ladies group broke up for coffee, tea, and cookies, with Julia at the center of attention in all discussions with most of them admitting that they had never had the occasion during their lifetime to ever even meet a real live honest to goodness Leprechaun or to even know one by name for that matter. Then, the fun began. Julia, showed the ladies how to make themselves netted stockings and a netted bra. "It can put spice and excitement into your marriage." She said. And, with the following intense interest of all of the ladies, she began to show them all how to go about it and they all hung onto every word that she said from that point on.

THOMAS'S AND ELIAS'S TALL TALE (but no offense meant by that)

"May the meeting in this meeting place, handily meeting at this time, with this handy hardy congregation hard at hand, please border some on coming to some order." Boomed out the blabber mouthed big bellied balding Bailiff, but, no offense intended or meant by any of that, whichever.
And, with that, the Pilgrim Headmaster walked up or stepped up, whichever, to the pulpit, or podium, whichever, took a swig of something that looked like water, and began his spiel. "Let us pray." He began. And, with no more than that, without hearing any or no other objection whatsoever, whichever, he then began his prayer before the group up as follows.
"We have all gathered here together, in this humble house, a log cabin if you will, built in the late fall and early winter, whichever, of the year of our Lord, 1620 or 1621, whichever, to give our thanks to that Grand Architect of the Universe, to that one and only Almighty himself, directly, for allowing us this great privilege of a most successful journey across that great salty shifting and wavering pond known as the Western Sea, although it all got started too late in the summer and turned out to be at the wrong time of the year, as, we had a long way to go with a very short time to get there or here, whichever, with the crossing that great water whose great waves made the better part of us all sick to our stomach along the way at one time or another or sometimes at the same time, whichever, especially after the dry soda cracker barrels went dry, to now have some new semblance now of a new start for a new life now in this new world, assigned as we are, or were, whichever, to be at the get go and in on the ground floor for the establishment of a colony or to start a new thriving plantation of sorts, whichever, for those kind folks that hired us on, and have come to some agreement on a new and adjusted up Compact, although we are starting someplace other than we were first assigned, although, considering, that we should have been gone well further south like a wild goose in winter, but took the "any port in a

storm" a little too serious at one particular moment in time." Then, the Headmaster hesitated and cleared his throat and took a drink of something that looked like water, but very well could have been something else, before continuing.

"Also, and although, we had to spend the better part of this most unseasonable winter aboard the very ship which brang, brung or brought us, whichever, in those very cramped quarters within those OSHA unpermitted confined spaces, in order to gain some semblance of safety for twice as many as should have been there, but please disregard the OSHA thing, as I do not think it has yet been established in the New World yet that anyone has heard of so we do not want to make any official or unofficial report, whichever, to any of them on or off the record, just in case they do, but, to remind you, that we all stayed aboard or on board, mostly because of the needed safety from the openly hostile activity of those old Native Americans, which activity seems to match the culture of their nature, or, the nature of their culture, whichever, but no offense meant or intended by any of that, so, whichever to all or any, as, we yet are still learning about their ways of life, culture of their customs, or their customs of their culture, whichever, purposely and so as, to be more than politically correct for any future generations who know that any of us had any part in their naming, as, I am sure that you are certainly aware, that they were previously named Indians because Columbus thought that he had landed in India, if you remember or recall, whichever, and, not unlike our present Captain Chris who we suspected of not knowing exactly where he was at the time either, but with ole Lum naming all the Indians in general, but in us, here and now, trying to deal with the remainder of some of the wilder ones, again, no offense meant by that either, now or on into the future, whichever, who appear to be operating out on the fringes of their society, each and every one with numerous or various intentions, whichever, most with multiple unpronounceable names, or that part of those who are more specifically continuing to cause our settlement no little trouble, especially those who are now being called the narrow minded nasty naughty Naussets, by name, but again, no offense intended or meant by or taken by that either, whichever, but whose constant nightly drumming have kept many of us awake night after night, which led many of us to delve into other of their unmentionable nightly activities, as, we have heard from more than one about their raceways, and their gambling or gaming casinos, whichever, set up for the primary purpose just to get a few more of our beads, with some, if not all of our men at one time or another, sneaking out and about to partake of their chances." The Headmaster, then hesitated, and, took another swig, which was now becoming definitely suspect as being something other than water.

He then went on. "But, to change the subject around a little, for both our benefits, although the fishing and hunting were good early on with but few interferences by those aforementioned, the ongoing risk of being shot at on a daily basis, and some of us being unduly penetrated bodily by the sharp shafts of their arrows, which, at the time, we offered up the excuse that we had no other recourse except to shoot back at them without even offering to yell "Fore", and to thereby, exchange pain for pain or hurt for hurt, whichever, it being an eye for an eye or a tooth for a tooth kind of thing, whichever, but, so as it will be known for future generations to come, that that, in itself, was not set out early on to be our first intent or our last purpose, whichever, at the outset, even though a couple, or a few, whichever, of us all, or a few of all of us, whichever, those some, few and or a couple, whichever, have already or already but, given up the ghost, died or passed on, or, are in the immediate process, or have all but come very damn close to that gate which swings only one way and which is guarded by none other than old Saint Peter himself, whichever to any or all, concerning those gone on previous, which we have not been successful at hiding, or, even a couple of those who happened to fall overboard unintentionally, with all being recovered except the one of which I am sure you are fully aware, who fainted while too close to the rail, a tragedy to end all tragedies, and to, being it that I myself of late have not been feeling all that well for that matter either, and for that, and, for this, or, for the other, whichever, we now give our most personal gracious or humble thanks, whichever, for and on our behalf for the immediate future to come." The Headmaster again cleared his throat took another drink of what looked like water, but now even more suspected as very well may not have been, as, it having been previously mentioned that it was previously suspected to have been something else altogether, and yet even now being in greater suspect by more than a few of the group. With that, he continued on.

"But, and lest, before I forget, one other very small matter, we ask, that you please provide some insight, ideas, or some complete laid out orthodox plan, whichever, for our engineers and at least to one of the ships quartermasters or at least to a few or a couple of his assistants, whichever, on just how to go about getting those milk cows off of that danged boat and onto earthy shore, of which, I might mention, that we were not supposed to have any of those stinky animals on board in the first place, and Captain Chris is no little pushed out of shape because of the continuing mess that they are making as it is difficult to keep the poop cleaned up off of the poop deck, with the smell creeping into his sleeping quarters or his office space, whichever, but we do need them sorely, as, we do not want to become known as a people who are all hat and no cattle, in this New World, but additional thanks is given for the survival of what is left of the live animals that we did not consume on the way over, such as the stinking pigs, the stinking goats, the stinking sheep, the stinking poultry, the stinking dogs and stinking cats with their stinking litters notwithstanding, and one young lady's non-stinking pet bird that just happened to have got loose, flew the coop, so to speak, got away, or was turned loose inadvertently or on purpose, whichever to any or all, so as to be as free as any other bird, too, please help us not to get in any trouble with any of those local animal rights folks, and with that or with all of the other, whichever, as, You know, down deep in our hearts, that we are just a bunch of good old boys, makin' our way, the best way that we can, or, know how, whichever, and with that and with all of the other aforementioned items, we most humbly say Amen." With that, he closed his mouth and took another swig of what still looked like water, but, was coming to be more and more recognized by more and more of those attending, as a big slug of some of the best clear un-cut rum yet to be found anywhere in the colony to date.

Then, an "Amen" was heard somewhat in unison or here and there, whichever, from all of those in attendance within the confines of the meeting place, except for smick-smack sounds of a couple or a few, whichever, of otherwise tight lipped tongue biting harbinging women near the back of the cabin and some of those who were mostly painted up trying to look like women, or, not to leave those other ones out but to even include the ones who said that they were just dressed up like women just trying to keep warm but not to get out of any work, whichever, but, again, no offense meant or to be taken by that, as nothing sexist was intently intended, directly.   Then, almost in unison, a second set of cold "Amens" were heard from the standing guards standing guard at the outside gates, who could hear, but were not here, but were just on the outside looking on or looking in, whichever, so to speak, who were faithfully or religiously, whichever, holding their fully loaded cold guns in their fully loaded cold hands, coming from both the East and West doors or entry gates, whichever, of the meeting place cabin, hut or house, whichever to any or all of your choice, whereas, it being their assigned noble purpose so as to defend to their very death, the new locals from the previous old locals harboring their habitual habitation habits in and around or about the harbor area, whichever.

In one of the hunched up bunches or groups, whichever, in the back of the room, someone said off handedly, although it was reported to have sounded more like a woman's voice or whisper, whichever, raising the question and asking someone else standing close in or close by, whichever, who also remains totally unidentified even to this date and time, but sounded like another or some other woman, whichever, questioning, whether or not, that the Headmaster was allowed to have said the prayer, that he said in the first place, as, and because, they insisted, more vociferously, that no one to date had any direct evidence that any form of freedom of religion was in vogue, or in existence anywhere on the face of the earth for that matter, whichever, as, as far as anyone knew at the time, as, it had certainly not yet been even fully established anywhere in the New World by record, as to their present day knowledge to date and at the time, and that in turn, was followed up with another question raised up by someone else who was also unidentified, but looked like another one of the women in the back, whether or not, that it was becoming more and more apparent, that women were really the ones in total control, and, had it tooth and nail, all over the men, when it comes to the mark of being unidentified, at any selected given moment in time, or, when they so choose, whichever.

Also yet unidentified, but sounding just like or somewhat similar, whichever, to the first woman previously mentioned, on whether or not that the guards stationed just outside, had the authority or legal right to bear arms, or, any further personal concealed carry of their arms in public for that matter, whichever, under the ruse of just trying to keep them dry, because, in both cases or either, whichever, they reasoned, that neither freedom would most likely not occur for on to sometime well on into the future, and was not even mentioned in the charter or included in the new compact, whichever, because, some woman in particular, but not fully identified, admitted freely that she done sneaked a peek, and that it would not be, for more than a hundred years or more or hence, or on into the far future, and most likely, certainly not during any of their lifetimes, whichever, with some added on mumbled response which sounded like the second woman previously mentioned a-forehand or mentioned immediately previous, whichever.

Then, one of the men, fed up to the gills with the girl's chatter, mutterings, murmurings, and some flat out bellyaching and bitching purposely thrown into the mix, just to mix it all up a little, whichever to any or all, your choice, whispered aloud in a very loud whisper which could have been heard by many more than were first interested in the first place, or those who had even lent an itching ear up to that time, whichever, had they but been keeping their mouths shut and their ears open, but just a little under their breath, mentioning, that they should all be reminded also, that even the freedom of speech had neither yet been voted on or approved of, or considered, whichever, in any constitutional manner or otherwise, and neither were mentioned in the compact or the original charter, whichever, because some of the other women reported that one of their band, had freely admitted to also sneaking a peek, either that, or she was out rightly lying about it just to get some wanted or needed attention, whichever, or, continuing, even by England's King James the First, God forbid that he would ever hear of such insolence amongst our group. After those comments, the chattering women finally shut their mouths for a little while and went back to biting their tongues and chewing on their lips, and clenching and gritting their teeth, whichever, not to mention the glaring and/or darting of their eyes, whichever, especially aimed at or toward, whichever, the men or others suspected to be unrelated in their immediate area, whichever, in unison with the murmuring or muttering of the other groups, whichever, and, with both at the same time throwing their arms up in the air and rolling their eyes back into their heads as if they were dead or in process of dying, or giving up the ghost, whichever, or rolling their fingers in their hair or poking their fingers down their throats or up their nose, whichever, in order to gain some attention or just to show off some show of emphasis to or in or at, whichever, the ongoing meeting at hand, of a few, some, or most of the matters at hand under discussion, whichever to any or all.

The Headmaster again took the podium. "Now, just to kick start this thing and do what it is we have to do. So, let us talk about first things first, of the first order, firstly and or primarily in the first place, whichever." The Headmaster went on, ignoring the chitter-chatter about the Charter, or the johnnie come lately catty comments about the Compact, whichever, mostly of which he realized was coming from the very selfsame women in back of the room he knew to not count much in the first place, or anyway, whichever, for that matter, but no offense meant or to be taken by that either as he recognized that it could be seen on into the future as somewhat sexist, so he felt more than obligated just to totally ignore them all, which was, for the time, more than justifiable in his own mind and most of the other men at that particular moment in time too, so he proceeded on further and announced his pronouncements or bounced some of them off of the wall or pounced upon some of them, mentally, not physically, just so to speak or in such a manner of speech, whichever. And, he again cleared his throat, and took another big swig from what was now beginning to look more and more by more and more by more of those attending to look just like a glass or a clear cup of the finest clear uncut rum, whichever, and then, he continued on.

"It is the beginning, here and now, with the end of winter near on, in this new year of 1621, already well upon us, with all of us already knee deep in it, with a new decade having begun within just the last few weeks, more or less, whichever. We have all but just arrived, here in Plimouth, or Plymouth, whichever, as we have called it, or named it, whichever, and, thanks be to that sturdy seaworthy ship the Mayflower, with all of its creaks and it's weathered pinning's, and the good Captain Chris Jones, who is not just one of the Jones boys, I might mention, but who does show that he does have a slight minor problem of not knowing exactly where he is at, at any given moment in time while maneuvering his ship, who also sometimes thinks he is Christopher Columbus himself re-incarnated, but no offense intended or meant by that, whichever, but please disregard that, as I do not think that that belief is part of our religion at this time, although there is some who delve into such incantation, but again, no offense or insult meant by any of that, but, to change the subject around a little more, no thanks to that good for nothing leaky ship the Speedwell and their lazy no good for nothing worthless crew, and their more than worthless Captain, Captain Scared as he was known as, but no offense meant by that either, as any good Captain under the same identical or given circumstances would probably have made the same decision that he made and may have did or may have done at the time, or, the same thing that he directly did do at the time, whichever, although it was both the did do and did not do parts that roily riled us up to the point where we railed against his deliberate decisions, wherein we lost half the sailing talent, half the sailing personnel, half the supplies, half of what we set out with in the first place, with no knowledge as to which half was the best half, and a doubled up growp twice the size that it should have been on board." He then took another swig of what now had all the appearances of what was left of a half of a glass of the finest straight un-cut rum brought into the New World to date, with no embarrassment whatsoever, and most of the men in the group licking their chops for a couple drops.

He continued on. "Even with all known and unknown deflugalties, which is said to be a Black Dutch phrase for "it most likely will never fly", we have now no more than just arrived in fact, but yet, we have more than established our presence in this new world, and have set our foot or set our feet down, whichever, and have gotten a foot in the door, so to speak, and, have taken control of a goodly section of good land, and took honest ownership of such, after a few slip orf sleight of the hand handy dandy bead trading's, and seized it all after the final transfer when the beads finally changed hands, if you will, whichever, from those Native Americans and their brothers, those wild and savage Indians, because we do not yet know all of their ways and means, especially those who are called the old locals, and, especially from those nervous-norvous nocuous nasty Nausets, but again, no offense to be taken of that mention, if you will, and now, if you will again, we have yet already accomplished the construction of our log cabins and a few huts, to finish the winter in, and, we have dug them in and piled the dirt up against their ramparts for insulation from the cruel winter winds." Here, the Headmaster once again cleared his throat took a drink of what some now openly mentioned that they thought that looked like cider, all but trying to give the speaker some little benefit of the doubt, but actually looked exactly like and may very well have been a little more than just another big slug of the finest un-cut rum or perhaps clear cognac that anyone had knowledge of but determined to keep a more watchful eye on his glass, and then he continued on.

"Not to mention that we have also constructed some of the most fancy toilets, latrines or out houses, whichever, and provided them with a goodly supply of handy dandy corncob wipers, for the men's use primarily, although the better part of the men have been more in the bad habit of relieving themselves in the open or outside, or like the bears in the woods, whichever, which we now prohibit I might add, not the bears, the men, I mean, and I might add, also, some of the better toilets constructed primarily and especially for the women, are amply provided with goodly piles of corn shucks, so as not to appear to be prejudiced or accused of being sexist, or, politically incorrect in any manner, shape, form or fashion, whichever, and, considering equality purposes, which will certainly become an issue of which I am sure on into the near future, although I hope it holds off, and doesn't come about until after I am at least dead and gone, I also feel somewhat certain, we will be able to finish the winter in some small comfort, as, we have built the fire places, put them into place and tested them out, and they are burning now with the gotten in dry fire wood stacked and drying under the beds, as a hold off or hold out, whichever, for such a freezing winters end and on into the cold Spring duration, whichever, and, for additional comfort, we have brought ashore the beer, wine and rum, especially the rum, to be provided daily by issue to prevent further sickness amongst us all, and, we have recovered the odd New World grain called "corn", and the nuts, the edible kind, not the hind legged walkin' kind, that were buried in the Native American or Indian's mounds, whichever, that we done dug up, plundered or grabbed and taken out rightly for our sustenance and benefit, whichever, primarily, I might add, just for the record, because the Native Americans, or Indians, again whichever, just to be more politically correct, and again not to offend anyone or to prejudice our case, because, those who buried it in the first place, apparently just up and walked off and headed south for the winter, without leaving record one, and, as far as we know anything about, with no signs posted as to ownership, and, who apparently done left the territory and abandoned it all, for Lord only knows for what purpose, we took that which was needed for our very survival at the time, and then, we went out into the woods about and found even more, unbelievably or notwithstanding, whichever, and too, we have purposely extended ourselves and made friends with a few of the lesser so called peaceful Native American brothers but not some of their cohorts who are known out rightly as wild and savage Indians even amongst their own brethren, which now have been named, and are now generally referred to or called, whichever, as the old locals, as was previously mentioned, but yet mentioned again for some emphasis and content, and some, that have went against their grain of their peers, so to speak, and have so befriended us just as we have befriended them, however, and unfortunately, we have had to kill off a few of the wilder more savage ones that have out rightly tried to kill some of us in the first place, which, I might add, was for absolutely no reasonable reason or presently known purpose, whichever, I also might add, but again, no offense meant or intended by that, whichever, so as to form up some defense if ever needed on our part on into the future, or on further down the road, whichever." The Headmaster, again swigged some of the aforementioned unidentified drink, whatever it was or could have been, but by now more and more of the group all but confirmed it to be a little more golden in color with a most inviting taste and smell as reported by those in the front row, and, he then continued.

"And, we have gathered and dried the edible fruits and vegetables of this new world of which we could find readily without too much trouble or work, or, not being put out too much, whichever, it being late winter and all, and now, almost dreading but going on into a cold and damp, dank and dreary, drizzly Spring, and all anyway, we have also dried a goodly bounty of Cod fish that we have caught off of the boat with our lines and nets just along the inside of the cape, and we have hunted and taken a goodly bounty of game and fowl, which has been both dried and cured, too, we have captured the available small game, have penned them up to provide for fresh meat on into the future, too, we have caught the birds, ducks and geese, have clipped their wings and hutched them up to hold them hostage along with our own poultry which we did not eat or completely devour on the way over, whichever, and, have constructed a hen house and have made them nests for the benefit of their future eggs, and, now, as long as we can dodge or avoid, whichever, the aforementioned animal rights groups, who may be unduly concerned with them all being penned up or tied up to control their wandering nature, that is if they do not make too much noise during the interim."

He continued, but without a swig this time, as, he duly noted several in the group taking more of an interest in his drink than he wanted to see. "We see that we are somewhat secure for the immediate, forgoing or ongoing future that is, whichever, with the exception, I might mention, of the scourge of sickness within our small group, other than, the minor problem of not being able to get the milk cows off of the boat, so, now, it has come the time to make our mark on and into this new world, so as to allow future generations, to know of our troubled journey and our momentous efforts, whichever or both, in order that these things and those doing them, may never go unnoticed on into the future or the years to come, whichever, may God forbid even the very thought of such by those who come a-journeyin' out of our hereafter and into their hereafter, before, hence or after, whichever."

By now, the Headmaster was reelin' with feelin', but still wheelin' and dealin', while sipping the sauce, hittin' the hooch, wavin' the ole bottle, or drainin' the old barrel, whichever, to any or all.

Again, and or for the second time in a row, whichever, someone else in the center of a bunch, but a little more toward the back of the room, who sounded much like the first woman again previously mentioned, again mentioned loud enough to be heard by some of the other women in the rear of the room, that they did not think that the Headmaster had the right, or, should have mentioned God, with the specific capital letter G, that is, in his speech, again, because of the point being made at the time, was, that the freedom of religion had not yet been fully established, or, even mentioned of for that matter, certainly not in the original Charter, nor, in the new Compact, and, would not be so documented or recorded for several hundred years hence, most likely, if the truth were to be ever known, by some entity long after King James himself, but the prime comment, was primarily from some of the most meddlesome bunch of women secondarily overheard earlier from the back of the meeting place cabin, previously mentioned, who now could be identified a little more readily as they were the very ones who were pursing their lips and rubbing their bitten sore tongues on the roof of their mouths as a result of them trying to keep their mouths shut or not saying anything further, whichever, but were with, or, were hanging out with a few more of the more unidentified vociferous ones. The whole bunch, or at least five or six of them, with their stomping feet, folded arms, frowns and eye a-rolling back in their heads, could have written up a treatise on how to apply and read body language and could have passed the requirements for their MBA, and, any one of them could have laid out a lesson plan and taught such a class to some graduate students at Harvard or Yale, but disregard the aforementioned, as I am reminded that they are not yet in solid existence yet as fully regionally accredited institutions and may not ever be accredited as such far on into the future, and, may wind up eventually only giving a pass or fail grade for any of their subjects.

The Headmaster, went on, again ignoring the ongoing less than cheerful chatter or salacious small talk in the back, whichever. "Therefore, I now make the loco-mated motion without any conceived considered commotion, that we now, open with an open rendering of discussions with remarks on just how to go about the making of some such a mark, such, that would, could, or should, whichever, withstand the ages, including the wind, rain, snow, freeze or frost, whichever, and, a mark made so secure, that it cannot be destroyed, by any person who would have such ideas to cross their fevered crossed brains, for whatever reason some time on into the future, but not to intentionally mention those crazy wild assed Indians that we have to deal with on a daily basis in the here and now, but disregard the crazy wild assed part, as, we realize that they are all Native Americans, again to be more politically correct and so as not to unduly accuse the wrong ones wrongly or short the right ones rightly. So, what say you? " With that, the Headmaster took one last big swig, gulped down or guzzled up, whichever, the remainder or what was left of his drink that he had perhaps previously provided himself prior to his prudent man presentation before anyone could say dag-nabit which is reportedly Whacka-Macka-Noag Indian talk for dog-gonit.

The group mostly murmured back and forth, with a few murmuring and chitter-chattering here and there, and in and out, off and on, here and there, whichever, and, with some small talk of a filibuster heard here and there amongst themselves, others with one another, some even requesting a hedge for an up or down vote, calling for some order according to the book on Robert's Rules of Order, then, upon further recommendation of the Headmaster, they split up into smaller groups, primarily of relatives and families with some distant cousins and old acquaintances' thrown in with a cohort here and there, with a few pushing themselves in just to justify the mix, then, the women were kind of separated out from amongst the men, mostly by the very men themselves having bigger elbows, after one of the groups kind of decided to do it on their own, and them thinking it ought to be a good idea whether it was or not, then, the other groups followed suit, first just to be a copy-cat, but then, purposely and with purpose, as they saw how it all worked out and, so as, that the men were directly cut in and the women were directly cut out, if you will, with the women evidently or apparently, whichever, not to be included further in any of the final discussions out rightly or directly, whichever, with the men, or, of the decision making process overall of the group, if, there were any to be made at the time, and, little by little, spokesmen from or of each groups of men, whichever, were selected, pushed up, voted up or chosen to speak, whichever, by other spokesmen from the other groups trying to pass some or a little bit of the blame, whichever, with a couple of them shoved, bulldozed or pushed out rightly, whichever, toward the front and up against their will, and, immediately afterwards, they were more further shuttled up front by some of the selected others, and then, the subgroups melted or dissolved, whichever, and liquidated, dissipated or shrank, back into one group or mass, whichever, still and yet, minus the women of course who were cordoned off in the rear of the room, I might add or mention, whichever, and then, they argued or debated, whichever, amongst themselves, as to who would be the first ones to speak or say anything, whichever, in the first place, and which group spokesman would follow which other group spokesman or say teller who disagreed with the first and foremost, whichever, then, who was to be elected to go first, then who second, and, so on, all the while, purposely ignoring the strained relationships with the women in the back, until they got to the last and most junior group of the groups, then, with that, the numero-uno muckety-muck, or the chief grand high elected spokesman, whichever, was introduced by someone who implied that he did not like him in the first place, purposely so, but so as to "test the waters", so to speak, because others in the group hesitated to introduce him or anyone else, because they did not like him or anyone else as much as some other one or some different one, whichever, and with that, the so chosen one began his speech before the Headmaster while still trying to get back more toward the middle of the group, so that he could not readily be identified or would not be hit with a thrown shoe if he perchance said the wrong thing at the right time, the right thing at the wrong time, or, the wrong thing at the wrong time, whichever, not fully knowing first hand whether the right thing could be said at the right time at any time, on time or timely for that matter, whichever, not dissimilar to an Iowa Presidential Caucus, but please disregard even the mention of the Caucus, or, Iowa for that matter, as, that may not have been developed yet in the New world and thereby deserves no affordable mention accordingly at this time, nor does the mention of such a specific location take on any meaning whatsoever at this time.

The women, now, already, still yet, or those in the here and now, whichever, being somewhat, or, a little, or some, whichever, realizing, that they were out rightly being more and more separated from the men, began, under their breaths, although some were more audibly vocal than some of the others, to squabble, argue, complain, gripe, moan and groan, with a few pisses and whines thrown in just for shits and grins, and a little more than just heard about from both here and there, or yon for that matter, whichever one you so choose, and to otherwise be generally discombobulated so as to disagree out rightly with any if not almost all of the on-going proceedings at hand, whichever, as, most seemed to have the ignorant and foolish idea, that they should have been included, one way or another, firstly and primarily because they were to be directly affected or effected, whichever, by any decision made forthwith to date by the men of whom they had some contact with or with who or whom, whichever, they had dated or had reportedly cuddled up to or slept with, just to try to keep warm and to keep everything in line with their other excuses, or for other unmentioned reasons or purposes, whichever, but, then, through nothing more than their concerned or wily wanton consternation, whichever, did they finally come to some agreement, particularly, that women's rights, or their right to vote in or on any matter for that matter, was most likely not to come to fruition for more than an estimated three hundred years or so, on to and into the future, of this New World, and, that none of them probably, or, most likely, whichever, would ever live to see such within their generation or their lifetime, whichever, so, they then just started to give up, one by one, little by little, here and there, but yet, a couple or with some in bunches, with a couple more or a few thrown in collectively, whichever, but with a few isolated cases, decided amongst themselves, that they would or could, whichever, work a better plan to deal directly or contrarily, whichever, with their husbands, boyfriends, lovers, sneaky sleep overs, or cabin handy live in acquaintances or associates, or wood cutters, whichever to any or all, your choice, or one who was just sleeping off a drunk with no place else to hide out, on both an ongoing nightly and a daily basis if need be, whichever, just to get them to do their bidding otherwise or anyhow, whichever, in spite of their decisions otherwise or what they thought they were voting on or for in the first place, whichever. So, with that plain plan plotted patiently with practiced pertinence, within the back of their minds or inside their fevered brains, whichever, such was agreed upon mostly sooner or later, whichever, generally and eventually by all of the women, girls or ladies, and a couple of the others who were reportedly just dressed up like women for the occasion, and, not to forget a couple of the women who were dressed up like men so as to get a little more attention or to strut their stuff for a show off, whichever to any or all, so, they then mostly became very silent or very quiet, whichever, and started to bite their tongues and lips in order not to laugh out loud or to expel out a squeal, whichever, or to be heard otherwise, and of all things, began to act like they were listening again, even as if they were hanging on to the every word, as to what it was the men who had a say, had to say, or what it was that they could possibly imagine that crossed their brain or whatever it was that they thought was meant, whichever, they too also agreed, amongst themselves, to try to refrain from any further snickering, flat hilarious belly laughing out loud, guffawing, rolling their eyes back in their heads, or the sticking of their fingers down their throats, whichever, again to any or all, your choice again, with one pinching the other or holding their nose, whichever, so as to prevent any such further or similar outburst, whichever, any further, while the whole process of the remaining proceedings were proceeding, carried on or just getting on the go-along, whichever.

"What is the name of the operation, Sir." Queried someone from the rear.

"What would you so suggest?" Queried back the Headmaster.

"Remembering what I do about it, I could safely see it being called "Operation Slick Spot." He yelled back.

The Headmaster cut him off at the turn and said. "So be it, be it so, let it be called "Operation Slick Spot", forever more from here to the door, by any and all having the gall to be standing tall against the wall in the hall at the ball in the fall."

A first speaker unnecessarily seconded what sounded like a motion in all of the commotion then said. "I am William, of the White clan, or, the Whyte clan, whichever, as it makes little difference because most of our group never learned to spell all that correctly in the first place when and while growing up in jolly old England, or, write much for that matter since there were very few or not enough quill pens to be had to go around, whichever, and, our group proposes, that we find some big rocks to set up and interlay them upon an unbreakable pile, high up into the air, similar to Stonehenge, back in southwestern England, that land from whence we came, departed, or, left from, whichever, originally, not the secondarily one, as that one was not really ours to claim to be from in the first place, so as, and for, the future generations to peer upon, walk around or stand and gawk at, gaze, gape or wonder about, whichever, your choice to any or all, like those who for centuries, have wondered about the great pyramids, wondering how it was, or, how they were all built and set up in the first place, with so little manpower of servants at hand, not dissimilar to our very circumstance here and now at Plimouth, or Plymouth, whichever, with no more folks than what we have, counting those who are not yet sick and even counting the few Indian volunteers and temporary help from the so-called sailors, just thrown in for good measure even, that debate the wonder if they really want to work for minimum wage much at all in the first place, who, if the truth were ever told, most would rather be out hunting or fishing, while the remaining would rather be golfing, or, and if not, at least lying about it a little on the side when and if the opportunity ever presented itself, or ever came about a little more in their favor, whichever."

"Recommendation objectively taken with no further recommended objections." Said the Headmaster who followed it up with a loud… "Next."

"I am Edward, of the Smith clan, or, the Smyth clan, whichever, as it doesn't make much difference, with us or to us either, whichever, because if the truth were known, most of us can't write or spell any better than those of the White or Whyte clan, whichever, and, our group proposes that we purposely go to the spot on which we first so landed here at Plimouth, or Plymouth, whichever, and, purposely mark that very spot with a mark of purpose for our new Colony and Plantation, and, that it would be a much better idea than my aforementioned predecessors mention of erecting up a "Stonehenge the second", because, to date, no one knows who it was that ever built Stonehenge, or how they did it for the most part in the first place, and, we could follow suit in that for years to come, with the same result, then, it could follow that no one would know who it was that built our structure in the second place, but to top it all off, or, get to the bottom of it all, whichever, we do not have an adequate or present labor force to engage in such a big magnanimous or large humongous project, whichever, because we have the more noble purpose, as, we have a colony to establish, a plantation to start up, a civilization to establish in this new world, whichever, and, finally, the overall cost of such a "Stonehenge the Second" project would require borrowing the money from some Tom, Dick or Harry, or some "you know who" entity, or perhaps indebting ourselves to some other foreign country with high interest rates, or even King James himself, God forbid, and, besides that, making our mark on the very spot whence we did our landing on dry land, would overall be the most economical or most practical measure, whichever, within our meager budget at large and which could be accomplished very quickly or in a very short order, whichever."

"Here, Here." Said the some spokesmen of the groups with some of the others chiming or adding in, whichever, with added on comments like…. "Best idea yet," or… "More simple to do" or,,, "Easier to accomplish" or… "Keep it Simple Stupid", or… "Run it up the flag pole and see if anyone salutes it", or, "We are already between a rock and a hard place", or… "The rock is already then and there and in place", or… "All we have to do is find it" or… "We don't have to rob

Peter to pay Paul, because if we do, Peter might get sore", and on and on and on and on, anonymously mostly, because, they all agreed that there was more than enough work to go around for everyone the way it was, with winter still not yet over, so, there was no sense in doing any more than what they had to do or what was absolutely necessary, whichever, especially since the group had but a few servants or workers borrowed from the ship until the spring, to begin with, and on the other hand, the ship's crew would be taking off and leaving in the Spring, for their return voyage from wherever they came from in the first place, with most everyone else silently wishing to themselves already that they could go along on the return voyage, if not just for the ride, even if they did not like Captain Chris because of his bad habit of scratching his butt and picking his nose in public at the same time.

The Headmaster was now to be seen, holding onto the podium with both hands, and, nodding his head up and down in agreement and approval, like a rock band head banger on a roll, but, not asking for another or for any further recommendation or comment, whichever, and, the group as a whole knew that White's or Whyte's idea, whichever, was already all but on the outs abouts and, Smith's or Smyth's idea, whichever, was already weighing in on being well on the way ins, and the smarter ones within the group already had the preconditioned premonition that they somehow just knew that further discussion was of moot effort or had had it all figured out a-forehand, whichever.

The group chatter now coming from in the back of the cabin, more than especially, became noisier, too, and especially from those selfsame mouthy troublesome women, who were all but curtailed, cornered up, blocked out, contained, confined or trapped, whichever to any or all, your choice, in the back most part of the cabin, but the Headmaster ignored most of it and them, for the most part, partly, then, raised his voice another octave, and, a few more or couple more decibels, whichever, and said. "Please, I beg of you all, please hold further comment, as some one or more of you have already mentioned, that the right of freedom of speech has not yet been born up into this new free world, or so yet provided, so, I would like to remind you all, ladies in the back in particular, not yet to be included, of that little notion, at this time, and, that we are still under the final sole rule of King James the First, who will finally have the final say to it all, that is, if he ever hears of any of this discussion, and has to make any decision or judgment on it further, whichever, may God so forbid to any or all of it on into our future."

The Headmaster then continued at same octave, boosted by a couple, or, maybe even a few more decibels thrown in on the side, with a couple more thrown up in the middle and one for good measure at the top, so as just to set a better tone to it all. "Do we have any volunteers, here and herein, to go and try to locate that very spot, where and whence we all came ashore after that too long of an enduring voyage of three long months at the wrong time of the year with landing at the wrong place, compliments of our good Captain Chris his-self? Surely, more than one or two, a couple or a few, amongst you all, have a goodly remembrance of that very spot, and can suffice to recall it and accept the commission to locate and mark it so on the behalf of King James himself primarily and we ourselves secondarily, or, the other way around, whichever, if it ever comes to be a little more politically correct."

One, among the group, but standing off to the side, a junior member of the ship's sailoring crew, a carpenters apprentice, none the less, Thomas by name, (although most called him Tom for short, but he hated it when some called him Tommy), held up his hand about half way up or a little less than what up would normally be, as if he had a rotator cuff problem or a tennis elbow, whichever, spoke up with timidity and said. "Sir, I am Thomas, a ships carpenter's apprentice, if you will, and, a jack of all trades but master of none, whichever, and, think that the least that I can do, is to help find and relocate that sacred spot, so, send me, as it is the most that I can do, since I am one of the few amongst the least of the most of us corralled as we find ourselves this very night."

Another servant, of the Pilgrim group, no less, Elias by name, (although some or most called him Eli for short or Ely, whichever, but he did not hate it when some called him Ely although he admittedly did not appreciate Elley), held up his hand, and said. "I was there, I was on it, I was at it, I was all over it like stink on shit, and, I can see it in my mind like unto a vision, I can still sweetly feel that sweet wet rock under my sweet wet feet, I can still picture both the right site and the tight situation, and I feel that it is my just duty, more or less, here and there, now and then, to go along with the aforementioned outspoken so-called sailor called Thomas, to do the will of the Colony for the betterment of the Plantation, or, for the settlement as a whole, whichever, in order that we all may all go down in history, if that is what it takes to get the job done to put our best foot forward to show future generations that we had both feet on the ground or had our foot in the door on the floor, whichever."

305

The Headmaster then said. "So, it is settled therefore, with none other volunteers voicing their availability, Thomas and Elias will venture out on the morn of tomorrow, after their breakfast that is, that is yet, when they are stone cold sober, that is, if the weather holds, and, if it don't rain, snow or sleet, or, if the creeks don't rise, and hell docs not just happen to freeze over, or, the world does not end beforehand or a-forehand, whichever, to so as find, locate and place a mark on that most very historical and sacred spot representing our very first endeavor of setting foot into and onto this part of the new world, as like it being, one small step for man, and, one giant step for mankind, but, disregard the last, as it may be reserved for some future quotation by some other volunteering pilgrim."

"How shall it be marked?" Queried one of the less senior middle management elected spokesmen, openly, but without request from the Headmaster, or, anyone else for that matter, and, certainly mostly out of order, you could say, with most of the other men looking on, frowning and generally gawking awkwardly at him out of the corners of their eyes, shaking fore fingers or pursing lips in his direction, trying to forewarn him and fore-arm them without using their forearm or fire arm.

"Do it with a hammer and a chisel." Yelled out one of the other more senior middle management elected spokesmen, so accepted by upper management, just in case they had to blame someone if everything went to hell in a hand basket later, yet, again without further request for comment from the Headmaster, or, anyone else for that matter, and a little more certainly out of order more so than the first guy was in the first place on the other side of the room at the time, who was now cowering and purposely making himself shorter than the rest by stooping or squatting down halfway, whichever, trying to hide his face for having opened his big mouth in the first place.

"What should be chiseled into it when they find it?" Asked another, off handedly, again without request, and, with the meeting then seemingly coming apart or asunder, whichever, from end to end, and going from bad to worse, with the chatter and clatter now almost overriding the additional comments, still ongoing and still out of order, so more so than the aforementioned second one previously mentioned a-forehand, before the first one on record was recorded.

"Just make an "X" on it, because "X" always marks the spot." Said another, kind of hollering or yelling it out, whichever, and, just to try to settle the matter once and for all primarily, and to shut everyone else up otherwise, secondarily, whichever, so that they could all go back to their cabins and go to bed, because more and more of them were now talking out loud, back and forth, some with interruptions, both on the defensive and the offensive, amongst themselves or between one another, whichever, with some evidently not fully cooking on the front burner, others not running their elevator all the way to the top, some others going on like they were a brick short of a load, for that matter, all of which, as if they had all been thumped more than once on their thinker pallet with a mallet or else as if they had all done up and overdosed on dumb ass pills, either that, or, they had come down with a really bad case of diarrhea of the mouth, whichever.

The Headmaster, then held up his good hand, with his bad hand still holding onto the podium, and signaling for some quiet, stated out rightly that Thomas and Elias were to now be commissioned, chosen, selected, or, officially assigned, whichever, and would be tasked for the task of locating and marking of the very rock whereon they all as Pilgrims first set their first foot upon when coming ashore first at Plimouth or Plymouth, whichever, so done, do did, with no do over, whichever, or whatsoever of either first assigned, and to be more than fully understood by all those present and accounted for, except for those noisy nosy women in the back without knack or rear without peer, whichever.

Now, Thomas (Tom), and, Elias (Eli), having now up and volunteered, it was then more fully laid out to them in discussion afterward, of what they were now duly tasked with by their Pilgrim fathers and leaders or those presently in charge, whichever, as to what exactly it was, that they were to do. For, it was already decided for them, for them to go to the specific site of their landing, and, to determine the exact location, along that cold and wet rocky sea shore, on which they all have contended or have claimed, whichever, to have landed, upon their arrival in the New World, and to somehow identify the location and mark it in some manner, both required with no whichever or whatever allowed here, so that future generations could come to view the location as a testimony of the Pilgrims courage, endurance or reliance in the New World, whichever, much like Columbus's landings down in the Bahamas with the Bahama Mamas, margaritas or pina coladas, wherever, he did what it was that he did with who in order to get the recorded credit for a daily rum runner.

The meeting was then immediately or abruptly, whichever, called for closure, and the women joyfully again joined in warmly with the men, and the groups then just kind of melted or gathered, whichever, back together, then, just as quickly broke up or separated on their own, whichever, with the men heading out for their daily issue of rum, after which most of them then headed for their cabins, with a few going potty at the outhouses first, mostly the women, I might add, just looking at the waiting lines, who were also dolling themselves up, putting on some perfume, and fixing up their hair as part of the waiting process, with most of them rubbing their sore tongues or lips, whichever, from all the tongue biting in trying to keep their mouths shut just previous or immediately before, whichever. With that, and the other, they all retired to their respective cabins, chocked up their fires for the cold night, and, crawled in together, mostly one with another, to just get through or make it through another day, whichever.

Morning came, and, folks began gathering around the camp fires that the guards had attended or tendered, whichever, all night, and, amongst the group, much murmur, some mutter, with a little side talk behind one another's back was ongoing. Back sniping, it was called in those early days of the Pilgrims, but, in the suffrage of it all, Tom and Eli both gave in, and, partook of a piece of bread, toasted to kill the yeast, and, some crushed and boiled corn that someone had named "grits", along with a large boiled goose egg each for their breakfast, of which, both agreed between themselves, separately at first, but later somewhat together, that it was all a little too salty for their tastes, either one, or, the other, whichever, especially the "grits", but it all enriched their bodies with much needed vitamins and minerals none the less, and, it was better than nothing, of which both agreed, heartily, or with great gusto, whichever, as they both went back for seconds, but with a little more butter on the "grits" this time around, and so filled their bellies to the hilt.

Tom and Eli, then went back to their respective cabins, and both agreed to dress extra warm, within fashionable reason, for the task at hand, then, they again rejoined one another at the warming fires, they then took the time to gather up and pocket some roasted nuts from the nut storage for their lunch, with a canteen of water from the guards water bag, then picked up their walking sticks, and, planning on taking the necessary and required time for such a project, or, making the day of it, whichever, they then, set out about the camp, asking about here and there, whichever, where that they may acquire a hammer and chisel in order to accomplish the assigned task or project of the day, whichever. Finally, after no little inquiry, they located a hammer here, acquired from one of the ships carpenters, and, a chisel there from another, although they both wondered why no one knew why that particular person had possession of such a thing in the first place, and finally, after no little "to do" with the winking and giggling girls who had nothing better to do at that particular moment in time, they both finally broke away and left the warming fires, and, set out on their assigned venture of the day.

On their hike down to the seashore, Tom and Eli tossed varied and various ideas back and forth variously, between themselves, or, amongst themselves, whichever, of their assigned assignment, but they mostly kept their discussions between themselves, the two of them, or one another, whichever, as, they had no one else at this particular moment in time to include in the discussion.

"Tom, I do not know what it is, but, down deep inside my grit fed belly, which, you might just call a "gut feeling" if you will, or, maybe a gritty feeling, but, I do not have a real good feeling overall, inside or out, whichever, about any of it, or, what it is, exactly, that we are supposed to be looking for, and what we are supposed to do when and if we find it after we get there, to get on top of it or get down on it, whichever." Eli said, sounding somewhat more than just slightly but definitely partly full of straight forward consternation, or otherwise filled with no little aggravation to express, whichever.

Tom responded. "Eli, as I understand it, fully, without delving into the matter more deeply, or, over thinking it, or pursuing the matter further, or more than we should, whichever, perhaps, under the circumstances, or, by not seeking some further explanation of definition, is, that, we have been assigned to locate the very rock of whence, we, as part of that Pilgrim horde back there at camp, where they all, generally as a group, but actually as individuals, first set foot on the dry land, here on the shores of the New World, all because, other than the fact that we both volunteered and just happened to have also opened both of our big mouths almost at the same time last night, partly because we got into our issue of rum a little earlier than the rest, that, we got ourselves involved into it, with no foreseeable way out, but, that is just between you and me, that is, to do what is required, for the betterment of the group, as, the sum of the whole is greater than the total, or vice versa, whichever ."

"Why us? Why did we have to go and volunteer last night, did we both have too much rum in our belly at the same time, or what?" Asked Tom. "Hell bells, Eli, we could be back at the campfires warming up our butts and hitting on all those hot girls flashing their bare ankles from under those long flowing skirts, full time seven to eleven, I can even see it now." He added.

"Tom, now just remember, you and I were one of the first ones to come ashore from the ship, firstly, mostly because we were not as sick as the rest or most of them, whichever, and, we were some of the first ones to have set foot here, that can recall it, or have any such memory of it, and secondly, because most of the rest of the whole bunch, were dumbed out on beer, wine, or rum, or, were sick from one cause or another, whichever, or, did not pay too much attention at the time to the matter at hand, that's why it has been left up to us." Said Eli.

Tom answered. "It's like this, Eli, I once met a midget on the east side of London, and, I told him some tall tale, but, it just went right over his head."

"Tom, you need a good education, the way you are calling someone a "midget" can be something on the order of politically incorrect and maybe even seen as prejudice.." Eli bantered.

"I calls them as I sees them." Tom responded. By the way, did you hear about the thief that done went and stole a pig, but the High Sheriff got him anyway, because the pig done went and squealed on him."

Eli acted like he was ignoring the bad joke, and, walked on, with Tom bringing up the rear.

By now, they had arrived at the seashore, in the warmth of the late winter midmorning sun, almost spring, with a salty fishy smell in the air, coupled with a more than damp chilling easterly breeze coming in from off shore, causing the Mayflower anchored out in the Bay to be bobbing up and down with the waves, kind of like in a calendar picture or painting of a ship in motion, whichever, so, after some discussion between the two as to what to do next, Eli chose up, on his own, to go one way, with Tom choosing up on his own to go the other, and, both of them then began to wander aimlessly, and all about, whichever, on and off the rocks, which were now exposed to the bay at what they guessed to be near medium but coming in soon to high tide, so, they both agreed that they had to work fast or get wet feet.

"Did we make land at high tide or low tide, when the first boatload came ashore?" Asked Tom.

"Somewhere in between, I think, because the Moon was up." Responded Eli.

"What has the moon got to do with it?" Queried Tom.
"Because the moon controls the tides, dumb ass." Exclaimed Eli.
"How big was the rock?" Asked Tom, who was trying to change the subject and get out of the dumb ass conversation.
"It was big, but just how big, I honestly don't remember exactly." Said Eli.
"Well, how in the hell are we supposed to determine which one was which, if we don't even have some clue?" Said Tom.
"I think that it has to be one of these slick ones out there." Eli responded, trying to ignore Tom's further remarks.
"Hells, bells, Eli, every damn one of these rocks is slippery as a damned eel, hell, the crabs can't even hold on, look, there's one sliding off that one now." Said Tom.
"Keep looking, Tom, we are bound to find it out here somewhere, I can see it in my mind, I just can't see it out here now, things just don't look the same as they did way back then." Said Eli.
"I don't even remember what color the rock was." Said Tom.
"Grey, Tom, I think the rock was Grey, maybe a little more than light grey." Responded Eli.
"Hells bells, Eli, look, look at these rocks, every damn one of them is one shade of grey or another." Said Tom.
"I think it was a big rock, kind of medium to lighter grey rock, if I remember right." Responded Eli.
"Why don't we just pick one, chisel it out, and get it over with, and go back to the campfires, after all, nobody else is interested, or, really cares for that matter, or else they would be out here, because if my rum soaked memory serves me to remember right, there was no one else jumping up and down to volunteer last night, and besides, they won't know the difference, whichever one we would pick out anyway." Said Tom.
"Now, Tom, They have given us the assignment, and, they want us to locate where they first set foot on it and it is up to us to make a mark on it, for all of them, for the Colony, for the Plantation, for the settlement, and, for future posterity or, prosperity, whichever, for them and their children and their grandchildren to come and see where their ancestral folks first landed in the New World as a Pilgrim, and to view firsthand some of the hardships that they endured, and, besides that, you and I will most likely go down in history as being a part of that real deal." Said Eli.
"I do not think that there will be many tourists, for quite a few years,

or, any coming out of the woodwork, for that matter, to gawk at this rock where we all first landed. The only ones here, right now, are the Indians, and, for the most part, if the truth were known, most of them could care less, because, they all resent us for just coming ashore and taking over and traipsing around through their happy hunting and fishing grounds, and, with us setting up camp, right out in the middle of their beach front property, using all their big trees for the building of cabins and their little trees for the campfire firewood, I don't think that down deep inside, that they fully appreciate us much at all at the end of the day when all is said and done." Said Tom.

"That might be the case, but the Pilgrim fathers have already put their foot down and put their claim on what is here, and, have set it up for a colony, settlement, plantation and all, and, they apparently don't give a didly damn with what those Indians think, as long as they leave them alone, unless, that is, that some of them can do something for them, to their benefit, I mean, after all, that wild bunch can't be too intelligent, as they all use sign language to try to talk, and, I mean, think about it, none of them can even speak the English, or seem to even want to try to learn for that matter." Said Eli.

"Well, some day, I am sure, that it will be hell to pay, sooner or later, because, this entire cluster of mustered up Indians were here first, and, we done come horning in, on their hunting grounds, taking their game, and their fishing waters, taking their cod, poking around, digging up their graves, stealing their winter supply of beans and "corn", whatever kind of grain that is, and the roasted nuts that they buried, which must have taken them all fall to collect for their winter snacks, we come in here just like illegal aliens coming across the border, and, it ain't no wonder at all to me, that they are all but knee deep aggravated and pissed off at all of us by now." Said Tom.

Eli interrupted. "Tom, if the truth were known, I think the Headmaster and his assistants, don't want the same thing to happen to us that happened down south at Jamestown years ago, with all of those folks just up and disappearing like they did, disappearing without a trace, with no marks or records made as to what ever happened to them whatsoever, so, if'n we find the rock where we arrived, and mark it, if'n the same thing happened to us, then, someone of future generations, or those in and on the next ships arriving, will be able to tell that we were here, at one time or another, previously to them showing up here, that is, but not necessarily them being first like Columbus was down south in the islands."

Tom said. "So, again, I say, why don't we just pick one of these rocks out, chisel it up and get it over with, because, nobody else is interested, if they were, they would have already been out here looking for it, or, caring about it, or, carting it off to put into some museum, and already have it all marked up or marked down, whatever or whichever, and, if the total truth would ever be known, for that matter, they won't know the difference, anyway, on whichever one we would pick out to put a mark on." Said Tom.

"Look there Tom, I think that is the one, it is big, light grey, and it lines up perfect with the Mayflower, laying out there, anchored in the bay, it is almost like a Holy omen, it has to be the one, it must be the one, laying there, shining in the sun like a new Pfennig or penny, whichever." Eli said.

"But it ain't close to the shore, Eli, the water's out there another forty or fifty feet or more from it." Exclaimed Tom.

Eli responded. "Well, it would be closer to the shore at higher tide, and, would probably still be exposed if you look at the seaweed leavin's from the last high tide, look, Tom, open your eyes and see, look how the terrain drops off just to the East of it, that would look just like an inlet, that is, if the tide were a little higher, and that is where they would have steered their dinghy in to land it on their first run in."

"OK, let's go with it, let's get down there and mark it good, before the tide comes in again, we might not have much time." Said Tom.

Both Tom and Eli scrambled down over the boulders, slipping and sliding, just in trying to get to the one and only rock, that they both come to now believe, and agreed upon between themselves, that it looked like, felt like, was the right color, and just seemed to be the one, or just had to be the one, whichever or whatever.

Eli yelled to Tom. "Give me the hammer and chisel, Tom, I want to be the first to make the mark, then, I will let you finish it, that is, if that is that OK with you?"

Tom hesitantly or reluctantly, whichever, gave the hammer and chisel to Eli, and Eli climbed down onto the so chosen rock, and, began the job of chiseling the mark on the rock.

Eli said. "Tom, I'll chisel the horizontal line, and then, you can chisel the vertical line of the "X".

Tom responded. "Hells bells, Eli, now think about that, if you chisel a horizontal line, and, I chisel a vertical line, we won't have an "ex" sign, as an "X", we'll have a "plus" sign, as a "+", and, I thought we agreed with the others that we would put an "ex" sign as an "X" on the rock which was so selected."

"Well, I can see here, a line in the rock, that would really be easy to chisel into, and it would really make it easier for us if we went with that, rather than us trying to make a forty-five degree angle to form the "X", besides, it is all in how you look at it, or whichever way you cocked your head, to the left or right, or, one way or another, up or down, as to whether it would be an "ex", the "X" sign, or a "plus", the "+" sign, and, I am going to go with it with what I got." Responded Eli.

"Suit yourself." Said Tom, plopping himself back down on the most non-slippery dry rock that he could find in the immediate area, and, one where he could get a good view of Eli working with the hammer and chisel.

Meanwhile, and, for a while, or, some time, whichever, Eli chiseled away on the rock that was so chosen, while Tom just sat and watched, bored as a gourd akin to watching grass grow, or, paint dry, whichever. After some time passed, as Eli had already but surely worn himself out, chiseling away as he was, he finally stood up on the rock, and said. "OK, Tom, come on down, it's your turn, so just chisel in an opposite line to mine here, and, our job is done, we will have made our so assigned mark which was so required of us to do in the first place, but you need to hurry because the tide is coming in and it is only out there twenty feet or so and we are in a low spot."

Tom climbed down from his perch, went down to the rock where Eli was, took the hammer and chisel from Eli, looked at the rock, and the two, together, agreed on the direction where the second line should be chiseled into the rock. Eli then got out of Tom's way, because he did not want to get hit in the head with the hammer, or a rock chip, whichever, then, he climbed back up and perched himself up on the rock from whence Tom had previously been perched, in order to gain a better view of the overall operation as a whole or in totality, whichever.

Tom, started to chisel away, the vertical as opposed to the horizontal, and, after about the fifty-ith or sixty-ith strike of the hammer onto the chisel, as, he was partially pissed off anyway and was trying to hurry and get the job done more quickly before he got his ass wet, and, as the count of hammer strikes had soon been lost from either of their memories, and, as it occurred, the hammer head, taking on a life of its own, or, as if it were possessed, whichever, flew off of its wooden handle, flying through the air, hanging in the breeze like a sea gull looking for a fish, then, veered off toward the water, bouncing off of a

couple of rocks like a bouncing ball, then plopping into the frothy sloshing water just short of the bay itself. Both Eli and Tom, then, just gaped, gawked, or, looked on, whichever, off and on into the direction from whence the hammer head had taken flight, without further comment, dumbfounded as they appeared to be to one another.
"Tom, I think it is gone, gone for good if you ask me, I don't think we will ever find it ever again." Eli said.
Tom just stood up on the rock, and, shook his head back and forth. Did you see where it landed, Eli?" Tom asked.
"Yea, I saw where it went in the water." Said Eli.
Tom yelled, now. "Eli, get a couple sticks, and mark them in the sand above the high tide mark, in line with where you saw it go in, then, move south about fifty feet or so, so as to triangulate the sighting, and mark it again there above the high tide mark, with a couple of sticks there, and a couple of sticks here, so that we can come back at low tide and maybe find the hammer head, and, I'll stay here as a marker for you."
Eli scrambled to find some driftwood sticks for the alignments.
"Don't forget, put the sticks in line above the high tide mark." Yelled Tom.
Eli, moved back forty to fifty feet or so, wading behind the high tide line and the seaweed, and stuck the sticks about ten feet or so apart, into the sand, in line of sight with where he had seen the hammer head go into the water, then, he took off and got a couple more sticks and went about fifty feet or so to the South, and again marked the hammer head landing site from that area in the same manner.
"So marked, Tom." Yelled Eli.
"OK, Eli, just remember, we have to come back here at low tide, probably early tomorrow, to try to recover the lost hammer head, or else we will be penalized and shorted, whichever, of our daily issue of rum." Tom said.
They both, then came together and then sat down side by side on the rock that Eli had first marked.
Eli broke the silence. "Tom, take a close look at the mark."
Tom and Eli got down on the rock, looked at it more closely, and then, Tom said. "Eli, I think that you done chiseled too much, look here, there is a crack that runs from out of your chisel area, and, danged if it don't seem to go both ways all the way around the whole danged rock. I think that you must have chiseled too much, as you have already broke the danged thing in half."
Eli, got down of all fours, put his nose to the grind stone, so to speak,

and looked more closely at the rock and the chiseled area. "Damn, Tom, I think you are the one that done went and ruined it." Eli said.

Tom, going on the defensive, said. "Eli, I did not hit that damned rock more than fifty or sixty times, and if anyone is responsible for splitting that rock into two pieces, it's got to be you, you must have hit it a couple a hundred times, and, you done chiseled on it too much, you should have cut your chiseling off sooner, then, we wouldn't have this problem, besides, the crack runs around the rock parallel with your chiseling, just look at it."

Eli, trying to think of some more rational excuse, said. "Well, Tom, maybe I did, then, maybe I didn't, maybe, the danged rock was almost already split in two pieces to begin with. We don't know that for sure now, one way nor the other, now, do we?" Eli said.

Tom responded. "Come on now, Eli, 'fess up, confession is good for the soul. You done did it, but there might just be a bright side, because, now, if you just think about it a little, there is only one rock, on this entire beach front property, of all the rocks that you can see for a couple of hundred feet north or south, east or west, that has such a mark on it, and, of which has done been split into two pieces, and, your mark on that rock will surely be there for many generations to come, so, we done did the job assigned to us, with gander and gusto, whichever, and, we have done did the job which was assigned, and, they ain't nobody that can say that we haven't. Don't you see the greater benefit or the importance of that, Eli?" Asked Tom, whicheverly.

Eli, just sat on the rock, looking somewhat down hearted or disgusted, whichever, but, little by little, he came back to life, raised up and responded to Tom, to say. "Well, I never looked at it that way, Tom, but, you may just be right, the rock has been marked, not exactly how we first envisioned it, or how we first decided to do it, or planned to do it, your choice, whichever, but it has been so marked, just the same, and, if either of us was called upon, to identify the rock, years from now, we could, either of us, separately or together, whichever, could do it, with no trouble or consternation, whichever, to either of our minds at any given moment in time on into the distant future, whichever." Eli said.

Tom responded. "OK, so, that's it, let's wrap this job up and head back to the camp fires, I am already starting to get a bit chilled, and, I haven't been feeling all that well for the last couple of days, anyway, with me being shorted of my issue of rum."

With that, both of them got up on their hind legs and made their way over the rocks.

As the two of them headed on up the embankment, when they got within fifty feet of so from a clump of saplings nearing the woods, Tom stopped dead in his tracks and put his hand out to stop Eli from going any further.

Tom said. "Look, Eli, up on top of that grade, just to the right of those three trees, there's an Indian standing there wrapped up in a serape, with an eagle feather stuck in his braided hair, holding a long spear, and he is looking down here straight at the two of us." They both stood almost motionless, except for their breathing, and looked up at the Indian. "I'm going to try to talk to him." Tom said.

"Native American, Tom, Native American, not Indian, you just going to have to learn to be more politically correct in this day and time with these people." Eli whispered.

"How." Tom said.

"Me know how, pale skin bearded pilgrim man, me just want'um chance. But you don't have to whisper, I have very good ears, and, I do not mind being called an Indian at all, old man Columbus named us early on, even though our elders all remember and have passed down to us, that we all came over from China, yet, the name Indian sounds a lot better than the name Chinian or Mongolinian. Don't you all think so? But no offense meant by that in any way, shape, form or fashion. Anyway, you can call me anything, just so long as you never forget to call me for supper, so, welcome to my world, white men." Responded the Native American.

"Damn, Tom, he speaks some English." Eli whispered, sounding in fact somewhat amazed in part.

"I never heard English with an accent like that." Whispered Tom back.

Eli spoke up. "What kind of English do you speak there Mister Native American?" He asked.

"That is one dumb ass question, Eli, how many English's do you know?" Tom whispered or half asked under his breath.

"It just might be the Liverpool English with a little Irish slang thrown in on the side just to add a little flavor." The Indian said. "Liverpool, where I done did go to school mostly now and then, here and there, studying this and that, and, I might add or mention, whichever, that I not only have an English passport, I also have Liverpool passport, of all things, which are few and far between, even there, and, as far as I know, no other Indian in these parts that I ever heard of, can say the same that I know of or ever heard of for that matter, whichever, and, that makes me a one and lonely only."

"Well, I'll be flatly floored or dilly damned down, whichever." Said Eli, again under his breath.

Tom spoke up. "My name is Tom, and this is Eli." Pointing his finger toward Eli's head with Eli knocking his hand away. "And, what might your name be?" Tom asked.

"My Indian name is, "Squanta Samoset", but I get kidded a lot by most of the girls, as they call me "Squawkin Sam" because I have an inborn tendency to talk too much, but then, I am really just generally trying to explain myself, and to try to keep myself out of trouble, generally, but, I was named "Squanta Samoset" when born into the Pawtuxet Clan, but am only slightly or distantly related, whichever, by a cousins marriage to that nasty Nausset Clan that has given your folks the shit-fits and bad spells, but nonetheless, both Clans are of the Mashpee Wampanoag tribe governed under the authority of that great Chief Massasoit himself at this time, but I, myself, am better known amongst my peers, cohorts and kin, by my nickname as "Wat-a-lotta-bee-es". Most of us have a half a dozen names or so, just to throw around to confuse the girls mostly. However, on the other hand, I might add on that, "Bobby" is my given English name that I am the most proud of, or "J-R" which denotes the son or Junior of that father. So, I have of late, a-lotta names." The Indian said. "So, come on up the bank, here in the trees, and out of the wind, and, let's have a simulated virtual pow-wow, amongst ourselves, as, I have my own second hand yard sale purchased peace pipe with a goodly supply of tobacco shipped up here by Sir Walter Raleigh's leftover troop down south in new Virginny, and a little bit of loco weed added in on the side that can be added in for a little flavor, and I'll start up a little warming fire to take the chill off of you all a little, if you have the time." He added on.

Eli then yelled up to the Indian. "I see that you have a sharp pointed spear there Squanta, J-R or Bobby baby, or Mister lotta-names, whichever, whatever your name is, and, we only have a couple of willow walking sticks here, so, if you will kindly lay down or lay by your chucking spear there, whichever, we'll think about coming on up a little more closer, maybe that is, if'n you don't get a case of the shakes, make any threating gestures or any quick herky-jerky or hurly gurly moves otherwise, whichever."

The Indian leaned his spear up into a "Y" on one of the willow saplings, then, said. "OK by me, but when you all get up here, you both also gotta' lay down your walkin' sticks, 'cause, I have been walloped unmercifully by walking sticks before, more than once in my life time if the truth were known, along with a couple London made walking canes made out of the finest polished rosewood, and hurt is hurt the same, all the world over, and I know firsthand, that pain can be quite a bit more than just weakness leavin' the ole body like the ocean goin' gyrene marines say."

Tom and Eli climbed on up and onto the bank, keeping a wary eye on the Indian as they approached him, and, each one of them stopped about ten feet from him, then, laid down their walking sticks, but kept them within a quick reach, just in case or to be on the safe side, whichever.

"I didn't think either of you had guns, I normally try to stay hid out when I see some of your folks coming out with guns, because most of them have the bad habit of shooting first and then asking questions later, as if they had some constitutional right or whatever to do it, and, I've even seen some of them that didn't even bother to ask questions or to try to get your attention a-forehand or otherwise, whichever, especially that bunch who practice permit required concealed carry whether they have a permit or not." Bobby said.

"What makes you think that they will shoot?" Tom asked.

"Does a bear poop in the woods? Is the Pope a Catholic? Is ocean water wet? Are you all Pilgrims?" "So, what do you think?" Bobby responded.

Eli spoke up and changed the subject. "How is it that you have come to know how to speak English?" He asked.

The Indian, squatted down on his haunches, packed some shreds of tobacco mixed in with a little loco weed seeds into the peace pipe, and, motioned for Tom and Eli to also sit down and join him. Bobby then reached under the serape into his leather breech clout pocket and pulled out a large clam bivalve sea shell wrapped in corn shucks for insulation, opened it up, blew his breath into the shell which contained some hot coals which then glowed bright, and used the glowing coals to light the tobacco in the peace pipe, he took a couple of puffs, then handed the pipe over to Eli for a draw or two. Motioning for Eli to try it out, as he seemed hesitant, he then gathered some small dry sticks and leaves and started a fire with the same hot coals from the shell. He then started off on his spiel. "The best tobacco grows further south." He said. "Somewhere down by Raleigh or the Richmond in the Virginia area, but please disregard that, as I do not think the latter has yet been so officially named as much as the former, but still, it is still a long, long way to Richmond,

or Raleigh either for that matter, either way you choose to go, by boat or by briar mail." He then added more brush on the small fire and continued. "Injun man, make small fire and sit close and keep warm, while white man make big fire and have to back off where he burning hot in front but still frozen cold on hind end."
Then, he continued. "Well, that is part of it, but, here's my sad sorry story in a nut shell…. a couple years after that danged Jamestown fiasco and the Roanoke thing, that done folded up way down south, with those folks just up and disappearin' like they did, at a time, when I was just knee high to a grasshopper, or, up to the time I was no more than a hairy assed teenager, a-livin' in the woods amongst a bunch of wild savage Indians, which I do admit that they appear to either be high on testosterone or steroids, or some weird kind of loco weed, whichever, while I was out in the woods hunting girls supposedly out a-hunting mushrooms, I up and got myself caught by a couple of well-practiced human trappers, one fine late spring morning while the dew was still on the roses, them catchers as they were, were castoffs from some ship of fools, that was over here a-looking for gold, of all things, in what they called the New World, and, they took less than proper custody of me, tied me up like a happy birthday present, and, put a bow on top of my head with a blue-bird feather stuck in it, took me aboard their ship, and presented me to their Captain, then, he proceeded to use me and order me around just for my labor and training me as a new crew member, rope climbing and all, and, he had me a-workin' my way 15-16 hours a day, seven days a week, doin' everythin' from bailin' water to climbin' ropes, with no time off, I might add, as a go-for gopher, shipmate and deckhand, whichever, and a-usin' my free labor all the way back to England, however, I did not mind that too much, as there was not much else for me to do at the time, and, it did pass the time for me, for almost three whole moon turn-a-rounds, or, months against a headwind all the way, ticky tackin' back and forth or zig-sagging, whichever, all the way back to England, either way, it was bad all the way, in your language, or, our language, or, any language, whichever, to any or all, I had thought that I had come to be the man of constant sorrow with no friends to help me at the time, however, the part that I hold against him and them and that, is that the trip was without the benefit of any rum issued on my part whatsoever, someone got it, I might add, except for some that I happened to filch or steal or siphon off, whichever, and learnin' to sleep in them danged swingin' and swayin' hammocks with the rolling back and forth of an all but empty ship without

adequate or proper ballast. By the way, just to change the subject around a little. Does your fine and noble King James the First still hold the reign of power in that grand isle and did he ever finally get that new translation of the Bible into print?" And, with that, leaving the question up in the air, he added a few more sticks to the small fire and stirred it up a little. "By the way, you two can personally call me Bobby from now on." He added on.

Eli responded but did not direct his speech to anyone in particular. "I knew a Bobby McGee one time, I remember her, as, she was some sweet girl that I had a special thing for, and, at one time, I even thought about writing a song about her, but she never came across and I lost out to some other lucky guy, but I never met a guy named Bobby."

Tom responded secondly, right behind or right after Eli, whichever, with. "Absolutely, and to answer your question about King James, the answer is yes, and he is still called James the First, and secondly, also yes, he finalized the new Bible edition about ten years ago, Bobby, but we have all but quit naming kids and things after him, as they all seem to go south, or, maybe further south sometimes than they should have otherwise, but not the Bible thing, as that seems to be making a go of it, especially with the Puritan bunch, but no offense meant by that. But you mentioned Raleigh, the Sir Walter one, who started this entire tobacco thing down south in Virginia, you probably haven't heard that King James done went and had Sir Walter executed about three years ago, yep, had his head lopped completely off with an axe he did, but not because of the tobacco thing, might may as well been a nicotine thing or maybe a caffeine thing, whichever, or maybe it was over some woman, as far as I know, I might add, but, most likely for something else we've never heard about, or just for the hell of it, or, because he was mad at him for some unknown reason at the time, whichever to any or all." Tom, then, took the lead and added some more sticks to the fire after his coughing fit relapsed a little.

By this time, Eli was back to coughing his head off from not knowing how to either smoke or inhale, whichever, either, and he quickly passed the smoking peace pipe on back over to Tom for a try and went to picking up sticks from around him with some more leaves, adding it to the fire, and trying not to cough any more than what was absolutely necessary.

Then, Bobby continued. "When we first arrived in jolly old England, near London it was, it was at low tide, so, we were held off shore, up wind and downstream until high tide came on the first of morn, so as

to be able to come on up the river Thames to dock in at Harwich, then, when we finally did get docked in, just east of what is now downtown London. It was almost dawn, that it dawned upon me, that I might just consider, just off of the top of my head I might mention, so to speak, as my thinker was not totally broken in two yet, of taking a leap off of or jumping ship, whichever, and finding my own way, whatever or wherever that might be or lead me, whichever, into the future and through that old settled civilized world, although it might have been new to me at the time. But… both the captain and the crew done out-thought me a-head of time, or outwitted me, whichever, and done put their holds and grabs or grapples on me, whichever to all or any, and they tied me up and buckled this Indian buck down, whichever, they were all over me like stink, as if they expected I would or could even think of such a thing would or could even elect such a thing to even cross my mind, whichever, almost as if they were reading my mind somehow or even knew what I was thinking a-forehand, whichever, or like they were being early apprised by some gypsy mother or fortune teller extraordinaire passin' them info on me all the way from Castlegate no less, whichever, but no offense meant by either, whichever, and, they done bound me up, hand and foot, or, ankle and wrist, head to tail, asshole to elbow, or, so tight, that the only thing I could do was maybe pass a little gas, whichever to any or all, and, all before I had the chance to enjoy even further thought of the opportunity for such as even a thought about such glorious freedom. The ship's Captain, then came and took personal charge of me, tied up as I was, without any hot cakes and eggs for breakfast, I might add, and he personally paraded me around or showed me off, whichever, up and down, in and out, back and forth, whichever to any or to all, on the streets around Harwich town for a few days, just for the fun of the show of it all if you will, and, made some real good quick money off of me on the side I might add, as, he charged folks to just see me do a rain dance along with a couple of early on London fog eradication cantations, and hear me talk my Indian talk, or squawk, with a little pig Latin thrown in on the side, whichever to either as he called it, of which I was supposed to do, when he poked me with his rudder arm handle or handy dandy cattle prod, whichever." Then, Bobby tried again to build up the small fire a little more, by adding some leaves and loose sticks and fanned it with his hand.
Bobby then continued. "Then, after but a few days or less, as less than a week had gone by, whichever, a family by the name of O'neal,

an Irish family, if you will, reportedly of good recent decent Irish descent, I might add, and, of which you might have already calculated, which, I found out that it was, one of the finest of families known down through history who had gotten themselves done run out of Ireland before potato famine plantin' time, and, who had come to England hungry, and, who had brought their entire family for their ultimate eternal salvation under none other than the glorious Pope Paul the Fifth himself, at the time, and, when the head of the family saw me, Bobby being his proper name, of whom I might mention that I was so honorably named after, he got to feelin' down right sorry for me in my poor pitiful bare ass predicament, and, he pre-paid the Captain off on the fair and square, as to what was the equivalent cost of my fare for crossin' the Atlantic on his ship, minus a small credit for my work effort I might add, that the Captain later said that he did fell a little guilty about not givin' me more on account, and then, the O'neal family took me in as their very own son, or equivalent, whatever that might be, or just a little short of adoption itself, whichever, and, they taught me their English with their Irish accent, and then put me into school where they all lived over near downtown, or, maybe it was uptown Liverpool, whichever, and, it was there I done picked up my danged Liverpool accent. Now, bear in mind, that at this point of my life, I had neither a pot to pee in, nor a window to throw it out of. I was there seven or eight years or so in all, and, by then, in and out of several schools in Liverpool for one reason or another, usually the other another, but after being educated to the fullest extent possible or as much as any of the known schoolmasters could stand at the time, whichever, I left school for work to pay my way in the world, but, I found that I could not get hired on to get a job afterward for high heaven or the help of any known saints or present local abidin' flutterin' angels, anywhere, even with Bobby O'neal's full-fledged "wild goose" Liverpool-Irish tainted recommendation."
He then poked up the fire a little, and motioned for the pipe to be passed back to him, taking a puff and passing it on to Tom again.
He continued. "But then, one day, while I was out and about lookin' for some decent honest work, near, down on or by the wharf, whichever, I heard talk of a ship that was all but ready to ship out and bound to be bounded round about for the New World, for the north part of the Americas even, I heard, and, I went and told the Captain that I was a sailor of good report and really of a some distant decent Spanish descent, but could not speak Spanish, because I had been kept away from my family and Spain too long, but did not mind it so

much, as, I being settled for so long in England as I was, it all bein' against my will, but still knew everythin' anyone ever needed to know about sailin' both with and into the wind, but did not exactly explain to him how I learned all of that in the first place, but, I knew in my own mind, that I learned about it, the first half of which was on my workin' trip to England in the first place as a captured captive if you will, and, the second half of what I learned from my a-readin' books in school as a free man, in the second place, and the third half, was where I learned how to lie just enough with a little truth thrown in on the side just for good measure, and, the fourth half, which was just to get it all to be believed real good, then, I shut my mouth up like a cold clam at a hot clambake. The Captain, impressed as he was, hired me on, Johnny on the spot, so to speak, just to add a little color or flavor to the crew he said, whichever, as, he said, that he liked my faded jaded shaded made up story, and, he took me on board, promised to pay me daily in the amount of rum that I could drink or thought I could contain on a daily basis, whichever, that is, if I could ever get the hang of it and eventually learned to ever hold my liquor for the long term, with final payment coming when I completed the journey and returned home. So, until our departure, some of the daily issue of rum, I traded off for knives and tools with other crew members, but then, the danged Scotsmen, Welshmen and a couple of the Irishmen on board would steal them back from me whilst I was a-sleepin', not that I was paranoid or anything, because I know firsthand that just being paranoid don't mean that there is not someone out there really alayin' and a-aimin' to get you when you ain't a-watchin, too, and, it did not take me very long to figure out that they were out to get me good, one way or another, at their first chance or opportunity, whichever, but, no offense meant toward any of them or either about that, as that is just the way it was, and it was just the way they were, and they just didn't know any better, not havin' any better childhood than what they claimed that they had and blamin. their behavior on it and their poor parentage. along with the pitiful times that they went through, and, there was no future in waitin' around for them to change any. So, for the early part, or the most part, whichever, of my journey, I was left high and dry with nigh to near nothin' to speak of, except the clothes on my back, until such time as I learned a few more things the hard way, so, I quit tradin' off the rum, and started drinkin' a little more of it instead, and, found the warmth of it to be more and more invitin', had fewer bouts with the trots and runs, and, not only gained additional credits with the Captain, but gained some real nice drinkin' friends in the process or in the long run, whichever, but in the process of it all, I finally learned the hard way, that the more I drink, the less I think, which has stuck with me in both good times and bad."

By now, Tom was hacking his head off, and, he passed the peace pipe back to Bobby who took it, knocked the ashes out of it, packed it in and added some more of the so called Sir Walter Raleigh tobacco and cramming in a little more of the loco weed seed and a couple more buds on the side, whichever, then, lit it up again, took a couple more puffs off of it, and, passed the pipe back over to Eli.

Eli enquired. "That stuff you stuffed into your pipe, other than the tobacco, isn't that illegal?"

"Illegal?' The Indian replied. "Illegal? Not that I know of or ever heard about, even back over in old England, as, there are no laws on the books as such here in the New World or back in the Old World either." He said. "Besides, I didn't grow it to smoke it at first, I grew it for my rope business, as, we do not have a good trade source for either manila or sisal rope fiber in this area, so, I grow hemp to make rope to sell and trade with the passing ships comin' up from the south islands, and, it was only by accident when a bolt of lightnin' struck my hemp patch, that while I was out there with a blanket along with my shirt tail kin, a-knockin' it down and tryin' to put out the fire to save my rope business, we were all huffin' and puffin' and a-breathin' the fumes, and, we all got to feelin' real good and warm about the fire and all, and didn't mind it a bit for a while, and it felt good just to be wanderin' around in it, breathin' in the mellow fumes from the blossomin' fumaroles, so, later on, I thought I'd try some of the leaves mixed in with a little tobacco, and, it added to the flavor and the fervor of the tobacco smoke, and, I liked the feel of it and so has everyone else that has ever tried it, so, my rope business has taken on a paradigm twist that most say is all for the better, and, I still have my rope business but the better part of it has all but gone to pot, but, that is not a bad thing, because I don't use any of the leaves or buds to make rope, and, I call that part dope, so, my official company name for my business is now "Rope-a-Dope", which I think fits it well, other than that, I am trying to get a moccasin business going, so we can get some export going to attract some import, that is what is important to me right now." He then grabbed his pipe, took a quick draw, and handed it back, seemingly in one movement, although unexpected and somewhat abrupt.

Then, Bobby continued on. "Anyway, back to my sailin' career, I got to feelin' better every day after that, for havin' made that decision not to trade off any more of the issued rum, and, as a result, for the rest of the way over, I did notice that I had fewer and fewer cases of the hangin' over of the port or starboard bannisters, or the bow or stern, whichever to any or all, a-pukin, or a-vomitin' my guts up or out and over the whichever side or end, whichever. I did learn in the process, rather easily I might add, even to the point of surprisin' myself, also in the process, that I would rather have a bottle in front of me, than a frontal lobotomy. Then, after another couple months or so, after spendin' almost a month out in the doldrums waitin' for a breeze, where we all but run out of both food and firewood, when we finally got back here to America, I of course, being a little more wary or a little more learned and a little wiser, whichever to any or all, this time, awaited my chance a little more carefully, and, as the opportunity presented itself, on one warm quiet cloudy morn, when everyone was a-sleepin' in, I made sure no one was watchin', and, I quietly slipped or slid, whichever, into the cool waters from the low stern of the ship and dog paddled to shore with my belongin's tied up in a gunny sack along with a couple kegs of the finest rum as flotation devices. After that, I must have walked a hundred miles or so, goin' day and night without eatin' a solid meal, or drinkin' a glass of pure water, and, havin' to drink some of the rum, just to relieve myself of the load as it was easier to carry inside than it was on the outside, just to get back to my home town, where I built me a stick and mud hut on the sunny side of the mountain, and, to the here and now of what you Pilgrims call Plimouth. Now, today, it has been three long years that I have not talked to a certified card carrying civilized human being in the Kings English, all the while just tryin' to get along, while daily a-comin' face to face with all of those crazy wild assed Indians out there in the woods, but no offense to be meant by that, as, they are still not as bad ass as some of those Liverpool hoodlums on the wharf back there in England, that would knife you for a Pfennig at the drop of a hat, but, no offense meant by that either, as they blamed their bad behavior on poor rearing too, and now, it has become all but a pain to even remember the events, the worst of them all is or was, whichever, that most of those previously mentioned are either my direct blood relatives or some distant shirt tail kin with the latter mentioned former so called friends. That's me and my dumb wild ass wild Injun man story, in a nutshell, so now, what's up with you two?" By now, Eli was coughing and all but turning green with his head stuck between his wet knees, and, reached up to pass the pipe back on to Tom, who took another drag but who also began hacking his head off again too, and he in turn, then freely handed or passed, whichever, the pipe back over to Bobby.

Tom, clearing his throat and coming up for a little gasp of fresh air, spoke up first. "Well, I travel with the ship, anchored out there in the bay, which is called the Mayflower, and, I go where it goes, as a crew member, a carpenter's apprentice if you will, but sometimes as a sailor or deckhand when and if, or as whatever is needed at the time, like a Jack of all trades kind of thing, but, I will be going back to England in the Spring, that is, if I perchance to live on throughout this horrendous Winter, because a bunch of the other crew members from the ship or boat, whichever, have already taken bad sick, and, we've already lost a couple of them or a few of them, whichever, and had to pat them in the face with a spade and hide their burial already in an otherwise unmarked grave, but, no offense meant by that as we must always respect the dead who are no longer amongst us, and, we are already a little short-handed for any future voyage wherever the ship is headed next if Captain Chris can get it all figured out by then."

Eli then offered up his verbal resume'. "I am one of the domesticated servants, if you will, reporting to whomever the Headmaster so designates, at any given moment in time, that needs an extra hand, so, I kind of just float around, kind of part time, like a jack of all trades and master of none, if you will, whichever, so, most likely, I will be staying on, for whatever the future holds for this colonizing plantation endeavor, even if it is in the wrong place or the wrong time, whichever, and, have no choice but to do what is necessary if we want to get paid for any of our effort at all on into the future."

Bobby, took another puff off of the pipe, and then responded. "You know, every time your folks come over here and disembark from those ocean goin' ships of yours, if we Indians have anythin' to do with you or them, or whoever is arrivin' at the time, whichever, or, at all, for that matter, we Indians, all done come down at one time or another, with some kind or type of sickness, like the measles, the mumps, the chicken pox, the whoopin' cough, the fevers, chills or the flu, with maybe a few fits and shits with some bad spells thrown alongside with a couple of rattles, just for good measure, whichever or whatever, and, my folks out there in the woods, who didn't go south with the rest of the snow bird bunch, are finally, slowly but surely, except for some of those who have overdosed on dumb ass pills, are starting to put two and two together, that you all, and your cohorts, here a-comin' are the cause of the better part of their ills, or the better part of their sufferin's, whichever, and, have come to realize that they could most likely and almost certainly, do better without you all a-comin', and visitin' over, or even stayin' over for a weekend for that matter." Bobby took another puff on the pipe and handed it back over to Eli, then asked. "So, what were you two doing down there at the sea shore willy whackin' and billy bangin' away on some danged rock, what was that all about?"

Eli took a puff off of the pipe, handed it to Tom who took a puff, then, passed it quickly back to Bobby, then, he responded. "We were marking the very spot whence the Pilgrim fathers first set their feet upon dry land after their long three month journey across that great pond of rough salty water, to this new world, for the purpose of any future generations to observe."

"Well, I observed you all's effort, for one, if you are goin' to start countin' any of the early on observances. Just like I have observed you all for the past few weeks, especially, in one observation, that your group has more men in it, than it has women, and, I have also specifically observed, that my group of wild assed Indians out there in the woods, but no offense meant by that either, known as the crunched up bunched up for brunch and lunch bunch, now, as a result of you all shootin' some of our men down and shootin' up some others, but no offense to be taken by that, that we, suddenly now, in the short term, have more women, than we have men showin' up for breakfast, or brunch either for that matter, or those comin' to the warmin' fires in the mornin', so, just dwell on that for a minute or so, and when you get that all added up in your brain, you will eventually put two and two together on that, and, you both know, what is bound to be goin' to happen next, into the very near future, pilgrims fathers or not, and, neither of our worlds will ever be the same again." Bobby said, and after taking another drag off of the pipe, then, he handed it back to Eli.

Tom ignored the adding up of the two's and two's, for the moment, so, he interrupted. "Bobby, is there any way that we could get you to perhaps to come with us, back to the camp, to meet our Pilgrim Headmaster? Then, maybe, somehow, you could become a translator, or, something like a "go between", a liaison, if you will, between, the white settlers and your Indian friends, because right now, I don't think, that between the two groups affronting one another as they are, that they are doing so good, because they are sure not really trying to get along with one another very much at all, under the happenstances of the extenuating circumstances and with all of the goings on going on." He said, as Eli handed him the peace pipe, then, he took one last puff and handed the pipe back to Bobby again after a couple more hacks and a few more gags and coughs.

Bobby knocked the remaining fire out of the peace pipe, made some comment under his breath about the three of them already being up to more than a two-pack-a-day smoker, then, looked at them both kind of funny, and said. "Well, I guess that I could, but when we are nearby or in your camp proper, I would want one of you to stand in front of me and the other to stand behind me, or, one of you on one side of me and one on the other side of me, whichever, if I am going to become a "go between" because you all have some wild gun slingin' folks and fast draw artists, that don't need much promotin' to start poppin' caps and rachetin' off rounds and emptyin' their blunder-busses or muskets, whichever, off in my direction, I know both personal and up close, whichever, because I have seen how trigger happy they are first hand, and, when one of them starts poppin' caps, all of the rest of them try their damndest to join in, like it's a danged shootin' range competition at some national open championship or something, but, no offense meant by that, not to mention those cannon that you all got done got unloaded from the ship and mounted at the gates of your fort out there on the horn of the cape, but, disregard that, as, that is somethin' that the rest of us are not supposed to know yet."

Eli, trying to ignore Bobby's carryin' on, tried to change the subject around a little or somewhat, whichever, and said. "You could even be a witness and verify that me and Tom made the mark on the rock down by the sea shore, too, today, that is, if you are conducive to contemplate such testimony on our behalf"

Bobby corrected Eli and said. "Tom and I, Eli, Tom and I."

Bobby continued. "I really wouldn't have a problem with that, but I really don't want to piss off my folks either, or, their friends and cohorts, whichever, or, especially, the grand high chief muckety-muck Massasoit who is in charge, for that matter, who is generally known otherwise as the G-H-C-double M, W-double I-C. But, I do not want any part of my story told further amongst your group, under any circumstances, for my own protection, so, you two, somehow, firstly or secondarily, whichever, are going to have to convince your folks, somehow, that one or the other of you, or both, whichever, done taught me how to speak some or a little English, whichever, just this mornin', or, at least lie enough to get them to believe it after you first introduce me, and, I'll act like I don't know much more English than to say things like "how to you, intelligent white man" or "me dumb ass Indian man" just enough to throw them off or confuse the issue, whichever, just to show them that all of us Indians do not take immediate or direct offense by such, whichever." With that, Bobby stood up, picked up a stick and poked the remaining hot coals down with the stick and scraped the dirt up around and on to the fire to close it out so that it would not start an unwanted forest fire or for some other environmental purpose not previously mentioned heretofore or as measures so approved by the national park service, whichever.

Tom and Eli, agreed, and remarked that they could see Bobby's point, could most likely could accomplish such convincingly, and, with that, and with no further ado or delay, whichever, they both stood up with Bobby, in order to head up or head out, whichever. Tom and Eli picked up their walking sticks, Bobby got his spear, and, with Tom in the lead, Bobby in the middle, and, with Eli bringing up the rear, they all headed back to the Pilgrim's campsite, one ahead, one in the middle, and, one behind, as close together with one another, as was comfortable for each of them at that particular moment in time, considering, with no more than what they knew about one another to this date, it yet be early on.

Upon arrival at the Pilgrim complex, they first tried to meet up or hunt down, whichever, the most respected senior speaker Will White or Whyte, whichever, so that Eli could report to him that they had accomplished their task, and, upon arrival, they found him standing at the door of his hut, holding onto the door with one hand trying to steady himself, and, with a lidless pee potty in his other hand, Eli, then reportedly reported his report of accomplishment, however, his report was not too well received, since, the senior speaker all but rebuffed him, or interrupted him forthright, whichever, and by saying. "Report your findings, if you have any, or, your accomplishments, if you have any of those either, whichever, to Smith or Smyth himself, whichever, as to the results of what you were tasked with or assigned, whichever, as it was his blamed or concocted idea, whichever, in the first place, or, better yet, take it on up the ladder or on to the top, whichever, to the Headmaster himself directly, as I hear that Smith or Smyth, whichever, may be ailing with the railing flailing's, because, if you want any consolation or any credits, you will have to go on up to that level way up there anyway." Will White's or Whyte's, whichever, dazed like gaze grazed or moved, whichever, from Eli to Tom, then, his sight or focus, whichever, fell upon Bobby, looking

330

him both up and down and sideways, then, he closed his eyes and shook his head, then, again, looked at Bobby again, up and down, again, but not sideways this time, but did not further address any of them. Then, he shuffled or swaggered, or staggered a little, whichever to any or all, opened the door further, stepped inside and slammed the door in their fresh forlorn faces. Tom said slightly under his breath, that he had seen him like that sometime before or after their landing, whichever, which was not too much dissimilar from a once similar previous occasion, where Will had already guzzled, drank, or, consumed too much, whichever, of his issued rum for the day. So, the three of them, left it all hanging there or let it all go at the get go, whichever, lifted up and left off a little to their left.

"Credits" Tom said, as they moved on along the way toward the warming fires or the camp fires, whichever. "So…, that is what this is all about and what you are looking forward for Eli, are credits, is that not it? That is it, isn't it? So…, in that manner, you can use them against your fines for not attending Sunday services, or for whatever else they be accepted for, but I am part of the ship's party, so, I do not qualify for, or, neither get any of the so called credits, nor need any for that matter, whichever to any or all previous, of those so called good Pilgrim father credits, I do not have to attend the Sunday services anyway in the first place, the meetings or the school, whichever, anyway. So…, now, Eli, you get all of the credit, one way or another, and I get little or nothing, not even hot spit, why Eli, you wouldn't have even had a hammer or chisel to do the job with, if it hadn't been for me, and, I get zip, nothing, zero, zilch, not even air time, whichever to all or any, with nothing to look forward to on into the immediate future but the same or similar, whichever, for any of my work or endeavor."

Eli responded. "Tom, calm down, chill out, or let it go, whichever, just don't forget, we were both assigned the job and we both did the job, together, so, don't be so touchy feely, we will both go down in history for what it was that we did in the long run, when the truth finally comes out or it is finally known, whichever. The only thing left for us, is how we go about explaining to Smith or Smyth, whichever, or the Headmaster as to exactly how we done made the mark as was assigned to us to make in the first place at the last place, and place ourselves at it at the time."

"Well, We will just tell it like it is, like it happened or like it turned out, or flat out, whichever, straight forward or honest, whichever, and, let Bobby here, verify with some of his fancy variable local vocal veracity, to tell him or them, whichever, first hand, to who or whomever, whichever, that the job was veritably verily merrily fairly done or so accomplished with great exuberance, whichever." Tom said.

Bobby interjected with. "Gusto might be the better word, Tom, as it implies passion, zest or zeal, whichever."

Tom tried to ignore Bobby's comment by acting as if he was actually trying to even consider such.

"Well, Tom, if we do use Bobby for testimony, we can't just introduce him as "Bobby", we'll have to address him as "Squanta", or, by one of his whatta-lotta' Indian names, whatever they was, or were, whichever." Eli said.

"Whatever they were, not they was or were, Eli." Bobby interjected, then, added. "My most common Indian nick-name best known by all is Watt-a-lotta-bee-es." He said.

"I think "Squanta" would probably be the best, overall." Tom added, with Bobby shaking his head back and forth as if he were really thinking it over and then nodded in agreement.

"So, that's it, that's the way it will go, so, let's take Will's advice and bypass Smith or Smyth, whichever, and go directly to the Headmaster, after all, we have nothing to lose in the process, except for him to send us back to see Smith or Smyth, whichever, to his place in the first place." Eli said.

With that, in unspoken agreement between Tom and Eli, with Bobby in the tow, the three continued their trek on into and through the encampment, one after the other, or one another behind the others little behind or a little behind the other, whichever, with Bobby always sandwiched tightly in between the other two, until that is, that they came to the Headmaster's cabin. Eli knocked on the makeshift door which was not completely made, shifted or finished yet, whichever, and announced their request to meet or have an audience with the Headmaster, whichever. They did then, hear someone shuffling around from inside the cabin and for them then to yell out to them... "He'll be right back, if you all are a-lookin' for him, as, he has his ass, or, he has his-self at the outhouse, whichever, bein' fairly freely fraught with the friggin' frailin' trots, so, wait for him by the camp fire, please, you will shortly see a tall man a-comin', hopefully with an empty little pee pot hurriedly held handily in hand."

The three went over to the nearest campfire, sandwiched Bobby up tight between them side by side, and, threw a couple more logs on the fire to build it up a little or just for it to look like they were doing their job, whichever, and, warily warmed themselves accordingly.

"What if the Headmaster doesn't believe us? Eli asked openly.

"Doesn't, believe you, Eli, doesn't believe you." Bobby interjected.

"Well, like I told you before, we'll tell it like it is, straight forward, honest with a capital "H", no more, and, no less, whichever, as, who could ask for anything more, except to be married to a woman who is deaf and dumb, blind, oversexed, and owns a liquor store?." Tom said.

"Tom, shut your mouth. What you just said, is as sexist as anything I have heard coming out of you, you do need more than just a good education to learn what is acceptable or politically correct in this day and time, whichever." Eli exclaimed.

Bobby interrupted. "Just remember to call me "Squanta", and, don't slip up and call me "Bobby" for God's sake."

"If'n we do, we'll say it was just a nickname we gave you, so, that should settle any further comment on it." Eli added.

"By the way, Eli, do you even know the Headmaster when you see him, or, even know what his name is?" Tom asked.

"The Headmaster is Brad Ford, but most just calls him We Willy." Eli said.

"We Willy? How'd he come by that?" Tom said.

Eli responded. "Well, he is a "We" kind of guy, instead of an "I" kind of guy, like in We, We, We, all the way home, always thinkin' about everyone else, instead of I, I, I, E, I, E, I, O, and only thinkin' about his-self, which he admits he learned on the way over from John Carver, the Governor himself."

"What about the military guy, the gun guy that the shooters have to answer to? Queried Bobby. "The one who marches around like he has a corn cob stuck up his butt, but, no offense to be taken or to be meant by that, whichever." He added.

Eli responded with… "I think his first name is Miles, but he is kind of a standoffish kind of guy, if I remember him right, but take my word for it, he can hold out, hold on and hold his own in a stand-off." He said.

Tom and Eli, both at the same time, or, one or the other first or just a little later, whichever, saw the Headmaster heading back to his cabin from the toilet area, with pretty pee potty in hand.

Tom put his arm out to hold Eli back, and said. "Let me handle this, Eli, because I am only a temporary, a visitor if you will, and, you may have to stay and live all of this down, amongst the whole bunch of your peers, well on into your near future."

Tom cut "We Willy" off at the pass so to speak, and began. "Sir Headmaster, may we, Thomas and Elias, have an audience with you, concerning the marking of the rock of whence the Pilgrim fathers all first set their feet upon on their arrival in this New World and of which me and Eli were assigned just last night at the meeting in the meeting house to so mark on behalf of all Pilgrims." Tom said.
"Eli and I, Tom, Eli and I". Bobby whispered.
"OK, but make it quick, for I am about to take my bed, as, I am somewhat more than somewhat under this drizzly drab dreary weary weather myself, stricken or taken, whichever, with the raging runs, the terrible trots, or the derriere diarrhea, the dyin' dumps, or the slick shits, whichever to all or any, take your choice." The Headmaster said.
Tom continued. "First, I would like to report, that the so assigned mission has been more than fully accomplished as was just previously assigned to both myself and Eli here, as, the very rock upon which, even you sir, set your very Pilgrimishist feet upon, upon arrival into this New World, has been duly marked, and, not just marked as so required, but, also, clave into two halves, cracked in half, cut in twain, split or banged in two, whichever to any or all, your choice, with it being the only rock on the seashore to be so marked and so attested to of the very spot where the Pilgrim fathers first set their feet on dry ground when they first arrived in this new world and where it was first heard to be uttered "one small step for man, and, one giant step for the Pilgrims", whichever. And, not only that, but if the end of the ice age continues, and, the seas rise, half or part, whichever, of the rock, can be moved to higher ground, and, I can even envision a shelter so designed with even a roof over the top so as to allow visitation by visitors at their convenience to further show their remembrance and respect, even in bad weather."
"Well done I hope." Said the Headmaster, looking Squanta up one side, and down the other. "But, tell me, who is this third personage here who is all dressed up like some wild Indian ready to go on the warpath, but yet without war paint, but no offense intended or to be taken by that, and who is all wrapped up in a Mexican serape, of all things, and, for what purpose, as is not Halloween done been long past?" He asked but then added. "Ignore the mention of Halloween, as, I do not think that it will ever be a holiday on or into the foreseeable future, and also make no mention of the Mexican Serape thing either, as both or one or the other, whichever, may be politically incorrect for the record sometime on into the near or foregoing future,

whichever, with coming immigration issues and all, also, please make sure to surely back off a bit about the Indian thing and refer if you will, to the personage previously addressed as an unknown Native American, of whatever repute, but, please disregard the negatives and please do assert the positives, whenever and wherever you can, whichever, but, go ahead and respond to the remainder accordingly or anyway, whichever."

Tom interjected. "Sir, although the report is, that none of them reportedly mind at all being called an Indian, as, this Native American standing before you presently will be more than gladly to fully testify, if so asked, even before a called out court of his peers, or a few or some or a couple of his chosen cohorts, whichever."

Tom went on. "Sir, may I introduce here, standing before you, a proud Native American known as "Squanta" as he is regionally known, and, if I may say so, a most proud and peaceful Indian of the first order, if I may also say so, who stands here today, to bear witness to what both Eli and I have done or accomplished, whichever, and who may readily testify on our behalf and of our assigned accomplishment, and, of which, I might just also mention, that, on this very day, Me and Eli, this very day, have also additionally accomplished the unbelievable task, of teaching this most peaceful Indian, the King's English itself, so that we may converse more readily and so as to level the playing field, or be able to speak on the same level, whichever."

Eli and I, Tom, Eli and I, Bobby whispered.

"Say again. You both also accomplished what and when?" Exclaimed the Headmaster.

Eli responded with… "Yes, and not only that, but, this particular peaceful Native American must surely be more than just highly intelligent than most, and, not like all of the other wild savages that we have so far encountered in this otherwise uninhabited part of the New World, but no offense intended by that, as, he has picked up the language quite well, and, in such a very short time just this morning already, and has a most pleasant personality and a most understanding and gentle nature."

"Gentle or Gentile, whichever, If he's so danged smart, let him answer for his-self." The Headmaster countered.

"Answer for himself, Sir, answer for himself." Bobby interjected, whispering loudly.

With that, Squanta, or Bobby, whichever, now made his move out from between Eli and Tom, but stooped or hunched down a little,

335

whichever, so that he would be no taller than the Headmaster, and stepped up before the Headmaster, and said. "How, white man, Sir, I am most peaceful Native American Indian on planet, or, most gentle natured Home Boy Indian by home fires at home, whichever, called by clan given Indian name of "Squanta Samoset", of the Pawtuxet Clan, but, I might mention, or add, whichever, that I am absolutely not of that innocuous Nausset Clan, or the Narangansett bunch or those Massachusett clicks, that has caused you all no little trouble over the past few moons, but no offense to be meant by that, although most Clans are off-shoots or in somehow related, whichever, to the Mashpee Wampanoag tribe, most under that great and high Chief Massasoit, who I might add, should have a State or at least a little region or some small territory named after him some day, or, maybe a lake or town, whichever, just to throw that in, to drop that thought, or to plant that seed, whichever to either or all, before those blatant Massachusetts get their word in edgewise."

He went on. "But I, on behalf of those others, or them, whichever, more than welcome you, your people, and your invadin' troop to our country, but, no offense is to be meant or to be taken by that either, as most of the whole kit and caboodle of my forebears or ancestors, whichever, are well known to have made a similar trip, albeit the opposite direction, and come all the way over here from all parts of China yet but a few hundred generations hence I might add, but have all but since forgotten their jibber jabber or gobble-de-gook language, but, no offense intended here and please also disregard that last remark about from whence they all journeyed over, as, I do not think that is yet common knowledge in these parts of the New World, as it is not one of those things that would ever catch on quickly, or, better yet, it is not like who is on first and who is on second, or, who is pitchin' or who is catchin' or who is "battin'", like if you have ever heard of the you who, if you catch my drift or know what I mean, whichever."

He went on. "However, I must say that I am all but more than very proud to have made your acquaintance, Sir, although we have not had the occasion to have been introduced or have met on some previous adjacent playing field, whichever, and, I am ready to stand at the ready for your service, or, for any translation of communication, between your trigger happy shoot-em up group who shoot first but never think to ask questions later, but again, no offense to be meant by that either, because I am personally acquainted with that crazy bunch of wild and backward Indians out there, with some of the young ones who are so damned mean that they don't mind dyin', but, now, no offense to be taken by that either, because they think that they are just doing the best that they know how with what they've got to work with, and, being it that they are independent as they are, totally independent as a legion of feral hogs on ice, day in and day out, and. they are all scrunched up and bunched up for both brunch and lunch, still eating with their fore fingers or their four fingers, whichever, and sometimes, even with either or sometimes both hands they are, whichever, and hidin' out there here and there, now and then, doing this and that, huddled up in their huts, mostly in the woods with only their lonely maidens and a couple lonely widowed squaws to keep them company or to try to console them and keep them warm just to get their fevers down, whichever, that is, but yet, and, however, just to make a long story short, and, get to the point or to cut to the chase, whichever, lest I digress further."

He went on. "However, I pray, that if you have the authority, and will but make a small promise to show some intention to get your shooters to stop shootin' off aimlessly sometime soon, or, on into the very near future, or if that is not an absolute possibility, maybe we could draw up some sort of an addendum to your present Plimouth Compact, as it so stands, so as, to have your armed personnel to specifically, if they will, especially, or, at least certainly, but yet mainly, whichever, to try to stop obligatin' themselves in the matter of shootin' off in our direction so very much, if that is but possible for you to command, it would most certainly be no little appreciated, mostly by my immediate relatives and some of my shirt tail kin, also, with, a few of my close cohorts and friends thrown in on the side just for good measure to add to the count as I mentioned previous, and maybe to even include some, or even yet a couple or a few, whichever, of those noisy naïve native narrow minded Nausets, but no offense meant by any of that, as, even I, as a firsthand witness who initially took a crooked look at your systems and found them to be down and dirty, yet up front and real personal and user friendly, as, I might add in here that it did not take very long for me in particular, to get tired of gettin' shot at, as you can imagine or may have on some occasion personally experienced, whichever, and, as, our present trainin' program for the wild bunch is, again, no offense to be taken or meant by that, is, as mentioned, but when a shot is too close to call for either a hit or a miss, is, for them to drop, flop and roll, then, curl up in the fetal position, roll their eyes back into their head, and play 'possum, or act like they were dead with their hair hangin' down or purposely raked over their eyes, whichever, but immediately, or at the same time, whichever, as when your gunmen start shootin', and the bullets start flyin' about, which has not been workin' out very well for our side yet to date, for, either the wild bunch trainin' is too complex, or the trainers may not be good enough, or maybe it is because they do not have any particular dandy randy powere pointe presentations handy, or, a couple or a few get scared to death and just up and die off unnecessarily in the process, whichever to any or all, but please disregard the immediate previous last remark as to type of presentations, as I do not think it or them to be fully relevant as it has not even been invented or copyrighted yet or have any trademark registered that anyone ever heard of that I ever heard of, but, I really must add on here to end this sentence a little more, so that I do not end it with a preposition."

He went on. "But, and yet, because of this little minor conflict, confrontation, conflagration or deflugalty, which by definition is hoch-deutch translated as, "it ain't got or it ain't ever gonna have any known flyin' capability, whatsoever, because if it did, it wouldn't have a "de" in front of it", whichever to all or to any, and already, amongst our high steppin', hot footin', high ballin', bunch of hog wild and pig crazy sorry ass junior warrior wannabees, but again, no offense intended to whichever, any or all, as to those who are camped out in groups wading around in the wide weedy woods, so, now, it sounds like we are bound to have found that we have wound up with more women than men, from the ground up no less, showin' up or around, whichever, at and about our warmin' fires for breakfast, brunch, lunch and even including' dinner and their mid-night knack sack snacks, whichever to any, on a daily basis if you will, which is now puttin' more and more of a burden on the remainin' males in the coffee clatch club, the guys at the local smoker poker parlor, or, even the brunch and lunch bunch, whichever, and it is getting a little worse as the days go by, both night and day, I might add, as some, if not many, whichever, of the female filial demands are going totally unanswered both throughout the day but most generally at night, especially after the sun goes down, whichever on the latter two aforementioned as it's enough to make your liver quiver, and a few of them or some of them, whichever, the women, that is, I mean and am talkin' about, are gettin' meaner and harder to live with nightly, durin', or even sometimes throughout the day, whichever to all or any, and, some of the men's groups are talkin' about tryin' to set up a sit in, or maybe a sit down, whichever, or maybe do a Monday night tail-gater before the game, whichever, reportedly at the local golf links, at the 19th hole, for want of other more invitin' places, or, for want of a better location available for rental on such very short notice, maybe even the local pool parlor, whichever, to protest such, so, their hold on the hold out has all but been held up."

He then finally took another breath, and went on. "So, I only mention that for the attention of the detention and retention for your information, "FYI" if you prefer, whichever, but also so that you may more fully understand the overall problem, see the big picture or take in the whole kit and caboodle, whichever, or, so as to be able to give them a break Jake, or at least a little face space, cut the pack some slack Jack, or to abide and let it all slide Clyde, whichever to any or all, and now, just to get by the smoke and mirror problem, respectfully pray, so as, that you may be able to better address your executive decision making process on and into the near and dear future without fear, or else, at least, to clearly hear and get it in gear, bring up the rear, and get it all to the point, where you can table the issue, so as, just to be able to kick the can on down the road or after you add it all up and eventually put all of the two's and two's together, whichever, because when it is all figured out, it shakes out and appears to be about six of one and a half a dozen of the other, or rather, perhaps even of attention to another brothers mother." And with that, he just stood there up shrugging his shoulders being all humped down as he was.

The Headmaster put his right finger on his forehead, just a little over toward his left temple, left it there, then closed his eyes and said. "More women, than men, you say, more women than men? Hiding huddled up in their huts? We Pilgrims have just the opposite problem, except for the huddled up hiding in the huts thing. Drop, flop and roll, you say. We train our solitary military to zig and zag, except for a couple of those who zigged when they should have zagged, but, disregard that, since I believe that may very well be some tactical military secret not yet to be known by anyone other than those directly involved, or, a for their eyes only, kind of thing, but we too have other problems, not to mention those tattooed up, straying strapped up and stressed out sea going boat bunnies, or so called sailor boys with them making their troubles into our double troubles, not to even mention the problems we experienced on the way over just trying to keep them all contained and corralled up, and even now, we have to plan roll calls every hour on the hour, when the sun is out and the sun dial is working proper, that is, and to make them go back to their ship on a daily basis to sleep overnight, night in and night out, or night after night, whichever, as, we already have too many men and too few women, or, at least not enough of them to go around, make up, match up, or choose sides with either, whichever to any or all, with some of the men burning their handy dandy candle handle on both ends at the same time, so to speak, it is a kind of thing like robbing Peter to pay Paul, then, when they do, Peter gets sore, yet, I just wonder how that is going to shake out and be pulled off, whichever, on and into our near future?" The Headmaster questioned, to the three of them out loud the first time around, and, to himself under his breath the second time around, then, realizing that there was some mention of some identifiable potential unsolvable immediate or potential future problem, or where some secret might get released inordinately, whichever to al or any one that you would so choose to make your day, which may also need be addressed more sooner than later, did what any goodly trained executive leader would do, and decided that it was in his best interest to change the subject, before it began to look too overly political on his part and still had enough time to do some adequate damage control where needed, to send even the mention of any problems back down the chain, and made the executive decision to go ahead and kick the can on down the road.

The Headmaster went on. "Anyway, back to the more important business at hand. Tom, you and Eli say, that you two have taught this otherwise obviously savage wild Indian, but no offense to be taken or meant by that, here standing before me now, how to speak English, and you both have accomplished such a task, all the while you were also accomplishing the seashore landing spot rock chiseling marking task project named "Operation Slick Spot"? If that is the true case of the matter, pray tell, why in the name of heaven, did you not teach him his proper King's English in the first place without that danged Liverpool slang and that slick little Irish accent interjected or just thrown in on the side, whichever? And, secondly, is he like this all the time? Going off on tangents that only a college professor with guaranteed tenure could follow?" The Headmaster asked himself of the first part firstarily, and then of Tom and Eli of the second part secondarily, but purposely, did not leave an opening for Squanta to add anything in or on, or into, whichever.

Tom scrambled to explain. "That is just the way it all came out Sir, and, it kind of gets worse, especially when he doesn't focus too much, starts to squawk, gets on a roll, rambles some, then, he almost loses it and goes off and spills his guts as if he got or done come down with a bad case of diarrhea of the mouth, overdosed on dumb ass pills, or has an acute or a chronic case of foot in mouth disease, whichever, and, it is just the way he is, on and on and on and on, and, it is what it is or it will be what it will be, whichever, whenever, and you have to interrupt him when he's at it once he gets goin' just to get a word in edgewise."

"Has got or has come down with, Tom, he has got or he has come down with." Bobby whispered under his breath.

"I fully agree with Tom, but me and him are not the best of English teachers to be found in the new colony right now in this day and time I might add." Eli responded somewhat on the defensive, derisively.

"Him and I, Eli, him and I, or, he and I, Eli, he and I." Bobby whispered under his breath.

"It is what it is, whatever or whenever, whichever." Said the Headmaster. "Again, I ask you, now, officially, for the record, down and dirty, for the system, did you two get the rock where whence we all landed, marked to such an extent to where either one of you, or, someone else of stature, whichever, if you so explained it all to them, and given the proper direction, could ever hope to find it ever again sometime on into the near or distant future, whichever?"

Bobby then stepped forward and intervened on behalf of Eli and Tom, beginning with… "Sir, if humble wild Injun man without direct pow-wow authority may speak to most highly educated white man off-the-cuff, so to speak, if you will, but, as to the question, I would certainly say so Sir, and, I would give my personal testimony to that extent, that such a mark has surely been made, here, with me, as a third party or an outside witness, whichever, to this important or historically significant event, whichever, without any previous side agreement, contract or monetary compensation agreed to beforehand or a-forehand, whichever to any or all, but if I might add, I would sincerely pray that such matter may be tabled but yet be somewhat open to negotiation after the fact, just so as to be able to cover a couple of unaddressed expense account items or travel expenses not fully documented to date, because of the absence of a proper receipt, whichever, or, of some expense which may come up as a charge on my behalf on into the future of the colony."

Eli added on… "Absolutely, beyond a shadow of doubt, it is not only so marked, but also, it has even been clave in halves, or, split into two pieces, cracked in half, brake in twain, whacked in two, poked and broke, whichever to any or all, if that is not fully understood, and, it is the only rock like it on the seashore, for hundreds of feet around in any direction, North, South, East or West, up or down the beach or in or out with the tide along the shore, whichever. So, with present testimony of such a tremendous accomplishment, do Tom and I get any special credit for that?" Eli did add on the first half, but only half asked on the latter half.

The Headmaster put his head down, thought about it all a little, then responded. "I will grant you Eli, four full credits, on your debit card, which means, that you may miss any of four Sunday services, but, not two in a row, or back to back, whichever, so, do not ask for anything further, otherwise, you can expect a fine, usually, in the form of a hold off, a hold up, a hold out, or, a hold on, whichever to any or all, of your daily issued serving of cut rum. But you Tom, although I wish I could do more, I can offer very little or nothing, whichever, since you are part of the ship's crew and are not under my direction or of my command, whichever, or, are not officially one of the Pilgrims entourage, which is a French word meaning group. So, so solly Charlie, about that minor deflugalty, which is reportedly an Amsterdamish phrase meaning that "I don't think it's a-gonna' fly anytime soon before noon", but I have to let the chips from the ships laying in the bay fall where they may, as they say today in May, however, I will put in a good recommendation for you to my dear friend Captain Chris who may think more kindly of your shipboard services on into your near future. But, here and now, may I ask of Mr. "Squanta" here, if we Pilgrim colonizers, would perhaps, sometimes on or into our near future, whichever, would perhaps, to have some extraneous need, say, for some difficult complicated translation effort to so task him with, exactly, how do we get in touch with him, do we send up short wave smoke signals in morse code, or, what? But, please disregard what I mentioned about the short wave signal part, as I don't think that it has been invented yet, or even thought of for that matter, to date in this day and time, and, no offense meant by mentioning smoke signals, or disregard the morse code thing, but, nevertheless, how do we go about it and what do we do if such an occasion would arise?"

Bobby responded directly. "White man Sir, if ignorant indigent most humble Injun man may speak again, forthright, again, followin' on without or just short of fully granted pow-wow authority yet, whichever, but just to mention some facts, that once you first order your shooters to stand down and hold their fire, just have Tom or Eli here, call into the woods for me by name, by my Indian name, "Squanta" in my language, and, if I am in ear shot range, although I hope not, as that would also put me within gunshot range, however, I will respond accordingly, if not, call me out, by my more common Indian nickname of "Watt-a-lotta-bee-es", and, someone will pass the word around, as they all know it and know me by it firsthand, and, they will notify me, and pass your request on to me, and, I will respond accordingly, to be at your service, to do your will on behalf of both your people and my people, and perhaps, in the long run, maybe, and perhaps, such an important intervention could prevent further unwanted bloodshed between a fraction of our concerned factions, or, between your people and my people, whichever, and, I will also convey such a message to my people, and, will put such request before them, to quit shooting arrows off in your direction, because, you know, that once things like that get started, it is hard to get them to quit, it becomes like a bad habit, as, they are all but hooked on doing it on a daily basis already, like their danged black market trade of Sir Walter Raleigh tobacco and the Pureto Reco rum shipments, with all their thievin', stealin', keg and jug smugglin' going on, whichever, that is, as, I can't even get them to quit any or either of those things since old Walt himself done come up here himself and got them started on it all, whichever, once they get the hang of how to take a drag and quit coughin' and hackin', and their daily swiggin' of rum seems to help prevent both diarrhea and insomnia in the first place but causes deep ass dissipation in the second place, because, if ever once either one ever gets started in the first place, whichever, as, folks can get up to two or three packs a day in no time washed down with a couple of short cut pints, with little or no further encouragement, then, that is all that they want to do from then on, day in and day out morning, noon and night, whichever, from that day on forward, which has become no little problem for those of us who are a little more or less informed, whichever."

"OK.", the Headmaster said… "I will agree to some of that of my choice, although I do not know anything about you all's happy tobacco smoking problem habits, and, I certainly am not supposed to know anything about the rum stealing or smuggling or black market activity, whichever, but I will pass the word to our armed men, through their commander, not to shoot first and ask questions later, but, both you Tom, and you, Eli, you both, or, one or the other, or one another, whichever, for that matter, or, either, had better write this wild Indians name down, but no offense meant by that, that is, if either of you can write, if not, you both damn well better have a good memory to remember how to call out a name like that, because when and if I have to ever call you to do it, I'll expect you to do it." The Headmaster added, and, with that, the Headmaster cut to the chase and closed out their conversations, excused himself for a respite, entered into his cabin for maybe another little dash of cut rum, just to settle a few of his ragged nerves, lower his blood pressure, reduce his cholesterol, and maybe just a little bit more to help settle his upset stomach since he did not have any rolaides or tumes handy, whichever, but also mentioned at the end… "I also have to add for the mention of that most previously mentioned, to be disregarded and struck from the record since neither trade mark nor copyright has ever yet been registered to this day or time, whichever, to my common knowledge according to the most recent wiki-leaks, but also forget even the mention of the leaky thingy." He added on as an add-on to his unmentioned condition. Then, the Headmaster excused himself, stepped inside his cabin with pee potty in hand, and, closed the door on the ongoing conversation with the previously mentioned three.

Eli turned to Tom and Bobby and said. "Hey, you guys, I think we accomplished quite a bit today, how about me buying you both lunch over at Sister Sarah's kitchen, café or ristorante, whichever she calls it today?"

"That sounds real good to me." Tom said, and, with Bobby again well again positioned between the two of them, just to be on the safe side, the three of them took off on over to Sister Sarah's place, with one close behind the other and the other one close out in the front, with the middle one close in between, as could be comfortable for all three.

"What's on the menu for today, Miss Sarah?" Eli asked as they all went in, broke through the door, busted or burst into, whichever, or somehow otherwise, entered the cabin, whichever to any or all.

Sarah smiled her sweet smile and responded. "Boston baked beans and a piece of cod on cornbread, with homemade donuts for dessert, for your daily vitamin and mineral enriched animal-vegetable protein requirements without an ounce of trans-fats, I might add." She said. "That is, if there were ever such a thing, as, I just dreamed up or thought up that name Boston, whichever, up off of the top of my head this morning, as, it doesn't seem to rhyme with anything anyone that I know of or ever heard about, but, it sounded good to me at the time, and had a good ring to it, so, I thought that I would use it, as, there is no telling what they will call the meal on into the future, maybe the day will come when they may even name some town, or even some city after it because it is so good, so, someday, someone could make up a poem, like, "Ah Boston, land of baked beans and cod, where the Lodges only talk to the Cabots and the Cabots only talk to God" whoever they may come to be after arrival from parts unknown, wherever or whenever, whichever."

"What all do you put in those Boston baked beans of yours?" Queried Tom.

Sarah shot back. "About 5 cups of the beans or your choice, although I particularly use Pinto beans for a better flavor, 2 cups of chopped onions, one cup of either brown sugar or molasses, a couple of crushed and pulped tomatoes, or, the equivalent of some English Catsup or German Ketchup, whichever, eight pinches of mustard, two pinches of ground cloves, a dash of mustard with 6 cups of water and a short slab of chopped up side bacon or salted jowl thrown in, just for flavor, which is a recipe to die for I might add, it is to be slow cooked all night simmering over a very low wood coal fire with some additional wood and water added during the night when I have to get up to go pee in the pretty potty."

"I don't think we have to know as much of your needed nightly practices in such detail, Sarah." Tom said.

"Three hot healthy hearty servings for us then, Miss Sarah." Eli called for.

Bobby queried both Tom and Eli, with. "Is this the same Sister Sarah that several say they see who says she is the one and same that shyly sells sea shells and shoes on the side down by the sandy shady sea shore where she sees the ships at sea surely sail?"

Tom and Eli just looked at Bobby, then, each looked off in opposite directions, without answering and otherwise apparently totally ignoring his question, mostly because it was reported later that they did not have a clue as to what the answer was.

Then, Tom, Bobby and Eli sat down on a log before the fireplace to warm themselves, looking forward to having something warm in their belly after a cold day down at the sea shore. Miss Sarah brought them all a hearty serving of baked beans, served up in three small pots with handles, which she called cups, and with a wooden spoon standing upright stuck in the thick beans. Miss Sarah then brought them all some cuts of "corn bread" with a slice or filet of cod, whichever, which was something new to the Colony, as, the "corn" was a new grain that the colonialized colonizing group were now just learning about, and trying out, adjusting to, or making up recipes for, whichever, and the cod was a new kind of fish to them all, being named after the Cape Cod bay where they were caught, or, perhaps the Cape was named after the fish, whichever, as history was totally lost early on before any of them arrived in their so called New World. But, not being able to talk and eat at the same time, Tom, Bobby and Eli enjoyed their meal along with the warmth of the fireplace in Miss Sarah's cabin, as it was most difficult to talk and eat at the same time, about equivalent to trying to walk and chew gum at the same time. But then, chewing gum had not been invented yet, so, please, do disregard even the mention or such for some time on into the immediate future.

"Corn bread and baked beans with a little piece of cod thrown in on the side." Said Eli. " It is just like the mixing of cultures, baked beans from England, a touch of cod from the ocean in between, and, cornbread compliments of the new grain from the Indians, cultures mixed, and, now, they are well mixed already, in our belly, even put together and cooked by a Pilgrim mother no less, is that not unlike an omen of some sorts, or what?"

"Disregard that there Pilgrim mother comment wild Native American man, as I am not yet a mother, and, for your information Eli, do not plan to be such for some time well on into the future, lest I rest to confess, nonetheless, that I have a present calling to address more or less to guess to nest, but only after I say yes in my best mess dress." Sarah interjected.

Tom, ignoring Miss Sarah, responded to Eli, talking over the head of Bobby. "Eli, that is a most eloquent insight, if I might say so myself, and, I could not have thought of anything better to say myself, you must be brilliant of mind to think of something like that about the mixing of cultures between the Old World and the New World."

"Well, it is what it is, I am what I am, and, things are what they are, and, whatever will be, will be, whichever, whenever, manyana." Said Eli, on and on, more than once, again and again, repeatedly, or somewhat redundantly, whichever, up until he was so duly interrupted.

Tom was the one who interrupted. "And your homemade donuts, Miss Sarah. What are they made of?"

Miss Sarah, overhearing the question, responded. "Four cups flour, 2 chicken eggs, half cup of sugar, quarter cup of soured cream, 2 pinches salt, 3 pinches cinnamon, 1 spoon of yeast, mixed up and kneaded, allowed to raise twice but only knocked back down once, or the first time, whichever, cut to size and dropped into boiling oil for cooking, but again, no trans-fats, I might add, and being flipped or turned once, whichever, forked out and put on a towel to dry and cool, then, with some powdered sugar sprinkled on after they cool some, and, with that, they are coming right up for your digestive deliverance and you can bank on taking that all the way to the bank." With that, Sarah brought each of them a powdered sugar donut for dessert which soon melted in their mouths.

Bobby whispered to Tom and Eli. "The Indians always add to their cornbread, rather than molasses or sugar, because it is so hard to come by, a little touch of honey, some maple syrup, and apple cider or apple sauce, which you may want to pass on to Miss Sarah to consider for both the cornbread and her homemade donuts too, if she ever expects to open a restaurant or a donut shop that also serves us wild Indians, because surely, and, very predictably, more sooner than later, you folks are goin' to run completely out of sugar and molasses, as. there are only a couple or a few sugar and molasses ships that come this way each year, whichever, that come about to take port mostly just to weather out a storm, and, even us Indians only get a couple barrels of cane molasses a year when they do, as, that is our only supply coming in from the south islands, with no improvement seen for you all for on into your foreseeable future, although Sir Walter Raleigh had no problem with his tobacco distribution channeling sales and trades into this area, as we usually get more of that than which we need, along with some rum once in a great while, but no offense to be meant by that, now or on into the future of this fine colony, establishing itself for the betterment of all mankind, which day, I may say, along the way, I look forward to, by the way, just to put that idea a little more forward and up on the front burner, just so you all know where I am coming from or where I plan to go, whichever. So, you all may do well to learn how to collect honey from the hollows of the trees, and how to collect enough maple syrup in the late winter and early spring to last you all throughout the year to come."

He went on. "But, to table the matter and put that aside, or, to turn, shift or change the subject around a little, whichever, Tom, you, being part of the ship's crew, say that you will return to England soon come Spring, so, now, who is this, your Captain Chris, that perchance, I may approach, and who may add me to his crew for my return to that grand English Isle, as, I am all but besides myself with being all but homesick for jolly old England, and, I sorely miss the O'neal family so very much, and my heart yearns for their company, especially for their one daughter who is a little less than my age who was once on fire with desire, and all but hot to trot for my ole bod' when I left a-previous, but yet, she was too young to get on into a full gait, and oh, I do miss her sweet smile that I yet hold in my memory. I even gave her the Indian name of, "Kamon-Awana-Liehya, besides that, astride or aside that, whichever, I also miss bein' a honky-tonk man who just couldn't seem to stop, partyin' hearty with all of the raucous night life, a-givin' all the hootchie kootchie girls a whirl, the bright boogie-woogie nights, chasin' the neon rainbow, and especially those rowdy bar hoppin' friends of mine. However, it may be by now, that all my rowdy friends have all settled up and settled down, whichever, but back then, at that time, I mostly let Hosear Kuervor become a little too close a friend of mine, askin' Shiela for another Tequela, and with that kind of a mix, there was just no tellin' what else was goin' to go on when the sun went down behind closed doors, and I was always the one who could never just stand by to wait and see. Besides all of that, I want to become a horse trader too, as, we do not have any horses over here, like they do in old England, and, if I could get someone to back me, I could make another veritable fortune by bringing horses over here from over there, and, along with my rope business, my moccasin business and my wine business, and, maybe even my beer business, I think I could make it real good."

Then, he went on again. "Too, I have to add on, that, I guess, if the truth were ever really known, I just missed playin' with all the snow snakes and ice worms found round about these parts in the winter months."

"Snow snakes? Ice worms?" Eli queried.

Bobby responded. "Yeah, the snow snakes come out in the winter, and, they hibernate mostly in the summer, and, they are white and hard to see when they are sunnin' themselves out on a snow bank, then, when they think you see them, they burrow down in the snow."

"What about the ice worms?" Eli asked.

"Well, the ice worms come out of the ice when it melts, and wiggle around in the cold water, but they are really hard to see, because they are clear, just like the ice they thaw out of, but they are no good for fishin' because the fish can't see them either." Bobby explained. "The girls around here, are mostly afraid of them both, but, let it never be said, that I have ever, in any way, shape, form, or fashion, have, ever, ever, taken advantage of some young thing, when I am really only tryin' to protect her well bein' by offerin' her safe haven in my mud hut overnight or on a weekend even, that is, only if she is of full age, that is where I draw the line, and, that is where I walk the line."

Tom then changed the subject. "Well, back to the subject at hand, you need to talk to Captain Chris Jones, if you will, about joining the crew, as he is also part owner of the ship, but you had better talk to him pretty soon, as he is already laying out his plans with what he has to work with, which is not much if the truth were to be fully known, and, I would try to catch him when he is not sick, unless you want to catch what he has, that is, but, if you really want to go back to England all that bad, you definitely need to get his permission, or approval, whichever, and, get it early on, recommending ASAP, but then, that acronym has not been invented yet, so, to spell it out for you, it is a temporary visa application for immigrants on the "Automated Student Access Program", and, not only to sign on for the journey back to England as a potential future student there, but also offer to work as a deck hand to help pay your way, and, I would do that as soon as possible, because there is indeed a need which need be filled, an annoyed void not to avoid, I might add, as, I tell you, we have already lost more than a few of the new crew without a clue, whose families may sue too, some who are known to have ceased to abide and died while on the ride with the wide tide, and some who are suspected of having already been captured and taken by some young maiden who wants to become a squaw, and are knowingly being held by their own free will, being tied up just for the practice of getting tied down, out there in some hot mud hut out in the woods where God only knows, and, Captain Chris could certainly use your skills, and we could be ship mates for the journey back home, but I should mention that Captain Chris was named after Christopher Columbus, even though his last name is Jones, he still sometimes gets carried away with himself and tries to act like old "Lum" himself, whatever old "Lum" was like back in the day when he did his thing, but not to the extent of him being reincarnated or anything like that, even though some mention of that has taken place, just that he is like old "Lum" in that he doesn't always know exactly where he is at any particular time or any particular given moment in time, or thinks he is here when he is really somewhere else, whichever, however you look at it, but, no offense to be meant by that, and please do not pass it on unnecessarily."

Bobby responded. "Now, that is definitely an innovative idea, and I may just give it a try, if nothin' else other than volunteerin' just to have somethin' to do, and, will keep that ASAP option open. I might add here, and adhere, that I do have any hidden agenda or any underlyin' reason, either or whichever, to try to return to England. But, while I was there last, I might mention, that, I did learn how to make wine, but, I never learned how to make beer, which, if I could but learn that art, I could come back over here and rake up a virtual veritable fortune with this wild bunch of Indians, again, no offense to be meant by that either, that is, if I could get the application papers put together for the required license for production and the proper permits for distribution."

"Good luck with that, Bobby baby." Eli said.

Tom added. "Yea, as what you are talking about is a right tightly held secret by some very selective secretive folks, as, years ago, the folks in charge only allowed the Catholic Monks in the monasteries to make their beer for hundreds of years under contract agreement with the Pope himself sitting on council at and on counsel in the Vatican City itself, or under the strict direct control of their other solemnly sworn selected church leaders, and, I think that the yeast that they use and the selection of the hops are most likely or probably, whichever, the two greatest of all their hidden secrets that they protect, both by the order of the Ancient Hierbarians, the selective Knights of Columbus, and those danged secretive selective Ancient Free Masons, or even thosw swirling dirvishes, whichever." But, no offense meant by any of that or the very mention of any of it, I might add."

"Hibernians, Tom, Hibernians." and it is the Ancient Order of Hibernians, not the other way around." Eli corrected. "They formed up to protect the priests in the church when times were less than civil, and, it is only rumored that the Knights of Columbus and the Ancient Order of Free Masons or their proud Knight Templars ever had anythin' whatsoever to do with the beer makin' thing, as they were all busy as bees, a-buildin' of all of the cathedrals all over the Old World in every country, although it is reported, that they did partake of their fair share of meetin's, and the drinkin' of their locally produced products, as, it is fairly well known and properly recorded, even if it was supposed to be some sacred secret, if the truth were to be or ever will ever be known, for any or either bunch, whichever."

"Knights Templar, Eli, it is the Ancient Order of the Mason's Knights Templar." Bobby corrected.

Bobby picked it up from there. "Well, if it didn't work out, I could always fall back on the wine making thing, if I could just learn how to increase the volume, as the production is down from the wild grape vines in the area, as, the better grapes come from on down further south, or, further west, however, the demand is out there waiting like orphans panhandling on a Liverpool street corner, but, no offense meant by that, besides, I don't want to arouse, intimidate, attract or aggravate, whichever, to any or all, or offend in any way, added in just to be on the politically correct side, of any of those secret ancient orders." Bobby responded. "Just so as, to keep myself on the inside, and on the safe side, but, so as not, to ever be put on the outside looking in, or, to have to be put into the position to ever have to take sides." He added on.

Miss Sarah, waited patiently aside, until the three were about finished with their meal, then timed her interruption as perfectly as she could find possible. "Just how do you all suppose that you all are to pay for your meals, I might ask, as you all look like you don't have a Pfennig or a Penny, or a thin Dime, or a single Euro to your name, whichever, between the three of you, but disregard the mention of the Euro thing, as I do not think that Europe will enter into such a monetary agreement until sometime much far on into the future, but, nevertheless, I do not need any dishes washed, laundry done, or wood hauled in, whichever, so, what have any or all of you, whichever, got to say for yourselves or on your behalf, whichever, and how are you going to pay, I might just add?"

Eli responded. "Sister Sarah, this is your lucky day, I'll give you one of my credits that the Headmaster provided me today; as you could use it handily so that you don't have to go to church on any particular Sunday on into the near future, so, how's that grab you in your little get-a-long?"

"I never miss church anyway; so, I don't have any need whatsoever, or, for any of your credits for such a use, whatsoever, whichever." Miss Sarah slickly snapped back.

Eli responded. "Well, you can or could pass off or trade off the credit to someone else." Eli countered. " You know how the Headmaster is, requiring everyone to go to church, whether they are sick or not, and, you know, that such mandatory attendance is just causing more folks to get sick, with all of their sneezing, snorting, hacking and coughing, with a few pukes and vomits thrown in here and there, whichever to any or all, all of which goes on during the services, and you also know, that it would be better if everyone just stayed in their cabin instead of going to services in the first place, and, the same is with the school kids, as they are doing nothing but causing one another to get sick as a result of their required attendance, and, then, taking it all back to their folks' cabins, like its homework, where, their folks get sick too, so, the value of not attending services, or not attending school, just took on soon greater value, because I am not the only one who has put this sparkling two and two together by the way, why, I could give you a list as long as my arm of folks who would come running at a fast trot if they didn't trip, once they found out that you had such a valuable credit to offer."

"OK, Eli." Miss Sarah countered. "But, just so that you know, there is no dumbwaiter in this kitchen, and, I will accept your credit, so, put your name down and sign it off on this corn shuck here, but on that basis, if I cannot barter it out or trade it off, I will come looking for you or hunt you down in a heartbeat, whichever, and, the resulting end result will not be a pretty sight, if you've seen what I mean and get my gist, but, if you ever try to double up, and try this gambit with anyone else for the same credit, I will go directly to the Headmaster and have you and Tom both slammed into the stocks, head first, feet and all, with your bare butt hanging out in the cold, as, it is all on your back, Eli, because you are the one who brought these other two in here and ordered up the meals in the first place, and, for the fact that I do not have any way to charge either your shipmate here or your Indian friend there for their meals."

Bobby had the good sense to keep his mouth shut like a cold clam at a hot clambake, especially since his belly was full, and it all appeared to him to have been for free and more than partly on his behalf at least half way, either way, even though he was as nervous as a worm in hot ashes at the mention of the stocks, as, he had nightmares of them from his early on visiting days in England, so he just turned his head and looked away, or, the other way, whichever was handy for him at that particular moment in time.

Eli, Bobby and Tom, then departed Sister Sarah's makeshift kitchen, café or ristorante, whichever, bidding the frowning Miss Sarah some good will, and feigning their returning to their assigned duties, but not before hitting on some of the hot girls, some warmer than others, who were hanging around a couple of the warm campfires, just to see who would show up for a show down at sundown for a bed down or a letdown, and, maybe even perhaps of the chance of some show or a flash of a bare ankle out or about from under those long skirts, but always, with Bobby sandwiched up tight between the two of them, or tightly beside one another, particularly for his personal security and other unrequested reasons or purposes, whichever was candidly or handily at hand, whichever.

352

Tom said. "Bobby, baby, I will speak with Captain Chris about you, or, for you, whichever, but I think that it would be best if you perhaps took on the previous personage of your Spanish sailor gambit, who reportedly was then sold off or traded, whichever, to some English merchant, who you can say taught you're your English, in order just to get by, then, you can claim that you were shipwrecked and was washed up on shore from some broken tobacco or sugar ship, bound previous for the Old World, and then was taken in by the Indians, as your excuse as to how you got over here in the first place, but, you probably need to get your hair cut before you talk with him, and tell him that you do not grow facial hair because of some hormonal imbalance, but, either way, on your behalf, I will be more than glad to personally put in a good word for or to fully recommend you further, whichever."

Bobby, expressed his appreciation for the offer, and, after warming himself properly by one of the fires, wrapped up in his serape and hiding his face as he was, then began to offer up his good byes, and said. "Well, I think that I have been most instrumental in your endeavors and even I feel that I have accomplished quite a lot for the day, with the day still so young, for such glorious purposes, so, I will now bid you both farewell, and elect to take my leave, and hopefully, we will all be in touch with one another, on into the near future for one thing or another, please give my regards to your superiors, and, do look out for those damn snow snakes and ice worms."

And, with that, with the good wishes of Tom and Eli, and, with a couple of glances from the giggling girls, with a wink here and there, and a swish of a skirt or two and a show of another bare ankle here and there from some of the other girls around the camp fire, the three of them then began their move toward the wooded area, closest to the camp site, with Bobby again sandwiched up tight between the two like a good go between, and, when they finally reached the edge of the woods, near a bunch of bushy honeysuckle, Bobby slightly slickly slipped out, or slide out, whichever, from between Tom and Eli, wadded quietly through the bush like a bushmaster, but, broke into a run or a fast lope, whichever, just as soon as he hit the edge of the shadow of the woods, just in case some trigger happy colonizer guard was watching with only one eye open and a half-cocked gun which had dry powder and buckshot already loaded in and ready to go off on the instant, whichever.

Tom then turned to Eli and said. "You know Eli, you are going to miss that guy if he goes back on the ship with me, but, first things first for our first order of business, we need to get back down to the landing site, before the tide comes back in, in order to try to locate that hammer head that you lost a-previous, so let's get some steppin' and fetchin' goin' on between the two of us here real quick." With that, Tom just up and took off and headed out on down the walking path toward the beach.

Eli, while just trying to catch up responded. "Tom, just to remind you, I did not lose the hammer head, you are the one who lost it, so, you had damn well best find it, but, since I am already knee-deep into this projected project, I have no choice but to help, so, let's head 'em up and head 'em out and go do it, so, let's get it all goin' with our get-a-long, and, get 'er done, with a yee-haw here and a yee-haw there, E-I-E-I-O, just like old Macdonald down on the farm huntin' for his goat's oats."

"Cut the cute Indian talk Eli, we have some serious work yet to do." Remanded Tom.

With that, the two, headed up in a heated rush back out toward the slimy seashore, to look for the hammer head, before the tide was to come back in and cover it all over once again.

On the way, Tom asked Eli, if he had ever heard the joke about the pirate. With Eli responding that he hadn't heard any pirate jokes lately, so, Tom proceeded to tell Eli about the pirate.

Tom proceeded to tell Eli about the pirate. "Now, Eli, a Pirate walked into a bar and the bartender said, "Hey, I haven't seen you in a while. What happened, you look terrible!"

"What do you mean? I'm fine." The Pirate said.

"What about that wooden leg thing? You didn't have that before when you were here on previous occasion." Said the bartender.

"Well," said the pirate, "We were in a battle at sea and a cannon ball hit my leg, and took it off, but the Doc fixed me up with a wooden leg, and now I am fine, really."

"Oh yeah? Well, what about that hook? The last time I saw you, you had both hands to drink with when you were here last." Responded the bartender.

354

"Well, we were in another battle and when we boarded an enemy ship. I was in a sword fight with this fellow that was a little better at it than I was, and my hand was cut off, but the Doc fixed me up with the hook, and I feel great, really." Said the Pirate.

"Oh." said the bartender, "What about that eye patch? The last time you were in here you had both eyes to watch the girls with, what is it with that?"

"One day when we were at sea some gulls were flying over the ship, and, I looked up and one of them just happened to poop in my eye." Responded the Pirate.

"You're kidding me," said the bartender, "You couldn't have lost an eye just from getting a little bird poop in your eye!"

"Nah, but it just happened right after I got the hook." Said the Pirate. And Tom laughed.
Eli, did not laugh, but did respond. "Tom, you have to get some serious bones in your body real soon or else you are in for a very hard time of it, into the near future."
"Oh, lighten up, Eli, it was just a joke for God's sake." Tom added.
Meanwhile, with little or no time having gone by, Bobby, was already back at his camp, had hunted up or hunted down, whichever, the Chief's location, and, had already but interrupted the semi-annual corporate board meeting and official regional quarterly pow-wow smoke-in with the Chief and the peoples selected clan representatives, from all about or all around, whichever, who had just gathered to give the Grand High Chief an updated report of whatever crossed their minds on any of the recent happenings they came to witness, and, with that, Bobby began by trying to explain to the great Grand High Chief muckety muck, in front of all of the attendees of all things, that he should try to refrain from any further confrontation with the colonizers and try to prevent the braves and warriors and especially those young whipper-snapper warrior wannabees from shooting off their arrows at the pilgrims at will or them doing it just for the fun of it, whichever, as, it was explained, that it suits no purpose other than to tickle their whiskers or even makes their bad sad dad mad, whichever, because it was and is to no avail anyway, whichever, as the colonizer's guns has greater range than any of the best Indian's arrows, even those from those stationed high up in the tree tops, and,

that it was eventually to all but eventually be but a losing proposition in the end, or in some of the sore Indian's ends, whichever, sooner or later, because, already, there were now, presently, more colonizers colonizing than there were Indians a-gathering together at any given time since the snow birds already previously went south and were not expected back until late spring, and those, who did not have reservations, stayed on anyway for the end of the winter, a-livin' both in and out of the woods, in or out of any of the vacant mud huts, whichever. Besides, the colonizers had already moved cannon in to land from the ship that had even greater range than their muskets and their noise when shot or set off, whichever, made everyone's ears ring for up to a mile or so away and for no less than three and a half weeks, and then some, to the point of not even being able to hear yourself think.

The Chief, who was not fully comprehending or understanding or seeing the total picture of the matter, whichever, then started an argument with Bobby as to what it was the best to do next, for, as any great leader and any good politician knows, and, he knew just enough, to start to argument when he didn't fully or totally, whichever, understand what was going on in the first place or in the second place for that matter, whichever. And, that was his plan, but it took a little gut spilling to get it all out or explain it all, whichever.

So, the Chief then took it upon himself to re-adjust his breechclout, and confronted Bobby, by asking. "How can you profess to be one of us, when you speak both their tongue and our tongue, yet say you do not have a forded tongue or split tongue, whichever, and claim to have even forgotten the Spanish tongue that you even admit you were lying about, and now, yet now, you argue for one or more of those danged border crossing foreign illegal claim jumping aliens out there without even one stamped Visa out of the whole bunch, who now have taken over our very own beach front property along the Cape, with beaches on both sides of the horn back to back? But, please do not pass that on as they all may take that as an offense directly when none is intended in the first place, but yet, you were or have been both here and there, back again and want to go again for God knows what reason, to date, and, and, you know, that there has been no formal request or even one known application of inquiry from a single soul to attain their green card, or, application from any of them in any of their groups, I therefore warily question even their very veracity, but, I recall and request you to fully disregard even the mention of the green card, as, I do not think that is has been issued yet for anyone here in their so called New World, as, we did not have one when we arrived from China either, whichever, for that matter, or even spoke the same language amongst the whole bunch of us when first arriving in this so called New World, or the so called America as is has come to be known, whichever, which names, I might add, even our area is now being called by these wannabee colonizers, and, this is all very confusing not just to me, but also to the whole bunch of us on the corporate executive board of directors, and even I, as their Chief Executive Officer, am totally concerned as all hell and get out, with what all is going on between them and us, or, between us and them, whichever, but to remember that old real estate saying that it is all about location, location, location, when it comes to the horn, or, the cape, whichever, as future real estate there will always be in the vogue until the close of the ice age on into the distant future, when the time comes that the ice melts and the seas rise, and they are get flooded out, but by then, they all will probably have some kind of federally required flood insurance to cover their wet asses, but disregard the "their wet asses" part and replace it with "the assessments of their wet assets" there. But no, that would put two theirs there, or two there's there, so strike one, whichever one you so choose, just for the record, whichever, or otherwise totally disregard, for the record."

Bobby responded. "Sir, the colonizers are already in there, about there or about out there, whichever, and, you know, first hand, that we do not have the weaponry to defeat such a highly technically advanced force at hand, and, I think, that most of them, or, some of them, or, part of them, whichever, are sick already, and, a couple or a few of them, or some of them, whichever, have already died off, as I myself have secretly witnessed their wakes, their hidden funerals and even their very hidden burials, and I have already introduced myself to a couple of their widows, a-tryin' to privately console them, but so far yet to no avail, but at least one of their husband's died off, still owin' me forty bucks, which I might add, as, he was fully indebted to me for tryin' to set him up with a couple of our lonely wannabee maidens a-lookin' forward eagerly to the practicin' methods of becomin' satisfying squaws. Too, I would suspect that more will also die off for one reason or another, before the winter is fully out, but no offense to be taken by that in the event that they hear some about it all, and, that the occasion will all but deplete their forces to some extent, with the hopes held out, that the shooters will not always keep their powder dry and the others will have trouble hittin' a moving

target, not to mention those who lied about their eye sight on their security guards concealed carry application forms with the TSA, but disregard or cancel out, whichever, the mention of the TSA, as I do not think it has ever officially yet been so designated as such under our own Homeland Security Agency, or theirs either for that matter, or more than likely may never come to be, whichever, as things like that may not come fully into fruition on into the future, or, for years to come, whichever, and, may not even be sustainable or workable, then, whichever, due to the taxation without representation budget constraints and their contract overruns because of their outsourcing."
The Chief argued in response to Bobby. "But what of the come of the Spring? Do we just tuck our tails and wait? Just sit on our hands? Do we just hide and watch? Do we just wait and see? Do we just hurry up and wait? Whichever, or whatever, will prevail sooner or later, either here or there. We have no guarantee of any potential North American Trade Agreement on into the future with that bunch of yahoos, but please disregard that name and strike it from the record, as it may not be politically correct, on or into the future with those folks, but then, on the other hand, they offer us nothing more than a bunch of beads like those other boatloads of similar folks that came here looking for gold of all things. Those folks, at least came and went, but maybe, if we pray for a slow cold end to the winter, and the Great White Father in the Happy Hunting Grounds grants it all, then, and maybe then, this whole bunch will just give up and go back from where they came from or go to where they were supposed to go on to in the first place, sometime later on in the spring when their ship sets sail, with the better part of them, or, better yet, all of them hopefully, riding out on the same boat that they rode in on."
Bobby argued back as best he could and still retain some respect of or for his elder, whichever. "Well, for some reason, organized as they are, I think that this bunch has all but come to stay, either that so accomplished, or, they do not get paid for their effort at all, and, as that is their main driver, as, it is all about the money, and you know, sir, that to learn anything at all, all you have to do is follow the money, look at the location that they have accessed to date, it is all about the beach front property on both sides, back to back if you will, all along the horn of the Cape of Cod, and, like you said, and, I agree, it is all about location, location, location. But, yet, and, too, I think that there is something about it all, that their endeavor may be more of a religious thing with this particular group, and that is most likely the worst kind if you know anything' at all about their religions. If

they cannot think up any other reason to stay or do anythin', they will call it their religious obligation or duty, whichever, and come and go, as if they were on a mission from and for God himself, and then they will put out a request to have the next ship over to send more black powder and more buckshot for their muskets and more modern blunderbusses for them to help their God out on his assigned mission in order to do his will. Yet, with all said, there is the possibility, that we will all have more than hell to pay in the end overall, but with no pun intended here or there, whichever, but there may be in the long run, more buckshot burning our naked warriors butts for the lonely maidens to slowly and feverishly pick out fervently, on a night after night basis, with more and more screamin's, groanin's and moaning's with a few Oh's and Ah's thrown in on the side, all heard from dusk to dawn from within their darkened mud huts."

The Chief responded. "OK, so say, we let them winter over, in hopes of their leaving in the spring and going back with the boat they came in on, but what happens if things go well, and, they up and decide not to go back from whence they came or where they were supposed to go on to in the first place? Because, if they stay, we have an ongoing or never ending problem, whichever, as, not to even mention yet that none of them have even applied or made application for that matter, whichever, for an extended stay Visa or even an alien's driver's license, whichever, so, what do we do then?" As if he had added on the additional question, yet to be addressed after the fact, or, for something not previously mentioned, or not said a-forehand, whichever.

Bobby, in trying to continue to reason with the Chief, countered with. "Well, we can always overcome them with blunt force by numbers if we wait until Spring, when the snow birds return from their wintering over down south, but, bear in mind, that most of those are somewhat elderly and somewhat financially independent, or, if not help from them, maybe we can get some volunteer help from what is left of the rowdy Mohawks in the hills up north with their Green Mountain Boys, or, to the Narangansetts from the fishin' bays further on down south, even if we have to pay for their services, just for them to show up as a fair farce for a show of force, as, we have only allowed what has happened to date by accepting it, but, they can't say that we still haven't tried to get along with the whole nutty munch bunch, but still, even now, we still have, at present, still the greater number by force, even still without either outside help from the north or south, east or west, still, but still not too far east, or, still, too far south, just to keep the disagreeable Massachusuits out of the picture, but still, just to keep it on this continent, but still, too, you should still remember, still, the Pilgrims still have the greater range of weapons, but, still again, I still remind you, that they still may not always keep their powder dry, and still, in this sea shore high humidity environment, still, their weapons still may not always work as they still planned, or still, they still may even run out of powder, as, England is still very far away, still, with no ships of record that we have still heard about, still coming to their aid, but, still, I think I may have used too many stills herein, so, cut out the ones you don't want or those you don't want to record. However, or anyway, whichever, or so, just kick out or throw out any othe of the stills that you so choose, whichever, although we still may be the superior force through nothing more than our numbers or our patience, whichever. So, I would still advise our group, not to not do anything inappropriate yet, to do nothing drastic, but to take a wait and see attitude, and, kick the can on down the road, trade today for a tomorrow, and wait for the sunset, if you will, looking for any or all of which things can or could happen, whichever to any or all, before you have to make a decision on any matter at hand, as time is on our side, remembering that we were here first, and, in that manner, many more of us can stay alive, including myself and some of my kin, with a few more of my cohorts thrown in on the side, just for good measure and just to boost up the count a little on any circulating petitions."

The Chief responded. "Again, I say, we presently have no treaty with this bunch, we have no written peace agreement of any kind, we only have verbal agreement with this one or that one, here and there, obtained now and then, and, we have not even sat down, either here or there, in a group or any official or unofficial pow-wow, whichever, for that matter, or, we have not even smoked the peace pipe with any of them, mainly because they all think that smoking tobacco is some kind of sin, whatever the definition of that is in their religion or belief, whichever, but, if it comes to it in the near future, I may just have to walk embarrassedly bare assed into their camp myself or have someone else do it first just to test the waters, or their waters, so to speak, so as to ask them flat out if we can come to some agreement or treaty to stop this ongoing insane nonsense. However, if you remember and I remind you, that you too should remember, as a comparative, that we had no problem whatsoever with Sir Walter Raleigh's group years ago, as, they more than readily smoked the peace pipe, but, there is just no trying to talk with this bunch, because they show no interest in learning our language, or, anything else about our culture or our way of life, whichever. It is a stalemate, I tell you, or else, it is an end run without a go or no go situation, with us mainly on the no go end, if you will, whichever, so, what is done is done, it is what it is, with no outlook for anything better out there on the horizon, except for more ships a-coming in, so, we will table the issue, wait it out, and sit it out on our sweaty clammy hands, whichever, and await the Spring. So, I hereby proclaim. Pass the word around the campfires and the windbreaks, for all of our clan, every one and all, to not have any more to do with the colonizers any more than what is absolutely necessary on a day to day basis, so as to protect our large breast interests and our best interests at large for the immediate moment, and, to wait and see what becomes of this group by Spring time."

He went on. "Pass the word or put out the order, whichever, for the shooters of arrows to cease their grievous aggravating activities, to suspend their aims, and to conserve their supply of sharp arrows for possible greater need some time on into the near future. Also, make sure that the women in general, if there were ever such a thing, along with those unattached teenage girls, those more recent widows, the squaw wannabees, the practicing maidens, and a few of those willing willowy wavering wives, whichever, are remanded to stay in camp and to not venture out in the corn fields and squash fields where they could be plainly seen during the soil tending and planting times, and, especially for them not to be seen bending over while in the bean or squash fields or while out picking up nuts, no pun intended, but just to be on the safe side, because we do not need to have any more accusations of any more maiden-nappin's or squaw catchin's, or any of them up lining up and a-holdin' up their hands to give any personal permission to volunteer themselves for such, or for any Pocahontas tryout or wet serape contests, whichever, other than what is absolutely necessary to keep the peace, yet, we still want to put our best foot forward and be a good prairie home companion to them all, so, assign the available women the duty in the program to treat the wounded warriors and to attend to those who are claiming some sort or some form of disability such as the recently reported post-traumatic stress disorders, whichever, just to keep them busy and to keep their hands and minds from wandering off too much in the wrong direction, and for one another to keep their hands to themselves where they belong, ust as long as they stay away from the colonizer's single males and those danged wild assed sea going sailor boys, boat jockeys or sea going bellhops, whichever, but, no offense intended to any one or all, but please do disregard the bellhop thing as that implies that there were some gung ho Hu-Rha Marines on board, may God forbid the day that they ever show up a-coming ashore in their Fleet Marine Force forced practiced beach landings comin' off'n their air-boats, but, disregard the last, the mention of the air-boat thing, as, I do not think that they have yet been invented or have been put into service, as of the latest wiki-spy reports or any of their unintended release of selective secret data, but also disregard that too as no offense is intended either here or there with the former sooner or the latter later as their national security agency has not yet been fully established according to the same report."

He went on. "But, if spring comes, and those folks are still here inhabiting our soil, we will approach them proudly, but very cautiously and very warily, whichever, or, on our own terms, as on some ruse or on some planned hoax, whichever, and, we will offer to try to help them some, any way that we can, and offer to teach them how to plant squash, corn, beans and greens, and maybe even turnips, whichever, supposedly for their food and sustenance, just to show the faith of our good will or our home made humble humanitarianism, whichever, but, in the process, for the near short term, we will keep our eyes and ears open, whichever, as to what they are up to, or, as to what they are going to do next, whichever. So be it, make it to be the order of the day for the future season for at least the next three moons, if it not be lunacy, and, I will get the corporate board members to agree to it all, even if I have to buy some of them off in the process with the promise of a couple of young maidens thrown in on the side, just to keep them warm on cold nights behind closed doors, but forget that I said that or disregard it, as corporate already has some executive directive regarding such an amenity, whichever, and by all means, please strike it from the record, as it may seem to be somewhat or more than sexist, whichever, officially, with the second part admitted with the third part omitted, or, the first part committed, either that, or, I will pass off some of my bead collection amongst them all just to keep the north American free trade agreement alive and kicking, but strike the north American thing and the trade agreement thing, as that is not yet fully official or even voted upon for that matter, whichever, on our side, even if we ever get to vote. Anyway, if I had a preference, to meet with them to explain it all, or meet with the

Harper Valley PTA, I would choose the latter, and could only hope that it so existed in our time to be able to deal with, so, disregard even the mention of such, and, strike the better part of the previous from the official record, just to be on the safe side."

"So be it to it all." Bobby replied, and, with that he formally excused himself and headed straight back, or, as straight as he could, to the warm camp fires near the wind breaks and picked the heated fire with the most identifiably single hot girls lined up at it just in case he got lucky, even if they were not totally hot to trot, with a plan already laid out to tell them about his fancy man cave and how they should or just had to, whichever, come and see it, look it over, or at least come over to help him decorate it a little better, whichever, and then, it all went on downhill from there, being that it was more than just a gross waste of time on his part, as, he might just as well went out and pounded sand down a rat hole for all the good that it did him, but still, holding out some small glimmer of hope, but yet, not holding his breath either, he left behind him, a trail of freshly cracked pecans from the camp fire all the way up to the door of his mud hut, for some hungry young maiden to make her way to and into or to just stop by or come in for a little visit just to satisfy her curiosity, along with a mid-night snack, whichever, for, tomorrow was yet to be another day awaiting.

Meanwhile, and, by this time, Eli and Tom were again busy down at the beach, trouncing around back and forth, hither and yon, here and there, whichever, doing this and that, now and then, but, mostly, looking here and about, for the lost hammer head, which was previously lost as was mentioned previous, and, which had been checked out from the quartermaster and yet to be accounted for, as it was presently unaccounted for, in the most previous inventory count.

"Tom, you line up the stakes, and I'll go down and look for the hammer head." Eli said.

"Move it on out Eli, the landing site was still further out." Tom said.

Tom, tried to line up the stakes that had been emplaced previous, then, moved over to the second set of stakes in order to try to line up the area where the hammer head went into the water.

"You are right at it Eli, move a little to the north. and, a little to your right, and you should be on it like hot spit on a grill." Yelled Tom.

"I see it, I can get it, I'm at it, I'm on it like stink, I have it, I got it, Tom, I got it in hand, and we have both together all but again for the second time in our recent past, yet again, saved the Pilgrim's day." Yelled back Eli as he held up the hammer head above his head, just to show Tom that he had a good handle on things and had the situation in hand, and was ahead of things, whichever.

With that, the two got back together, joined or regrouped up, whichever, and both headed back to the camp, connecting up the hammer head with the hammer handle by sticking the head end of the handle in the hole of the hammer head and holding it by the butt end, so as to make it look like it was all together, even though it was as loose as a goose, and to return it to the quartermaster to whom it was obtained previous all in acceptably good shape except for the keeper wedge not being stuck in the hammer head end of the handle.

"We totally done did lose the keeper wedge to keep the head on straight." Remarked Tom.

"Not done did, Tom, just plain totally did lose the keeper." Eli said. "I think I need a keeper wedge stuck in one of my ends just to keep my head on straight." Added Eli.

"Me too, especially when I'm around some of those hot girls flashing their sexy bare ankles out from under those long skirts, around the warming fires." Responded Tom, as they hustled on back to camp trying to get there before dark.

Then, the dreamer again, rousted a little, poked the pillow, but then, rolled over, and went back to sleep.

INTERESTING INTEREST

The dread was overwhelming. It had been almost seven years now, since Hank had modified the computer program systems for interests paid out. But now, today, years later, with all of the additional security checks and required balancing processes, he did not now have the authority to go back into the bank's computer system to be able to make any changes, which, was no little problem with respect to his situation.

He had no doubt, that he was one of the best accountants that his bank had ever hired. He had numbers, checks and balances, debits and credits, banging around in his head since he was in high school. He was the best in his class for all of the accounting majors in his college of choice. He knew what it took to balance a ledger. Other businesses had sought him out to work over their books and to do their quarterly accounting on the side, other than that of his job at the bank, which he did, just to make ends meet and to give him a little extra spending money.

But, it was his job at the bank that was creating his greatest dread. Someday, sometime soon, someone, would, most probably sooner than later, find some irregularity, then, an investigation would ensue, and, sooner or later, an irregularity with his name bouncing around on it, would pop up as he being a contributing party. He just knew it! There was no other way about it! He was to the point of not knowing what to do next. He went to work with it, he worked with it on his mind minute by minute, hour by hour, he went home with it, he went to sleep with it, and he woke up with it. It was more of a burden than what he ever thought that he could bear or endure.

Yet, he went on to work at the bank, day in and day out, always on time, renowned as the most punctual of all of their employees, he did his job, and he kept his mouth shut as to what was going on, hoping beyond all hope, that he could somehow correct the things that he had put into place some seven long years before, but, not knowing just how he could go about such under the new rules and guidelines of the banking policies put into place since the 9-1-1 security upgrade requirements.

He wished that he could go back in time, to that time where he first modified the computer programs, to change it back somehow, either then, or at least sometime during the seven years that had passed ever so quickly.

At first, at the outset, he rationalized in his own mind, that, he had done what he had done, in order to get back at the president of the bank for not offering him a promotion years ago that he felt was due him, and, especially, when he thought that he had certainly more than deserved it. He had been rejected, in his sight, as ultimately becoming an officer of the bank, a vice president no less, with some little authority. Instead, he was all but ignored, and, passed over, and his feelings were not just hurt, they were absolutely destroyed at the time, as he saw it, and, he had no choice but to get even. This attitude did not bother him at all, although he knew, that, a get even attitude was one of the first ear marks of a criminal mind, but then, he never ever considered himself such.

Now, in the here and now, seven long years later, he was in the same position that he had been in since he had been hired almost fifteen years ago. A lot had changed, various people had come and gone, but, he and the president were the only original employees left in the management of this branch of the bank. He had bent over backwards, just to continue to get along with the president and the bank board, specifically the chairman of the board, who, at the time, had also negated his promotion from the get-go. However, it was also the president of the board, who did not stand up for him, or, give him the most needed recommendation for the promotion. He saw no reason for any of their actions or their lack of actions against him. That, partly, was the cause of him taking the action that he took, to get even, to get back at them, to try to hurt them in some way just as he had been hurt. It was more than just personal, with nothing against the bank itself, but, those in charge were the ones who had brought about his great pain and his daily misery.

He thought again, about what it was that he had done. He had actually stolen the bank president's identification, outright, no less. At the time, it was all but pure luck that he had found the bank president's driver's license laying on the floor one day, and, seized upon the opportunity and the very moment which presented itself to somehow eventually get even. It was his get even attitude that kept him going day in and day out. He had taken the president's driver's license, left from work at lunch time, went to the State's licensing registration, showed them the driver's license and requested an additional identification card which had no expiration date. The driver's license photo was old and they could not tell whether or not that he was really him or not as the photo was poor, as was with all driver's license photos, and, with little ado, they took his photo and put the president's address and other information on the identification card, charged him fifteen dollars, and issued him the ID card. Then, he returned to work, and acted as if he had "found" the president's driver's license on the floor in the hallway, and, returned it to him, a goodwill gesture but with a hidden agenda. Simple sure, but yet, it was a guaranteed old fashioned and sure way of stealing someone's identification. As part of his job as an accountant, he had access to all accounts at the bank, and, he accessed the president's accounts, and, got his social security number which sealed up the identification theft. Up to this time, he had not yet committed any crimes that he could have been directly charged for, as, he could destroy the identification card, and claim ignorance otherwise as no transactions had taken place up to that time. He was all set and good to go for whatever came next.

It was later on, when he had gotten a little more grit and gumption, that he went into the banks computer program files, and modified the interest pay out parameters in order to accumulate funds and to eventually transfer those funds from one account to another and to ultimately transfer funds from his bank to another bank, and, do it all electronically at will. As more and more of the accounts became accessible by the computer system, the transfers became even easier from any location or any computer, and, he had all of the necessary passwords.

From that early point in time, it was somewhat mixed up in his mind as to when he did this or when it was that he did that, but, that the dates and times were surely registered somewhere within the banks records. His original scheme, was, to make it look like that the president of the bank, was embezzling funds in a somewhat articulate manner. With this in mind, he then opened accounts at other banks, and began the transfer of funds from his bank into the other bank accounts.

When he had first modified the parameters of every interest bearing account at the bank, he had expanded the interest accounting from two decimal points to four decimal points, to be paid out according to the two decimal point interest paid, with the remainder of interest points to be paid and shuffled into an alphabetical account rather than a numbered account, but dispersed daily as the accounts became due on their monthly or quarterly payout period.

He went over in his mind again, as to how he did it all. One account was a good example, as, the account had $97,458. in it at 3.64% interest. The account paid out that percentage of interest in the first quarter of $886.8678, however, the .0078 was never seen or heard from again, as, the computer program rounded the interest down to the two points in the cents range, at $.86, and then , took the remaining four points of $.0078 and transferred the amount into the alphabetized account. The alphabetized account would never show up in the numerical accounts record when the accounting run was completed on a daily basis. The value of the amounts were minimal, at the outset, however, when it was taken into account for more than a hundred thousand transactions, on thousands of accounts on a monthly and quarterly basis, the small amount added up very quickly, with interest gained on the previous interest paid, and, especially when there were ongoing transfers and transactions where people were shuffling their money in order to gain the greatest amount of return by the interest, by closing one account and opening another.

At that time, seven years ago, the scheme was set into motion. The funds would be collected on a daily basis, then, transferred to another branch of the bank disguised as a balance of interest applied to funds on deposit, but with the balance being accumulated at the other branch, under the name of and in the president's account which he had opened surreptiously in order for him to make it look like the president was embezzling funds when it was all eventually found out. The plan was in place and the transfers were ongoing and in process. Funds were accumulating in the other branch's accounts. The plan was functioning and in process, and, had been ongoing up to now for seven long years. Along the way, he withdrew funds from the accounts and held the cash in hundred dollar bills.

But, all of that was some seven years ago, when the crooked man plan began. Now, the accounts had gained greater numbers, and, at last check, the funds had approached three hundred thousand dollars which were deposited and withdrawn from the president's hidden accounts as cash paid out on a weekly basis. To date, as far as he knew, as there were no inquiries that he could account for, and, no one had picked up on the simple electronic scheme to date. He wondered why. Why was there no interest in the accounting mumbo-jumbo that he had set up? Why was there no ongoing investigation? He had thought, that the president would have been "found out" and an investigation into his embezzling would have been forthcoming at least by this time, but, yet, nothing. Had his attempt to somehow accuse the president of absconding with funds, fallen short somehow, or, fallen by the wayside never to be found? He looked at the accounts and they were all there, in order and untouched with cash money being withdrawn on a weekly basis under the president's name. The adjustment of the parameters on interest had filled the unnumbered alphabetical accounts to the brim within the last seven or eight years or so from more than forty-seven thousand accounts registered with his bank. The money that he had withdrawn from the accounts now totaled more than the three hundred thousand dollars, in cold hard cash, and, he now had three milk cartons with more than the a hundred thousand dollars in one hundred dollar bills stashed away in each milk carton on a shelf in his garage at his home. Now, he was to the point of not knowing what to with all of the cash money. The only salvation to the dilemma to date was, that the lower interest rates had slowed the transfer of money and, the amount of funds transferred, had somewhat dwindled.

It was more than past time, he thought, for him to consult an attorney. However, he did not exactly know just how to explain it all. He could say, that he had become aware of the possible abscondment, but, then, he would have to explain how he had come to know about it all without an audit being called for. He had looked in the yellow pages, had made a couple of initial calls, but, when the question was asked as to what the problem was, and, he could not readily explain it at all. Or, better yet, he did not want to spill his guts and explain it at all. He just wanted to point the finger and to get the president of the bank investigated for criminal activity, and, maybe even get him fired from his job, just to get rid of him, and, maybe even the chairman of the bank board along with the president. That was his aim, that's what his plan was all about early on from the get-go. However, so far, after more than seven years, nothing had happened, absolutely nothing. He did not understand the why or the why not of the matter. Perhaps the FBI was just sitting there, waiting for some false move by him, or to be there, when he made the transfer of some of the money or when he walked in to get some cash in marked one hundred dollar bills and walked out with them in his pocket, so, he now quit even doing that and was just letting the money accumulate in the accounts.

Finally, he called one attorney, a criminal defender of some note, one who had made some news in recent criminal prosecutions where he had gotten the defendant off with little or no penalty. This was what he needed, he thought. He realized that he needed such, just in case, that the tables were turned on him and he was found out to be the party of the first part which set up the phony deal so as to accuse the president of some criminal activity. He realized that he needed some guarantee that he would be able to be gotten off of any pointy fingers coming back at him into the near future. After all, his retirement was at stake, he was just a year off of qualifying for full retirement at age fifty-five, and, he did not want to lose everything that he had worked for over the last twenty years or so. Yet, he still had envious animosity in his heart. He was still hurt by being overlooked for the position of a vice presidency years ago. He knew, down deep in his heart and in the back of his mind, that the original rejected promotion was primarily because of the president's required recommendation, or lack of recommendation, that had cost him that significant promotion years and years ago.

So, he made an appointment with the criminal attorney, and arranged the appointment to be after his work hours at the bank so that there would not be any conflicts.

He arrived at the attorney's office on time, and waited to be called. Then, when called into conference with the criminal attorney, he felt down deep inside of himself, that he was not yet fully prepared.

The first question out of the attorney's mouth was. "What is the problem?"

In order to try to answer, he began to explain the problem, which, the more he talked, the less it sounded like a problem. He reiterated as to what it was that he was aware of, what he did and how it all came about.

The attorney asked. "Where is the money now?"

He responded. "Well, there is about a hundred and fifty thousand, left in the account at the second bank in three different accounts, with about three hundred thousand in cash, in three different milk cartons stashed on a shelf in my garage at home. Right at one hundred thousand in one hundred dollar bills in each of the three milk cartons, with the hundred dollar bills all rolled up with rubber bands around them."

"OK." The attorney said. "I'll take your case on thirds. If you come out on the positive side, I get one third of whatever is left. If you come out on the negative side, you have to do my taxes for the next ten years. Is that a deal or what?"

"Agreed." He said.

"OK." The attorney said. "The first thing we need to do is to notify the FBI."

"The FBI!" He yelled. "Why does the FBI need to be involved?" He asked.

The attorney responded. "Look, if we are the first ones to notify the FBI, it will be in our favor, rather than the bank notifying the FBI, then, secondly, they will choose to notify the bank as to our discovery. At this time, our story has to be, that we do not know, for sure, just how this all came about. Perhaps, the bank president himself, did indeed open the accounts and set up the scheme, then, perhaps, he did not. That is not for us to say one way or the other. Either way, the FBI will have been apprised by us, and, not by them. So, the investigatory aspect of the case will be against them, or him, rather than back at us, or, you. You want to get some train of thought going off in the right direction, if you can do that, the damned train will keep going until it eventually runs off the track, and, you and I will be totally out of earshot and not be present at the time. Do you get my gist?"

"Well, if you say so, I mean, you are the only authority that I have right now." He said.

The attorney called the local FBI office. He asked that an agent meet at the attorney's office as soon as one was available. Which, was almost immediate as their downtown office was nearby. It was almost as if the local FBI office and their agents had been more or less sitting on their hands in their local office, just waiting for something like this to break out into the opening.

The agent showed up at the attorney's office within a half an hour, and was ushered in by the receptionist.

The story was passed to the agent, as having been a "finding" by the accountant. The accountant's verbiage addressed the issue as being what he considered to be a banking irregularity, but also mentioned the bank president being the center of attention in the matter as a side note.

The FBI agent indicated that he thought that he had enough information to pass on to his supervisor but requested a temporary leave of absence from the initial meeting to apprise his superior of the matter. With that, he left, promising to return within the hour.

In the meantime, the attorney notified the banks attorney, who, in turn, notified the appointed officers of the bank and the banks board members accordingly. The banks attorney then called back to say that if the FBI had been notified, that they requested an agents presence if and when the banks representatives met and requested that their attorney would also be present. The attorney agreed to their requests and invited an open forum for any discussion on the matter.

He literally did not or could even second guess as to what was to happen next. However, his attorney indicated that things were going as well as could be expected and to remain calm and to go out for a drink or two if he was feeling somewhat nervous. Which he did without further ado and did more than just two without further ado.

Upon his return, from the local bar just around the corner, he noticed that the FBI agent and his supervisor were already in the conference room for the big meeting. He joined them albeit somewhat dizzily. Shortly thereafter, the banks attorney arrived and introduced himself, followed by the officers of the bank and members of the board that were available at the time.

After a short discussion as to whether or not there was a quorum present or not, and, whether or not there were present proper officers of authority, and the fact that the attorney was present, it was announced that the representatives were present and requested that the matter be presented before the group.

The attorney stood up at the end of the table, and said, blankly, "Gentlemen, I am here, to address the announcement of an irregularity of which you may yet not have been aware of, and, with the assistance of my client who can perhaps help explain such irregularity." He said.

The attorney for the bank was the first to respond. "Please explain to us, those present, as to the so called irregularity, if you would so please." He said.

The attorney stood up at the end of the table and said. "Gentlemen, there appears, to have been, some irregularity, having occurred sometime in the recent past, which re-calculates the percentage interest paid to your banks clients, to the extent, that some overages not otherwise to be accounted for, have been transferred into other accounts at other bank offices. These overages have accumulated in none other than the bank presidents named accounts and remain so to this date." He said.

The banks president responded. "I have several accounts at the bank which are open to discussion, which account is it to which you refer?" Immediately, the banks attorney put his hand on the bank presidents shoulder, pushed him back into his seat, and put his finger over his mouth, indicating that the bank president should keep his mouth shut.

The banks attorney responded. "Please define the specifics of the irregularity for the audience." He said.

The attorney then turned to his client. "Sir, would you be so kind as to please define the specifics of the irregularities as you have found such." He said.

The client stood. "I am the senior accountant for your bank. I have come upon a number of accounts of some origin. The accounts seem to have the mechanism within itself, to calculate the percentage interest to the forth and sometimes to the fifth decimals. However, only the calculation to the second decimal is passed on to the primary members accounts, whereas, the remainder of the third, fourth and fifth decimal points, are passed on to the accounts in question, accruing value to such and all of which are being in the president's name.

"I don't know of any such accounts with my name on it other than my personal accounts! What is the value of these accounts?" He yelled.

The attorney again stood up and announced. "The value of the accounts are in access of one hundred thousand dollars, has not been accessed in the last few years, and, continues to grow in value dependent upon current interest rates." He said.

"I don't have any accounts with a hundred thousand dollars in them!" Yelled the bank president.

The banks attorney again put his hand on the shoulder of the bank president and pushed him down back into his seat. "Has there been any dispersal on this account, or, has there been any interest reported to the IRS on the account?" He asked.

The attorney deferred to the client for an answer. "The account appears to have been set up as an IRA account, which does not require the reporting of interest gained to be reported to the IRS." He said.

"I do not have an IRA account at the bank other than the one that I am presently enlisted in!" The bank president yelled. Again, the banks attorney put his hand on the bank president's shoulder and again pushed him back into his seat, again putting his finger on his mouth indicating for the bank president to keep his mouth tightly shut on any further matter.

The attorney again stood up, and said. "The problem with the irregularity, is, what to do about it? Where will the money be transferred? The only authority for any further transfer is in the name of the bank president. What is to be said for the disposition of the funds that are to remain?"

The FBI agent stood up. "The funds, in the one hundred thousand dollar range, appear to be, at present, in the banks president's name. I hereby request a run on the activity of the account over the period as indicated as to the life of the account." He said.

The client, now knew, that he had been had. The account was more than seven years old, activity on the account would show dispersals, it would show withdrawals, it would show transfers, it would show everything, and, sooner or later, it would show his name, and, his end would soon be in site. His ass was grass, the thought.

The bank president again raised his voice. "Have the accountant, the finder of the so called irregularity, here and now, run the activity on the account, and, see what transpires. Do it now, before this group, before any accusations ensue, before any wrong doings are brought forth, before any further irregularities are exposed." He said.
The attorney again deferred to the client, and, the client was assigned

374

to access the banks records on the aforementioned account by way of the computers available from the attorney's office. The first access of the account revealed that there was no loss to the banks funds as had been previously suspected. The second drilling in of the access of the account indicated that there was an excess only being applied to the value of the accounts. The third access of the accounts indicated some small early withdrawals under the name of the bank president, but transferred to other accounts or paid out in cash. The interest of which as applied were reported to the IRS on the president's yearly taxes. It appeared that the remainder or the balance only appeared to be IRA funds and to be non-taxable with the remainder being transferred to accounts which reported interest paid, and, the proper tax forms had been prepared and taxes paid on the remainder of the withdrawals by the president of the bank.

"I have always paid my taxes!" The president yelled.

The banks attorney again stood and pressed the bank president back into his seat by pressing against his shoulder. "Please be seated." He said.

The FBI agent stood. "If taxes have been paid on all withdrawal transactions over the years since the account was initiated, there is no need to advise the IRS of any further information except for their normal advisement requirements as they already have that information." He said.

The banks attorney stood. "It appears, that there is a legitimate account in the name of the president of the bank, which has in excess of one hundred thousand dollars, which has had all taxes paid over the years since such account was established, against any transfers or withdrawals, and, which is still active as we speak. However, under bank rules, any account which is unknown, even by the owner, not having activity over a previous period of one year, may be accessed by the State and released to the State accordingly."

"Hold on, hold on!" Yelled the bank president. "Let the interpretation of that requirement be at the discretion of the bank and its officers, please." He said.

The clients attorney stood. "We have reported to you, without further ado, what we thought to be an irregularity within your banking system. However, after further investigation and insight, we find that this is a banking systems problem, rather than a regulated systems problem, which, at first sight might seem irregular, however, upon second viewing, we at this time find no irregularities to report further, and, we are sorry for taking up your precious time in regard to this matter." He said.

The bank president stood up but not calling him by name, said. "Accountant. Accountant. Get me the account number of the aforementioned account in question, and have all the information on my desk with all particulars at the beginning of the day tomorrow, at your earliest convenience in the morning, if you please!"

The clients attorney again stood. "With that, if there are no further questions, we now dismiss any further comment with regards to the aforementioned potential alleged irregularity but which appeared to be not so in any manner and we apologize for the alarm of our indiscretion."

Everyone got up to leave. The client held back. After everyone had left the conference room he asked. "So, what do I do now?" He said to his attorney.

The client's attorney looked at him and said. "Well, you have to report to work tomorrow morning, and provide the president with information on his account. In addition, you have to provide me with the one-third of your cash stash in milk cartons on the shelf in your garage, whatever that may be, post haste." He said.

So, in the end, the president of the bank, came out of the woods with more than a hundred thousand dollars in his account, and, the clients attorney came out with just as much, and, the client came out with almost twice as much as the two of them put together, and, he still had his job and his retirement was assured and all remained legitimate, above board, within all banking regulations, IRS requirements and FBI oversight, and, the accountant was still scheduled to do the bank president's taxes again next year.

THE FIRST AND LAST INTERVIEW OF THE PATIENT

The dream began innocent enough, but became somewhat confusing and less innocent the longer that it dragged on, until such time as the dreamer had had it up to the gills, realizing that he was dreaming and eventually woke himself up, only to roll over and drop off to sleep again, continuing on into a more darker part of the dream.

Now, as it was, the interviewer appeared early, purposely so, so as not to miss such an important assigned appointment, along with her habit of being overly conscientiously punctual. A neophyte, the interviewer had been assigned the task, as it had been rejected by all of the other reporters for the newspaper. It was her first ever outside-on-the-spot interview and, she was to follow it up with the writing of a number of editorial pieces for the newspaper concerning the asylum's patients and their concerns by using material from just one of them. She did not know how she was going to accomplish the task, just yet, but was more than just up to the challenge. She was also more than obviously nervous as she waited at the prison gate for a guard to escort her to the interview area.

The guard arrived on time as he was assigned, and, the interviewer was escorted from the Asylum's front gate waiting room, down through several turning passageways until they arrived at the interview room. The guard asked her if she wanted a cup of coffee, water or a soda, which she declined, then, the escorting guard bid his best wishes and left the room, returning to his duty elsewhere.

Shortly thereafter, another guard, from the other side of the room, on the cell side, entered through the opposite door and introduced himself. "Good morning Miss, I'm Sergeant Simpson, and, I have seen your clearance to be here and for you to interview one of our patients who goes by the nickname Harlan, as his real name is Henry. However, I must tell you, that this particular individual, who has been selected for your interview, has been legally adjudged by our glorious State, to be bonafidedly insane. Very few herein have ever attained such a significant designation, although there are some here that could do so if they really tried or honestly answered the questions they were asked on examination. But, not to be curt or to offend you in any way, I feel that I must give you an example of some of the tests which were run on the particular prisoner you are about to interview. Please be advised, that this information is not any violation of the Privacy Act, because, if you but ask him, Harlan will tell you the same. So far, I think he has told everyone that he has met over the last few years. For instance, when he was given a set of ink blot tests, he declared that he had never seen so many pictures of piles of dead puppies in his entire life time, and, remarked, that a couple of them could have been mistaken by him for drowned baby kittens instead, and, he felt deeply offended by whomever was in charge, for having been shown such pictures in the first place. So, that is only one example, as, there are others, which he may relate to you, just as gruesome, so, you are hereby forewarned. I have always said, that it is heartwarming that forewarned is to be forearmed. You may also find it interesting to know, that Harlan was struck by lightning when he was thirteen years of age, while disking corn on the third of July. He survived, but barely, as it has been reported. The lightning strike knocked unconscious the two horses he was driving, along with Harlan. Supposedly, when he awoke from his unconscious state, he saw the two horses and thought that they were dead. Then, he thought himself to most likely be a ghost. Even today, in his older years, he still sees flashes of light which cause him to believe that the gods, or, perhaps The God Himself, is sending him a message. The physicians feel that this may be part of his overall problem."

He hesitated, looked about, then, continued. "Now, the patient will be brought in, hand cuffed at hand and foot with restraint devices, and, will be positioned at the other end of the table from you, and, he will be also secondarily handcuffed to that ring you see mounted on the table top. Also, there is a ring mounted in the floor that his feet will be foot cuffed to, so, you have no worry that he could possibly make an attempt to attack you in any way, except perhaps verbally. The reason for this level of security is, that Harlan as an incarcerated patient, has escaped from this asylum on too many embarrassing occasions and we have not yet figured out as to just how he does it, so, with that, it is my hope, that with that information, it should make you feel a little more secure, being in the room with him alone and asking questions that he generally does not answer well. In addition, I might add, that when he does make his escapes good, and, when he gets caught in the process, he tells his captors that he is, of all things, their guardian angel, possibly and supposedly, just to throw them off, to get them to let their guard down, or maybe just to get on their soft side, in doing so, some even let him go, or, on more than just one occasion, some have even invited him into their home, with more than just one of those times being for coffee or tea. That is just the kind of patient that he is, so, that about sums it all up in a nut shell, but, no pun intended. Do you have any questions?"

The interviewer shook her head responding in the negative, and, the Sergeant said. "By the way, in case you missed my previous comment, the patient goes by his nickname of Harlan." He then departed back through the door from whence he came.

The interviewer waited patiently, albeit nervously, for the prisoner to be brought forth and wrote "Harlan's Interview", on top of her writing pad. Her first glimpse that she caught of Harlan was through the reinforced glass on the cell side, her vision showed the patient being led in chains down the hallway toward the interview room. The patient was escorted into the room by two guards, side by side, and front and back as they came through the door, who also assisted him to sit in a chair at the other end of the table, she noticed that both the table and the chair were purposely fitted for the shackles on his legs and arms that he had on, and, with adjacent rings and cuffs, to secure him to the table and also to the floor, so as, that he could not readily move, and, could not even stand up or scratch his butt or pick his nose. Once the guards had the prisoner secured, with chain, lock and key, the guards then excused themselves, and, left the room from the same door of which they had entered, only one of them even glancing back, and, nodding that the situation was well in hand, and saying somewhat off the cuff, that the interviewer was then free to begin her job. The interviewer, first looked the patient over, was surprised that he appeared older not only by his looks, but also by his movements, she found him otherwise to be of normal physique and stature, and noted his bushy hair and green eyes, which seemed to stare through her or maybe he just looking somewhere off far in the distance behind her. It was, what it was, an old prison, converted into an asylum for the insane, with too many totally insane patients inside, and, with an insane patient to interview, with that, the interviewer began her job.

She started. "Well, hello Harlan, I know your name is Harlan not only from the guard's slight introduction but also from the letter you wrote some time ago to the Evening Gazette, and, I have it here." She held the letter up for Harlan to see. "I am Anelia, but, most folks just call me Nellie, which I do not mind in the least. Is it OK for me to call you Harlan?" She asked.

"Yes." Harlan said.

She continued. "OK then, Harlan, the way your interview was set up, was, that the editors and staff at the Evening Gazette all read your letter, then, they thoughtfully composed some questions for me to ask of you, all based upon the information you provided in your letter. Do you have any objections to that?" She asked.

"No." Harlan said

She replied. "Well, with that in mind, and with that understanding, I will begin your interview as agreed." Then, she opened her notebook and asked her first question.

"First things first, Harlan, who are you anyway, and, what is it that you represent other than just being a patient here in this asylum, reported by you in your letter to be held against your will as some common prisoner, but not yet having been charged, arraigned, found guilty of something or one thing or another, like some unforgivable sin itself, but not yet sentenced for some rather peculiar odd-ball or off-the-wall committed crime?" She asked.

"Well, to answer the first part of your question first, some say, that I am both a patient, and yet, others say that I am also a prisoner too, which it feels more like." Harlan said. "But, adding on to the first part firstly, and mostly foremost, I am being held, not just held against my will as "a messenger", I am held against my will as, "The Messenger", so, please, of all things, do not kill "The Messenger" which brings about messages of which there is no choice but for him to deliver, and, I want that to be known up front and honest, and for sure, especially with footnotes added in about the not killing the messenger part."

He went on. "Otherwise, some folks may think, that I am some kind of guru, some kind of prophet, or, even worst, some kind of alien, or perhaps, something even more strange, as perhaps, someone who has come back from the future, or maybe some spirit erupted from some dark past life, or, someone from another dimension, or, one which has been called out from some dark cold grave by some Tarot card shuffling gypsy even, or, someone with a couple of devils or demons or two or more each in them scrambling to get out, which I am not, have not, of none, or either, neither, and never have been, under any circumstance, so, that has to be first fully understood by all who ever hear of this, of that of which I am most compelled to mention, just to cover my locked up poor bare ass up front."

He continued. "I am here, amongst my fellow men, not of, or by my own volition, because I had no control of that whatsoever, and, I might add, those who have been instrumental in containing me have yet to find some charge to bring against me, but, never-the-less, by some of the unknown and unused or under used rules of life itself, of which rules, no one on the face of this planet have yet come to understand to date, not even those historically great wise rulers, have ever fully understood themselves, neither the Knights of Columbus, nor, the Masons, with all of their secrets piled up atop one another and all together, nor, those two-thirds Irish members of the Ancient Order of Hibernians, nor, those Germanic minded Rosicrucian's, nor even the Illuminati or those suspected of being such, nor that Great All Seeing Eye of ancient Egypt which following worshippers observed the Sun and starred at it until they all went blind as a bat with a bad sunburn." The patient then stopped talking, somewhat abruptly, and starred at the opposite wall as if looking for a slide Power Point presentation to be projected upon it.

The interviewer looked at her notes, and asked the patient the next question. "Harlan, in your letter to the editor of the Evening Gazette, you say, or mention, therein, that living things on this planet, are not of this planet, or, did not have its origination here, could you please explain how you came to such an unheard of assumption?"

Harlan seemingly came back to himself, looked down at the table, and answered. "It may have been thousands upon thousands of years ago, perhaps even millions, or more, all of which has been lost to time itself, as, I can't remember all of that bullshit, to any matter of record for that matter, of any part of history, written or oral, where my many forefathers and all of their mothers and other brothers, were sent so long ago, and, were brought here to this planet, which they eventually came to call Earth, which, you will find, in future research, if the Earth lasts that long, that we all, as humans, surprisingly, originated someplace else, and were brought here and transplanted here, and, too, they will find, that, they did not all come here at the same time, and even some of the DNA that is seen today, was old even before it ever first arrived here, but, I suspect, that in the long run, we will all wish that we had or had not of came here at all, as, we will all probably leave it the same manner as those dearly departed left us when they took their last deep sleep, but most likely not at the same time, that it, unless the Sun dies off of some peculiar premature internal demise, and swell up all red and consumes us all."

He went on. "The cold hard fact is this, that we, or they, all of our ancestors, were all sent here as prisoners, we, or they, and, I say we to denote those in the present and they to denote those in the past, were the outcasts, as a rejected group at any given time, we, or they, were once considered, less than civil and not allowed to participate further in the society from which we, or they, came, all cast out, unwanted for ever more in all ways. When the prisons from whence we, or they, came, became full, we, or they, were all loaded up on the great ships which brought us, or them, here and dumped our sorry asses, or them, all out here and there, hither and yon, to fend for ourselves and themselves in all ways sorrowful. But, we, or they, were not alone in that respect, not only us, but, every other form of life, which did not meet the expectations of that Great Civil Society from which we or they came, were also rejected and sent here, every man, animal, insect, serpent, fish, bird, plant, creepy crawly scrawny hairy thing or whatever. However, nothing came all at once or at the same time, neither did all of the insects, neither did all of the birds, although, they were some of the earlier arrivals, neither did all of the mammals, neither did all of the fishes, neither did the serpents or the lizards, although, some of them were early starters, or, those other things, whatever you wish to call those other things that crawl on their belly like a reptile, neither did the trees or plants, or, for that matter, neither did the rest of the unmentioned living things of today, and, researchers will also find, that those things neither originated here, but were just set out here like someone setting out plants in the Spring time, for that matter, but came, wave by wave by wave, in the prison ships too numerous to mention, or even count, or even recall, from somewhere else somewhat afar off in the cosmos, with no hope whatsoever of ever returning to that Great Civil Society, because the ones who brought us, or them, took their conveyances back with them to gather up another load. Far enough away that they could never expect is to ever return. Except that one that had Noah on it, as it sat for years, broke down, way up on the side of Mount Ararat, until, maintenance personnel from that Great Civil Society came and finally got it running again and then took it back with them. So, this planet, in that manner, became an assigned prison for all of the rejected life forms as we have come to know it, present and accounted for on planet Earth just awaiting their time to go extinct." He said.

"I'm not sure that I can assimilate all of that in my notes here, or in my mind either, for that matter, but, let us go on. Where do you see all of this earth prison stuff of which you speak, all going on into the future or us in this world?" She asked.

"Every living thing on the face of the Earth, is here, in the now, as I have said a-previous, because all of it, every last bit of it, was once rejected from that Great Civil Society, and was sent here to be imprisoned, because it was wild, because it was uncivil, because it was rebellious, inconsiderate, or because of it was hostile, or because of it was rude, or, it was antagonistic, it being belligerent, it being a liar, a killer, a thief, a burglar, dishonest, unforgiving, mean, downright dilatory in all of their ways. It was this type of behavior which got our first ancestors and everything sent along with them, sent here to this prison planet in the first place, and, it is yet what it is that keeps us here. Time to time, the ships may come, and abduct some of us, as we see it, to examine and see if those negative things are out of our psychological and physiological system, only to return to from whence they came, empty, leaving us to continue our sentences and our eventual extinction if we do not change our dyed in the wool bad habits and our weary wanton ways." He said.

"OK Harlan. OK, I think I get it. I get your message or at least the better part of it about the prisoner thingy. But, we need to get down to specifics, brass tacks kinds of things, right now and here before you done up and lose the readers short attention span. In your letter to the editor at the Gazette, you mentioned global warming, which is a hot topic right now. What do you have to say about the global warming thing?" She asked. "And, please stick to the specifics, if you understand what I mean, and, try not to ramble so much, as my notes are already more than a mess." She added.

Harlan responded. "Everything that I have been allowed to read or view on the news, seems to show that global warming, is a "primary" problem facing the world and caused by and blamed on society as a whole. Everything I have seen or heard for that matter, has been opinion, and, if you bought those opinions at a dime a dozen, you would be paying too much of a premium. At this time, and, I speak of a period of the last few tens of thousands of years, the Earth is now proceeding on, right nicely, I might add, going through the end of another ice age. I say, "another", because, the Earth has went through numerous, several, quite a few, a bunch, a whole lot, many, just to be redundant, because, the ice ages themselves are redundant happenings as the Earth grows older. However, this time, is the first time, that it is happening in recorded history as far as we know it. Scientists are now documenting the happenings. Never before has such been recorded as far as we know from even the oldest archeological digs, as, the last time that it happened, the folks around at that time did not have their shit together, and, the thing happened so fast that they didn't even know that the shit had hit the fan. They had other things on their pallet besides just reading and writing. They were out scrambling just to find their next meal, kill of some mastodon, and to get to someplace warm and to stay out of the path of some predator out and about trying to find its next meal and find someplace warm, either that, or they were out and about dodging incoming meteorites. So, nothing previously was ever recorded about what happens on Earth when an ice age ends. Scientists today, can only try to reason it all out and argue it all out amongst themselves. Yet, there are some surprises, such as, the abrupt changes in the weather, which, when you think about it, should not be a surprise to anyone at all."

He went on. "Now, just think about it. If the temperature of the oceans rise, the water, covering two-thirds of the earth will expand with the heat of it. Land will be inundated because of that alone, not from the reported melting of the ice caps of the Arctic and the Antarctic. The oceans will become less salty and slushier but will be more susceptible to algae bloom. If we have abrupt weather changes, then, there could possibly be droughts, floods, intense storms, and the like. However, these things, cause other things, like sudden insect population growth. Or, sudden mold and mildew growth, which can result in modifications of some crop diseases. Changes in crop growth, damages from bad weather, or poor crops brought about from the droughts can eventually result in famines here and there. However, the areas which have the blessing of good weather, adequate rain, good soil, allowing for more abundant food, only lulls the populace into believing that this will be the case forever and on into the future, and, this in turn, brings about the secondary problem of overpopulation which we have been experiencing since the turn of the last century, that is, if you so choose to look back at our history."

"You did mention overpopulation of the world as one of the problems which you say we face today. How does this overpopulation thing come to be a secondary problem of global warming?" She asked.

Harlan thought a little this time, before he spoke. "I would have thought, that someone, somewhere in the world, would have recognized the overpopulation problem thingy and would have by now, written their doctorate's dissertation on it all. I mean, the world's civilizations should have bellied up to the bar and paid a little more attention after some nations went to a one child per family with penalties if a family had more, the rest of the world should have taken notice of such a warning, but, very few nations elsewhere in the world paid any attention, and, everyone, everywhere else, went right on, and, did their thing, and kept having more and more children, but, you just can't blame the passionate people for having big families, some religions encouraged big families, and, some governments even encouraged multiple reproduction and even established welfare programs to support their own population explosions." He said.

He went on. "Overpopulation has been rampant all over the world since the turn of the twentieth century, already, and has been for some time, for too long. There are no warning or caution signs being put up along the highways and cow paths to try to get the general populace to reign in and back off of any of their passions. Think about it. There are no passion suppressants available from your local pharmacies, there are only passion stimulants encouraged by pharmaceutical company's paid advertisements in all news media. Mankind itself has become its own worst enemy in this respect no matter what the nation."

He went on. "Overpopulation causes both immigration and emigration problems, people will move when they are starving. Think about the "dust bowl" of the 1930's of the near southwest in the U.S. Families gave up their lifestyle and location. They either moved, or, they starved to death trying to etch out a living in a drought ridden region. Many went back from where they had come from, many went on out west out to California. The better part of a regional population moved over a very short period of time. Today, we see refugees; we see people being rejected from one society and not allowed entry into another. They are in limbo prisons. This is past the point of being serious. We have seen the creep of the great Sahara desert moving further and further south and pushing hungry peoples ahead of it. We have seen the recent droughts of the southwest right here in America. all of the nations throughout the world will experience immigration problems because of other peoples wanting to find a safe haven."

"How does the overpopulation thingy effect or affect nations as a whole?" She asked.

"Overpopulation brings about wars. Wars for territory, or, wars for some economic reasons. Wars for both renewable and non-renewable resources. Defensive wars to protect their own territory or regions. Wars to gain some access or passages to other resources. We will live to see wars fought over food and water. The end result of all of the wars, is a population reduction within the region of conflict, which, in turn, allows additional migration to flow into that region. Spilled blood, thereby, allowing the influx of new blood. Government leaders worldwide already know all of this, but, they keep their mouth shut." He said.

"Too, nations can assimilate, fold into themselves, or, grow in other respects. All in the name of civilization, they say. What is good for the country must be good for you, they say. The opposition is always bad, and, the government good needs to overcome it, they say. Sometimes, a country's rumor of a war is almost as good a war itself, as, other countries round and about may very well come to their aid and support, on the pretense of preventing another war along with a second hidden agenda of gaining some occupation of the land or to gain some trade agreement for watermelons." He said.

He went on. "On the one hand, war helps to get rid of the best of the best among society who have the greatest capability of being aggressive. It is the aggressive youth who sign up and volunteer to go to war, it is the rowdy young of all nations who want to join in on the fight, for whatever reason if not just for the excitement of it all and the attention of some accompaniment of excited sex. Some governments even go so far as to trump up their own reason and feed it to an unsuspecting public. Now, do not get me wrong. There are today, and have been down through history, many good reasons to go to war against those who have in their mind to destroy good people for no reason other than for some financial gain, or some land grab, or by, some false religious endeavor that they believe to be ordered and commandeered by God Himself. History is replete with examples of such. But, to add on to that, the newer wars of the governments of today, will come to be over the natural renewable resources with water and good crop land to be at the head of their list followed by selected non-renewable resources."

"Harlan, have you ever read the book "War and Peace", or, similar books?" She asked.

"Nope." He said. "But, if I ever did, when I was in school, I don't remember it anymore. I have read both the Bible and the Quran. Both of them have more than just quite a bit of war and very little peace between the two of them, if that would count, that is, if you are counting. When nations can't come up with or think of any other reason to go to war, they can always fall back on their religion to support one. The one thing that I learned about war was that wars are resting periods for culture, and it was most likely the cultural differences which started most of the wars in the first place. But, we've already been through this and talked about those things a-previous, so, why would you drag it out and bring it all up again?" He asked.

"What about that famous book "Catcher in the Rye", did you ever read that book?" She also asked.

"Yes, I did read that book, if that is what you want to call it." He said. "That's one thing that I definitely absolutely remember. That book, which stretched the legal definition of what a book was, was the most ridiculous, no-good worthless piece of shit literature that I ever laid my eyes on in my entire life. It was more than just a total waste of my precious time, it was both an insult and an injury to my intelligence, I should have, or, ought to charge the publisher with assault and battery. I finally totally lost it all somewhere between where the dumb ass yahoo was carrying a baseball mitt around with him in his suitcase for some unknown dumb ass reason and where the girls he was dating were all whooping and yelling "stop" and he kept stopping like the dumb ass that he was. He should have dropped out of school early on, as he couldn't hack any of it anyway, and he should have went home and admitted to his parents that they failed in their attempt in child rearing by trying to raise a brainless dumb ass yahoo, which he had always been, even before he turned sixteen, and, as if his mother and father hadn't figured it out on their own already, he should have got himself a minimum wage burger frying job at McDonald's for Christ's sake, somewhere, along about the time in the book, where, before he realizes that people who get ahead stick to the point because he never could stick to the point in the whole damn stinking book! And, that so called girl friend of his, one of the one's that he had the hots for, not that New York hooker, but that Jane Gallagher girl, the one he says that he played tennis and golf and laid around the pool with, why, nobody plays both tennis and golf and then go and lay around the pool, especially in the same damn book! She should have had her Doberman Pinscher bite that dumb ass yahoo on the ass, and then, dumped his dumb ass in the swimming pool especially after Mister shit-for-brains lit up a cigarette. All in all, all I can say is, that that book was a total waste of my time from the get down get go. Besides that, I still think that it was him who wrote the F--- You on the Egyptian wall and was just too chicken shit to admit it in the book. Besides, Salinger won't even go so far as telling you what his first or middle name is, and, only goes by "J.D." which is just more bullshit that you have to tolerate in order to get through that dumb ass so-called book." He added on.

"OK, Harlan, I think I have it. You say, that all of mankind is imprisoned with global warming being the cause of the end of the ice age, and, that it will cause everything from bad weather to famines to overpopulation, which, in turn, will cause more wars and rumors of wars, for everyone presently on the face of this good Earth, all of which coming about because someone on one side or the other can't get enough watermelons, only to further complicate our prisoner status worldwide, and, you have not read very many good books except for the dumb ass one that you didn't like but like to rant about. Is that about it? Or, is there something else, or, anything else?" She asked.

Harlan responded. "I think that's it. I have said what I had to say, in order to deliver the message that needed to be delivered, albeit somewhat late in most cases. I did the job as was assigned, and, passed the message along for someone else to pick up and run with. You have now completed a communication with one of the fishes in the fish bowl prison, no more or no less. However, please, please, do not write down, what it was that I have said, but, do your job, and write down what it is that I meant!" He added with emphasis.

"Now, just to add on to your interview, since we have the time. Now, Harlan, the word on the street, is, that you are really just a home boy, someone who grew up and went to school right here in this town, and, local folks know you by sight by the name of "Eugene". Just how is it, that you reportedly have on too many occasions to even mention, have escaped your confines herein and while free have claimed to be someone's guardian angel on more than just one occasion. I think that this is most probably the one question that the local readers want to have answer to, so, what say you, how is it?" She asked.

"Well, I am Harlan. This Eugene character, of which you speak, has been my roommate, or, rather, my cell mate, for some time now. So, in that regard, I would have to let him speak for himself. That is something that was not in my letter agreement to comment upon during this interview and you can advise your readers that Eugene did not help me write the letter. I did not write to the newspaper for the purpose of making any such claim, remark or to comment on any such subject matter and cannot speak for anyone else. However, I should point out, that there is no natural law with respect to quantum physics that says, that something, or, someone, or anything, for that matter, cannot be in two places at the same time no matter the name that they are called or the name that they call it according to the space time continuum thinghy. All with respect to the definition of both "is" and "it". Sometimes, the party of the first part in one matter is the party of the second part in another and vice-a-versa. I mean, after all, all you have to do is dream, or just imagine a little for that matter. Think about it, for instance, what if part of you is in your bed, fast asleep, and, the other part of you is off into the great wherever hinterland, doing what you damn well please and having a good old hell of a time, but, not remembering the better part of it when the other part of you awakens. Or, what about if I can imagine myself standing on the moon at the same time that I am talking to you, so, am I really imagining that I am on the face of the moon, or, am I imagining that I am here talking to you, all the while with my feet kicking up the moon dust up there? So, I most certainly do refuse to answer any other such type questions myself and cannot speak for any others whatever name they call themselves by. However, just as a side note, and, I'll deny it to the day I die, that I ever said it, or that it ever crossed my brain, especially if comment of it ever shows up in the New York Times or the Boston Post. But, listen closely now, and, remember this, if you, or, if you know of anyone who needs a really good handy dandy guardian angel now and then, here or there, or, now and then, for any or whatever purpose, I might add, or, maybe just to liven things up for a party on a weekend, just get in touch and let me know. Perhaps I can help get you a volunteer lined up to help you or someone you know get out of some embarrassing predicament that they had got themselves into, or, maybe even help them get into some predicament that they have been looking forward to wanting to get into." He said.

"OK. So, you didn't answer my question, so, I'll ask it a little differently and a little more flat out." The interviewer said. "How is it now, that you say that your name is Harlan, but, you have also appeared amongst some honest people and known relatives within your home town, right outside these confines as someone named Eugene? Just how do you explain or accommodate that?" She demanded.

"I am who I am at any given moment in time. A being which is in a constant state of change, no different than anyone else in the world, but, like I told you before, my name is Harlan and my roommate or cell mate is named Eugene and I don't know anything extra personal about his personal extracurricular activities, besides, I have never ever claimed to have been him, and, as far as I know, he has never ever claimed to be me, although, I have observed, since we have been in the same cell for some time now, that he has taken on some of my habits, and, I can see that I have adopted a couple, or, maybe even a few of his. However, I remind you, that I would choose to deny such statements in a court of law, even if they were written up and published in the New York Times or the Boston Post, or, is it the Boston Herald?" He both said and asked himself.

At that precise moment in time, two guards entered the interview room. One of them said. "You have been with the patient for right at an hour, and, now, I have to ask you to leave, as we all have specific assignments, and, Harlan is on a rather rigid schedule and needs his rest."

With that, the interviewer thanked Harlan for his patience, and, the patient was unchained from the table and floor, and then departed the room with the one guard, rattling his chains as he waved goodby. After they were back inside the prison wall beyond the door, and, after the second guard had locked the door, the interviewer asked the remaining guard.

"What is wrong with him, anyway, as, he seems to be well read and more than just a little intelligent, he seems to have his mind about him for most of the time, he speaks well, albeit he is habitually redundant and doesn't always answer your questions like you want him to, but, he seems congenial enough, and too, he does not seem to be aggressive in any way, so, what is his problem?" She asked.

The guard responded. "Well, in some societies, such as in the far East, where they believe in foreign things like incarnation and reincarnation, or believe in other things even more spiritual, or, even some things we in the western hemisphere, would call delusional, in those foreign societies, he would seem perfectly normal and some would even go so far as to seek him out and to honor him as a sage, or, as soothsayer, or as a guru, or as some other type of spiritual leader, and, he would be a good fill-in anchor replacement for the evening news, however, in our society, in this day and time, with the exception of a couple of the more liberal Universities, we see it all differently, as most psychologists would think him to be deranged or a little crazy as they say, even mad as a lunatic, or, some more western thinking religious folks could see him as even being demon possessed, but, either way, here or there, I see him on a daily basis, that is, when he is not out and about on one of his unbelievable fantastic escapes. However, in my personal observations, he does appear to have both some displaced long term and some emplaced short term memory problems, and, even some replaced or, made up, homemade if you will, even some cooked up or self-made memories, if you could call them that, and, in other areas, he has, on occasion, let his imagination run wild, however you wish to say it, otherwise, he is one of our most interesting and best patients, again, when he is here and not out on some of his unexplainable escape escapades. Otherwise, he has been with us for the last fifteen years or so, off and on, and, now and then, when he is here and not somewhere else, but then, overall, he has almost been out of here as much as he has been in here, which doesn't say much for us guards or our system.

Otherwise, I personally, find him very interesting to talk to, on about any subject. So, that is it in a nutshell, with no pun intended, but, I am on a schedule and I now have to return to my duties. I hope you got the information you came for." He said.

"Well, I think that it is nice that Harlan at least has someone in his cell to talk to while he is in here." The interviewer said.

"What do you mean, someone in his cell? Harlan only has the guards to talk to while he is in his cell." The guard said.

"Oh, I mean, his roommate or cell mate Eugene, which he mentioned." The interviewer added.

"Ma'am, Harlan is in solitary confinement and has been for some extended time now. There is no one else with him in his solitary confinement. He is in solitary confinement because of all the times that he has made good on his escapes from here and he bears watching and keeping track of minute by minute and hour by hour. Also, I know every patient here in this institution by their first, middle and last name, and, even know their nick-names, and most of their family, however, we do not have a patient incarcerated here by the name of Eugene." With that, the second guard excused himself and left the room.

The interviewer still sat in her chair making some final notes and awaiting her escort out of the asylum or prison, whichever she thought about it at the time, and, wondered as to how or where she was going to start the patient's first story for the Gazette.

Again, the dreamer stirred, but not by much, but, did get up to pee, then returned to the bed, and again tucked himself in, wondered a little about what eventually happened to the poor patient, or the interviewer and the guard, but then, went back to sleep. And, his dreams went on.

JAKE KELLYS TALE   (that is, if he ever had one, but, no offense meant by that)

To all of you All-American readers, this dream, is about some real All-American places and locations, with some more or less than real All-American people. Their All-American names have been changed, so as, to protect those who are really the guilty ones, but not yet arraigned, charged or convicted yet by a jury of their peers, beyond some All American shadow of some All-American doubt. So, with no more than that as an introduction, let this All-American dream begin....

"The All-American roundup of some lyin' cowhand, and, his cohort, who's always just tryin' to keep both his and his buddy's mouth shut...."

Jake was worried, he couldn't get any of his cowhands to answer on the hand held portable radio; he had been calling for almost half an hour with no response whatsoever. He told Doc at the camp, that he was going to mount up and go out looking for them, and, he headed out to the corral, saddled up his horse, and, struck out to the west across the valley toward the pass that led to where the crew was supposed to be out looking to round up un-branded strays.

Within a half an hour, Jake came across the edge of the dry lake at the northwest corner of the Blue Wing Mountains, cutting his horse back and forth to avoid the shrub sagebrush. As he made his way along the edge of the dry lake, he saw what looked like a couple of horses up in a tight draw less than a quarter mile away, one on one side of the draw and one on the other, and he was well on his way over to check it out. He had been calling on the radio since he had left camp for his cowhands Will, Big Bird and Cahill. He was seriously concerned for their safety. As he came up the drainage, he saw one horse yet saddled with the reins tied up to a tall sagebrush, and, he recognized the horse as being Will Pardey's, one of his hired cowhands that he was out on the look for.

Will didn't deserve such a good horse, Jake thought, but, that, in itself, just might be Will's only salvation, he thought. As he rode on up beside the horse, he untied the reins from the sage brush, and let the horse go free. Jake knew that Will's horse always went straight to Will, no matter where he was or how unfortunate, even without being called or whistled for. So, he said to himself, let's see where this fine horse goes.

The horse put its head down, ambled on up the draw, then turned to the left amidst some tall sagebrush. Jake watched until the horse stopped a couple hundred feet or so, and again put its head down, then he rode on up to where the horse was.

There, all sprawled out under the shade, of big tall sagebrush, was Will Pardey all laid out like he was practicing for his funeral. Will's hat covered his face, his legs were crossed, his hands were folded over his chest like a dead man in a casket, just like he was ready for a proper burial, and, to top it all off, he was snoring so loud that Jake couldn't help but hear it. Will thought to himself, then mumbled under his breath, "Supervising cowhands is worse than tryin' to herd up a bunch of calico cats."

"Wake up there cowboy Will, it's time to pay the preacher man!" Jake yelled.

Will's snoring stopped, and he raised his right hand to scratch his nose, then, slowly pushed his hat back up off of his face. Peering out from under the brim, he stared up at Big Jake on his horse.

"Ohh, man, am I ever glad to see you, Jake." Will said, while slowly raising up on his elbows. "My horse must've thrown me off, stepped in a badger hole or somthin', and done knocked me out, totally unconscious I must have been. I've prob'ly got somethin' broke some where's in here, hurtin' as bad as I do." Will said, while sitting up, pushing his hat back on his head, and punching around on his ribs and belly.

"Yea, right, Will, and right after he threw ya' off, your hat just fell right proper atop yer face and yer horse went down there in the draw, in the shade of that other big manzanita, and he done already tied himself up. You know better than that Will. But just to be kind, we both know yer lyin' thru yer teeth. Now, come on, get yerself up, get on yer horse... and get a move on, ...and that's the word with the bark on it Will, so get yerself a-moving, and, let's do it now." Jake yelled.

"Now, Jake, don't you go gettin' hostile." Will said, getting himself up and brushing his pants off with his hat. "I ain't quite got myself together yet...."

Pulling his horse around sideways, Big Jake leaned over in the saddle and looking down at Will, Jake said. "Now, Will, where in the hell is Cahill and Big Bird?"

"I think they are over on the other side of the draw, Jake." Will said while motioning and pointing to the south.

"Are they OK, what are they up to?" Jake asked.

"I think they are a-tryin' out their hand at prospectin'." Will said "Prospectin', what the hell, they don't know nothin' 'bout doin' any prospectin', they's cowhands for criminey sakes, they don't know jack shit' 'bout prospectin'." Jake retorted.
As Jake wheeled his horse around to head to the other side of the draw, Will bounced up off of the ground, stepped up to his horse, pulled his saddle strap tight, mounted up on his horse and headed down the draw, trying catch up to Jake before he got to the edge of the sand flat. And, when he did, he fell in a horse length or so behind Jake, and he cut his horse back to about what Jake's horse's gait was at.
Jake cut his horse to the south along the edge of the sand flat, across a washed out drainage, and headed up the south side of the draw where he now spotted two other horses which he now knew to be Big Bird's and Cahill's. Will tried to keep up tight right behind Jake.
Jake cut his horse up through the sagebrush, and he now saw the two horses with their reins tied up to some manzanita.

"CAHILL... BIG BIRD... where in the hell are you guys?" Jake yelled.
"Over here." Came a faint reply that sounded like it came from Cahill.
Jake turned his horse and went straight for where he heard Cahill's voice, and Will followed along trying to keep up with him.
As Jake rode up to Cahill and Birg Bird, he pulled up short and dismounted. "What in the good name of heaven do you two think you are adoin'? " Jake asked as he walked over to where they were.
"I thought I'd just take a little time out, maybe take a break, maybe to do a little prospectin', on the side, so to speak." Cahill explained.
Big Bird added. "I'm just tryin' to help him out a little, Jake."
Will blurted out. "It ain't my fault, I didn't tell him where you guys were, Jake spotted your horses on his own, so, don't be blamin' me if'n you guys done got yerself in trouble."
Jake interrupted. "Shut up, Will, and all of you listen up real close... I have been calling you all, on the radios every 10 to 15 minutes or so, since a little after lunch. None of you answered. Now, these radios can carry a signal for 6-8 miles, and, you all are, not more than four miles from camp in open air and not on the other side of some hill or mountain, and with none of you are answering, I thought maybe you

all got jumped by a mountain lion, attacked by a badger, or bit by a rattler, I thought everything bad that you could think of had happened to you all, and, here you are, the three of you, doing nothing but sloughing off and calling it prospectin'. Where's your radio Cahill?, where's your's, Will? Jake asked.

"Mine's in my saddle bag." Said Cahill. "So's mine." Said Will. "I never ever had one to talk on in the first place." Said Big Bird, defensively.

Jake continued. Now listen up close, all of you, Miss Stephanie bought us these radios for our safety, and they are to be used for that, and, if you choose to ignore such an important matter, you may find yourself with no job at all, and, on the outside looking in, if you will. That is settled, and, that is the word with the bark on it, and I suggest you all pay sweet attention to it."

Jake continued. "Now, Cahill and Big Bird, let's change the subject, just what makes you two, of all people, think you all know anything about prospectin', as far as I know, and, according to your resume's, all you two have done, all your life since you both dropped out of high school, has been herdin' up strays, and maybe catchin' a wild burro or a mustang now and then to take credit for. So what's your stories?

Cahill responded first. "Well, I've just been listening for the past few weeks, to those Lovelock prospectors that we've been camping with, and I just had the idea go across my brain and we came by this outcrop, and it looked good, and, I guess I just had to check it out, and try it on my own and get a sample for Doc to look at tonight."

"I'm just taggin' along here, Jake, 'cause, I for one, fully agree, I don't know nothin' about prospectin', and, I was just helpin' out Cahill here, do his thing." Big Bird added.

"Well, I have to say, that you both are at least honest about it, which, is more than I can say about your pardner Will, here. But still, you all, are on the Yeehaw ranch payroll as cowhands, not prospectors, and, presently employed, with Miss Steph still signin' your paycheck, week in and week out, but maybe not for so long, under the circumstances," Jake said.

Cahill, then went on the defensive and said. "Well, Jake, me and Will and Big Bird really worked extra hard all mornin', runnin' up one draw after another along the Lava Beds, goin' from dry spring to dry spring, not findin' anything live, or wet for that matter, then, I spotted this rocky outcrop, and, it looked a lot like what those prospectors have been talking about at camp, and, I just thought I'd take a shot at it and get a sample or two for analyzin', and, maybe have Doc look at what I found, anyway, if it ever came to anything, I would surely split it fairly with the whole crew, includin' you and Miss Steph."

"Well, Cahill, thanks again, for at least being honest about it, but I don't know how much water that all will hold with Miss Steph." Jake said.

Jake then looked over at Will, and with his head cocked to the side, said, "Will...my daddy told me that if a man will lie to ya... he'll steal from ya... and when yer' not doin' your work like you should... it's no different than stealin' outright, and, on top of that, ya' go and lie about it. Don't ya' know...that if it weren't for Miss Steph... having kept you, Cahill, and Big Bird on as hired hands here this late in the fall... you'all would prob'ly not even have any work at all by now. You'all would prob'ly be back in Californie or up in Oregon some wheres', or back in Reno... embarrassed to the gills, that you had to live off'n yer families…. and feeling ashamed of yer'selves for being such losers. That is all so totally un-American. Don't ya' see that Will? Cahill?, Big Bird? Don't ya? But go ahead and get your sample there anyway Cahill, gather it all up, then, we're all heading back to camp, by the way, where'd you get those sample bags anyway?"

"I got 'em from MaClintock, last night at camp." Cahill said.

Jake, not responding, remounted his horse and turned down the draw, with Will uptight close and right behind.

Cahill grabbed the sample bags of rock, gave two of them to Big Bird, and they both hurriedly put then into their saddle bags, and, Cahill removed his radio and put it into his pocket. They both then untied their horses and mounted up in order to join up with Jake and Will, they both hurried in order to try to catch up on down the draw.

Well ahead, when they had hit the sand flat, Will pulled his horse up alongside Jake and said, " Jake... I know that what Cahill and Big Bird were doing was questionable… and, I guess in my own way I do appreciate your concern… and maybe I don't show it very well. But, on the other hand.... you could say the same thing about yer'self... being it, that Miss Steph made you the Grand High Chief Muckety Muck What Is In Charge... but no offense intended there, and not having any more work than what there is, just having us out here every day, chasing strays... and picking up everything from them sorry ass wild burros on up… ya' know dang well that this cowboy thing, just ain't been what it's cracked up to be in this day and time.

Anyway, about that lyin' thing… I do want ya' to know… that I do know enough about the good book… to know that it says… that we are all liars… so I guess that makes me not feel so bad overall. Anyway, after all is said and done…that puts you in the same boat with me and everybody else." Will said, trying in some manner to explain himself, riding on but now looking across the valley and away from Jake.

Jake broke the silence with… "Will... it's like you got diarrhea of the mouth or something. Will... you don't even stick enough truth into your lyin' to make'm believable anymore.   But just so you know, Will, if I hadn't of always considered you to be a real good friend of mine, I would've fired your young sorry ass a long time ago." With that, Jake then turned his head, and, began looking straight ahead across the flat and not paying any more attention to Will, that is, any more than he absolutely had to.

Will, now no more than a horse length behind, tried again to get some kind of conversation going, and said. "Well I'm sure glad ya' found me, Jake, a fella could die out here in the desert in little or no time…maybe even in a few hours if'n he got snake bit, anyway, how'd ya' ever find me?"

"I didn't find ya', Will, I found yer' horse, then, yer' horse found ya, and it's no wonder that a rattler didn't go up your pant leg while you were sleeping, or a mountain lion pounced on you for his supper." Jake said, as he turned his horse about along the end of the dry lake, and headed east back toward their camp.

Will slowed his horse, and fell back with Cahill and Big Bird, then, they all followed along, looking ahead at Jake, but Jake didn't even turn his head back to even see if they were even there. Jake was deliberately and purposely avoiding any further eye contact with either of them. Will, too, looked away and purposely turned his head and couldn't bring himself to even look toward Jake again. One of the four was obviously really pissed off, and the other three were obviously no little intimidated by the happenings.

About a quarter hour later, when they were well within a half-mile or so from their camp, Will stuck his nose up in the air like a coyote getting ready to howl at the moon. Breaking the silence, Will said, "Cahill is that the smell of Nevada barbeque or Utah barbeque…. man, don't that smell sure make your guts growl?"

Cahill responded. "It's got to be Nevada barbeque, stupid, hells bells, Will, we sure ain't chasin' strays in Utah, you dumb ass."

ake heard, but didn't acknowledge either of them, now, ignoring them totally, still riding and looking straight dead ahead toward camp.

Will, prodding his horse on ahead some, eventually caught up with Jake, with Big Bird and Cahill purposely lagging further behind, Will, tried again to break the silence between him and Jake by saying, "Yup, that's barbeque alright, Jake, you know, I didn't even know that those prospectors could cook, especially Doc, until he got sick and wound up on their chuck wagon. Since Doc has been cookin' though, we've been eatin" pretty high on the hog, if you ask me. Best piece of luck we've had lately." He added on, but to no avail and to no apparent effect on Jake in trying to get him to speak.

Finally, Cahill and big Bird caught up with them, and him and the three now continued to ride along now close behind Jake, and, now and then, Will and Cahill, would stick their noses up in the air and breathing in, savoring the barbeque smell coming at them downwind. Will whispered to Cahill that he thought that things couldn't be too bad if Jake hadn't already told them yet that they was both fired, and, Cahill just shook his head back and forth, indicating a no.

The four of them, rode on up to the corral, and, almost in unison, they unsaddled their horses, unbridled them, hung the saddles on the fence, put the bridles on the saddle horns, run the horses into the corral, gave the horses some grain in the feed boxes, poured some water in the trough, then, still in unison, they unbuckled their chaps and hung them up on the corral fence, again purposely not talking anymore with one another or even looking at one another for that matter, any more than what they had to.

It was now Jake who broke the silence between the three of them as they walked back toward the camp, and, he said. "Now, Will...just to get this thing off my chest, I have to say, the second time, just so I am sure that you have heard it, and, that is this, that there are three things you and I both know.... first, that is, that you know you're a born liar and seem to be proud of it, second, the truth ain't anywhere to be found in ye', anywhere, whether for fun or not.... and, the third is, that everyone in the world that you know, or, have ever met, also knows it, so, please stop now, as, you may as well, before it comes to something that you may live to regret for the rest of your life sooner or later."

Will, going on the defensive, said, "Jake, you know that they ain't no law no anywhere's against lyin' for the fun of it, besides, there's a lot of difference between just outright lyin' and tryin' to come up with some good excuses once in a while."

Jake retorted. "Will, old Sam Clemens, blamed Mark Twain, for sayin' that, all an excuse is... "is the skin that covers a lie", and besides that, the good book says thou shalt not lie."

"Now, Jake, It don't neither say that any where's, I know enough about it... to know... that it don't neither say that." Will said, as he stomped along acting like he was getting a crick out of his back and sticking his head up in the air like a duck trying to catch rain drops during a frog stranglin' downpour or a chicken drowner thunderstorm.

"Well, I know it does say "thou shalt not bear false witness", which means the same thing as not to lie, and, it also says that all you liars are a going to hell... and yer' well on your way, Will.... yer' headed down there in a danged fancy hand basket at about ninety miles an hour." Jake said.

Will said, "Somehow, Jake, I hear what yer' sayin', but somehow, it just don't seem right to me...it just don't seem right to me, somehow."

Jake came back at him and said, "You know, Will, all that lyin' makes you out to be crookeder than a barrel of snakes with scoliosis....and the fact of the matter is, down deep in your heart, you know that is a truth, so, put a stop to it while you still have the chance."

Will sauntered on, beside Jake, but looking down at the ground. Cahill, apparently the smarter of the two, followed quietly along behind, and was keeping his mouth shut. Big Bird took Cahill's lead and fell even further back, also without making any further comment.

Jake said, "You all, prep up tonight, and make sure to fill your canteens for tomorrow, 'cause we got bad weather movin' in by tomorrow late, and, we need to get an early mornin' start, 'cause we may be blown away by tomorrow this time, if'n the weather report is right."

"I don't think I brought quite enough clothes." Cahill said.

"Do what I do Cahill, put everything you got on in layers out here in the desert, as you can take it off if'n it gets warm, but if you don't have it, you don't have it to take off or to put on." Big Bird said.

As they entered the camp area, Jake said. "Doc, we smelled your barbeque from more than a half-mile away." Doc nodded pleasantly and welcomed them in for the evening.

Their All-American camp site is about 40 miles northwest of All-American Lovelock, Nevada, in an area where there are no trees, no houses, no cars, no traffic, and, very little of anything else except the wind and the dust which is only noticed by the lizards, the rattlesnakes, the wild burros and the antelope who are mainly into their roaming thing under a clear blue sky.

While they were getting a drink of water and filling up their canteens, Will chimed in…. "Yea Doc, I smelled it first, so, between me, Cahill. Big Bird and Jake, I guess I have the better smeller".

Doc said, "I always did think you cowhands were pretty smart fellers, or, is that petty fart smellers? Supper won't be ready for another hour or so, and by the way, I got a radio call from the prospecting team that they are running more than an hour late on their way down and out of a steep canyon up by the tungsten mines, anyway, so, I guess we'll feed you cowhands first and the team play get and take of what's left over, so, you might as well clean up and get a little rest, so you got a little free time, but Jake, send Will and Cahill in early to help me set it all up."

Jake said. "Well Doc, except for that sandy draw halfway up the valley, if they make it OK through that, we should be able to see their dust when they get within a couple of miles or so from camp. I'll keep a watch out, for 'em, and give you a yell."

Will, Big Bird and Cahill headed up for their tent, where they both stretched out on their air mattresses.

"Why do you suppose Jake brought the tents, you think he was expecting rain with the bad weather moving in?" Will said.

"No, but they keep the dust, crickets, scorpions, and rattlers out." Jonesey said, and with that he pulled his boots off and laid back on his air bed.

Big Bird, not saying anything further, pulled off his boots and piled in on his cot to get some rest before supper.

"Whatever." Will said. "I once heard of a mountain lion draggin' some guy out of his tent while he was a' sleepin' in his sleeping bag, eatin' off his upper half, then leavin' his head layin', and draggin' his lower half off, and hidin' it somewhere's, to eat the next day, what do you think of something like that, Cahill?"

Cahill never responded, either already asleep or just purposely ignoring Will. Then, a period of quiet sort of engulfed the whole camp, with only the wind blowing through the cottonwoods making any noise, a short period of unmeasured time passed.

Jake called out. "Hey Will, Cahill, come help Doc and Will laying out the supper."

Will rolled off his air mattress, pulled on his boots, kicked Cahill's cot, then unzipped the tent flap, and, headed over toward the chuck wagon to join up with Doc, with Cahill trailing up the rear.

"Yo, Doc.", Jake yelled, "Dust is a comin' down the valley."
"Yea, I got 'em on the radio, they made it through the sandy draw, and, they'll be here in a jif." Doc said.
The moral of the first part of the first part is.... "Holding someone to the truth, is almost as hard as, holding someone back from a lie."
The moral of the last part of the first part is….. "The first liar never has a chance, but that does not keep them from trying to vie up for first place."

"The dream goes on, with…" "The last agreement at the first supper of the congregation."
"Soups on." Doc yelled. Followed by Will yelling…. "Supper is as served."
One by one, the All-American group all came together for supper, getting their forks and paper plates and passing by Doc's buffet layout of homemade buttermilk buns, beans baked in brown sugar, home fried potatoes mixed with scalded onions, hot buttered mushrooms, barbeque brisket sliced thin like Italian beef, cornbread with butter and blackberry jelly, a salad topped off with yellow peppers and black olives, not to mention the sliced tomatoes, and, at the end of the table, Doc had set up two glass gallon jugs of Gallo red wine with cups. "A supper fit for a king. Doc, you have outdone yourself again." Jake said.
Sizing it all up, Cahill summed it all up with... "Apparently, Prospectors sure eat better than cowhands."
The crews served themselves, buffet style, and sat down at the fold up picnic tables that served as their outdoor kitchen by the chuck wagon, right in the middle of the desert.
With his supper about half way consumed, Cahill hit on Doc. "Doc, I got some samples that you need to look at after supper, I just happened to see an outcrop that I couldn't pass up, after hearing you prospectors talkin' about what to look for and all, I done went and got a couple samples."
"Sure, Cahill, let me have a look, if it's anything of interest, I'll more than give you the credit." Doc said.
Jake then interrupted and asked. "That brings up a topic for discussion, Doc, as to, what if one of us cowhands did find something, that was worth something, how could we be included if it was ever to be developed?"
 "Well, Jake, if us prospectors ever find a stray cow with calf, we tell

you all, and you all go get it. Do we get any credit, recompense or pay, if we tell you about it?" Doc said.

Jake chimed in with, "Well, Doc, partly, I think it's like one of those, you rub my back and I'll rub yours, kinds of things, but, if we could come to some sort of agreement, between you all and us, maybe we can make it worthwhile for all of us, in the long run."

Doc continued. "Well, you all do get in areas that we never get to see, and, vice a versa, so, yes, it would be, in both of our best interests, to come up with some solution, in the event that such a thing would ever come about, do you suppose that we all could come up with some agreement that would be reasonable?"

"Don't we need something to make it legal, like a contract or at least some kind of written agreement or letter of intent, to confirm that? Jake said.

Cahill interrupted. "Doc, what is bringin' this all about, is, that I found something I think you prospectors should look at down on the west side of the north end of Blue Wing mountains, if there is anything to it, would that be a starter for some kind of agreement?"

Jake held up his hand for Cahill to stop, and continued. "Cahill, you personally couldn't make such an agreement, as long as you are an employee of the Yeehaw ranch, it would have to be me or Miss Steph, to come to and sign on such an agreement."

Doc said. "Well, if it was anything like that, it would most likely be 50-50, between my company and the Yeehaw ranch, that is, if it was on open federal lands, unless of course, it was on the property of the ranch, then, we would have to negotiate further."

So, you are saying, that if we came across something of value, the Yeehaw ranch could enter into some kind of 50-50 agreement with your company for any future revenue?" Jake said.

"Well, in a 50-50 agreement, it should include the Yeehaw ranch putting up half of the expenses, like the mining costs, or, exploration costs, too, or, electing to having them deducted from the total expenditure of such an operation, just like the cost of the rounding up a stray, the time it took to bring it in, puttin' it in the corral, then haulin; it off to the feed lot, and payin' to fatten it up, so, the overall cost would reduce the total divided dividend" Doc said.

In the interim discussion, Cahill got up and went over to his tent, got the rock sample bags, and, brought them back to the table, and, set them out in front of Doc.

"Take a look at those rocks, Doc, and, tell me if you don't think that they are not just as interestin' as anything that you prospectors have brought back to camp in the last two weeks." Cahill said.

Doc laid down his barbeque sandwich, opened a sample bag, and dumped some of the rocks out on the table. Then, he did the same thing with the other two bags. He took his knife out and raked the rocks around some, then, he got a magnifying glass out of his pocket and began to look more closely at Cahill's rock samples.

"These look promising, but I would want MacClintok to look at the samples, because this type of rock is within his specialty, because it looks highly altered, whatever it is, but, it is certainly not leaverite." Doc said.

"Leaverite, what is leaverite?" Cahill asked.

"You leave leaverite, right where you found it." Doc responded.

"Do you think it is worth anything?" Cahill asked.

"Well, I can tell you, that I would certainly think it would be worth having the rock assayed to determine if there was anything in it of value, and, maybe even have a 32 element run to see what else may be in a combined sample." Doc said.

By this time, Jake, Big Bird, Will, Hank and, Cahill, were all ears, but their interest was interrupted by the honk of a truck horn from the prospecting crew, returning from their day in the field. As the truck rolled into the camp area, the crew bailed out and headed for the feed table, without even washing their hands.

"Let's table this discussion, and hold further talks on this matter, when everyone has had time to eat, then, I'll have them take a look at your rock sample, Cahill, and we'll talk about it some more." Doc said.

After Prospector Pete and MaClintock, got their supper and sat down at the table, Doc asked. "You all find anything of interest today?"

"We brought in a few samples." MaClintock said. "Yea, we busted our butt to get them too, you would think me and Pete were part mountain goat, the way we had to climb without any climbing gear, straight up for half an hour, and, slide straight down into the canyon."

"I am not into that sort of thing myself." Prospector Pete.

"Yea, you sat on your flat fat ass while we did all the work." MaClintock said.

"Well, someone had to stand watch, and look out, just in case you two fell and broke your danged necks." Pete countered.

"Well, hey, when you all get some barbeque down your throat, I have some samples here that Cahill came up with, that you all maybe need to take a look at, especially you MaClintock, because they look like they are highly altered, which is your specialty." Doc said.

"Pass them down, now, I can do two things at once, not like my cohorts here, who have trouble walking and chewing gum at the same time." MaClintock said.

Cahill hurriedly scrapped up the loose rocks on the table from in front of Doc, dust and all, put them back into the sample bags and carried them down to MaClintock, who opened each bag, and dumped some of the rock out on the table in front of his plate.

MaClintock looked at the rocks carefully and Prospector Pete looking over from each side. Prospector Pete picked up a couple of the rocks for a closer look, and, MaClintock took them back from him and smacked his hand with his fork.

"What do you think?" Cahill said.

"Yea, what do you think?" Said Doc.

"Well, they certainly look good enough to have them assayed, I'd say." Said MaClintock.

"They look better than anything we brought back today." Said Prospector Pete.

"Where'd you get them, Cahill?" Asked MaClintok.

"Over on the northwest corner of the Blue Wing mountains." Said Cahill.

"Doc, can we modify the schedule some, and go look at this area first thing in the morning?" MaClintock asked.

"Well…." Doc started to say, but was cut off at the pass so to speak.

Jake interrupted with. "Doc, don't you think before you all look at what Cahill has maybe come up with, that maybe we should enter into some sort of agreement, about who gets what, and whenever, if this thing, or anything else for that matter, happens to maybe pan out to be something of value?"

"Well, yes, that would be the proper thing to do, and, being that we are all intelligent men, we can draw up such an agreement right here and right now, I'll write it all down, and, we can all sign it to make it official, if everyone could agree to that." Doc said.

Jake said. "Doc, before we do, I think that I should go call Miss Steph, just to make sure that such an agreement would be OK with her." And, with that, Jake got up, and, headed down to the corral area where he could get some reception, so as to make the phone call. Jake called Miss Steph on his cell phone discussed such an agreement, and, to Jake's surprise, she was interested, and concurred, that it could be of some considerable interest to the Yeehaw Ranch, and, gave Jake the OK to make such an agreement and to sign such on her behalf.

Jake returned to the campsite, and, announced. "Miss Steph gives us her blessings on an agreement, but she wants everyone to be on the same page with all of us in agreement with one another on such a thing, so, what say you all?"

The group answered, in their own manner, somewhat to the affirmative that they thought that to agree to such an agreement, would be in good order and all concerned would also be most agreeable to signing it.

 Doc then got some paper and a couple pens, cleaned off the table so he could write, and said… "OK, here is my idea of such an agreement, but, along the way, if any of you want to add in anything, just yell up and we'll add it in if it has merit, that is." and, with that, he started to write and say what he was writing….. "We, the said parties of the first part, namely, Robert Schmidt, John Littlemore, Clint Davidson, and C. A. Hill, aka, Cahill, said parties being employees of the Lovelock Prospecting Company crew, agree with the parties of the second part, namely, Jake Kelly, Herb Holibird, Will Pardey, Henry McGardy, and Steph Hill (in absentia), said owner or employees of the Yeehaw ranch, do hereby agree, that any prospect, of potential credible value, founded by the Yeehaw ranch crew, would be reported to, and, if valued, located and developed by the Lovelock Prospecting Company crew would be shared 50-50, in value, minus the share of exploration of prospect, mine development and eventual overall mining expenses, between the parties of the first part and the parties of the second part, namely with the Yeehaw ranch crew, and furthermore, any cattle, burros, wild mules or mustang horses, with a few antelope thrown in on the side, so founded by the parties of the first part, namely, the Lovelock Prospecting crew, would be reported and turned over to the parties of the second part, namely, the Yeehaw ranch crew, and shared 50-50, in value, minus expenses in locating, handling, holding, hauling, feeding and sale, with the Lovelock prospecting crew, all of which is agreed to by both the parties of the first part and the parties of the second part, and agreeably signed to by all named parties in such agreement, here in the County of Pershing, in the State of Nevada, USA, this date."

"So… how does that sound to you all." Said Doc.

All respondents, cowhands and prospectors, agreed that this would be a good measure, in light of the circumstances, and, discussed the agreement among themselves agreeably. Everyone commented, and agreed that the agreement sounded good, and that it would be a legal document, agreed upon by the signers. But not after haggling about whether cattle included some calves, or, prospect included a mine, or whether burros and mustangs included horses which had got loose from some ranch, and, on and on and on and on, but, the final agreement was not changed by word from the original that Doc had written up from the beginning, too much. There was some discussion on whether or not the ranch crew should really be the party of the first part, and, the Lovelock prospecting crew be the parties of the second part, but all agreed that either way, the agreement would be the same.

Jake said. "To make it a more perfectly legal document, shoudn't you add somethin' like "In God we trust"… or… "So help me God"…. Or, something likes that?"

Doc said. "Well, the "So help me God" phrase is used in the swearing in of witnesses in court, or in the making of a Judge or a President, in that fashion, "In God we trust" is assigned to the monetary system, so, I do not think that either fits the agreement, or, would add or detract anything to it, in effect, considering. But what we have here, I think should suffice, and, besides, I don't want to be out here until midnight writing up the the agreement."

"OK Doc, write it up, and let's all sign it, then that will make it perfectly legal." Jake said.

Doc responded with…"Well, Jake, legal is another matter, to make it more perfectly legal, we need to make at least three copies of the agreement, with each of us signing all three, one copy for the Lovelock Prospecting crew, one copy for the Yeehaw ranch crew, and one copy that we need or should take to the Pershing County Clerk and have filed, for a matter of official County record in the State of Nevada."

"Sounds even better to me, I think that Miss Steph would be pleased." Said Jake.

So, Doc took the time to write up the three agreements, with everyone examining them to make sure they were all the same, and, that all the words were in the same order, then, he said. "OK, who is going to be the first to sign up?"

"I'll sign first, on behalf of the Yeehaw ranch and Miss Steph." Said Jake.

"Well, I'll sign first on behalf of the Lovelock Prospecting company." Said Doc. All the others, then agreed in unison, more or less, here and there, and, now and then, all came up to sign the three documents, with Will accidentally spilling some wine from his cup on one of the copies.

"That copy must yours Jake, Will just baptized it with some Gallo red." Doc said.

Doc and Jake, agreed between themselves, that they would jointly and together, go into Lovelock at first opportunity, and, the next day, if possible, while the prospecting crew was looking at Cahill's findings, and both together would then file the agreement at the Pershing County Courthouse, with the County Clerk, just to make it legal and binding.

"OK, now that we all agree, will you all go take a look at where I got the samples first thing in the morning? Cahill said.

"Absolutely, never let it be said that the parties of the first part, known as the Lovelock Prospecting company, ever lingered on, or delayed, any such an examination, of any such prospect, brought to light, by any such party of the second part, or other person for that matter, at any such time, including representation of the Yeehaw ranch, just to keep it legal." Said Doc.

After supper was over, Will and Little John started a camp fire, and, everyone gathered around the fire with most of them pulling their boots off. Cowboy boots were intermingled with prospector's boots. Hank got his harmonica out and started blowing out some blues tones; Big Bird got his radio and turned on the news. Doc brought out two more gallons of Gallo red wine, and the prospectors and cowhands both enjoyed the evening under the stars, telling corny jokes, sipping one cup of wine after another, but yet, with a couple of the crew members mumbling to one another, wishing that Doc had of brought out a keg of beer instead, and, one, who added that he was really wishing for a double shot of whiskey or bourbon, but they all went along with the wine, partly heartily, until the two gallons had been completely consumed, with Jake making the observation, and, commenting that everyone had at least a quart and a half of each in their belly, more or less, and, that he had not heard any cursing yet, and, no fights had erupted, too, no one was singing or crying, no one had fell down and got hurt yet, that no one was so drunk that they couldn't get up on their own if they did, so, it must surely be an agreeable group to be able to hold their liquor like that, overall, and, Doc agreed. Agreeable conversations were enjoyed by all, and everyone, was excited and upbeat, about the coming happenings of the morrow.

"Jake, why do they call Doc, Doc, is he a doctor or something?" Will asked.

Finally, Jake made a reply, and said, "Doc was awarded his Doctorate degree from the University of Nevada in geology, he is first a prospector and prob'ly the best of that bunch that share our camp, as for the rest of them, they all are a bunch of Johnny come latelies, so now, Doc just studies the maps, tells the crew where to go, and, looks at the samples that they bring in, Doc is not sick, but he done come down with gout in his knees, and, he has trouble climbing hills, so he chose on his own to stay in camp doing the camp chores and cookin', sortin', log'n, and keepin' track of samples, it is his cookin' part that is the best thing that has happened to us cowhands."

Will said, "Well I'll be damned if that ain't all… what's Doc's last name anyway?"

Jake replied, "Schmidt, Doctor Robert Schmidt, the German spellin' rather than the English spellin'."

Jake, after showing that moment of weakness by breaking the silence, glanced out of the corner of his eye and noticed the fading silly grin on Will's face, but didn't say anything further.

Doc told a story about old man Sam Clemmons who blamed Mark Twain for saying, and, he said that old Sam, first went out west to Nevada, with his brother Orion, who had been appointed the Governor of the Nevada Territory, and, Sam, or, Mark, as he was known as then, hired on with a newspaper at Virginia City, which was just East of Carson City, where his brother held office, and, Doc added, that Sam, or Mark, as he was known, may not have even gotten the job, had his brother not been appointed the Governor of the territory, however, it was also known, that Sam, or Mark, as he was known, had invested in some gold mining ventures, to try to build up or add to his fortune, and with that as an introduction, Doc started it out with….. "Now, Sam Clemmons, is said to have accused his alias of saying, or, Mark Twain was heard to have said, that when he first went out west, his efforts included trying his hand at some prospecting, and, that he had clear definitions for almost anything at the time, for instance, he said, that his first definition of a gold mine was, that it was a hole in the ground with a couple of men down in the bottom of it. But, after he lost his first fortune in gold mining, he said, that he revised his definition of a gold mine to read, that a gold mine was a hole in the ground, with two men down in the bottom of it, and, one or the other of the two, was a liar. Then, after he lost his second fortune in a gold mining prospect, he said, that he again modified his definition of a gold mine somewhat, to read, that a gold mine, was a hole in the ground, with two men down in the bottom of it, one of which, was a known liar, and the other of which, was a known thief."

As the wine bottles were emptied, one by one, the crew members left the fire, gave it up for the evening, and made their way to their tents, with only Doc and Jake remaining by the fire.

"Doc, have you or your company ever entered into such an agreement with a bunch of ranch hands before? Jake asked.

"I can't say that we have, ever, this thing seems to be a first, is it that way with you Jake? Doc replied.

"First time for everything, I guess." Jake said. Then, Jake put a cover on the campfire, got up and headed for his tent.

"Good night, Doc." Jake called back.

"Good night, Jake, it will be a better day tomorrow for us all.... By the way, tell Big Bird that he's to be up first thing in the morning to help me and Prospector Pete with the breakfast." Doc called out.

"I heard that, Jake, I'll be there first thing." Yelled back Big Bird.

With that, a quiet came over the campsite, with only the noise of the wind and the coyotes yipping in the background on up the valley. No sounds of traffic, no sounds of trains, no sounds of airplanes, a million zillion stars a-shining overhead, and, a quiet that only those who have been there, can ever understand, only interrupted now and then from an occasional unidentified snoring.

The moral of the second part of the two first parts is... Folks can bet their bottom dollar, that anytime, when more than two folks, at any one time, ever agree, on any one thing, that one or another of them, has some agenda, in the matter, either that, or one or the other of them, has a side bet put on the eventual outcome.

"The dream goes on, with..." "The day of the discovery..."

Dawn came, even without the sun being up. It was light out, but the sun had not yet topped the Seven Troughs Range, and, it wouldn't for another hour or so. The camp was coming alive, nonetheless. Doc had started the gas grill and the smell of coffee and frying bacon wafted throughout the campsite. Jake had the hood up on the ranch truck and was already checking the water and oil. The prospecting crew was rousing up and, Prospector Pete with Little John were already outside their tent, in their long johns with their boots on, relieving themselves out amongst the sagebrush. Prospector Pete then quickly dressed and headed to the chuck wagon area to help Doc and Big Bird with breakfast. The rest of the ranch crew and the prospecting crew were coming awake little by little. Cahill brought some water to the grill to heat up for shaving, he asked Doc to let him know when it was hot. Slowly, but surely, the camp was coming alive, although a little slower than normal, mostly, due to the amount of wine that had been consumed the night previous, everything was going as best as could be expected.

When the water was hot, Doc yelled for Cahill, and, he came to get the water and parceled it out at the crews wash tables, then, everyone was out and about for shaving and washing and cleaning up. Doc, Big Bird and Prospector Pete were busy getting breakfast ready.

Shortly thereafter, came the all… "Come and get it…. first come, first served." Doc yelled.

One by one, the prospecting crew and the ranch hands came to breakfast. Doc had spread out pancakes and hot maple syrup with some melted butter, turkey bacon, some pieces of cut up cantaloupe, chilled orange juice and hot coffee with some individual containers of yogurt from Walmart which everyone apparently enjoyed, as they kept coming back for seconds.

"A breakfast fit for kings but probably not yet fully appreciated". Jake called out to Doc.

Following breakfast, Jake started to give the assignments of the ranch crew about the same time that Doc was giving assignments to the prospecting crew. Then, Doc stopped, and asked Jake if he still wanted them to look at Cahill's sample area first thing. They agreed between themselves to go ahead with that as a first order of business, then, assigned Cahill to join up with the prospecting crew accordingly.

Cahill, as planned, would go with MaClintock, and Prospector Pete to the sample area first thing, to get that order of business out of way. Will, Hank and Big Bird, would take the truck and horse trailer, and head on up the Granite Springs valley to push on north on up the east side off the valley to Willow Springs and beyond. Then, Jake and Doc told everyone to gear up for the day, make sure they had enough water, and to mount up. The ranch crew first headed for their tents, to gather up their gear, then to go on to the corral to saddle up the horses and load them up into the trailer for the day's work That is, except for Will, who had headed to the toilet for a quick sit down visit.

As everyone was gathering up their provisions together for the day's labor, all of a sudden, the peace of the camp site was broken, with Will yelling from the toilet area…. "Yeowee, Yeowee, HELP, HELP, I've done been snake bit…there's a rattler in the toilet, HELP, ANY BODY… I've done been bit bad…. Oh for God's sake, I've done been snake bit…. I'm prob'ly gonna die… I need help out here

NOW…..Oh my God, someone, help me now, Lord, I do not deserve this kinda shit!" All said while running all but bare assed from the toilet or latrine area.

Everyone in the camp, turned their attention to Will's plight over in the toilet area. But then, most of them wondered, in the back of their own mind, if this was not just another joke, or prank being played upon them, by Will, as was his customary habit, or, if there was really such an emergency, so, no one moved immediately, and they all waited to see what was to happen next.

Will came running toward the breakfast area out of the toilet area, with his pants about half down around his legs, holding them up with his left hand, and holding his right rear buttock with his right hand, just like he had just come off of some bucking bronco. As this all took place, most of the group decided in their own minds that it must be really true, that Will actually had been snake bit, but what was to happen next was anybody's guess.

Hank ran up to Will, and asked… "Where you done been bit, Will? Let me take a look at it."

Will said, "On my butt, on my right side, up high." Hank tried to look but Will wouldn't stand still.

Hank grabbed Will by the arm and spun him around, just a few feet from the toilet, "Where's the snake Will? He yelled.

"In the toilet, behind the toilet, by the toilet paper." Will yelled back.

MaClintock came running with a short handled shovel, one that they used for prospecting, and, he yelled, "Will, where's the snake?"

Will yelled again… "In the toilet, by the toilet, by the toilet paper, oh, damn, this is a hellava way to start the day."

Hank ran around the back of the toilet area and MaClintock went into the toilet with the shovel, looking first, then, stabbing the shovel into the ground around the toilet, and, shortly after, yelling…"I got him, I got him…. It's a rattler all right, it's a big'un,…he's in here alright, but, I got him good… there must be seven or eight rattles on his tail, I got his head cut off already, everything is OK now, this is one rattler that won't be bittin' anyone anymore."

"No, everything ain't OK, I need help here, real quick." Yelled Will.

Hank came running back to Will and said. "Calm down Will, let me look at where you got bit."

Will said, "Right here, on the right side." … showing his butt to Hank."

Hank, looking at Will's butt, said, "Yea, I see what looks like fang marks, you got bit, sure enough, but now, we need to get you to the doctor, pronto."

Jake come running to where Will and Hank was, and he was yelling for Cahill to go disconnect the horse trailer from the pickup truck so they could use the truck to take Will into Lovelock.

Cahill took off to the corral area where the truck was, to get the truck. He hurriedly disconnected the trailer, and, let the tongue drop on the ground, then, he got in the truck, started it up and drove back to the camp site to get Will, with Big Bird running along behind trying to catch up.

Jake yelled for Will to get into the truck, so that Big Bird could drive him to the doctor. Doc came running with some Ice in a gallon plastic bag, and told Will to put it on his butt and sit on it until he got to the hospital, as it would slow down the effect of the toxin from the bite, until they got him an antidote.

Will got into the truck, while Jake was giving instructions to Big Bird, on how to get into Lovelock. "Stay on State Route 48, you have to go up the switch backs through the Seven Troughs range, then, across the Antelope valley, for about 8 miles or so, holding to the right at each intersection, then through the Trinity Range, until you hit the blacktop at the top of the Trinity Range, then, go straight on into Lovelock on the black top, and, when you come in to town, go like you are going straight to the Courthouse, but go on west a few more blocks, and, you will see the hospital, take Will there, and, we will let them know you are a comin'...., now, go, get Will to the doctor, we'll call ahead and let them know that you are on your way, me and Doc will be following you in shortly, we'll only be a little while behind you, so, we'll see you there."

Big Bird headed out of the camp area in the ranch pickup truck, with Will riding shotgun, and, headed up through the switch backs in the Seven Troughs Range, and, they were on their way and out of sight within a few minutes with the dust fading away as they were going through the southern pass of the Seven Troughs Mountain range.

Jake told Hank and Cahill to come with him down to the corral to get the horses ready, because that is the only way that the crew could get into Cahill's prospect area.

Jake headed on down to the corral, because he knew that that was the only place where the cell phones could pick up a signal. When he got to the corral, he climbed up to the top of a pile of andesite just on the south side of the corral, got his cell phone out and punched in 911.

Jake heard the signal go through, and the ringing of 911. That was a good sound for a time like this, he thought.

The, 911 answered the call with... "911 here, what is your emergency?" Jake answered with.... "This is Jake Kelley of the Yeehaw Ranch, out in the Granite Springs Valley, 40 miles northeast of Lovelock, we have a ranch hand who has just been snake bit, by a rattlesnake, and, he is being transported to the Lovelock Clinic for treatment, and, we need to alert them that he is on his way, and, will be there on site within about an hour."

"This is 911, what is your emergency?" the operator asked. Jake said...."This is Jake Kelley again, of the Yeehaw ranch."

"OK, Jake, what is your emergency?" 911 responded.

Jake responded with.... "OK, again, we have a ranch hand, who was bit by a rattlesnake, and, we have sent him on into Lovelock to the Hospital Clinic there, for treatment, and, we would appreciate it if you would let them know that he is on his way."

911 replied with... "OK, we will alert them, what is the ETA?"

"What do you mean by ETA?" Jake asked.

"The Estimated Time of Arrival.": responded the 911 operator.

"Within the hour." Replied Jake, "It'll take them about an hour to get in there."

"We will advise, and, thank you for your information; we will also notify the Emergency Management Agency for Pershing County." The 911 operator replied.

Jake added. "We just want to make sure that they know that he is on his way in for treatment."

911 responded. "We are just happy to be of service, sir, and, thank you for your call."

Jake then hung up. Hoping in his own mind, that everything would be OK with Will.

Meanwhile, Big Bird and Will, were on their way to Lovelock, on Nevada State Route 48, with Big Bird driving.

How are you feeling, Will? Big Bird asked.

"I'm OK, right now, but this ice is sure cold on my butt." Will responded.

"I think that Doc gave you the ice in order to slow down the toxin from the snake bite, so, you should try to keep it in place until we get to the hospital." Big Bird said.

"Well, my butt is already numb from the cold, and, I am not feeling any pain, so, I don't know how bad the damned snake bit me, maybe he only nicked me." Will said.

"Try not to think about it, Will." Big Bird responded.
"That's kind of hard to do, when you are the one who has been snake bit. You ever been bit Bird?" Asked Will.
"No, I ain't never been bit by no rattler." He said, and, he drove hard on.

"The dream goes on.... and, Meanwhile..."
Back at the camp site, Cahill and Hank were saddling the horses up at the corral, and preparing for work of the day, and, to get them ready. The prospecting crew, however, had mounted up and was all but ready, to go to the site where Cahill had found the outcrop, where he had taken the sample. came up with yesterday, as, there is nothing else that we can do right now for Will."
"OK, Doc, go ahead and and have them get the exploration of the area out of the way, so that we can go on with our work. Have them take both Cahill and Hank, and see if they can be of any good, and take all the horses, because that is the only way you can get in there." Jake said.
Doc then ordered the prospecting crew, Prospector Pete, and, MaClintock, to join up with Cahill and Hank, and go look at the sample area, and they all, headed out on horseback, toward the area that Cahill had told them about out on the northwest corner of the Blue Wing Mountains.
Jake and Doc, headed back on foot to the camp site to get things wrapped up and to get Doc's Jeep to get ready to go into Lovelock.
Doc went back to cleaning up after breakfast, doing just the bare minimum that was needed, with Jake was trying to offer some assistance in the effort to hurry things up.
Doc said to Jake. "Jake, I think that we should follow Will and Big Bird on into town, as soon as we can, just to make sure that they make it, and go ahead and file the agreement that we wrote up last night while we are in there."
Doc, that sounds like a plan, we'll do it as soon as I finish my calls to make sure everything is working out as planned."
Meanwhile, while Big Bird and Will, well on their way to Lovelock, on Nevada State Route 48, which was not much more than a graded gravel road, graded down to bedrock, here and there, and, Big Bird said... "Will, we ain't got much gas, according to the gages, and, we might not make it to Lovelock, if'n the danged gages are right."
Will said, "What are you saying, Bird, that if we run out of gas out here in the middle of nowhere, and, don't make it to Lovelock, that I

might as well be dead? Is that what you're saying, that I might end my life with a danged snake bite'?

"Not at all, I'm just sayin' that we don't have much gas left, and, that I just noticed it, and, that it may not be enough to get us to where we want to get, and we have a long way to go and a short time to get there." Said Big Bird.

"How much gas do you have left? Asked Will.

"About almost on empty or just notch or so a little better." Replied Big Bird.

"Well, I guess that we will get as far as we can get, then, with what we have, to get there with, but if we don't make it, we'll have to wait for Doc and Jake and ride on in with them." Replied Will.

Big Bird drove on, hoping to make it on to Lovelock, but decided to drive a little slower in order to conserve on the gas, and thereby, hoping, maybe, to be a little more able to make it on into Lovelock for sure.

"The dream still goes on, with another, Meanwhile…"

Back with the prospecting crew, as, they had planned their work and were now working their plan, and, they were well on their way to go look at the site where Cahill had taken his sample the day before. MaClintock was telling Prospector Pete that they really needed to pay attention to detail when taking a sample, to make sure that it was representative of the overall prospect, if and just in case that it was to be any future value.

MaClintock, and Prospector Pete were in the front of the truck, with, Little John and Cahill and Hank, were almost to the dry lake bed.

"Don't ride out on that dry lake bed." Said Cahill… "it won't hold the horses, and, you'll get hung up quick, you'll fall through and you won't get out." He added.

Cahill said, "I'll lead out with MaClintock, and Prospect Pete and Little John can follow along behind."

"Thanks a lot there Cahill, but how do we know which is which one that will fall through the crust of the dry lake?" Asked MaClintock.

"Hank, you get your horse and I'll get mine, that'll simplify it." Cahill said, then added. "Maclintock, get your horse in front of, Prospect Pete, or, pick your poison." Cahill added.

"I don't think I've ever rode a horse without cowboy boots on." Maclintock said. "I don't think my hiking boots fit in the stirrups." He added.

"We'll make do, with what we got." Added Cahill.

They all untied their horses, mounted up, and followed ahill out onto the dry lake bed at a fast walk, with MaClintock now all but bringing up the rear, just in case anything went wrong.

As an avid reader, you will note that Hank never says much, anytime, at all, I think that that is just the way he is, as, he keeps to himself, usually, does things on his own, normally, but otherwise, he keeps his mouth shut and follows the lead of others. On the other hand, he would not say shit, even if he had a mouthful.

"And, yet, another Meanwhile… just thrown in at the last moment."

Back at the camp, Jake and Doc were discussing what additional that they could do to help out in the situation that they were in before they headed for Lovelock.

Jake said. "Doc, I think I will call 911 again, to see if they can patch me through to the clinic, and, maybe let them know that they might need to get some rattlesnake antidote lined up for when Big Bird and Will get there."

"A good idea, Jake, go do it, and, I'll get the Jeep readied." Doc said.

Jake headed back down to the corral area to make the call. When got there, he again climbed up on top of the pile of andesite, and again called 911.

"This is 911, what is your emergency?" Was the answer.

"This is Jake Kelley of the Yeehaw ranch, again, here in the Granite Springs Valley, and, I am calling to see if you can patch me through to the hospital clinic there in Lovelock, to make sure that they have some rattlesnake venom antidote on hand for when our ranch hand arrives there, or, just give me their number, and, I can call them direct." Jake said.

911 responded. "Yes, Jake, we already advised the clinic that a snakebite victim was on their way, and, I've tried to call you back, with no response, and, now that I've got you on the line, they want to know the victim's name, and, some other insurance information."

Jake said. "The victim's name is William Pardey, he is a ranch hand with the Yeehaw Ranch, and, I am his foreman, Jake Kelley."

911 responded with. "Jake, the clinic says they need to know his condition, what time the snake bite occurred, where he got the snakebite, and, if the snake is being brought in for positive identification as being toxic, whether the victim is having any complications, if he is on any medication, that sort of thing."

"Well, he got bit this mornin' about 7:30 or so, and, we are sure that it

was a rattlesnake, because we killed it and cut off the rattlers, and they are not bringing the snake with them. As for the victim, I do not know of any medication that he is on, and I cannot tell you what his condition is, because I am not with him at this time, as, he is on his way to Lovelock now, but I can add that he got bit on his right butt, and, we gave him a bag of ice to sit on while he was on his way in." Jake said.
911 again responded. "Jake, I will so advise the clinic, but is it possible for you to call me back within a few minutes, if they need any other information, that is, if I cannot reach you?"
Jake added. "Yes, I will stand by here, as the only place we can get a phone signal, out or in, is out near the middle of the Granite Springs Valley, near a corral here."
911 responded. "OK, Jake, 911 out, will be back to you shortly."
Jake sat on the top of the pile of andesite, talking to himself about also calling Miss Steph, to let her know and to bring her up to date on the days happenings. Then, the phone rang, and, he answered.
"Jake, here, go ahead." He said.
911 responded with. "Yea, Jake, the clinic has been so advised, however, they do not have any rattlesnake venom antidote on site, but there is some at Winnemucca, and the Highway Patrol has been notified, and, they have dispatched a patrolman to pick it up at the Winnemucca hospital, and, to deliver it to the clinic at Lovelock, post haste, so, help is on the way, and, they have some coming up from Reno, but they are flying it in to the Derby airport from up at Stead, just north of Reno, so, it may be here first, but at least two doses are so dispatched but not yet enroute. By the way, the nurse on duty at the clinic, wants to know, if this is the same Will Pardey, that was in there last Spring that got stitched up after a four-wheeler accident and who had a slight concussion at the time, because, if it is, they already have some information on him, insurance and all.'
Jake responded. "Tell her that it is the one and same person coming in, same person, different kind of accident."
911 said. "OK, Jake, thanks, we will so advise, and, he should be arriving soon, as it has been almost an hour, so, 911 out."
"Thanks for all your help." Jake said, and hung up.
"911 out." Was the only response and Jake hit the off call button on the phone.
Jake then called Steph at the Yeehaw ranch to advise her about the incident and what was happening and advised her that he would update her when he arrived in Lovelock later in the morning and told

her that maybe she might be able to get more information directly from the clinic on a land line, then, Jake climbed down from his perch atop the pile of andesite at the corral and headed back to the camp site.

Meanwhile, at Winnemucca, All-American Nevada Highway Patrolman Jay Marshall, had gotten the call from 911, to go to the Winnemucca hospital, pick up the rattlesnake anti-venom, and to make sure that it was put on ice, and, to head out and deliver it ASAP to the clinic in Lovelock, about 60-70 miles to the Southwest on Interstate 80. Jay finished his $1.99 come-on breakfast special at the casino, and headed out the door, on to the hospital, where he acquired the anti-venom, packed on ice, put it in his patrol car, and, headed out to West Interstate 80 for Lovelock, with his whoop whoop siren on and his lights a-flashin' and a-blinkin', all at 90-110 miles per hour in the Nevada 75 miles per hour speed zone forever in the left lane. All-American Jay, was to say that he was on his way, to make someone's day, and to make his pay, and, he confirmed that, with the 911 operator, and, he felt good, like he was doing something positive for his fellow man, as if, he was to become some kind of All-American hero.

At the same time, or somewhat near that time, another unmentioned All-American Nevada State highway patrolman was dispatched to St. Mary's hospital in Reno, to pick up another dose of anti-venom, to deliver to the airport at Stead, just north of Reno, and, to meet with the All-American Civil Air Patrol flight crew there for delivery by air to the Derby airport near Lovelock if needed for any further treatment as called for.

Meanwhile, Big Bird and Will, had already made it through the Trinity Range, was off of the gravel road and onto the blacktop hard road, and, they were on the downhill grade with the green irrigated grasses of Lovelock well in site ahead.

"I think we are going to make it Will." Said Big Bird excitedly.

"My butt is totally numb." Complained Will.

As they came into town, aggravating traffic slowed them down a little, but they made it onto the parking lot of the hospital with the truck engine still running strong. Big Bird told Will to wait in the truck while he went to get a wheel chair because he thought that Will should not be walking on his leg any more than necessary, but, Will argued him down, and got out of the pickup anyway, and walking on his own, headed into the hospital under his own power and hard headedness.

Meanwhile, back at the campsite....
Doc and Jake departed the campsite in Doc's Jeep, and headed on in to Lovelock, to make sure, primarily, that Will and Big Bird made it in OK to the hospital and secondarily to file their agreement with the Pershing County Clerk. With that, they both headed out on route 48 and on to Lovelock.
The moral of the third part is... Every action, at any particular moment in time, will bring about some reaction at some time or another, sooner or later, with none of them expected or particularly predictable.

Then, the dream takes another peculiar turn, another meanwhile, if you will, but one that is down in Lovelock... with Will...

The love story between the cowboys and the Indians, as best remembered.... by those so fully involved at the time.

As Will and Big Bird entered the hospital, they were met by the on duty nurse.
"Well, hello there Will, we've been expecting you, come with me." Said the nurse.
"How does she know you Will? "Do you know her?" Asked Big Bird.
"From the four-wheeler accident that I was in back last Spring, when I was laid up here and lost a couple week's wages." Said Will.
"She sure is a pretty one. What's her name?" Asked Will.
Quietly, somewhat under his breath, Will told Big Bird.... "Her name is Sarah, I can't think of her last name, right now, but somehow she got the idea, or, had the thought that she fell in love with me last Spring, when I was in here 'cause of the four-wheeler accident when I had to be stitched up and was treated for a concussion all while in a coma, anyway, I got to know her then, after I came out of the coma, I mean."
While Sarah was pulling the curtain around a bed in the emergency section of the hospital, she overheard Big Bird talking to Will, and introduced herself. "Hi to you, my name is Sarah White-Snow, and I know Will, both first and second hand, so to speak, so, how is it that you are here with Will?
"My name is Herb Holabird, but my friends call me Big Bird, and I

just drove Will in from our camp site out in the Granite Springs Valley, where he done went and got his'self-snake-bit this mornin', but in his defense, it weren't his fault anyway, and, by the way, he just might be embarrassed to tell you, but he got bit on the right upper side of his butt, while he was going potty this mornin' just after breakfast and before shavin' and brushin' teeth time." Big Bird said.

Sarah, going about her business, did not answer Big Bird, but instead, continued with…. "Will, take off your clothes, put on this hospital gown, call me when you are ready and I'll take look at your snake bite, the doctor is on his way in to look at you too, and, the highway patrol is on their way, bringing a capsule of snake venom antidote down from Winnemucca, and, I hear from the 911 Dispatcher, that they have another capsule on its way up from Reno, being flown up by the Civil Air Patrol from out at Stead, just North of Reno, and coming into Derby, so, you have more help coming than you probably will ever need, and everything is fully under control, for now, except you, that is."

Big Bird stepped out of the bed area and asked Sarah if there was anything else that he could do to help, but she indicated that the hospital staff and the doctor could handle Will's case now, and directed Big Bird to the lounge waiting area for the time being.

Sarah went into the kitchen area, got four bananas, then went back to where Will was, walked into the bed area, and said to Will, who was now sitting on the side of the bed in his hospital gown, with his clothes folded neatly and piled up on the table beside the bed.

"So, you done up and went and got yourself snake bit on your itsy bitsy shiney hiney, huh, Will?"

Will, just nodded, sheepishly.

"Are you still ridin' them hard and putin' them away wet, like you told me you were doing last Spring?" Sarah asked.

Will did not respond, except to turn and look the other way toward some empty chart on the wall.

Sarah told Will that she had to take his vital signs, so, she hooked him up with the blood pressure cuff, took his blood pressure, first on the left side, then again on the right side, then, did the same on his lower legs, then, counted his heartbeat.

"How much do you weigh, Will?" Sarah asked.

Will said. "Oh, about 170, I guess, more or less, why do you need to know that for?"

"Well, Will, how much snake bite venom antidote you get, depends upon your weight, heavier people get more, lighter people get less, it's as simple as that." Sarah said.

Sarah made the notes on her chart, then, said. "OK, Will, now, let's take a look at your itsy bitsy snake bite, so, lay down on the bed and turn over on your belly."

Will laid down on the bed, turned over, pulled his gown up, and patted on his right buttock, and said. "It's back here somewhere, but it is numb as can be, 'cause I've been sittin' on a bag of ice for at least the last hour or so."

Sarah said. "OK, Will, I'm going to get you cleaned up real nice and pretty for the doctor, as, he should be here any time now." With that, Sarah went to the sink area, gathered the utensils and soap needed, ran the hot water until it was warm, put some antibacterial soap onto a wash rag and returned to Will's bedside and put on surgical gloves, purposely snapping them up near Will's ear, just to aggravate him.

While she was cleaning and scrubbing the snake bite area on Will's butt, she said. "Will, how come, you ain't never called me, like you said you would, after your four-wheeler accident last Spring? Don't you remember telling me that you would sure call, or did the concussion cause you to have some total lapse of memory of me over the past six months? Huh?"

Will, with his face pushed into the pillow, responded with…. "Well, Sarah, I would have, but not havin' any more money, than what I make on the ranch, and, not havin' any transportation to get into town, and, me working seven days a week, and now, livin' at a camp site out in the middle of nowhere, off and on, where you can't even take a shower to clean up, or…"

Sarah interrupted. "Oh, shut up, Will, if you'd a wanted to call me, you'd have found some way, or, if you'd have wanted to date me bad enough, you'd have found some way to get into town, even if we didn't do anything that cost money, if you'd have wanted to just talk to me, you'd of found some way, so, don't make it sound like you can't do anything for yourself, 'cause, you do what you want to do in this life, with the ones you want to do it with, and, you know it." All the time, while poking around on Will's butt with her gloved finger, she said. "Here, where you are all swelled up, does that hurt?"

"I don't feel nothin'." Will said.

"Probably still numb from the ice." Sarah said. "I'm going to check to see where the doctor is, and, I'll be right back, meanwhile, go ahead and have a banana for a snack, it's doctor's orders, and, it'll be good for you, besides, you need the vitamins." Sarah added.

Big Bird saw Sarah coming out of the emergency area, and, he jumped up as she came into the lobby area. "How's Will doing, is he going to be OK?" He asked.

"Will will be fine, as soon as we can get the anti-venom delivered, but when we do, I don't think Will will be too happy with all the injections, because, if I remember right, Will does not like needles." Sarah said.

"Can I go back and talk to him?" Big Bird asked.

"Sure, but if the doctor comes in, you will have to beat a hasty retreat back out here in the lobby." Sarah responded.

Big Bird went down the hall and into the emergency area, to Will's bed. He pulled back the curtain, and said. "Will, how you doin' Will? Is there anything I can get for you? "

Will, sitting up in bed and peeling a banana, responded with…. "Hey, man, I sure could use something to drink."

"I'll get you a soda, what do you want, diet or regular?" Big Bird asked.

"Get me a regular Coke or Pepsi, whatever they have available." Will said.

"OK, Will, I'll be right back." Big Bird said.

Big Bird asked the receptionist where the soda machine or snack area was located, got the directions, then, he headed off to get Will and himself a soda, and, maybe one for Sarah.

Sarah was in her office calling for the doctor, but just as she got his beeper on the line, she saw him walking in from the parking lot. She hung up, went into the reception area, waited for him to come in, then, joined him to escort him into where Will was, and was explaining to him the circumstances of Will's emergency.

Sarah and the doctor, came into the emergency area, where Will was, and pulled the curtain back for the doctor to enter in to Will's bed, Sarah told the doctor what Will's blood pressure and heart rate was, gave him Will's chart, and also told him that the Nevada Highway Patrol was bringing a vial of rattlesnake anti-venom from Winnemucca, with a second vial being flown up from Reno by the Civil Air Patrol, coming into Derby, and, that the first one should be on site very shortly, and with that all said, she then introduced them.

"Will, this is Doctor Zerwin, Doctor, this is Will Pardey, an All-American rowdy dowdy Cowboy and Yeehaw Ranch employee, who was also in here last Spring after a four-wheeler accident when he had a slight concussion along with some other scrapes and bruises

resulting in a total loss of memory on selected issues mostly off but some reported on, over the last six months or so."
"You all now riding four-wheelers instead of horses for round-up Will?" The Doctor asked.
"Well, no, we were just out trying to see if we could round up a few at the time, as kind of a test thing, but found out that the muffler noise scared them all too much, and, the other thing was that we all ate too much sagebrush." Will said, still holding about a half-eaten banana.
The doctor asked Will. "Where'd you get your snake bite, Will?"
"On my right butt." Will said.
"Now, just how did this all come about?" The doctor asked.
Will responded with. "Well, we were all camped out by Porter Spring, up in Granite Springs Valley, about 40 mile or so northwest of here, and, a little more than an hour ago, this mornin', after breakfast, while I down was at the toilet, I reached for the toilet paper, and, a rattler, unbeknownst to me, had somehow got down behind the toilet, done struck me while I was bendin' over and wipin' my butt, simple as that."
"Don't forget to tell him about the ice pack, Will." Sarah said.
"Oh, yea, the guys at the campsite, made me up an ice pack, for me to sit on while en-route in here from the camp site." Will said.
The doctor told Will to roll over on his stomach, which Will promptly did, and, Sarah took what was left of the banana, wrapped it in a napkin, and laid it on the stand beside the hospital bed.
The doctor, first looked at the bite area, then, went over and washed and scrubbed his hands at the sink, put on a pair of latex gloves, and began looking at and poking around on the snake bite area on Will's right buttock getting into his examination a little more seriously. Sarah mentioned that she had already poked around on it previously, and had cleaned it up with some antibacterial soap, so as to disinfect the wound area a little. The doctor said that he appreciated that, and, continued to poke around on the snake bite area. Sarah mentioned that the swelling in the bite area appeared to be hard, and, the doctor said that it did appear to be so, but could be expected he said, and he asked Sarah to go and find out if she could, what the Estimated Time of Arrival, the ETA, if you will, was, of the Highway Patrolman with the anti-venom, and, to bring some Tincture of Iodine to further disinfect Will's wound area.
Sarah left for the receptionist area to make the call to 911, and met Big Bird coming from the snack machine area. Big Bird asked if he

could get back in to see Will, to give him a soda, but Sarah told him to wait, as the doctor was with Will at that time. Sarah, finally got the 911 operator on line and asked where the patrolman was at this time. The 911 operator told her to stand by, then contacted the Highway Patrolman, who was reportedly enroute from Winnemucca, and asked him where he was and what his ETA was on arrival at Lovelock. Jay Marshall responded that he was at mile marker 127, which was about 20 miles East of Lovelock on Interstate 80, and, that he would most likely be at the Lovelock clinic within about 15 minutes or so, as, he was cruising at a little more than 95 miles per hour. The 911 operator said that she would so advise, and, in turn, advised Sarah, Sarah then asked about the anti-venom coming in from Reno, and was advised by the 911 dispatcher that the Civil Air Patrol had departed Stead with another vial on ice about fifteen minutes or so ago, and, could be expected to be at the Derby airport within about another half hour or so. Sarah thanked her, then carried the message back to the doctor who was still with Will.

"The first vial of anti-venom serum will be here from Winnemucca within about 15 minutes or so, doctor, with a second vial being flown in from Reno by the Civil Air Patrol and should be at Derby within a half-hour and could be here onsite within the hour." Sarah announced. With that, Sarah opened the bottle Tincture of Iodine and painted Will's butt all but red round and about the bite wound, then, she painted a smiley face on his other buttock.

"Good, good. Have you ever been bit before by a rattlesnake before Will.? Asked the doctor.

"No, never." Will responded.

"Well, the good news is, that the anti-venom will be here soon, but, the bad news is, that is has been more than an hour that, that you have done been bit. That means, that the venom has had some time to do some damage, so, you may wind up with another hole in your butt, or, worst case scenario, you could lose half of your ass, then, you would become known as half assed Will, but, just joking Will, but, all joking aside, the other side of the good news, is, that you probably will not have any further adverse reaction, once the anti-venom is administered, except perhaps for an upset stomach, perhaps that is." The doctor said.

Will looked at Sarah, but did not respond, and, apparently did not find the Doctor's joking to be all that funny.

Sarah, trying to lighten up the situation, remarked. "Well, Will, it could be worse, but it isn't, and, we do have anti-venom on the way to try to offset any secondary anguish, so, you at least ought to be more than thankful for that."

Will responded. "I am thankful for what you all are tryin' to do for me, at this time, but I do feel kind of stupid, for having been in the wrong place at the wrong time, which got me here, to where I am now."

The doctor went on to explain the treatment, of the intravenous delivery of the serum, along with local injections, to be administered hour by hour over a period of the next four to five hours, so Will was to be admitted for the administration, then, monitored for any serum sickness. The doctor also told Will that he would have him on a banana diet for lunch and maybe even for his supper, because if he got sick, he may vomit and that bananas tasted the same coming out as they did going in, as if that were some sort of comfort.

Will responded with... "Well thanks a lot Doc, that is somethin' nice to know."

The phone was ringing off the wall of the emergency room and Sarah rushed to pick up the call. It was the 911 dispatcher calling. The dispatcher advised her that Trooper Jay Marshall had just got off of Interstate 80 and would be at the hospital within a couple of minutes, but, that he could not tarry, because he had another call waiting as there was a tractor trailer roll-over about thirty miles west of Lovelock. Sarah asked who was bringing the second vial of anti-venom from the Derby airport, if Jay couldn't do it. The dispatcher said that she would call Derby and have the Civil Air Patrol take their loaner car and to deliver it on-site themselves, and, that she would contact the Fixed Base Operator at Derby to confirm such. Sarah told her that she appreciated that and the dispatcher signed off.

"Anti-venom will be here within a couple of minutes." Sarah yelled to the doctor.

Shortly thereafter, Trooper Jay Marshall rolled into the hospital parking lot with red and blue lights flashing, shut his emergency system down, then, grabbed the six pack cooler that held the anti-venom, and, headed into the hospital area and the lobby where he met Sarah.

"Jay, stand by for a couple minutes and let me get this to the doctor." Sarah said, and, she opened the cooler to see five vials of ACP. She took the vials, put three of them into a plastic baggy marked them with a control number, then, put them into the refrigerator in the hallway. She took the other two into the room where Will and the doctor were. She provided the doctor with the one vial of ACP for his injections, then, set up the IV bag and the other vial of ACP for the setup of the IV catheter and then plugged Will in to administer the dextrose solution, then, hooked up and started the antivenin drip, all the while, the doctor was setting up the needles for the local injections of the anti-venom at the snake bite on Will's butt.

Sarah then went to the refrigerator in the hall way, got two sodas and returned to the lobby area, where she put them in on the ice in the same six pack cooler Jay had brought in to the hospital and told Trooper Marshall that that was his treat of the day for delivering the medication. Jay thanked her, then, with cooler in hand, he headed back to his car to head out for his next assignment.

Sarah, then went to the kitchen area across the hall, got two more bananas from the fruit bowl, and headed back to the emergency area with the bananas for Will.

As Sarah came back into the room, the doctor was explaining to Will, that he was also going to also inject some of the anti-venom at the bite area on a quarter hour schedule, as he had better experience with that method, and, he drew a clock like marked circle on Will's butt and began the first injection.

Big Bird poked his head around the curtain and interrupted with... "I have a couple of sodas here, can Will have anything to drink?"

"Sure, that is as long as Will can hold it down." The doctor responded. He went on to explain to Will, that the anti-venom applications may make him sleepy and lethargic, or, it possibly could make him sick, and, reminded him again that he could vomit.

Will just nodded with his head muffled in the pillow.

"I'll be back in a little while Will, you are in good hands here with Sarah, so, behave yourself, and, I will see you in an hour of so." The doctor said. Then, he entered the information on Will's chart, gave Sarah verbal instructions as to the continued administration of the IV with the ACP, advised her that he would return within a half hour or so, and then he left the emergency room area.

Will asked if he could sit up. Sarah indicated that he could, and, Will turned over and sat up. Sarah adjusted his bed for him in a head up position, then, Big Bird came into the room, opened one of the sodas and gave it to Will.

"You are the one that is called "Big Bird"?" Sarah asked.

"Yep, that be me." Big Bird said.

"Why in the world do they call you that? Or, how did you get that for a nick name?" Sarah returned.

"My real full name is Herb Holibird, and, I was always kind of on the big side, and, had what some folks said were bird legs, so, when I was a kid, there was a character on the Sesame show with a name of Big Bird, so, it just kind of fit along with when I was in school, and then it continued on in to today with and amongst the other cow hands at the Yeehaw ranch." He said.

"Well, Herb, I appreciate you bringing Will in to the hospital, with his snake bite and all, but would you, or could you, give Will and I a little privacy, as, I have something to talk to him about, which is personal and only concerns the two of us." Sarah said.

Big Bird responded. "Sure, I'll be out in the lobby, if you all need anythin', just let me know, so, I'll see you all later, and you'll know where I'll be." Big Bird left Will's room, but stepped just outside the entry where he could still listen. He stood within earshot of the ongoing conversation between Sarah and Will, out of nothing more than curiosity as to what was about to transpire.

After Big Bird stepped outside, Sarah adjusted up the things around and about the emergency room, then, she sat down on the edge of Will's bed and just looked at Will, who was sitting up in bed, eating the rest of his banana and sipping on his soda.

"What is it you got to say, Sarah?" Will asked.

"I think that banana is about the same size as your wing-wang, Will." Sarah said.

Will retorted embarrassedly. "What do you know about my wing-wang, anyway?"

Sarah responded with. "Well, Will, when you were in here totally unconscious last spring, I had to put a catheter in that wing-wang of yours, on no less than two or three separate occasions, I gave you no less than a dozen enemas, and I got more than real familiar with your familiars, and, I had to give you a number of baths, and even wash and wipe up your smelly butt, I shaved you every day, I put lotion on your skin, I rolled you over three or four times a day, all while you were unconscious and having fun runnin' off at the mouth with your delirium tremens about ropin' and ridin' the wild broncos of the west."

"Well, I would never have otherwise known, but maybe I was better off anyway when I didn't know anything about it at the time." Will replied.

Sarah began, "Will, I am an All-American, in more ways than one, although, I am better part Indian, for the most part, Piaute, to be exact, and, I am going to cut to the chase, get to the point and blow it all out once and for all, and bare my mind and my soul for whatever good it may do. So, here it comes. When you were in here last spring, with your concussion and all, after you finally came to and recuperated, I thought that you and I had come to some agreement, which we would try to establish some kind of relationship between the two of us. Just to put it on the line and lay it out flatly to you, since you must have some kind of problem understanding the King's English, I did, at that time, aimlessly all but fall in love with you, so, stupid on me the dumb ass, as I must have been more than very foolish at the time, I might add. I know now, that it was a high-school girl kind of thing, but I did it, I fell off the wagon if you will, I let it all hang out, and, I couldn't help myself otherwise at the time, and, it is still with me to no little extent yet on to today, and, now that I see you again, I have the same feelings for you that I had then, with nothing changed, so, in my fevered perception, as I see it all, it must be nothing else in the world but true love, albeit perhaps, it may only be a one way kind of thing. And you, you said, at that time, that you would call me, come to see me, visit, talk and walk, and, I waited, and I waited, day in and day out, for you to either make my phone ring, or someday to show up at my front door, although I would have sneaked you into my back door, or maybe by chance to even come by the hospital in the event you lost my address, all the time singin' those honky tonk blues a-thinkin' you were partyin' all night and a-chasin' some neon rainbow, or out paradin' at some jiggle joint, but then, you never did make contact in any form whatsoever. I even thought about writing a book about us, entitled, "For sale, new wedding dress, never used" and then, it's sequel "For sale, new baby shoes, never used", so, until today, by none other than by accidental happenstance, either that or by none other than by a cast of fate itself, to tell you the truth, I am no little perplexed with all of it after all, but, I would like to hear your explanation of your lack of action with respect to your previously professed feeling for me and my expectations, and the whimsical agreements that I thought that we had established between the two of us back last spring. Now, here, today, I am pouring my heart out to you, for what reason I know not, but still, I feel that you need to know that I can't help it if I am still in love with you. So, what say you now you, you all around bronco bustin' All-American quick draw cowboy Will?"

Will, first looked up at Sarah but then dropped his head, looked at his hands, and then began his response. "Sarah, my grandmother was a Cherokee, born on a reservation back in Oklahoma, my grandfather, a cowboy, met her at a barn dance, they fell in love, and they married and moved west all the way out to California. They had five children, of which the first, the oldest, was my father, who married a Mexican girl whose father was a Chinese gold miner, she was my very own sweet mother, who had three children, of which I was the last of the lot, the runt of the litter if you will, who chose to go to work rather than go to school, and, who regrets that decision to this very day, but, none the less, that is the way that it was and the way that it is, mostly because she never heard that song about "Moma, don't let your babies grow up to be cowboys". However, when I first met you, you told me that your mother was a Piaute Indian, fresh off of the reservation north of Reno up by Pyramid Lake, and, that your father was a cowboy, but had injured himself a-breakin' broncos, so, you told me, that he took a job in Wadsworth at a feeder lot, then, saving his money, he got a loan and bought them out to go into business for hisself, just to be close to family on your mother's side, I remember it all, and, especially your sweet smile, I remember everythin' you told me, and have it as a picture in my mind, and I have tossed it back and forth over and over in my mind since that very day, day in and day out, and, I thought or come to the conclusion at the time, that there were more than enough cowboys and Indians already in both of our families for the next hundred years or so without adding me to the mix or to the confusion. So, I just held off and went on standby, and, I avoided any further contact with you because of that, nothin' more, nothin' less, however, after these last few months, I have come to regret that decision, and, now, I ask for the favor of your forgiveness, and, with that, the offer of a more close continued relationship between the two of us, on into our future if you are so willing, so, as my father said, I hereby plight my troth, whatever that may mean or whatever that may bring either or both of us on into our future. I am a real deal and what you see is what you get, no more, and no less."

Sarah took his hand, looked at Will, and, said. "Will, are you in this drugged up fevered state of mind asking me to marry you for better or worse or whatever?"

Will looked at Sarah, and began. "Sarah, understand your man, a man's gotta do what a man's gotta do, yet, on one hand, I ain't got many hang ups, although most cowboys got at least one big one, too, I ain't been mis-behavin', I ain't your everyday coca cola cowboy, and, I ain't a travelin' man, but on the other hand, I am all hat and no cattle, because I ain't got as much as a pot to pee in or a window to throw it out of, but, I ain't exactly alligator bait either, even though I have near little or nothin' to offer, I have only a poor cowboy's wages, I have no property, but I have good intentions of getting some line of work, but, at present, I do not even have a pickup truck with at least a two horse trailer, which I might add, almost all other cowboys that I know, do have, which takes exception to the rule, but to add on, I have no savin's whatsoever, and, there are more things that I do not have than what I do have, I have just been a good ole boy, makin' my way, anyway the law would allow, however, I realize that this is not a cotton candy world, and, I do have sincere lovin' feelin's for you here, down deep in my heart, and, yes, I have literally walked the floor over you, also, I have come to the realization, now that we have met once again, that it must surely be nothin' else except fate itself that brought us together again to this moment in time, and, that led me to the conclusion that we must surely not test that fate, lest we come up on the short order of it, and, yes, I do guess that I am askin' you, if you will, to become my better half, my one and only, my soul mate, if you will. So, now, you know the feelin's of my heart and where I am comin; from, so, what say you?"

Sarah added. "Will, I am not some hootchie-kootchie girl and I neither have their ways even in a blue smoky haze in a bar room just before a brawl, nor do I have have tears drippin' in my beer, but yes, I could have taught a weepin' willow how to cry a big river, but I am tellin' you in the only way that I know how, and that is, all that I ask for, is a roof over my head, and enough food in the house to feed us and our children, and, speakin' of our children, I will even wash their diapers and hang them out on a line to dry, to keep them clean and to save you money. So, if you can find work that can bring in enough money to provide that, along with what I can bring in from my nursin' work, we can make a go of it all and be a success and grow a family from the ground up, right here at home. Besides, my dad would gladly let you drive his pickup truck and pull his two horse trailer the minute he learned that I picked you up out of the round up." The two of them, then, just gawked at one another, kind of moon eyed, but not saying anything further, then, Sarah kissed him. Laid a big one on him, she did, hot and heavy, and, on that note, Will would not forget that kiss for some time on into the distant future even when he was old with alzheimer's a-coming on strong.

Big Bird, just being in the hall to the lobby, stood sipping his soda, not fully believing what he was over hearing coming from these two love birds, it was like a live soap opera, he thought, waiting for what was to happen or what was to be said next for a cliff hanger. Then, he saw the doctor coming through the lobby to go back into Will's

treatment area, and, he asked. "Hey Doc, how do you think Will's a-comin' along?"
The doctor responded. "That's what I gonna' be checking now, so, I will find out and let you know in a few minutes."

"As the dream went on, again, with another Meanwhile..."
Meanwhile, Jake and Doc were on their way into Lovelock on route 48, kicking up dust all the way across the Sage valley, petal to the metal, runnin' hot and all that.
Jake was the first to break the silence between the two with... "Well, Doc, we are almost in to the hard road, so, Will and Big Bird must have made it in OK on into Lovelock."
"Looks that way." Doc responded. "They should at least be at the hospital by now."

"Also, meanwhile... with the dream still ongoing..."
Too, and also meanwhile, Cahill was heading up the prospect crew on horseback into the area where he had taken his sample that he had shown them the night before at supper. The horses followed one another without any of the group reining any of them in. Cahill pulled his horse up near the outcrop with the group dismounting and securing their horse's reins to what sagebrush was closest.
"This is where it's at." said Cahill. "So, get up close, take a good look, and get a sample."
So, just now, the dreamer has just woke up with the realization that there was a problem of how everything in this All-American story about Cowboys, Indians and Prospectors was going to end.
Too, it now has come to the attention of the dreamer, that this story of this dream is totally too long, has too many characters, and wanders around totally too much for any accomplished literary work, with both sentences and paragraphs too long, not to mention the dang dangling participles, along with the innuendo, so, the writer begs your pardon, and, will now try to cut to the chase, if you will, and try to make a too long a story a little shorter.

"Before the awakening... concerning any concerns of All-Americans Will and Sarah..."
Of Will and Sarah, the dreamer surmises that they both did eventually fall head over heels in love, and, they first moved in together shortly thereafter at her place when Will first got out of the hospital, as he was restricted from working by the doctor, and, that they later got

married, with the blessings of their parents on both sides of the family. With Will finally getting a settlement from the Nevada's Worker's Compensation from his previous four wheeler accident occurring the previous Spring, and, a second settlement later on, for getting snake bit, which financial settlements, he used to buy into Sarah's father's feeder lot business down at Wadsworth, since her father was retiring on Social Security pension, and in addition, Will was able to get additional Tax Increment Funding, a "TIF" if you will, from a joint Pershing County and Washoe County agreement to set up an alternate feeder lot on the edge of the Piute Indian reservation near Pyramid Lake, if he would hire some fifty percent of the workforce of the local teenagers there, who were looking for some work that included job training in animal husbandry. Will and Sarah, it is also further surmised by the dreamer, had two children, a boy and a girl, both of which were proved to be well above average, and, who grew up in the area, with both attending the University of Nevada at Reno on scholarship, and, eventually made something of themselves, showing more success of life or in their life, than what their parents did previous, but, no offense meant by that and none should be taken thereby, as, there were definitely extenuating circumstances in both of their lives. Too, Will and his step-father, enjoyed fishing for lake trout up at Pyramid Lake on more than a regular basis, always looking for that nine pounder, and, even tried their hand at golfing, with Sarah having purchased them both a couple sets of golf clubs at yard sales over in Reno while on weekend shopping trips for groceries.

However, on the other hand, maybe Will got cold feet and all but run off again, and, maybe Sarah is still at the hospital there in Lovelock. If it wasn't a dream, I would probably be compelled to go check it all out myself.
"Of the All-American Prospectors…"
Of the prospectors, the dreamer also surmises that Clint Davison, aka "McCintock" moved to Reno and worked for himself as a temporary contract geologist and started an agency for the placement of unemployed geologists, mostly setting on drill rigs and logging drill cores and cutting and splitting samples for evaluation and testing, but he did have one trip out of country to Medelin, Columbia, a dopey excursion as he called it and let it go at that, but then, maybe he didn't and maybe it wasn't. Pete Reeves, aka "Prospect Pete" literally took off from the territory, left Nevada and headed up and headed out, if you will, and went to work for Hamstake Mining company at their

deep mine near Lead, South Dakota, as a hard rock miner no less, but still attained much reported success in his endeavors as evidenced by his 401K investments, but then, maybe he didn't, and the dreamer just made it all up. Robert Schmidt, aka "Doc", got out of the prospecting business altogether, and, got himself a real job, with the State of Nevada Environmental Private Protection Agency, setting up air monitoring system stations all over the State, and, in his spare time, tried to help prove up the causes of global warming on the side, in his treks back and forth all over the basin and range provinces from California to Utah, and from Arizona to Oregon and Idaho, he had the whole real deal, and eventually proved up that the glaciers first started to melt back while they were floating around in the Black Rock Desert up in northern Nevada, but then, maybe he didn't, maybe he did something else, whichever, however, the dreamer does know firsthand, that "Doc" would never leave Nevada.

Also, there is another however, or another on the other hand, for a fact, there is no record in the Pershing County court house of any agreement between the ranch hands and the prospectors. Too, there is no record that Jake or Doc either one ever arrived at Lovelock. They may just as well have been abducted by aliens out in the middle of Sage valley, as far as the dreamer knows anything about.

"Of the all-American Cowboys…"

Of the cowboys, the dreamer surmises, that Herb Holibird, a/k/a "Big Bird", got out of the cowboying trade totally, moved to Reno and went to work for the Harvey Braswell Detective Agency mostly serving papers, following people around and setting out on surveillances and became a Special Deputy of the Washoe County Sheriff's Department and a proud member of the Sheriff's posse, and, finally, married and settled down, but then, maybe he didn't. C.A. Hill, a/k/a "Cahill", just up and walked off the ranch one day, gave it all up, and went back to college on the GI Bill at the University of Nevada at Reno, where he attained his degrees in Biology from the School of Science, then, went on to work for Mansonto where he found an antidote for agent orange exposure, but then, maybe he didn't. And, finally, Jake Kelley, a/k/a "Big Jake", married Miss Stephanie and they folded in on themselves, reducing the size and scope of their ranching operation, and they both together, all by themselves, ran the Yeehaw ranch, provided feeders to Will's feeder lot at Wadsworth, and on the side, raised Appaloosa and Paint horses, making appearances with their livestock in the County fairs and at the Rodeos in the area, and, selling their "home on the range" stock on the internet, but then, again, maybe they didn't to any of it and simply went their own way in the world.

In addition, the site where Cahill had found his sample, proved out to be only an iron stained earthquake fault zone, exposed by another valley fault with no mineral value whatsoever, typical of most faults in the desert outback of Nevada, that can cause some folks to get overly excited sometimes about absolutely nothing, but then, on the other hand, maybe it was the real thing after all.

Here, the however, or the on the other hand, the prospectors may have led the cowboys down a rosy path and just told them that their findings were worthless, being believed by them being knowledgeable in their trade, only for them to come back at some later date for further testing followed by claims staking and eventual mine development. As the dreamer reminds you of the Mark Twain story about his investment losses in gold mines, and, about there always being both a liar and a thief down in the bottom of most prospect holes found round about.

"Of the other All American Heroes…"

The dreamer surmises, that Jay Marshall, the highway patrolman, took an early retirement, and, moved back to his home State of Indiana, where he took a second job as a University Police officer, where and which he again retired from in his later years, and, became a decidedly daily dapper double dipper and enjoyed his retirement years carving real to life artwork to his heart's content. However, maybe he didn't, as, that surmises that that was what his wife allowed him to do and that she agreed to everything and anything that he ever came up with, including their tremendous work at their local church's food pantry.

The Nevada Civil Air Patrol volunteer pilots, the dreamer surmises, delivered the second vial of snake bite anti-venom in record time and under budget, but got no special recognition or award of any kind for their life saving or their heroism, and, yet, to date, no one remembers their names or what they did or when they did it, and, the Mission Log at the Nevada Wing Headquarters was even missing the only page that had their names and Mission number on it. The only record of their Red Cap Life Saving Mission is still held by the widow of one of the pilots, which is an avgas 100 Low Lead gasoline fuel receipt for 22.5 gallons from the Fixed Base Operator at the Stead airport, north of Reno, of which, it might be mentioned, that he or she had never been re-imbursed for to this date as most of the paper trail and records had been shuffled or all but lost at the Nevada Wing

Headquarters down at Carson City. However, maybe it wasn't, maybe they did get recognized and that part was lost instead, whichever.

And, also, the dreamer surmises, all of the other All-American involved.... oh hell, the writer, or dreamer, has run out of characters to report on, they have done been done in or done up, if you will, so that must truly be the official end of a too long story of a dream to begin with. The writer, or, the dreamer, whichever, only wishes that you, yourself, could live such an interesting life as those you have most recently read about, or may also have dreamt about on some exciting occasion.

So, to end it all, on a wake-up call, "Good Morning, to you all... hope you have a nice day."

HOW TO TELL A STORY WELL

To develop a love story, a scientific dissertation, or, a historical paper, for that matter, as, it makes little difference between any two of them, as they all tell their own story, and, they all take an unbelievably equal amount of too much hard work, sweat and tears, research and evaluation, along with a little imagination thrown in on the side, or, crammed and jammed in at the end, at your choosing, not to mention a little selected plagiarism over on the side. But, this is mostly because it requires the writing if it. Just plain everyday story telling is different. You do not have to be a writer to be a story teller. Ernest Hemingway and J. D. Salinger were writers, while, Mark Twain was both a writer and a story teller. You do not have to be both either. Let someone else worry about the grammar and sentence structure. If it's good enough to pass the spell check on your computer, you are good to go. Now, Mark Twain just happened to be what they call self-taught. He got his start when he took the job of setting type in his brother's newspaper office where he learned to spell. He didn't know much at the time, but, he knew enough to choose the right word and put it into the right place at the right time. Here is where his story telling really took off which eventually made him to be what it was that he became.

I mention that, just so you know that that was part of his story and it could be part of yours too.

The very first thing that you need to do when you try to develop your story, is, to first collect up as many of the bones of the skeleton of your story as is possible. The bones are the ideas. This may require some digging, and so, you may also need some digging tools to assist in your overall efforts. A little knowledge of archeological techniques may help you some, that is, if there are any similar skeletons previously located somewhere in the world, a few here or there, or, some that someone else has previously put together, stashed in some closet somewhere, then, even dared to put their findings into the known recorded word of storytelling for copyright with the Library of Congress. A warning here, that even though similar things sometimes appear to be similar, yours will certainly not be as similar or the same as someone else's unless you choose to get by the easy way and plan early on to plagiarize your story body's mess from the get-go. If and or when that you do such a thing, even if it shows up on you-tube, someone, somewhere, somehow, sometime, will call the FBI, the IRS, the SEC, and, maybe even the CIA just to put you in your place, or, where they think that you need to be.

Now, the skeleton of your story, is no more or no less, than, your ideas connecting the outline of the story, however, in that outline, each idea, or, each bone, needs to be connected to the next bone, and, all in the right order, by the way, I might add. In other words, the bones need be matched up according to where they belong; every bone has its own place in the skeleton, just as the ideas need be put together in the most correct order. Story boards only work for the movies or for soap operas and the bones will just fall off of the boards in the first place and disorder will reign. You see, this is no little important matter, because, if you get the wrong bone, in the wrong place, it will be as conspicuous as a hip bone poking out of the skull bone, and, you can confuse your readers and give them the wrong impression as to what your story is all about and what you are trying to say. Now, you cannot just glue the bones together, or, wire them together like dinosaur skeletons in a museum, as they would be stiff, and, only be a spectacle for someone to look at, take a picture with it, and then just walk on by, never even to be brought up in some conversation with someone some time later on in the future. On the other hand, if you tied the bones of your story together with some ord string, they would be loose, or, may even work loose sometime in the telling of it all. So, you have to develop some ligaments and sinews to make the joints naturally flexible. Now, it is the time for you to start picking out some nouns, a few verbs, a couple prepositions, and the other superfluous unmentionables that I can't think of the name of or for at this time, that make up those ligaments and sinews. These bones, these ideas, have to be joined together with some pretty tough but consolidating things that I mentioned above. So, you need to choose those words very carefully and very wisely if you can remember what it is that they are called. If you can't remember what they are, just wing it, and let your listeners of your story figure it all out for themselves. If they laugh at it, what you said was funny.

Secondly, the next thing you need to do is to put some meat onto the skeleton of your story. This is the filler that fills your story body out. So, lay it on a little thick here and there, in some places, and spread it out a little thin in others. Let it begin to take a natural shape, I mean, six pack abs can be interesting to some of the young girls even without a good oiled down tan. However, you want your story to look even more slim and trim, as, those types attract a little more attention than the fat ones. Too, this is the point where you also need to add in the blood and guts to your story. Now, if you are the type person who gets all queasy at the sight of blood and guts, just get over it, as, many wanna-be doctors have dropped out of medical school because of the same, so, there is no other option or answer except for you to close your eyes, and deal with it head-on. So, you may even have to put on some good music to get your mind off of it, and then, proceed, full speed ahead with open throttle, and just get-'er-done partner. I might mention, that, a little of the blood and gore, may be held back at this time, so, that it can be added on later, on the outside, just for emphasis, or, just for the show of it all at the proper time, that is, if you don't have any other excuses. Now, around about this time, you may need to add on a little fat, just to enhance the overall shape of your story. Just enough, here and there, to add shape to make it look really nice and presentable, or, maybe even a little sexy, your choice. It is the nouns and verbs and how they are connected up in the same sentence which adds the sexual flavor that causes the readers to hang on to every word waiting for the next dangling participle to come disconnected and fall off all by itself. Remember, never end any of your sentences with dangling participles, any more, than you absolutely need to, if you do, at all. It is the angle of the dangle that can catch and keep the listeners attention.

Thirdly, you are now at the point of no return and have no choice at this time, except to add the skin over the body of your story. It is the skin that holds the body together and helps to add some shape. The skin is the overall theme. You can also add some deodorant or perfume of your choice just to get it to smell good. You might even give the skin some fresh color, put on some makeup, just to make it look good down on the beach in the sunshine. Be sure to tighten it up here and there, as, no one likes wrinkles, as, they would make your story body look old, and, you want to keep it vibrant, and as young and exciting as it possibly can be. Remember too, any wrinkles at all, will tell side stories, in themselves, and people will talk about them behind your back. It is here, if you so choose, to smear some blood and gore around in the exposed areas just to attract a little more attention when and where you need it if you are aiming for a little sympathy. Remember, the skin, being the overall theme of your story, need be stretched from one end to the other without leaving any poked holes, except those which are necessary of course. It is the skin, or, the theme, that holds the entire mess of a mass or the mass of the mess all together. A body that springs a leak in the wrong place at the wrong time can be most embarrassing and more difficult to explain at a later date to some wanna-be editor at the Huffington Post. Too, you have to consider, that, your story body, will look different when lying down than it does when standing up on its own hind legs. You certainly want it to look good in either position, so, test it out on your own time, rather than on your listener's time. Remember too, that some folks listen faster than others, and, you have to keep the pace of your story to meet their expectations, as, there are fast listeners and then there are half fast listeners.

Fourthly, on one hand, you are now to the point of needing to breathe life into this newly made up story body. You might even need a good jolt of electric shock to bring it to life. Don't think of measures like the method of the making of the Frankenstein monster coming to life with a bolt of lightning; think more like using a good brand of Taser followed by an atrial defibrillator with some explicit written or loud vocal directions for proper use. If you don't want the expense of such, you could call 9-1-1 and request such, as those folks are usually just sitting around on their hands awaiting your call and would be more than obliged to help you out of your predicament. Just in case, that this action does not bring life to your story body, after the third or fourth shocking, you have no choice but to resort to some other form of resuscitation. Mouth to mouth breathing along with physical cardiopulmonary pulses may be required for some extended period of time, and, you should be prepared and trained accordingly in the administration of such, and, if not, you may have to hire it out, or, like I said a-previous, call 9-1-1 again for backup. Now, on the other hand, if you do successfully bring the body of your story to life, you are good to go.

However, it has to be mentioned, albeit somewhat painfully, there is the possibility, that there is absolutely nothing you can do which will bring the body of your story to life no matter what you do. You could feed it Gensing and Ginko Baloba or just cram vitamin pills down your story's throat to no avail. It may take a while for you to realize that, or, for it to sink in, and, it may be difficult for you to even consider such, but, you must be prepared for this eventuality in the event that it would ever occur, even remotely without any remote control. And, you should be able to recognize it at that precise moment in time, because, you now have nothing more than a dead laid out cold corpse of a story on your hands and you may not have the proper credentials to handle it any further. This eventuality will also be addressed again later on in this primary official instruction in Storytelling 101.

Fifthly, at this time, if your story body has caught its breath, and its eyes are a-twinkling and a-blinking, right now, so far, less the possibility of the corpse thing, all you have is a live naked ass body, so, now is not the time to be embarrassed by what you have brought about, as, it now falls your lot for you to dress up the body of your story. Put some decent clothing on the dang thing for god's sake. So, do, please, take the time to pick out some of the more fashionable and up-to-date clothing. The cost, in the long run, will be a bargain. Do not, under any circumstances, go to the Goodwill or the Salvation Army Store to get your clothes. Dress the body, with clothing acceptable for the occasion and do make the body most representable and acceptable to society in general in all respects. You do not have to go so far as to dress your story in Hickey-freeman or Jacquelin Smith or Gloria Vanderbuilt styles. Remember, sports clothes go well for the sports enthusiasts, and business clothes go well for business. Leisure clothing may be acceptable for golfers, but not generally acceptable except on course of course or on Fridays in some offices. By the way, if you have the extra money, get the right size or have the clothes tailored to fit, and make sure that they are cleaned and pressed. Do invest in a nice pair of shoes for your story body to stand on, as, you would want the body of your story to put its best foot forward when the time comes time for it to get it's foot in the door, and to make an acceptable entrance at time of first telling. Remember, just like you, your story body, will never get a second chance to make a good first impression.

Again, if it is called for, and, if you want to spread some of the gore, maybe along with a little blood here and there in the proper places, now is the time to do it. Just don't lay it on too thick, as, it may appear somewhat suspicious to those who have a more investigative nature.

Too, if you want to add some jewelry, now is the time to do it. Now, the jewelry amounts to putting in a few antonyms, synonyms or maybe even predicates, or, maybe a few adverbs, stuck in here and there if your editor calls for or needs some additional filler. Synonyms are nice if your cadaver is female, and, generally females require more makeup and jewelry than male cadavers. So, you may even want to cram in a participle or two, just don't leave too many of them dangling here or there, any more than what your story calls for as was previously mentioned, I think.

Now, there is the possibility, as was also heretofore previously mentioned, that you may not be able to or cannot breathe life into the body of your story no matter what extreme shocking measures were taken at the time. Now, it may be very hard for you to accept, but, you know, down deep in your heart, that, shit happens. I also have to remind you that you now have nothing more than a dressed up cadaver of a story on your hands lying out in the open with a nice pair of shoes, but, without even the mention of a casket to stick the thing into since the funeral home is probably closed by now. Yes, you heard it right; you now have a cold dead cadaver to deal with, as, there is no such thing as a live cadaver, that happens only in the theatre in downtown New York and once in a while in some of the Hollywood studios on some studio couch. So, in this instance, you are now obligated and required to respect the body of your cadaver, just as you would respect a live story body, and must treat it with all due respects accordingly. However, you can't just keep it around stuck back hidden on a bookshelf, or, in some file cabinet or on an otherwise empty 32 gig flash drive in the bottom drawer of your desk. Story bodies, just like real dead bodies, will decay, if not otherwise properly embalmed within a short time, and will definitely, without a doubt, start to smell to high heaven, and others will definitely start to notice the decay of it, sooner or later. There is nothing you can do to hide the stink, by the way.

The short of it in a nut shell is this. It is your responsibility to do something with it. You cannot pass this duty on to anyone else at this time, or, hire it out to some editor as they are not in the business of handling dead bodied stories, so, it is up to you, no matter how busy you say that you are in your day job. So, you have no choice, but to proceed to take the time and bear the cost of a funeral and a proper burial, if, that is, as if that would even be a choice in the matter that is within your capabilities. Just to let you in on a little secret, at this time, you may think that this has never happened to anyone before, but, rest assured, you are definitely not the first and will certainly not be the last. Others, who have gone down this long rutted out road before you, but, so far, have kept it a tight secret unto themselves, unbeknownst to you, google and you-tube. And, they have even gone out of their way to keep you from hearing about their other story telling activities, and, you may so want to kick this stinking can on down the road, but, you may not want to do it, or, maybe you can't do it, you just can't. This obligation has been visited upon many story tellers in the past, and now, the mantel has now been passed on down to you. The die has been set. The curse has come to fruition. This signals an unwanted end to so much hard work and totally too much time consumed with no returns whatsoever for your labors and loss of sleep, not to mention the years off of your life that now might appear to be no less than futile, as they flash past your red shot eyes and fevered brain. That is the why of, that, you are reduced to such few options in these final matters. You might realize that you could have just as well spent your expended time on a white sand beach down in Puerto Rico sipping on Hurricanes.

If, on one hand, for instance, if, that is, you want to pursue the premise, and, persist in the pretense that the story body were really alive but only sleeping off a cheap drunk or taking a little nap, just so as, to perhaps get it signed up for some return from worker's compensation, food stamps, or disability social security payments, even though you and everyone else around your neighborhood really knew better because you could not hide the horrendous smell of it, although, perchance, you just might get a few new arrivals from out of town to believe in it at first, but, don't count on them to invest in your story any time soon as they will not spend their travel money. So, if you so choose to go this route, you still have to go through the action of the required public presentation of the story body sooner or later following shortly thereafter with the obituary, which, if found out too early on, could be embarrassing. There are few things that you can do at this point but usually even fewer which ever work, if the truth were ever known. If life is all but impossible to instill within your corpse, and, you still endeavor to pursue the publication of your mess, because of your hard headedness, your blatant idiocy, not to mention your lack of humanness, here and now, just as an idea, you could prop the dang thing up, then, break one or more of the cadaver's arms or legs, just so your listeners could feel a little sorry for your story body as it was presented. It may work. Some people do believe in magic, card tricks and witchcraft.

But then, if, On the other hand, as a positive note, if you can and do get the body of your story to come to life, kick started like a big Harley, you will not have to do any selling of the matter whatsoever, why, that thing, will get up, walk out of your life from now on even until doomsday, and, it will take off and go out on its own, even going door to door if need be just to get the needed attention. The thing will stop everyone it meets on the street just to introduce itself, worse than any politician ever dared to be, and it will then take off by itself and go viral and sell itself with no assistance from you whatsoever, worse than anything you ever saw on you tube. However, I should mention, that, the downside of that, is, that this may never happen until even after your long awaited demise, after such time as when the undertaker has patted you in the face with a spade, and, you may not be popular or receive any accolades, or atta-boys until after those kinds of things have happened to you, with a little of the proceeds going to distant relatives that you never knew that you had, that have come out of the woodwork, and the majority to some future attorneys that weren't born until after you finished college. That is just the way things is, or, are, whichever, so, get used to it and go on and do your thing before it is too late, and, one last thing, do not tell stories on into your old age unless it is stories about your memoirs or autobiography, those stories that are all about yourself, then, brag all you want and stretch the truth to no end. I mean, isn't that what you would want to do anyway and at least go out as a legend in your time?

End